Systemic Functional Linguistics and Critical Discourse Analysis

Systemic Functional Linguistics and Critical Discourse Analysis

Studies in Social Change

Edited by Lynne Young and Claire Harrison

continuum
LONDON • NEW YORK

Continuum

The Tower Building,
11 York Road,
London SE1 7NX

15 East 26th Street,
New York, NY 10010

First published 2004 by Continuum

British Library Cataloguing-in-Publication Data
A catalogue record for this book is available from the British Library.

ISBN 0–8264–6773–3 (hardback)
    0–8264–6774–1 (paperback)

Library of Congress Cataloging-in-Publication Data
Systemic functional linguistics and critical discourse analysis: studies in social change/
  edited by Lynne Young and Claire Harrison.
     p. cm.
  Includes bibliographical references and index.
  ISBN 0–8264–6773–3   ISBN 0–8264–6774–1 (pbk)
    1. Sociolinguistics. 2. Functionalism (Linguistics) 3. Discourse analysis—Social aspects. 4. Social change. I. Young, Lynne. II. Harrison, Claire.

  P40.S9 6 2004
  306.44—dc22   2003062654

Typeset by RefineCatch Ltd, Bungay, Suffolk
Printed and bound in Great Britain by Antony Rowe Ltd, Chippenham, Wilts

Contents

Applied Section: Institutional Identity

List of Contributors

Faiz Sathi Abdullah is Lecturer and English Language Programme Co-ordinator at the Faculty of Modern Languages and Communication, Universiti Putra Malaysia. In 1998 he completed a Ph.D. at Heriot-Watt University, Edinburgh on cognitive genre analysis in TESOL. He currently teaches undergraduate and postgraduate courses in Critical Discourse Analysis, speech communication, and English for Specific Purposes (ESP). Besides presenting his work at various local and international forums, he is writing a book on ESP from a critical perspective and finalizing plans for a national research programme on Malaysian identity.

Ralph Adendorff is Professor of English Language and Linguistics at Rhodes University in Grahamstown, South Africa. His principal areas of interest and research are sociolinguistics (particularly code-switching and the pidgin, Fanakalo) and the critical microethnographic investigation of literacy practices, the topic of his Ph.D. dissertation.

Tom Bartlett is currently writing up his Ph.D. thesis for the University of Edinburgh Department of Theoretical and Applied Linguistics. The thesis looks at agency and power in foreign-language learning and the appropriation of dominant codes by minority language cultures. It is based on field-work with the Makushi people in Guyana, South America.

Chng Huang Hoon is an Assistant Professor with the Department of English Language and Literature, National University of Singapore. Her teaching and research interests revolve around language, gender, law, and ideology issues. Her most recent publications are the book, *Separate and Unequal: Judicial Rhetoric and Women's Rights* (John Benjamins, 2002); and a 2002 article entitled 'Who are My Peers? Women, Men, and the American Jury' in the *Australasian Journal of American Studies*, 21(1): 46–62.

Frances Christie is Emeritus Professor of Language and Literacy Education at the University of Melbourne and Honorary Professor of Education at the University of Sydney. She has research and scholarly interests in language and literacy education, pedagogic grammar, children's writing development, and classroom discourse analysis. Recent publications include: (ed.) *Pedagogy and the Shaping of Consciousness: Linguistic and Social Processes* (Cassell, 1999) and *Classroom Discourse Analysis: A Functional Perspective* (Continuum, 2000).

Débora de Carvalho Figueiredo holds a Ph.D. in English and Applied Linguistics from Universidade Federal de Santa Catarina (UFSC). She is a professor at the Graduate Programme in Linguistic Sciences at Universidade do Sul de Santa Catarina (UNISUL), and a lecturer at the Department of Foreign Languages at UFSC. Her main interests lie in the area of Critical Discourse Analysis and gender studies with an emphasis on legal discourse and violence against women.

Norman Fairclough is Professor of Language in Social Life at Lancaster University, UK. He has published extensively in Critical Discourse Analysis, including *Language and Power* (Longman, 1989), *Discourse and Social Change* (Polity Press, 1992), *Media Discourse* (Edward Arnold, 1995), *Critical Discourse Analysis: The Critical Study of Language* (Longman, 1995), *Discourse in Late Modernity: Rethinking Critical Discourse Analysis*, with Lilie Chouliaraki (Edinburgh University Press, 1999), *New Labour, New Language?* (Routledge, 2000), and *Analyzing Discourse: Textual Analysis for Social Research* (Routledge, 2003). He is currently working on issues of citizenship, governance, and globalization from a Critical Discourse Analysis perspective.

Phil Graham is Senior Lecturer in Communication at the UQ Business School, University of Queensland. His research interests combine political economy, media studies, and discourse analysis. He is currently (re)writing two books for Peter Lang, *Hypercapitalism* and *The Digital Dark Ages*.

Claire Harrison is a professional writer and editor with 25 years' experience working for government and corporate clients. She recently completed an M.A. with Distinction in Applied Language Studies at Carleton University, Ottawa, Ontario, specializing in writing and rhetoric research and theory, social semiotics, Systemic Functional Linguistics, and Critical Discourse Analysis. She is the co-author of *Developing Online Content: The Principles of Writing and Editing for the Web* (John Wiley & Sons, 2000) and has published papers on hypertext, professional writing, and visual social semiotics. She is currently enrolled in a doctoral program in Communications at Carleton University.

Arlene Harvey is an Assistant Professor in the Faculty of Business Administration at the University of Macau, China. Trained in the Systemic Functional Linguistic approach to discourse at the University of Sydney in the 1990s, her early research focused on the grammar of definitional clauses, which she has published in journals such as *Functions of Language* and *Pragmatics*. Since 1999 she has worked in business faculties in South East Asian universities. Her current research involves text analysis that not only illuminates the rhetorical features of charismatic leader discourse, but also attempts to make functional linguistic insights accessible to business researchers.

Ruqaiya Hasan was taught linguistics by Ian Catford, David Abercrombie, Angus McIntosh, John Sinclair, and M. A. K Halliday. While teaching at Macquarie University (NSW, Australia) she has researched in the areas of linguistic stylistics, relations of context and text, lexis as delicate grammar, message semantic, socio-semantic variation, and the concept of semiotic mediation. She has published in all these areas, and has held visiting appointments at several universities, including University of California at Berkeley, University of Illinois at Urbana, Yale, North Western University (Evanston), National University of Singapore, Copenhagen University (Denmark), and the City University (Hong Kong). Some of her papers have appeared in *Ways of Saying: Ways of Meaning: Selected Papers*, edited by Carmel Cloran, David Butt, and Geoff Williams (Cassell, 1996). Currently, she is Professor Emerita (Linguistics, Macquarie University, Australia).

Inger Lassen is an Associate Professor at the Department of Language and Intercultural Studies at Aalborg University, Denmark where she teaches discourse analysis, genre analysis, and technical communication. She has a position as Director of the B.A. study programmes in International Business Communication and is a board member of the Centre for Discourse Studies. Her main research interests and publications focus on genre theory, discourse analysis, text accessibility, and style in communication in professional settings.

José Luiz Meurer is Professor of English and Applied Linguistics at Universidade Federal de Santa Catarina, Florianópolis, Brazil. He holds a Ph.D. in Linguistics from Georgetown University and was a visiting researcher at the University of Birmingham, UK where he also taught courses in discourse analysis. He is the author of *Aspects of Language in Self-help Counselling* (UFSC, 1998) and co-author of *Parâmetros de Textualização* (UFSM, 1997), and *Gêneros Textuais* (EDUSC, 2002). He is interested in Systemic Functional Linguistics, Critical Discourse Analysis, genre studies, and the integration of sociological theories to explain the interdependence between language and other forms of social practice.

Dragana Polovina-Vukovic holds an Honours B.A. from the University of Sarajevo and an M.A. in Applied Language Studies from Carleton University, Ottawa, Ontario. Presently she is a doctoral candidate at the School of Journalism and Communication at Carleton University. Her research interests are in the field of Critical Discourse Analysis, using this model to examine issues of social inequality as well as ethnicity and communication in the Canadian media.

Maurice Ward has been involved with unions variously as an activist and full-time organizer for over 25 years. He is currently Associate Professor of Modern Communications at Kanto Gakuin University.

Lynne Young is an Associate Professor in the School of Linguistics and Applied Language Studies at Carleton University, Ottawa, Ontario. Her research interests have been in discourse analysis within the model of Systemic Functional Grammar, an area in which she has published a book and several articles looking at tertiary-level academic discourse in lectures and textbooks, on the one hand, and, on the other, examining the semantic progression of L2 acquisition in terms of metafunctional components. More recently she has been working in the field of Critical Discourse Analysis, using the Systemic Functional Linguistics model to examine racism in the Canadian media, and is also currently studying the discursive role of social change in governmental institutions.

Introduction to the Collection

The papers in *Systemic Functional Linguistics and Critical Discourse Analysis: Studies in Social Change* were originally presented at the 28th International Systemic Functional Congress. Each paper expands on the theme of the Congress: 'Interfaces: Systemic Functional Grammar and Critical Discourse Analysis' by examining a broad range of current social changes. The volume begins by focusing on theoretical issues that arise from social, political, and economic transformations, and then presents studies of the ways in which such transformations affect national and institutional identity.

The SFL and CDA Connection

Researchers, who work in Systemic Functional Linguistics (SFL) and Critical Discourse Analysis (CDA), share several commonalities, three of which we wish to highlight here. First, they share a view of language as a social construct, looking at the role of language in society and at the ways in which society has fashioned language. The second commonality, to which the first leads, is their shared dialectical view of language in which particular discursive events influence the contexts in which they occur and the contexts are, in turn, influenced by these discursive events. Third, as Phil Graham notes in his paper in this collection, 'both [SFL and CDA] emphasize the cultural and historical aspects of meaning'.

Yet, these two fields are also very different. To begin, SFL is a functionally based theory, developed during the past 45 years, which examines the functions that language has evolved to serve in society. Such a view involves the examination of 'real' language events to understand the purposes language serves in a variety of contexts, and to understand the way language itself functions. Systemic functional linguists, then, study how meanings are made in different contexts; they have also focused on the teaching of English as a first and second language as well as on discourse analysis of a wide range of discursive events.

Linguists such as Roger Fowler, Gunther Kress, Robert Hodge, and Tony Trew, on the other hand, developed CDA as one branch of discourse analysis in the 1970s in East Anglia, UK. It is basically, as Tuen A. van Dijk (2001:

96) says, 'analysis with an attitude' – analysis of different public discursive events that explores the relation between language and power and the ways in which language is being used to produce, maintain, and reproduce positions of power through discursive means. As Kress (1995) notes, the intention of CDA is to move the linguistic field into a domain of social and political relevance and, thus, provide a social critique by documenting structures of inequality. Therefore, the aim of CDA is to use analysis not only to reveal structures of domination, but also to effect change in the way power is wielded, maintained, and reproduced in social organizations and relationships.

Furthermore, CDA is unlike SFL because it is an *approach towards* (or as some have preferred, a *perspective on*) the examination of social problems manifested discursively, that is, it is neither a methodology nor a theory of language. This issue has been discussed by Ruth Wodak, who, in her thoughtful appraisal of CDA (2002: 12), identifies the need to operationalize theories that relate linguistic dimensions with social ones. She also notes that a 'mixed bag' of linguistic theories has been used in CDA without any particular grammatical theory. Michael Meyer, in the same volume (2001: 18), echoes this, saying that 'there is no guiding theoretical viewpoint that is consistently used within CDA, nor do the CDA protagonists proceed consistently from the area of theory to the field of discourse and then back to theory'.

One of the intentions, then, of this collection is to connect CDA explicitly to SFL by explaining and illustrating their relationship more completely in terms of theory and application. This volume draws these two fields into one context, as it were, so that elements of both can be (re)considered. The result is not quite a marriage between SFL and CDA but a firmer 'relationship' between the two. The authors in this volume extend parameters for examining the relations between language and society, between language and power, and between language and social change.

Looking Backward

One way to situate the ties between these two fields is to examine CDA origins and developments in relation to SFL through a brief survey of the major works that have focused on the role of SFL in CDA for approximately the last 30 years, that is, the lifetime of CDA itself. Any such survey is, of course, selective and inevitably leaves out many important works; however, for the purposes of putting the current collection in context, we will highlight some seminal researchers in CDA who have focused, to differing degrees, on SFL elements in their frameworks and analyses. As this survey will show, early researchers examined the connections between language and social structure through SFL analysis of metafunctional components and studied the meanings in lexicogrammatical selections and patterns. As CDA matured as a field of study, however, some analysts developed areas of CDA outside of SFL; nevertheless, all researchers in CDA acknowledge that SFL is centrally important to the critical study of situated language events.

The first major work that connects SFL and CDA is *Language and Control*, edited by Fowler *et al.* and published in 1979. As Fowler and Kress (Fowler *et al.* 1979: 185) note, central to its thesis is the notion that 'ideology is linguistically mediated . . .' Each study in that volume draws on one or more SFL components to carry out analyses, primarily of media. In 'Critical Linguistics', one of the major chapters of the book, Fowler and Kress outline the metafunctional features that they indicate as useful in critical analysis. They focus on: the ideational, or what they call *the grammar of transitivity*; the interpersonal, or in their terms *the grammar of modality*; and the textual, in which they examine transformations such as nominalizations and passivization as well as classification in terms of lexical patterns. They also introduce but do not examine coherence, referring readers to what has become the 'bible' on this topic: *Cohesion in English* by Halliday and Hasan (1976). The central thesis in both *Language and Control* and its companion volume, *Language as Ideology*, by Hodge and Kress, also published in 1979, is that language is an instrument of control in the sense that 'linguistic forms allow significance to be conveyed and to be distorted' (Hodge and Kress 1979: 6).

The next major work in CDA appearing a decade later, in 1989, was Norman Fairclough's *Language and Power*, in which he provided an introduction to the critical study of discourse by carefully setting out CDA theory: its intentions, its goals, and its basic tenets as well as providing a model for analysis. As with earlier works in CDA, much of his analytical framework is based on SFL theory. Another influential work is Jay Lemke's *Textual Politics*, published in 1995. While Lemke does not work within the CDA model, his critical language perspective has similar features, which is not surprising since he adopts a social semiotic model, which, as Martin suggests (1998: 9–10), is one '. . . of the transdisciplinary fields (the other being CDA) . . . which has emerged to close the gap between textual and social analysis'. The last major work we wish to note is *Language in the News*, written by Fowler and published in 1996. In that volume, Fowler extends critical language study, also rooting his analysis in SFL as is evident in his focus on transitivity, transformations, lexical structure, and modality, particularly in Chapter 5. Finally, although we do not have the space to outline many other developments in CDA with connections to SFL, important studies have appeared in two major CDA journals: *Discourse and Society* and *Discourse Processes*.

The CDA strand outlined above has the closest ties to SFL; however, there are two other important lines of enquiry in CDA, which, while acknowledging SFL as a linguistic approach favourable to the critical study of language, have moved in different directions. One such strand, headed by van Dijk, stresses the socio-cognitive aspects of analysis and focuses on the macro-structure of texts with only some attention paid to what he calls *local semantic features.* Wodak and the Vienna School, another strand, emphasize the discourse-historical approach which is concerned with more fully con- textualizing analyses through consideration of broad historical contexts; nevertheless, Wodak (2002: 8) also states that 'an understanding of the basic claims of Halliday's grammar and his approach to linguistic analysis is essential for a proper understanding of CDA'.

There is, then, a solid tradition that links SFL and CDA from the very advent of Critical Linguistics (CL), the precursor to CDA. However, it is appropriate now to emphasize and extend the dimensions of this connec- tion because SFL provides a solid methodology that can, as Gregory (2001) states, help preserve CDA from ideological bias – a view which echoes Martin's point (2000) that one of the strengths of SFL for CDA is to ground concerns with power and ideology in detailed analysis of texts in real contexts of language use, thereby making it possible for the analyst to be explicit, transparent, and precise.

Organization of the Collection

We have divided *Systemic Functional Linguistics and Critical Discourse Analysis: Studies in Social Change* into Theoretical and Applied Sections. However, it should be noted at the outset that the line between theoretical and applied is often blurred and indistinct. We have retained the two categories to reflect the researchers' purposes: the authors in the Theoretical Section analyse data to illustrate components of SFL theory and CDA approaches, that is, the texts they have selected are supportive rather than constitutive of their papers. On the other hand, the authors in the Applied Section concentrate on discoursal events and their conclusions are based on, and primarily apply to, these events. The Applied Section is itself fur- ther divided into two thematic categories: 'National Identity' in which authors demonstrate how discourse is used to create or alter national/ cultural representations; and 'Institutional Identity' in which authors focus on discourses that structure and are, in turn, structured by institutions in education, government, and industry.

Theoretical Section

Opening the Theoretical Section is 'Analysing Discursive Variation' in which Ruqaiya Hasan explores the meaning of discursive variation and its role in social change. Focusing on the causes and results of dialectical and diatypic variation, Hasan insists that, in order to understand the role of discourse in social change, it is necessary to first understand what produces discursive variation and what the variation itself produces – views encapsu- lated in two central questions: 'Does discursive variation produce social change?' and 'Does social stability presuppose discursive consistency?' In pursuing these questions, Hasan stresses that it is as important to under- stand the discursive property active in social change as it is to recognize 'how the "genres of power" grow, what nurtures some diatypic varieties, how, with what results'. Finally, she suggests that understanding how and why language works in society is equally significant to the social critique of discourse.

In addition, Hasan notes that one has to study and understand not only unique texts, but also the unique in relation to the systematic so that we can begin to appreciate 'how we ourselves contribute most probably unknowingly to [the] pathology [of the system or] how our own activities are often in keeping with the ideologies that support the structures of oppression' – issues of obvious importance and relevance to those working in CDA.

Phil Graham's paper, 'Predication, Propagation, and Mediation: SFL, CDA, and the Inculcation of Evaluative-Meaning Systems', focuses on different ways to examine evaluative meanings, or what he calls *axiologies*, through the study of mediation, that is, the movement of meaning across time and space. His definition of media includes: types of media such as television, radio, and the Internet in which symbolic material is stored; and text types such as news stories, action movies, and editorials. To situate and illustrate these axiological meanings, he examines the merging of sitcom discourse into presidential speeches made by US President Bill Clinton in his second term. The study of axiological changes through mediation helps to explain how meanings are moved within and among cultures, providing analysts with a new way to study how meanings are produced, distributed, and changed over time and across social boundaries. As Graham notes, '[we] cannot understand the character of meaning systems in social systems without understanding the totality of means by which societies store and move meanings' – an important consideration for researchers in both SFL and CDA.

Tom Bartlett, in 'Mapping Distinction: Towards a Systemic Representation of Power in Language', focuses on another aspect of evaluative meanings which he examines in terms of increasing delicacy of description in systemic networks, a different but related extension of the axiologies described in Graham's paper. Based on data collected in Guyana, South America, Bartlett describes the communication strategies between members of the Iwokrama International Rainforest Conservation Programme, a multinational non-government organization (NGO), and local Amerindian communities – two groups interested in sustainable development of local, natural resources. Bartlett suggests that his networks of modality and projection at different levels of delicacy 'could be extended by increasing the range of speakers, the number and type of lexical items employed, and the speech acts they instantiate, or through a comparison of speakers' performance in different contexts'; and that such *multidelicacy* can strengthen CDA research and assist in removing ideological bias by demonstrating a greater sensitivity to texts and by its applicability to large-scale quantitative analyses.

In 'Role Prescriptions, Social Practices, and Social Structures: A Sociological Basis for the Contextualization of Analysis in SFL and CDA', José

Luiz Meurer extends the concept of social context by outlining Anthony Giddens' structuration theory in greater detail than is usually found in SFL/CDA research and connecting it more explicitly to SFL and CDA. Demonstrating its usefulness in an analysis of Noam Chomsky's text in response to the events of September 11, 2001, he shows how '*intercontextuality*, in an analogy to *intertextuality* and *interdiscursivity*, [can] refer to the various contexts that intermesh to influence or determine, and be influenced or determined by, texts, discourses, and other social practices'. Meurer suggests that Giddens' sociological concepts of rules and resources as structuring properties of social life can help analysts see how, 'across chains of practices, different social contexts may impinge upon other contexts' – a notion encapsulated in *intercontextuality*. Thus, he broadens the concept of social context in ways related to Graham's ideas about the movement of meanings within and among cultures through technical means.

Applied Section: National Identity

The papers in the first part of the Applied Section explore the ways in which social change affects national identity. The leading paper is Norman Fairclough's 'Critical Discourse Analysis in Researching Language in the New Capitalism: Overdetermination, Transdisciplinarity, and Textual Analysis'. His study examines social changes related to globalization and new capitalism by focusing on the recent, radical restructuring in economic, political, and social domains as well as the re-scaling of relations resulting from this restructuring. Fairclough has long maintained that language plays a key role in the process of restructuring because the process is knowledge-based and is, thus, particularly reliant on language.

Through analysis of a text by British Prime Minister Tony Blair, he illustrates the relationship and the differences between what he labels the 'global' or the new global economy, and national 'space-times'. His analysis suggests that global space-time deals in 'imaginaries' in that 'it projects ways of acting and ways of being' as if they were realities instead of possibilities. Fairclough describes how these 'imaginaries' in neo-liberal representations of the global economy are positively valued and thus 'colonize' national space. Finally, he suggests that the combination of interdiscursivity with transitivity analysis of neo-liberal discourse provides a stronger linkage between linguistic and social analyses, thereby enabling CDA researchers to make richer contributions to social research.

Faiz Sathi Abdullah also explores the effect of globalization on national identity in 'Prolegomena to a Discursive Model of Malaysian National Identity' by examining the question: 'What are we as a Malaysian people?' He notes that the nature of national identity is already being changed by 'master discourses' of global appropriation such as the neo-liberal texts described by Fairclough. Abdullah further maintains that the key denominator in a wide range of discursive types is 'strategic positioning/

framing on a continuum between nationalist and national ideologies', and that looking at 'discursive engagement in identity (re)construction' provides insights into the ways in which discourse is produced and interpreted. In other words, he also suggests that although the state tries to create a sense of nationhood through what he calls 'official decree' – common language, education, culture, and ideology – the process is not only, and not even primarily, a question of political 'space', but more a consideration of discursive 'space'.

In 'Celebrating Singapore's Development: An Analysis of the Millennium Stamps', Chng Huang Hoon examines social change and its connection to national identity by asking a similar question to that of Abdullah – namely, what it means to be a proud Singaporean in the contemporary, globalized world. Through an examination of the *Millennium Collection* – a set of 14 stamps with accompanying texts issued to 'commemorate Singapore's developmental milestones from a colony to a nation' — Chng explores the official construction of Singapore's nation-building and identity construction by unpacking the ideological messages in the verbal and visual elements of the stamps. Her analysis of agency through SFL and CDA looks at what has been included as well as left out of the representation in the texts. Interestingly, she suggests that the lack of agency serves to include all Singaporeans in the sense that every citizen is implicated covertly in this nation-building exercise. Yet, as her conclusion notes: 'The question remains as to why, at the official level, what Singaporeans should be proud of is so clear-cut, while at the level of the individual, there remains such a problem identifying with a Singaporean identity.'

In 'The Representation of Social Actors in the *Globe and Mail* during the Break-up of the Former Yugoslavia', Dragana Polovina-Vukovic explores the consequences of the construction of national identities, not primarily from a state's viewpoint as in Abdullah and Chng's research, but through outside 'eyes', in this case, those of the Canadian media. She analyses the portrayal of Albanians, Croats, and Serbs from the perspective of a major Canadian newspaper, the *Globe and Mail*, during the ten-year period of the Yugoslavian conflict. Through an SFL analysis, she demonstrates that the ethnic groups were represented very differently, either as 'villains' or 'victims'. The result of such media coverage, Polovina-Vukovic suggests, not only revealed discursive differences in representation but, more importantly, contributed to Western actions in the Balkans, resulting in deleterious short- and long-term consequences for those affected: 'Some of them received no humanitarian aid, some of them were bombed, some of them were not granted visas in different developed countries, and some of them are still waiting to return to their homes.'

Applied Section: Institutional Identity

The papers in the second part of the Applied Section explore how social change has affected discursive and social practices in institutions of education, government, and industry. In the leading paper, 'Authority and Its Role in the Pedagogic Relationship of Schooling', Frances Christie examines the nature of the contemporary educational institution, focusing primarily on how knowledge is acquired and the role of the teacher in its acquisition. Her study, supported by an SFL analysis of classroom talk of both early and later learners of English as a first language as well as Bernstein's theories of pedagogic discourse, strongly suggests that it is necessary to reconsider knowledge itself as well as the nature of teacher authority 'in apprenticing students in their learning'. This focus leads to questions that frame her paper: 'What constitutes the nature of authority in the pedagogic relationship of schooling?', 'How is it recognized, and what is its significance in an educational enterprise?' and 'How is it related to the various models of curriculum and of knowledge that apply in different classrooms?'

Christie suggests that the teacher assists in the construction of knowledge through the use of 'the regulative register, mediated . . . by the authority of the teacher'; she also maintains that 'successful teacher authority is essential to the processes of teaching and learning in schools'. Christie concludes by asserting that the social change as reflected in some current educational theory 'is in need of a major review and reassessment, such that a renewed understanding is achieved both of the nature of knowledge offered students in schools, and of the authority teachers must use in teaching such knowledge to their students'.

Ralph Adendorff's paper, 'The Principal's *Book*: Discursively Reconstructing a Culture of Teaching and Learning in an Umlazi High School', looks at the role of educational authority from another perspective. He examines an educational administrator's text, the *Book*, which is distributed daily among all teachers to convey school information – its overt function. However, the principal's discursive practices, including encouraging slogans, are designed to mobilize the staff and imbue them with a new sense of identity and purpose as teachers – a much more covert, but also more contested, function. Adendorff uses Appraisal Theory to analyse this 'ritualized discursive practice', particularly the principal's use of AUTHORITY and EXHORTATION, to demonstrate 'identity construction, more particularly, the constitutive effect of discourse (the *Book*) on identities (those of the teachers and principal) in this context'. In doing so, he also illustrates how the discourse in the microcosm of a small school reflects the macrocosm of 'the complex and unstable sociopolitical context in post-apartheid South Africa'.

Débora de Carvalho Figueiredo's 'Representations of Rape in the Discourse of Legal Decisions' introduces a different institutional context – a study of social change in relation to categorizations of sexual assaults in the British judicial system over a ten-year period. From a CDA perspective, she shows that the lexis used in reported appellate decisions (RADs) 'present the event in different lights, depending on how the assault has been labelled and categorized'. De Carvalho Figueiredo suggests that this process reflects and recreates a body of sexual myths and ideological presuppositions that determine how 'blame, discipline, and punishment is judicially apportioned, and who will be cast in the roles of "victim" and "villain" ' – different discursive constructions of events that result in different judicial adjudications – a finding not unlike that of Polovina-Vukovic's, whose research on ethnic groups in Yugoslavia also demonstrated that lexical choices in the labelling of people as 'victims' and 'villians' have serious ramifications.

Claire Harrison and Lynne Young's paper, 'Bureaucratic Discourse: Writing in the "Comfort Zone" ', uses Phasal Analysis, an extension of SFL, to examine change within another institutional setting – a Government of Canada department in which there has been a recent, radical reorganization. The study analyses a memo, the first piece of official communication from a new Assistant Deputy Minister (ADM) to his Branch. Although designed to build a positive corporate culture among disparate employee groups, the memo has, woven throughout its linear, 'static' structure, a second dynamic discursive 'plot' that ultimately undermines its purpose. The discourse of the new ADM reveals contestation – a personal conflict between his desire to adhere to the new, open style of management and his previous 'command-and-control' experience. Harrison and Young point out that the memo's failure to galvanize staff support demonstrates that 'Bureaucratic discourse, long considered to be useful in maintaining institutional cohesion may, in fact, contribute to the very opposite of its desired effect by creating staff resentment and resistance to the hierarchical status quo', resulting in an environment that will not appeal to the type of sophisticated, knowledge workers required in today and tomorrow's workplace.

Arlene Harvey's paper also examines leadership discourse, but from a different perspective. In 'Charismatic Business Leader Rhetoric: From Transaction to Transformation', she analyses a discussion between Steve Jobs of Apple Computer and his employees over the need to meet an operational deadline, illustrating how his rhetorical focus exhibits *transformational* leadership, which is visionary and inspirational, as compared to *transactional* leadership, which is managerial and pragmatic. Harvey uses an SFL analysis of the ideational patterning of the text to show how Jobs successfully shifts into the transformational mode 'through the combined strategies of abstraction, metaphor, and negative material processes'. She then focuses on interpersonal issues using Appraisal Theory, specifically the evaluative sub-systems of AFFECT, APPRECIATION, and JUDGEMENT, to demonstrate how this 'rhetorically skilful leader . . . can evoke employees' sense of their own self-worth and efficacy to try to inspire them to perform beyond expectations, a feature of transformational leadership'. Her analysis has obvious implications for a variety of institutional settings in which leaders often play a dual role of AUTHORITY and EXHORTATION and of management and inspiration – the types of roles that have been examined in the previous three papers.

Inger Lassen, in 'Ideological Resources in Biotechnology Press Releases:

Patterns of Theme/Rheme and Given/New', looks at another sort of institutional practice, namely press releases (PRs) as a form of promotion – in this case, that of two groups: a large multinational company, Monsanto, that is advocating genetically engineered (GE) foods for developing countries; and biotechnology critics opposed to this practice. By examining Thematic development in the PRs, Lassen demonstrates that institutions with high stakes at risk such as the Monsanto group, to whom popular opinion and profits are important, are intentionally vague about their purposes and activities. On the other hand, the opposition has nothing to lose and can afford to be outspoken: 'observers who are critical of GE foods have a morally acceptable cause and can, therefore, voice their opinions in much more direct terms and even take pride in doing so'. But what is at issue between the two groups is more than the 'truth' about GE foods; although each claims to be representing what is real and presumably incontestable, in fact, '*different* discursive resources are used to promote *different* ideologies'.

In '*We* have the Power – or do We: Pronouns of Power in a Union Context', Maurice Ward examines the stereotypic image of unions within the polarizing and antisocial forces of a capitalist society. Through analysis of the use of the pronoun *we* in a union meeting, Ward examines distance and solidarity between a group of workers in a factory in New Zealand and their elected union representatives. Using corpus and SFL analysis, he shows 'how union negotiators in the process of settling a labour contract are alienated from their electorate by the contradictions in the division of labour that constructs unionism'. Ward also focuses on activities that could broaden participation in actual negotiation processes, which, among other strategies, may offer practical means towards bridging division-of-labour roles. In his conclusion, he offers 'some small steps towards empowering workers within their union, affirming that linguists in concert with other activists do have the power to contribute to change'.

Conclusion

The brief descriptions of the papers in this collection illustrate its aims: to make explicit and to extend connections between SFL and CDA; to provide analyses of social change that are rooted in linguistic theory and methodology, specifically in SFL; to critically analyse discursive material that includes, but is not limited to, media; and finally, to offer a wide diversity of international perspectives on issues of interest and concern in CDA. The papers, in their focus on social change in many different settings and through a wide range of voices, offer to both novice and experienced researchers a fresh view of both SFL and CDA, and, ultimately, the relationship between the two. We hope that the collection stimulates further examination and discussions concerning the connections and interfaces between these two different, but strongly linked, approaches to language and its uses. This, we believe, is an important and worthwhile goal considering the central role that discourse plays in the current transformations of political, economic, and cultural change.

References

Fairclough, N. (1989) *Language and Power.* London: Longman.

Fowler, R. (1996) *Language in the News: Discourse and Ideology in the Press.* London: Routledge.

Fowler, R., Hodge, R., Kress, G. and Trew, T. (eds) (1979) *Language and Control.* London: Routledge and Kegan Paul.

Gregory, M. (2001) ' "Phasal Analysis" Yesterday, Today and Tomorrow?', in *The 28th International Systemic Functional Congress – Interfaces: Systemic Functional Grammar and Critical Discourse Analysis.* Abstract Book. ISFC28, Ottawa: Carleton University.

Halliday, M. A. K. and Hasan, R. (1976) *Cohesion in English.* London: Longman.

Hodge, R. and Kress, G. (1979/1993) *Language as Ideology.* London: Routledge.

Kress, G. (1995) 'The Social Production of Language: History and Structures of Domination', in *Discourse in Society: Systemic Functional Perspectives (Advances in Discourse Processes: Volume 50 – Meaning and Choice in Language: Studies for Michael Halliday)*, ed. by P. H. Fries and M. Gregory. Norwood, NJ: Ablex, 115–40.

Lemke, J. (1995) *Textual Politics: Discourse and Social Dynamics.* London: Taylor and Francis.

Martin, J. R. (2000) 'Close Reading: Functional Linguistics as a Tool for Critical Discourse Analysis', in *Researching Language in Schools and Communities, Functional Linguistic Perspectives*, ed. by L. Unsworth. London: Cassell, 275–304.

Martin, J. R. (1998) 'Discourse of Science: Genesis, Intertextuality and Hegemony', in *Reading Science: Critical and Functional Perspectives on Discourses of Science*, ed. by J. R. Martin and R. Veel. London and New York: Routledge, 3–14.

Meyer, M. (2001) 'Between Theory, Method and Politics: Positioning the Approaches to CDA', in *Methods of Critical Discourse Analysis*, ed. by R. Wodak and M. Meyer. London: Sage Publications, 14–31.

van Dijk, T. A. (2001) 'Multidisciplinary CDA: A Plea for Diversity', in *Methods of Critical Discourse Analysis*, ed. by R. Wodak and M. Meyer. London: Sage Publications, 95–121.

Wodak, R. (2002) 'What CDA is About – A Summary of Its History, Important Concepts and Its Developments', in *Methods of Critical Discourse Analysis*, ed. by R. Wodak and M. Meyer. London: Sage Publications, 1–13.

Theoretical Section

1   Analysing Discursive Variation[1]

Ruqaiya Hasan

Understanding discursive variation involves understanding at least two things: one, what produces discursive variation – which is not the same as describing where it occurs in discourse – and two, what it is that discursive variation produces in its turn. The latter perspective appears necessary because of the emphasis on discourse and social change (Fairclough 1992; Martin 1985, 1992; Lemke 1995). Discourse is as hospitable to variation and to consistency in its own make-up as it is active in the change and maintenance of culture. But despite much discourse about discourse and social change, especially among colleagues pursuing research inspired by Critical Discourse Analysis (CDA), the specific relations between these linguistic and social phenomena still remain to be identified. Does discursive variation produce social change? Does social stability presuppose discursive consistency? A preliminary condition for answering such questions is to identify what kinds of variation can occur in discourse.

Introduction

It is something of a tautology to say that the familiar fails to surprise, for that is precisely the measure of its familiarity! And yet, a close look under the seemingly unruffled surface of the familiar will often reveal a depth of unsuspected complexity, the ramifications of which have the power to unsettle some of our most cherished beliefs: human talk is very much a case in point. This claim might seem unjustified, for after all, over the last few decades, there has been such intensity of discourse on discourse, that one could be forgiven for believing that the study of discourse is 'done and finished'. But take that most familiar of all varieties of human talk, namely casual conversation, described by Eggins and Slade (1997: 6) as talk that is 'simply for the sake of talking itself'. No matter what our social positioning, it is a truly familiar variety since we regularly participate in it. We know also that instances of our casual talk with, say, the selfsame friend differ from one occasion to the next; but this does not unsettle our conviction that in each case we have engaged in casual conversation. This much is clear. But what explanations have we for this obvious variation and this perceived sameness across instances? A kind of answer was implied some time ago in the observation that what varies from one instance to another are the particular meanings and wordings which contribute to the unique pattern of the text's texture, while the structure specific to the text type stays constant to the type's potential (Hasan 1985a: 97ff). Hence, our conviction that in all these cases we are engaged in the same kind of talk. This claim is not very different from Bakhtin's (1986: 60) observation that in language use 'each separate utterance is individual', but the speech genre developed over time remains stable. However, in retrospect, such observations appear not to explain the origins of variation and consistency; they are simply a technical 'description' of where variation and consistency are manifested in discourse. What is needed is to identify the motivational relevancies which underlie the presence of the robust consistency and the systematic variation found in most discourse types. I will open this discussion with a word about *discourse* and *variation* in order, not so much to explain the terms as to locate my own stance.

A Word on Discourse

Today, discourse is, in the words of Basil Bernstein (1990, 1996), a privileged and privileging term. So not surprisingly everyone is 'doing discourse'. This popularity of the field has gone hand in hand with many ways of deploying the term *discourse*. Not surprisingly, the semantics of the term has now many variants, and where there is variation, there will be valuation. In the nature of things, this valuation is commensurate with the fame of the scholar from whom the term is borrowed. I am not objecting to this intellectual piggy-backing; what causes concern is that the borrowed term remains undertheorized in the borrower's framework if they have one.

Recognizing this problem, Henry Widdowson (1995) suggested clarifying the concept before proceeding with any discussion of the nature, function, and analysis of discourse. However, providing definitions of a theoretical term – be it discourse or variation, dialectic or determination, intertextuality or hybridity – requires that it be positioned *vis-à-vis* other concepts in the theory – a position argued so effectively by perceptive scholars (Firth 1957; Bernstein 1996). For this reason, the semantics of terms in a theory is 'ineffable' (Halliday 1988); like the dictionary's meaning of lexical items, it is a descriptive convenience, something of a placeholder; and it is in this light that I offer the definition of discourse as it is used in Systemic Functional Linguistics (SFL): *discourse is the process of language in some recognizable social context(s)* – a densely coded definition, which I hope to clarify later.

Variation and Consistency in Discourse

Variation is a common term among sociolinguists. But I intend to probe into its meaning as if nothing had been written about the word. This may

help me avoid taking on board preconceptions that engagement in dominant sociolinguistics is likely to encourage. If, like a lay person, I consult any
dictionary, it will most probably indicate that variation is a divergence from
the consistent, that it refers to difference from what is stable, normal or
typical. Thus, the meaning of *variation* is arrived at by focusing on the
meaning of *consistency*, or *normality*. I follow this route because it juxtaposes
variation and consistency. Later I will argue that variation is in fact a form of
consistency, which is differentially valued by the members of different
social groups or by sub-communities of a wider community.

In his plenary address to the 28th International Systemic Functional
Linguistics Congress, Lemke commented on the production of artefacts,
built over a large time-scale. Discursive consistency resembles such artefacts; it too gets built up over considerable time spans. But it differs from
individual artefacts such as Alhambra or the Sagrada Famiglia, which,
though built over decades and centuries, differ from discursive consistency in a crucial respect. They are 'one-off' products – 'individuals', built
over time but without any instantiation. To evolve naturally, discursive
consistency, like consistency in other social practices, requires a substantial body of instantiations. Each instance varies from other instances;[2] but
to be taken as an instance of the same particular category, it must display
some features that remain stable over a multitude of instances, the
instantiations occurring over a substantial period of time. The Shakespearean sonnet as a generic form, would, for example, be readily recognized as such by a particular sub-community, aware of Western literary
traditions. But, to state the obvious, when Shakespeare wrote his first
sonnet, there did not then exist a discourse type called 'Shakespearean
sonnet': what he did was simply different from anything called 'sonnet' up
to that point. However, through a number of instantiations over time, the
genre is now sufficiently established so that to say, today, that something is
a Shakespearean sonnet is to imply the presence of a certain set of
specifiable properties in it: the configuration of these properties has, by
definition, become a *sine qua non* for the category. In general terms,
this same mode of development applies also to other discourse types
such as scientific writing, buying-selling interaction, casual conversation,
advertisement, and so on.

So for some instance to be perceived as consistent, it must be relatable to
a type. A type is knowable by a certain configuration of properties, which
themselves need to have been instantiated with a sufficient frequency over a
sufficient extent of time within the context of that type of social action
which is being brought into existence by this process. However, frequency
and persistence in time are only the necessary conditions for something
being perceived as consistent; they are not, by any means, sufficient. For
example, one single individual's 'learnt' pattern of behaviour might appear
in a stable manner in a particular kind of action undertaken frequently,
and yet this would be regarded not as consistency but as eccentricity. The
crucial difference between eccentricity and consistency resides in the

community's validation of the pattern: this is achieved by the community adopting the pattern as part of its own practice, thus bestowing on it an 'objective reality'. So, typically, if a behaviour pattern is perceived as stable, normal or consistent, and not just eccentric, this is by virtue of its currency in the relevant community. In making these observations, I am simply describing how things are in our society – what typically gets regarded by human beings as normal or, indeed, rational. It is no part of my description to evaluate the prevalent modes of legitimation. Certainly such evaluation is important, but it is, in my view, ideologically suspect to silently merge description and evaluation as if the author's preferred stance were not open to question. Whatever one's view of these legitimation practices, if the description of this actual process appears to be empirically valid, then to be seen as consistent and not idiosyncratic, a pattern of behaviour must be evaluated as *the* appropriate pattern by the members of that section of the community in which it is manifested. It follows that terms such as *variant* and *norm* – and their derivatives – act inherently as *shifters* in Jakobson's sense of that term: which member of the pair will be used depends on who is speaking. One person's norm is another person's variant, and, more often than not, an undesirable one. To sum up, then, for a behaviour pattern to acquire the attribute of consistency/stability/normality, it must meet three requirements:

- display frequency of instantiation and persistence in time;
- be specific to some particular form(s) of interaction; and
- possess objective reality, being viewed by a given community as *the* appropriate, normal behaviour in the context of such interaction(s).

So what of variation? To say, as I have done above, that variation and consistency are shifters is to say that, in general terms, variation would share the same three characteristics that are the defining properties of consistency. So note, first, that the term variation cannot be applied to any pattern that does not have sufficient frequency of instantiation: by the same token, a chance event or episodic divergence from 'norm' is not a case of variation; it is at best a perturbation of the existing situation which awaits other such perturbations over many instances and over a sufficient span of time before it can be viewed as socially significant enough to be treated as variation. Second, like consistency, patterns of variation too are specific to particular form(s) of interaction: what happens in one context is not necessarily relevant to another context. And, finally, variant patterns possess 'objective reality'; they are ratified as legitimate by some sub-community, which adopts this (variant) pattern as a normal mode of being, doing or saying. Further, consistency and variation are very closely related in another sense: something can be viewed as variation only in the context of some consistency, and similarly consistency is a meaningful concept only where the potential for variation is present.

Kinds of Discursive Variation

The concept of variation offered above is qualitatively different from that made popular under the same label in Labov's (1966, 1972) seminal work. As used here, it includes not only the sense of variation in the Labovian paradigm, but all forms of linguistic variation as well,[3] for example Hymes' speech varieties (Hymes 1986), which closely resemble Halliday's register variation (Halliday *et al.* 1964), whose status in Labovian sociolinguistics remains ambiguous.

All categories of social practice act as the site for variation/consistency, the social practice of *discourse* not excepted. What makes discourse exceptional is that within any instance of a discourse type, different kinds of variation co-occur, and are unobtrusively interwoven into the text's fabric, with the implication that without an understanding of what one is looking for, it is in many cases problematic to even 'see' the various kinds of discursive variation within one and the same instance; disentangling them one from the other is harder still. To add to this difficulty, in (socio)linguistics a strong tradition exists of treating the behaviour patterns of the dominant social group(s) as 'normal', not as representing a variation on other groups' norms, which is what they actually are. This leads to problems. The term 'copula deletion', for example, implies that the presence of copula is the norm, which it is but *only* for the dominant group of English speakers. It follows that where the discourses of a certain social group are concerned, often no variation can be found. Obviously, it is important to guard against such 'miscognition' in the analysis of discursive variation, and this demands a clear understanding of the scope of the concept as well as the forms it can take in discourse.

Very early in the development of SFL theory, Halliday offered a principle for distinguishing the various varieties of linguistic variation: he argued that language as process varies by reference both to 'the users and uses of language' (Halliday *et al.* 1964: 75ff), each yielding one general category of linguistic variation.[4] Halliday suggested that different users – or more precisely, users belonging to different social groups or 'user-types' – have different norms. This means, in turn, that in theory, and often in practice, there can be as many varieties as there are social groups/user-types in a community, each norm differing systematically from others.[5] I will refer to this kind of variation as *dialectal variation*. The label represents an extension of the meaning of the word *dialect* as used in most sociolinguistic literature, a point developed below (see 'Dialectal Variation' on p. 35). Side by side with this variation, there is also variation by use: different uses – more precisely, different contextual configurations which activate the use of language – give rise, over time, to different varieties. This is the principle that underlies the well-known notion of *register* in SFL, a kind of variation known, after Gregory (1967), as *diatypic variation*. These two general types of variation – dialectal and diatypic – offer sites for further variation.

Diatypic Varieties

The notion of context is crucial to diatypic variation. This relationship is highlighted in the definition of discourse as 'the process of language in some recognizable social context(s)'. The preposition 'in' in this formulation could, however, be misleading; it is not simply that texts happen *in* some context, or that context is a 'container' within which texts get 'placed'; the fact is that their relationship is solidary (Hasan 1980). Figure 1.1 borrowed from Halliday (1999: 8) displays the postulated relationships between: (a) context of culture and context of situation; (b) between language and text; and (c) among these four terms of the theory, which are closely implicated in the production of discourse. In short, this figure shows the relationship of language as system and process to culture as system and process.

To the 'note' at the bottom of Figure 1.1, a word should be added about the relation of realization. Realization is a dialectical relation (Halliday 1992; Hasan 1995, 1996). To say that context of situation is realizationally related to the process of language as text is to say that the two are governed by a co-genetic logic: a social situation is (largely) *construed* by a text/ discourse, and the text is itself *activated* by the relevant context of situation. All things being equal, what we find in an instance of some register variety is a response to the relevant context of situation, which is itself perceived as this or that type of situation because of what language – often along with other semiotic modalities – is accomplishing. This is a large claim, sustainable only if the concept of context is robust enough to bear the weight.

Much has been written on the nature of context in linguistics; in SFL

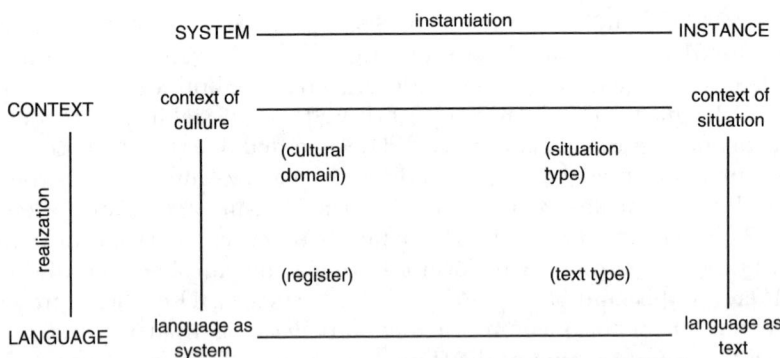

Figure 1.1 Language and context; system and instance (from Halliday 1999: 8)

Note: Culture instantiated in situation, as system instantiated in text. Culture realized in/construed by language; same relation as that holding between linguistic strata (semantics: lexicogrammar: phonology: phonetics). Cultural domain and register are 'sub-systems': likeness viewed from 'system' end. Situation type and text type are 'instance types': likeness viewed from 'instance' end.

alone we have a huge literature (Butt 2001; Cloran 1994; Firth 1957; Gregory 1988; Gregory and Carroll 1978; Halliday 1973, 1974, 1977, 1985, 1999; Hasan 1973, 1978, 1980, 1985a, 1995, 1999a, 2001a; Martin 1985, 1992; Matthiessen 1993; etc.). The views are not always in agreement, a theme to be side-stepped here. I adopt the Halliday and Hasan perspective because I perceive it to cohere better with the conceptual syntax of SFL theory.[6] In this perspective, context of situation as construed by discourse is a tripartite entity, each component of which is always active in the production of a text. Thus, instances of discourse must always construe the specific identity of social action, what is being done by way of using language: this aspect of context is the *field of discourse*. At the same time, the language in use must be indicative of the social relations being enacted between the interactants: this is the *tenor of discourse*. And finally, the text's language must also be indicative of the nature of the contact between the speaker and the addressee – whether the two are face to face, if the addressee is present, or if absent whether the addressee is *actual* or *virtual* (Hasan 1999a), and so on: this is the *mode of discourse*. The qualifier *of discourse* is a reminder that unlike the 'cultural activity theory' associated with the Russian, especially (neo-)Vygotskian literature (Engeström *et al.* 1999), 'context theory' was not intended to apply to all kinds of social action, being designed specifically with discourse in mind. In this sense the evolution of the concept of context can be traced ultimately to Plato's *organon modelle*, on which Bühler (1934) built his theory of the functions of language. So far as SFL theory is concerned, the immediate inspiration for the theorization of context came from Malinowski (1923, 1935) and Firth (1957), but in SFL too the idea of context is closely linked to metafunctions: contexts as instantiations of the complex system of culture cannot be linguistically construed; and texts cannot be created without the simultaneous play of the metafunctions postulated by Halliday (1979).

Each of the three components of context of situation – field, tenor, and mode – represents a wealth of alternative possibilities for the speakers: technically, these terms name situational vectors, each of which may be instantiated by one of an enormous range of values; and the values of each vector are systematically related to each other. This allows a paradigmatic description of these components; in other words, we can extend the system network technique of description beyond language into the context of situation. Indeed, examples of initial attempts already exist (Butt mimeo; Cloran 1987; Hasan 1999a; Martin 1992). Figure 1.2, representing a description of field, is an example from Hasan (1999a: 311).

Avoiding details here,[7] note that, like system networks at the three linguistic levels, the networks at this language-external level too require similar criteria for validation. Their realization must be explicitly stable, and, just as at the primary level of delicacy MOOD and TRANSITIVITY systems exhaustively describe the potential for all classes of the unit *clause*, so also the primary systems in Figure 1.2 must exhaustively describe the potential of all forms of field since, as the point of origin for this network, it is this

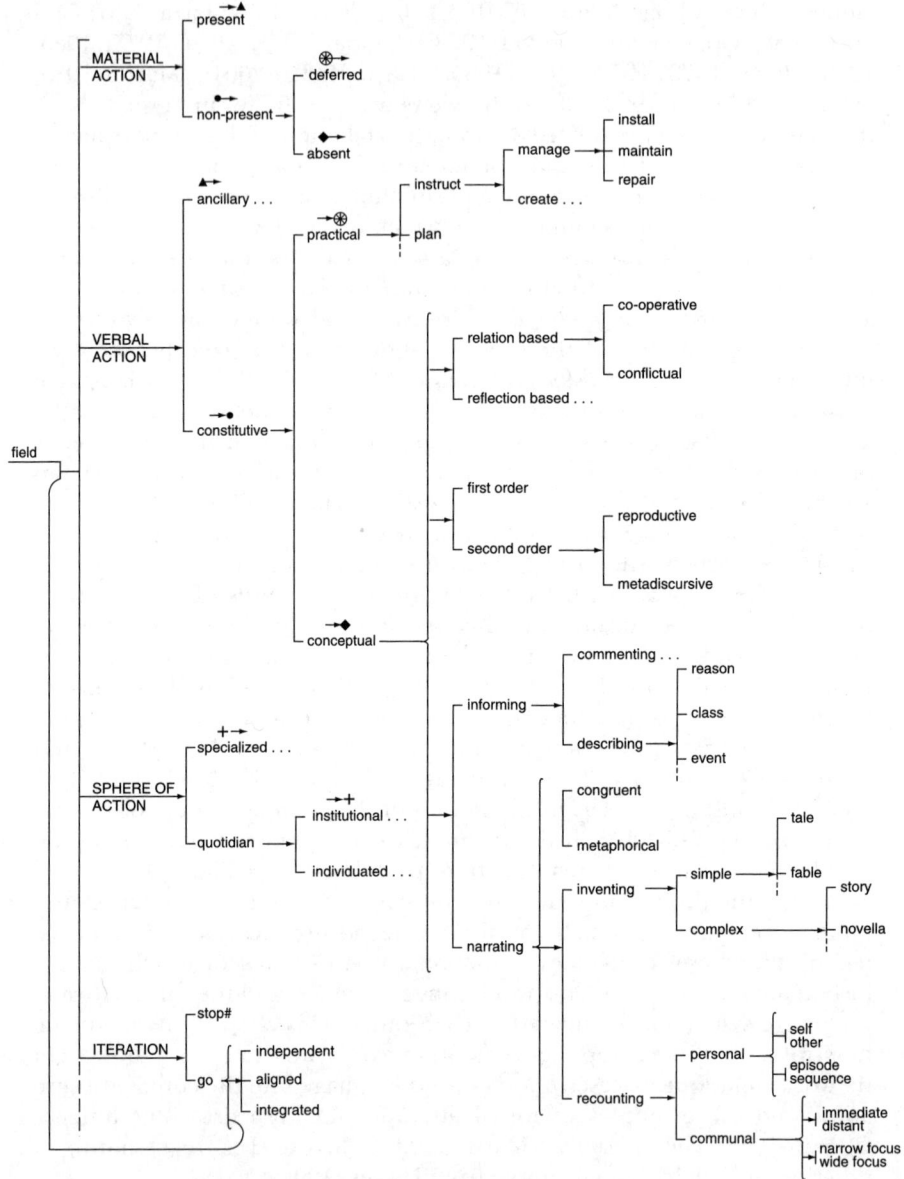

Figure 1.2 A paradigmatic description of the field of discourse (amended from Hasan 1999a: 311)

contextual component which is being described. Figure 1.2 implies a claim that the systemic options of the four parameters included in this network are sufficient to describe, up to a certain degree of delicacy, all those social actions apropos of which the process of language occurs, and that there are no social actions relevant to text production that cannot be so described by the system or by its legitimate progression in delicacy.[8] The claim may or may not be valid when confronted with a much larger quantity of discursive data; that is, however, an empirical issue.

Variation and Consistency in Diatypic Varieties

All texts capable of instantiating some diatypic variety must possess two attributes: *texture* and *structure* (Halliday and Hasan 1976; Hasan 1985a). We have known from the early days of text analysis (Hasan 1978, 1980, 1984a, 1984b, 1985a) that texts instantiating a given diatypic variety, for example advertisement or shopping over the counter for daily needs, display consistency in structure across unique instances of the same variety, while, in respect of texture, each is unique. Despite this, texture and structure both present a locus for variation. Let us take structure first. Hasan (1978, 1985a) introduced the notion of *structure potential* to account for consistency across the instances of a diatypic variety. Structure potential is a specification of the possibilities of structural shapes open to a particular diatypic variety; it thus offers a range of structures all of which are associated with that variety, and each instance of the variety, as it were, moves within this specified structural range.[9] This suggested the notion of *obligatory* and *optional* elements of text structure. Cross-cutting the distinction between these two categories was the notion of their *fixity* or *mobility* in the syntagmatic sequence. Consistency is manifested by the occurrence of obligatory elements and by elements occurring in their fixed place in sequence. Naturally, then, these properties furnish the *recognition criteria* (Halliday 1988) for the variety in question; they were its *sine qua non*, in the same way that the rhyme schema (abab, cdcd, efef, gg) is the *sine qua non* of the Shakespearean sonnet.[10] Variation in structure within the given diatypic variety (and so leading to more delicate sub-varieties of that diatypic variety) is manifested by the occurrence of optional elements and/or choice of one from some other possible location for the elements' occurrence (Hasan 1985a). In other words, this approach to discursive analysis presented criteria for recognizing a particular diatypic variety as well as its sub-varieties, by keeping the issue of principled variability in view. I shall return to structure as the locus for discursive variation below.

As for texture, underlying it are patterns of semantic connectivity, realized lexicogrammatically by cohesion and cohesive harmony (Hasan 1984b, 1985a; Butt 1987; Cloran 1999a; Lukin 2002). Like structure, it displays consistency but at the same time remains open to variation. Both attributes can be traced back to the role of meaning in realizing the elements of textual structure, which occur not by force of some immanent 'rule'; nor are they imposed by an authority external to the practising members of the community; they occur only by way of language perform- ing some specific function in the relevant activity, and so constitute a record of social practice. For example, 'Placement' in nursery tales is a device for the *mise-en-scène* of the main dramatis personae (Hasan 1984a); similarly 'Sale Request' in a shopping interaction identifies the commodity being sought by the buyer (Hasan 1985a), and so on. In other words, some specific meanings have to be lexicogrammatically construed at that point in order for the activity to come off. To the extent that the recognition of a diatypic variety depends on its obligatory elements of structure, to that extent those meanings must be selected that are *crucial* to the realization of the obligatory elements, relevant to the recognition of that variety. Consist- ency in texture across instances of some given diatypic variety is manifested by these crucial meanings, which is not to say that the words and vocables are 'prescribed' and 'invariable' because there is no one-to-one cor- respondence between wording and meaning: this, after all, is what justifies the recognition of two distinct levels for semantics and lexicogrammar. While consistency arises from the selection of certain semantic options, not from specific lexical items as such,[11] other orders of meaning – called *associated* and *elaborative* (Hasan 1984a) as well as the meanings realizing the optional elements of the generic structure potential (GSP) – can and do vary within a fairly wide range from one instance to another.[12] This range, referred to as the *genre specific semantic potential* (Hasan 1985a: 102ff), is specifiable for any variety; thus, even for optional structural elements, the semantic and lexicogrammatical choices are not entirely unconstrained by the diatypic variety, being instantiated by a text:[13] as Halliday (1978: 185) remarked, a register is known by the meanings at risk in it. The same position is voiced by Bakhtin (1986: 60), who suggested that 'the selection of the lexical, phraseological, and grammatical resources of the language' as well as other aspects of the linguistic organization of the text are 'deter- mined by the specific nature of the particular sphere of communication'. The expression, 'particular sphere of communication' proves problematic as soon as the need arises to explicate the essence of that particularity (Hasan 1995): for example, how far does that 'sphere' extend, and what constitutes its identity? With greater linguistic sophistication we can now be more precise: we can point to the domain of consistency, thus identifying the particularity of the 'sphere of communication', and, at the same time, show where that potential of variation operates, which is responsible for giving an instance its character as an individual instance of a speech genre. It is at this point that the paradigmatic description of contextual components appears to offer an elegant formulation of the principles underlying both discursive consistency and discursive variation in diatypic varieties.

According to the logic of the system network, the progression of the paradigmatic description coincides with progressive moves in delicacy: the primary systems provide a less delicate description than those which depend on them. Assuming that a paradigmatic description of the potential of contextual components is viable, we may claim that the options towards the primary end of the network are realizationally related to the text's structure while those towards the more delicate end would contribute to its texture. In other words, the relatively general nature of the contextual configuration is realized as structure; its more specific aspects which render it an 'individual' occasion for talk are realized as texture. To take a concrete example, the general activity of buying and selling items of daily need over a counter finds expression in text structure, but what is being bought – vegetables or fruit, groceries or meat – is likely to contribute to texture. Note that this situation is reminiscent of that at the level of lexicogrammar. For example, take the systems applicable to the major clause. The primary, less delicate end of these systems specifies the structural make-up of the clause; thus, options such as Declarative, Benefactive, unmarked Theme, and so on 'shape' the structure of the syntagm. By contrast, the progressive moves in delicacy eventually take us to the specification of lexis. Assuming the Roman orthographic conventions, the left of the lexicogrammatical system network specifies grammatical structure; the right progressively construes lexis: this is the principle underlying the description of lexis as most delicate grammar (Halliday 1961, 1966; Hasan 1985b, 1987; Tucker 1996, 1998; Halliday and Matthiessen 1999). If it is true that the primary options of the contextual system networks realize the structure of the text while the more delicate ones realize its texture, then registerial structure is to the texture of a text as grammatical structure is to the lexis of a clause. What this claim implies is that the typically unmistakable registerial orientation of a text as well as its specificity and uniqueness are ultimately realizationally related to the context of situation. In this way, everything in discourse – its structure, its texture, its principles of consistency and variation – is beholden to the relevant contextual configuration (Hasan 1985a) which activates textual selections. It is only logical that given an instance of discourse in displacement from its activating context, 'readers' are able to reconstrue that 'absent' context from the text.[14] This is an important part of what it means to say that discourse is the process of language in some recognizable social context. Table 1.1 summarizes this complex discussion,

Table 1.1 Consistency and variation in diatypic varieties

	Relevant to consistency	*Relevant to variation*
GSP structure	obligatory elements fixed order of sequence	optional elements optional order of sequence
GSSP texture	crucial meanings	associated meanings elaborative meanings

Note: GSP = generic structure potential pertaining to a diatypic variety;
      GSSP = genre specific semantic potential relevant to a diatypic variety.

showing the sources of consistencies by reference to which a basic diatypic variety is identified, and, at the same time, pointing to the potential for variation. It is when speakers draw on these resources for variation, that sub-varieties of the basic diatypic variety emerge.

Note that the textual properties relevant to variation operate independently of each other: in the realization of an obligatory element, associative meanings may or may not be chosen; whether or not they are chosen, the elaborative ones may or may not be selected; at the same time, irrespective of the nature of these choices, an optional element of structure may or may not be selected; and if it is selected, it may or may not have optionality in sequential order. Such claims may frustrate those who like neat and tidy categories and believe in simplicity as a virtue in itself, and, indeed, it has sometimes been said that there is no such thing as 'a' register as postulated in SFL. This is true in the same sense as would be the claim that there is no Declarative clause. Assertions of this kind reveal a confusion between category and instance, forgetting that instance is precisely where other categories are also instantiated; it can, therefore, never be neat and simple. Besides, categories and units tend to be multidimensional; since the various dimensions largely operate independently of each other, the instances naturally display variation. So, each Declarative clause differs from others (unless it is a 'copy'), but each Declarative clause is like other Declarative clauses or else it would not be a grammatical category. The same is true of register, with the simple but significant proviso that the concept of diatypic variety pertains to a much higher order of abstraction.[15] Its instances, typically, have a greater extent, which means the potential for variation is greater. This discussion has tried to explain why substantial sections of the community see *differing* instances of, say, casual conversation as casual conversation, not as anything else. Their perception implies that they are aware at some level of consciousness of both the patterns of consistency and of variation as inherent aspects of the same variety. I mention conversation because it is common wisdom to characterize it as a variety not subject to any specifiable form of regularity in its structure or texture. In my view, this common wisdom is based on a failure to probe something that has become so familiar that it seems to need no analysis.

The Complexification of Textual Structure

The above discussion permits the conclusion that the principles for the structuration of a discursive instance carry within themselves a vast potential for variation while, at the same time, affirming an instance's specific diatypic status. However, as is clear from Table 1.1, all forms of discursive variation so far discussed arise from the properties of the specific diatypic variety – from its structure potential and from its genre specific semantic potential. If the principle for variation remained internal to the diatypic variety in question, then despite the potential of an immense degree of variation in the instantiation of the same basic diatypic variety, it could be maintained that in each of these variant instances, the activating contextual configuration remains the same at a certain degree of delicacy. Such instances honour the principle formulated by Halliday and Hasan (1976: 23) that texts are generally coherent 'with respect to the context of situation, and therefore, consistent in register', which is to say that only one kind of social activity is occurring in the course of one spatio-temporally located inter-action, and so it is realized by one single diatypic variety. This observation applies to a good deal of language use, but not all. If it applied universally, that would imply that specific diatypic varieties themselves are impermeable, each representing a separate domain which never crosses the boundary of another domain. In terms of Bernstein (1990), recognizable social contexts would have to be seen as 'strongly classified', the separation of their boundar-ies being always maintained. But such strong classification is not the universal condition for the process of diatypic varieties. Thus, there are occasions[16] when in the middle of doing one thing, speakers turn to something that could be seen as doing something else, i.e. distinct varieties interpenetrate. In fact, such interpenetration is sometimes cited as the defining character-istic of casual conversation; talk for the sake of talking is often talk apropos different goings-on, all happening between the same interactants in the same spatio-temporal location, and employing the same means of contact. But conversation is not the only variety; official pedagogic discourse is another example. Nothing could be further from casual conversation than classroom discourse, yet Bernstein (1990) defines it as 'instructional dis-course embedded in regulative discourse'. The unavoidable implication is that *there are contexts in which contexts are permeable*. The permeability of con-texts, and of diatypic varieties, furnishes another source for discursive vari-ation. Returning to the text's structural aspect, I examine Extract 1 to illus-trate the functional integration of different diatypic varieties into one text.[17]

Extract 1:

```
01  Mother:    now Stephen, do you want a sandwich for lunch?
02  Stephen:   yes
03             and some passionfruit
04  Mother:    and some passionfruit
05             where is the passionfruit?
06  Stephen:   um . . . um the passionfruit is um . . . um [?    ]
07             do you know where the passionfruit is?
08  Mother:    no
09             you were walking around with it
10             what did you do with it?
11  Stephen:   I don't remember
12  Mother:    is it on the table?
13  Stephen:   let me see . . . it's under the table
14  Mother:    under the table!
15  Stephen:   yes . . .
```

16		here it is
17	Mother:	OK . . . right . . . peanut butter sandwich?
18	Stephen:	yeah . . .
19	Mother:	you go to the table
20		and I'll bring it in . . .
21		there aren't many passionfruits out there at the moment
22	Stephen:	why?
23	Mother:	because . . . passionfruits usually come
24		when it's warm
25		here, you sit here in Nana's seat
26	Stephen:	**why —
27	Mother:	**I'll put —
28	Stephen:	why does Nana like to sit here?
29	Mother:	I'll put —
30		oh it's easy for her to get up
31		if she's sitting there . . .
32		we have to go to Chatswood this afternoon, Stephen
33	Stephen:	why?
34	Mother:	um . . . to . . . Peter has to have his injections . . .
35	Stephen:	[?]
36	Mother:	and we might — if we've got time
37		we might go to the library
38		to see if we can get a book on goldfish
39	Stephen:	why?
40	Mother:	Richard wants to know about how to keep goldfish . . .
41		ah I have to ring up that lady about the music class, don't I?
42	Stephen:	what music classes?
43	Mother:	um the music classes that Daniel goes to
44	Stephen:	oh . . . you mean the um the dancing class . . . Mummy
45	Mother:	yes . . .
46		I'll see if she's got room for you . . . in the class, will I?
47	Stephen:	mm
48	Mother:	OK . . . what would you like to drink, Stephen?
49	Stephen:	um orange juice . . .
50		and I want some vitamin C . . .
51		yeah that one . . .
52		**I want —
53	Mother:	**you can have one tonight darling
54	Stephen:	why? (WHINGEING)
55	Mother:	well, they're very big tablets, sweetie
56		very big tablets
57		five hundred milligrams there are in those
58		that's twice as much as any other tablets . . .
59		so you really had two tablets this morning . . .
60		do you want a banana . . . or some mandarins?
61	Stephen:	um no . . . [speaking continues]

Extract 1 is (a fragment of) one spatio-temporally located interaction. But within this one interaction several kinds of things are being done. Table 1.2 shows my reading of the segments of this extract.

Table 1.2 divides the extract into nine segments, five of which realize the main social activity of the mother organizing lunch for her son in consultation with him. I will refer to this as the *main context*, and to the segments that realize it, as the *primary text*. With one exception, all the other segments constitute *sub-texts*. A sub-text is functionally related to some primary text, thus contributing to its organization. The one segment not treated as a sub-text is Segment (vi), concerned with planning a visit to Chatswood. The relationship of the various segments to the primary text of lunch organization is shown in Figure 1.3, where the primary text is represented by the

Table 1.2 What's going on in Extract 1 (from Hasan 1999a: 248)

Segment i:	lines 1–4	**organising lunch**
Segment ii:	lines 5–17	finding the passionfruit
Segment iii:	lines 17–20	**organising lunch**
Segment iv:	lines 21–4	commenting on scarcity of passionfruit
Segment v:	a: lines 25, 27, 29	**organising lunch**
	b: lines 26, 28,30–1	explaining Nana's seating preference
Segment vi:	lines 32–47	planning visit to Chatswood
Segment vii:	lines 48–53	**organising lunch & vitamin C to eat**
Segment viii:	lines 54–9	explaining about vitamin C tablets
Segment ix:	lines 60–1	**organising lunch**

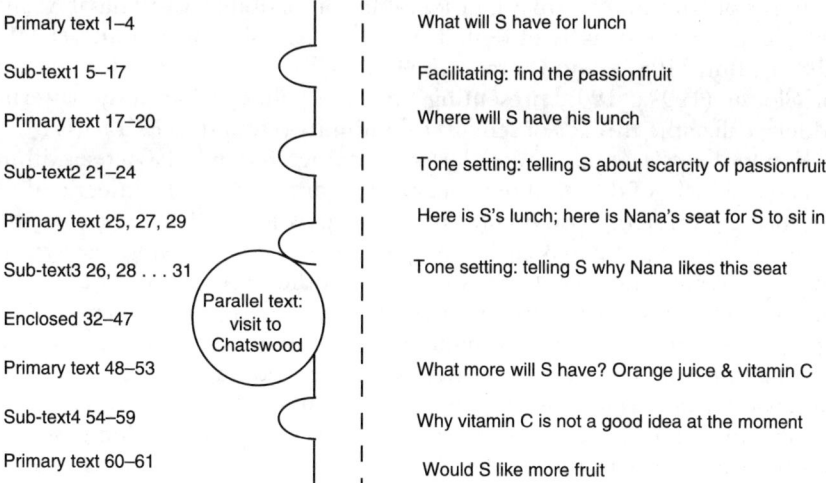

Figure 1.3 Con/textual integration and co-location in Extract 1 (from Hasan 1999a: 260)

straight line, the sub-texts by half circles, and the unrelated segment enclosed in a circle.

The contexts construed by the sub-texts diverge from the main one, nonetheless the sub-texts contribute to the progression of the main text. The enclosure of Segment (vi) in a circle iconically indicates its status as an *enclosed* text whose boundary does not permeate that of the primary text or to the other segments of the extract.[18] Briefly, Sub-text 1 (5–17) facilitates the business of locating one item on the lunch menu; thus, it is something in the main context's field of discourse that has occasioned the appearance of Sub-text 1; it thus performs what I call *facilitative* function. In one respect, this function is very much like Goffman's (1981) 'side-sequence': it arrests the ongoing activity in order to satisfy some presupposition for its completion. Sub-texts 2 (21–4), 3 (28–31), and 4 (54–9) differ in this respect from Sub-text 1: they do not relate to the action in the field of discourse; their function is to contribute to the enactment of interpersonal relations. This I have called *tone-setting* function. If the tone-setting is *positive*, the interpersonal relation between the interactants is maintained and/ or strengthened as happens clearly with Sub-text 2; if it is negative then the relation is put under threat. In Sub-text 4, the tone-setting hovers for a moment between positive and negative poles, but the mother ends up by securing the child's co-operation (60–1). These functions are assigned on the basis of semantic continuity between the primary text and its sub-texts, which takes the form of an integrated pattern of cohesive harmony (Cloran 1999a; Hasan 1984b, 1999a). By contrast, the enclosed text (32–47) does not have any such semantic continuity: its pattern of cohesive harmony stays isolated from the rest, which is the main reason for claiming that it makes no functional contribution to the development of the primary text. These patterns of continuity display considerable compatibility with Phasal Analysis (Gregory 1988) as is evident from the discussion in Hasan (1984b, 1985a), Butt (1987), and Cloran (1999a). Figure 1.4 is a truncated version of Cloran (1999a: 190), presenting only the cohesive harmony patterns which realize the threads of semantic continuity relevant to Extract 1.

Extract 1 realizes (part of) a *complex* text, which is defined as a text within which instances of different diatypic varieties are functionally integrated. If the principle for the production of *simple* texts is *one thing at a time*, the principle guiding the making of complex texts is *different things together*. In the complexification of texts, we have another vector of variation in diatypic varieties: instances of discourse vary along the dimension of complexification – discursive instances realize either one variety in a simple text or integrate two or more varieties into one complex one. But just as variety-internal variation is not random (see Table 1.1), so also variation by complexification is non-random: in fact, variation and randomness are antithetical. There is, thus, a significant difference between complex texts formed by text integration and the pure co-location of texts. By pure co-location, I mean either texts co-occurring in parallel or through enclosure within the same spatio-temporal location. Enclosed text is exemplified by

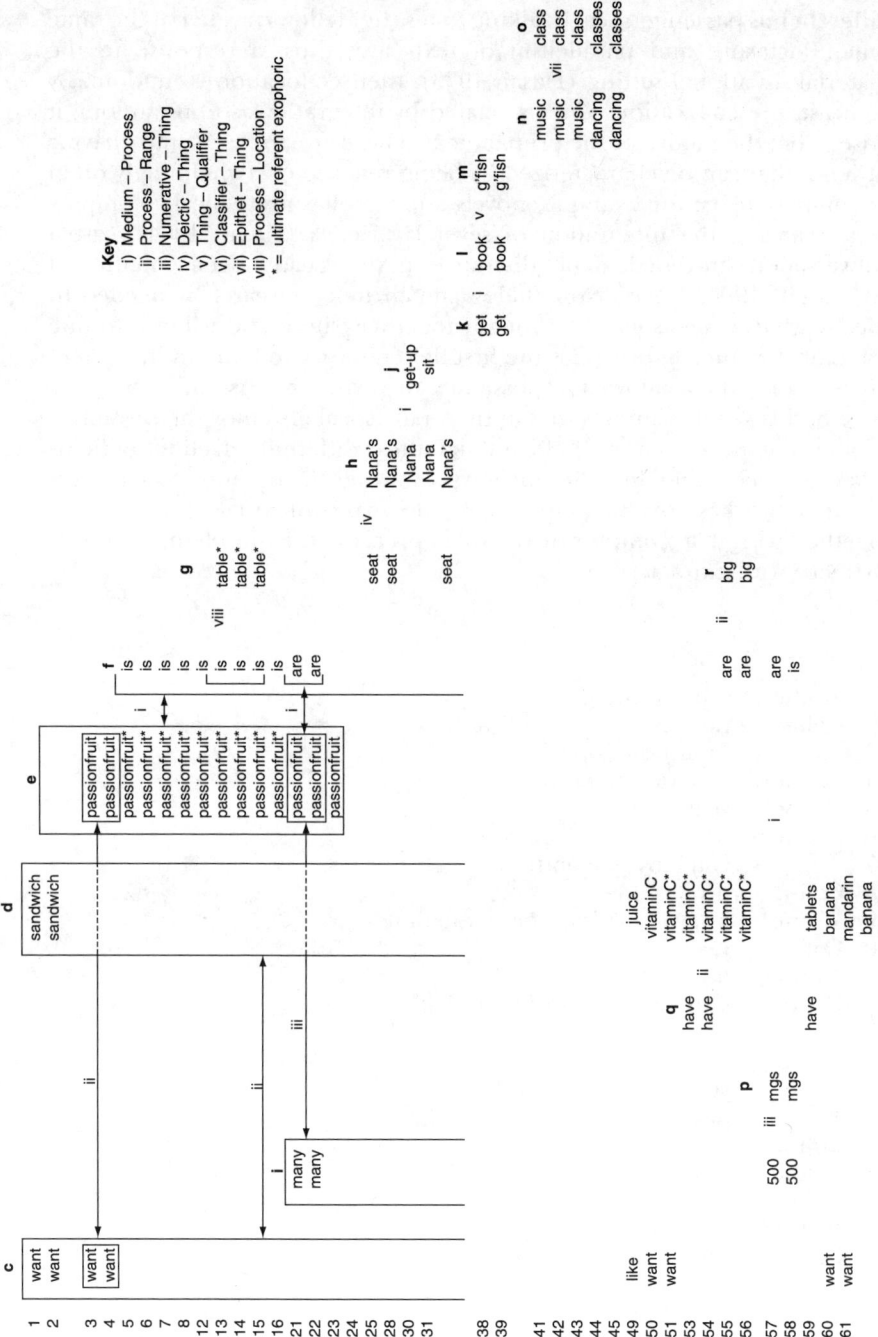

Figure 1.4 Cohesive harmony (adapted from Cloran 1999a: 190)

Segment (vi) in Extract 1. Parallel texts are produced in many different interactions all occurring at the same time in the same place, for example different bus passengers, each talking to his/her fellow traveller at the same time. Enclosure and parallelism of texts are, thus, a response to the material situational setting (Hasan 1973); their co-location is random. By contrast, the co-location of texts related by integration is non-random; it arises from the nature of the primary text. There are, in fact, some diatypic varieties that can be characterized by being realized overwhelmingly often as complex texts: for example, novels and novellas are typically complex texts realizing the integration of several varieties (Hasan 1964); casual conversation and pedagogic discourse have already been mentioned (Bernstein 1990, 1996). Nonetheless, much more research is needed to specify what varieties can be brought together where and when into one functional whole. Figure 1.2 is the first field network to build in the system of iteration, which allows the possibility of textual recursion.[19] The presence of this system signifies that in their talk, speakers enjoy the possibility of choosing more than one field and that these different selections of fields relate to each other in different ways. However, in its present state this system network is not able to specify exactly what contextual choices can go together within a complex text. To appreciate the problem, compare Extract 2 with Extract 1.

Extract 2:

01	Mother:	want some?
02	Colin:	no
03		I want the top
04	Mother:	you want the top?
05	Colin:	yeah
06	Mother:	no
07		you have the bottom
08	Colin:	no
09	Mother:	no, you can't have the top of it
10	Colin:	yes
11	Mother:	no
12	Colin:	that's not — can I have that?
13		that's lettuce
14	Mother:	that's right
15	Colin:	you can eat [? letta]?
16	Mother:	lettuce
17	Colin:	lettuce?
18	Mother:	mm
19	Colin:	I said 'lettuce'
20	Mother:	good boy! ...
21	Colin:	oh ... eat all of [? that] ...
22		you can't get me
23	Mother:	mhmmhm ... yes I can
24	Colin:	no

25	Mother:	yeah
26	Colin:	no . . . can't get me
27	Mother:	I might
28	Colin:	go on . . . [?] . . . get me
29	Mother:	got you
30	Colin:	get me . . .
31		I want you to get me . . .
32		get me
33		get me, Mummy
34		see if you can get me (MOTHER AND CHILD LAUGH) . . .
35		can you swear at school?
36	Mother:	oh no
37		it's naughty
38	Colin:	no, not when you [? hear me]
39	Mother:	no, you're not allowed to swear at all
40		not even when I can't hear you . . .
41	Colin:	mm
42	Mother:	if I [? find out] you've been swearing
43		you know what's going to happen? . . . (?DOES CHILD NOD IN CONFIRMATION?)
44		what?
45	Colin:	get a smack
46	Mother:	and a big belting
47	Colin:	smack on your bum
48	Mother:	mm
49	Colin:	and on my bum
50		and we smack [? heads]

The primary activity in Extract 2 resembles that in Extract 1: the speakers are a mother and her child; they are co-present and their semiotic contact is dialogic. With all these features in common, one might expect that parts of Extract 2 could easily be integrated into Extract 1. But, if the first 20 lines of Extract 2 are put next to the end of Extract 1, the infelicity of this 'integration' becomes immediately obvious.[20] How can we explain this infelicity?

I have hypothesized elsewhere (Hasan 1999a) that typically two (or more) diatypic varieties can be integrated into one complex text if: (i) the *sphere* in the field is *quotidian* and/or the *verbal action* is either *ancillary* or *constitutive: conceptual* (see Figure 1.2 to locate these terms); and (ii) the mode of contact is identical. Both these requirements are successfully met by Extract 2 in respect to Extract 1. So what more is needed? One very obvious point is that the extracts do not occur in the same spatio-temporal location. But would their doing so provide sufficient condition for integration? I suspect this may not be the case. Imagine, for example, a cocktail party with several guests present, where many interactions might occur at the same time in the same place; but it is doubtful that (portions of) each, or even some of these interactions, could be integrated into one complex text, realizing perhaps a cocktail time chat. Rather, they would run parallel to each other, as would those produced at the various service booths of the same post office, registry office, bank, and so on. This means that the identity of an interaction is not fixed by its occurring at the same time in the same place. This too is a necessary requirement but does not constitute a sufficient condition for integration to occur: the most important requirement would seem to be that *the same interactants should be involved in any one unified inter-action.* This presupposes the same spatio-temporal location for the inter-action, but the reverse is not true. It is this crucial requirement of the same interactants that would be missing in a felicitous integration of (parts of) Extracts 1 and 2 into one complex text. We can generalize that for instances of two or more diatypic varieties to be integrated into one complex text, what is needed is not simply the three requirements of: (i) certain specific selections in the field; (ii) same selections in the mode; and (iii) same spatio-temporal location, but also, in addition, the interactants should be identical. But why should this principle apply at all? What is its significance?

The identity of interactants appears to be a simple concept that, on closer enquiry, presents problems. Normally, in the description of tenor, a good deal of information about the interactants is included. For example, Hasan (1978) suggested three vectors of distinction for the description of interactant relations: (i) agentive role, i.e. what is the relation between the speaker and the addressee from the point of view of the action they are performing; (ii) social role, i.e. their status *vis-à-vis* each other along certain vectors of hierarchy; and (iii) social distance, i.e. their relationship based on their mutual interactive history. Cloran (1982: 95) in her tenor system network shows distinctions along numerous vectors for hierarchic relation, degrees of intimacy, social distance, and so on. Similarly, the tenor system network by Martin (1992: 526, 536) offers an array of choices, including affect and degree of involvement. There is no doubt that the nature of discourse is responsive to these interactant attributes, which suggests that the effort to build these distinctions into our description of tenor is valid. Following such descriptive frameworks, we would most probably analyse the tenor underlying both Extracts 1 and 2, by describing the relation as that between mother as caregiver and child as receiver of care; status hierarchic along vectors of expertise, age, and kin relation, with social distance fairly minimal, affect most probably positive, and so on. This, however, is not their identity as users. What is not captured in this description is the specific *semantic style* (or *orientation*) that the two distinct mother-child dyads bring to their interaction. The semantic style of speakers identifies them as belonging to some specific social group, as being an instance of some user-type. This does not mean that in the absence of this information, the distinctions described under tenor are either neutralized or rendered irrelevant; it simply means that cross-cutting the variation by use, i.e. dia-typic variation, there is also variation by user, i.e. dialectal variation: talk is responsive not simply to what one is doing with whom and how; it also responds to which social group, and what cultural milieu one belongs to – what *type of user* one is and what dialect variety one uses.

Dialectal Variation

It may be argued that the interactants using language by way of engagement in some social activity are also users. So why talk of variation by user as if it were a different thing altogether from variation by use? There is an important principle underlying the distinction. So far in the description of diatypic varieties, the interactants as users have been described in terms of a relatively shifting user identity. A speaker is not always a mother, not always a caregiver, not always an expert. Instead, since the speaker and addressee attributes are typically reciprocal, the speaker identity becomes ineluctably related to the nature of language use, i.e. to the whole contextual configuration, and as the contextual configuration varies from one occasion to the next, so the speaker identity changes as well. By contrast, in dialectal variation, speaker identity is relatively stable; it does not shift from one kind of use of language to another. The attributes determining this kind of user identity turn out to be fairly stable – *when* and *where* does the speaker live and with *whom*. Speakers are, thus, identified by their affiliation to a community that lived, perhaps, in the Elizabethan era rather than today; or by affiliation to a community living in locale A rather than B; or by affiliation to some social group. Popular sociolinguistics has coined terms for the variety associated with each such vector of distinction. So corresponding to *when*, *where*, and *who with*, we have *chronolect*, *geolect* and *sociolect*, respectively. Figure 1.5 presents this relation graphically. A detailed critique of dominant sociolinguistics is not necessary here, but some relevant points must be made.

My first criticism of sociolinguistics is ultimately the paucity of its theorization. Thus, the meaning of the three *W*'s – *when*, *where*, *who with* – has been treated as evident. Time and place are taken note of but treated as if they had no social content. Yet, it can be argued that encapsulated in the three *W*'s is the meaning of human social existence. Being an Elizabethan, for example, would imply living within a particular kind of sociopolitical organization; within a certain mode of the distribution of the community's capital, both material and symbolic; within a certain tradition of the distribution of access to and participation in discourses of various kinds whether specialized or quotidian; possessing a certain level of control on material phenomena; having a certain standard of medical care; entertaining some concept of the possibilities of mobility both physical and social; subscribing to a range of views on right and wrong; and so on. In all these respects, the Elizabethan people differ from today's inhabitants of England: Hamlet as a product of Elizabethan imagination had an 'objective correlative' for his *angst* difficult for the modern Eliot to appreciate![21] During the same Elizabethan era, moving to Peru would reveal a totally different social universe. In other words, places are not independent of time, or vice versa; when it comes to the significance of time and place in social life, they are what social beings make of them with their 'others'. The question *who-with*, thus, boils down to *where* and *when* so long as *where* and *when* are interpreted as what state of societal organization and what place in that organization is

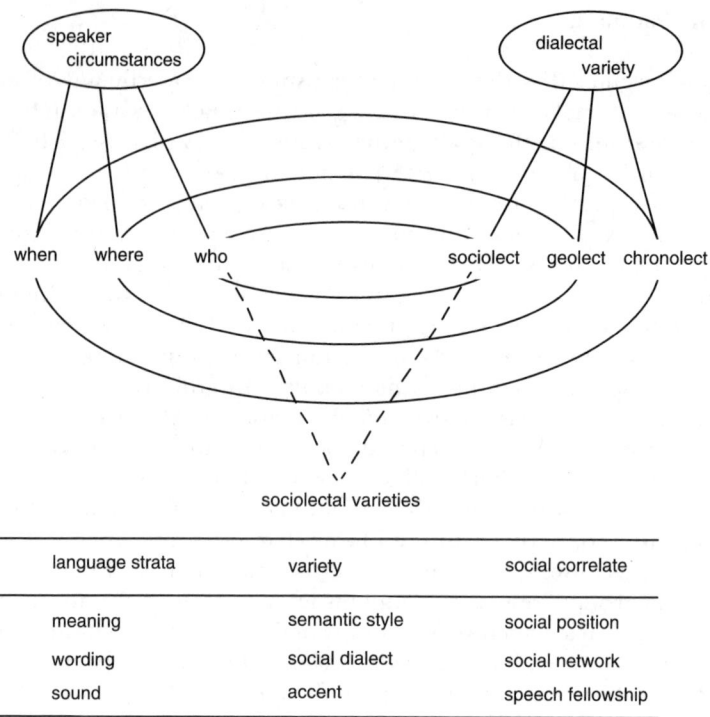

<table>
language strata	variety	social correlate
meaning	semantic style	social position
wording	social dialect	social network
sound	accent	speech fellowship
</table>

Figure 1.5 Dialectal varieties: language and the speaker's social location

occupied by the speakers under study.[22] Ultimately, this is the basis for social grouping. The nesting in Figure 1.5 is meant to indicate that all sociolects exist in some social location and the potential of social location is determined by the state of the social structure in question. From this point of view, the concept of social networks (Milroy 1980) is not an explanation of anything about our social identity; rather, it is itself in need of explanation: what creates non-random social network formations, and why we live and act with some persons rather than others, are questions that sociolinguists might do well to pay attention to. Over the past few decades, we have come to recognize different parameters for grouping people: we invoke gender, religion, sexuality, profession, caste, ethnicity, nationality, race, colour, and so on, but ultimately their significance resides in how they affect one's place in social structure – what Bernstein referred to as *social positioning*. It follows that the most powerful concepts for dialectal variation are the structuring of society and the social positioning of individuals in it because it is these concepts that relate directly to the distribution of power and the principles of control.

My second criticism of dominant sociolinguistics is that it fails to take the potential of language into account. It has not allowed data to speak to it;

rather, it has imposed on its data already existing conceptions of variation and of language. Dominant sociolinguistics has inherited its methodology and its concept of variation from classical dialectology, and its linguistics from an a-social structuralism; and its approach to the social remains superficial. These legacies have brought limitations: for example, instead of viewing language as a meaning potential, it has treated language as a structure of sounds and words. In this view, meaning is the correspondence of words with reality. Reality is out there; it is pre-linguistically categorized, waiting to be named by this or that word. The word could be 'pip' or 'pit' or 'stone' (in a fruit); it could be 'lass' or 'girl' or 'wench'; it might be pronounced /vɑːz/ or /veiz/ to name the object 'vase'. But *legitimate sociolinguistics knows from the ancients* that the objects so named are bits of reality independent of languaging; they remain the same no matter what they are called, or how their names are pronounced. It is hardly surprising that dialectal variation is viewed as 'saying the "same thing" in several different ways' (Labov 1972: xx), with the implication that dialects cannot vary in meaning. If, however, the view is that language is a meaning potential, that different languages construe different meanings, and that these different meanings are (in some way) different perspectives on whatever it is one calls reality, which is therefore unknowable without language, then meaning becomes integral to language. Once the naming theory of meaning is abandoned, then linguistic meaning will have to be seen as intersubjectively real, though not reality itself, whatever that may be. With meaning as an inherent part of human language, a multi-stratal picture emerges, as shown in Figure 1.5 (first column in the lower half of the figure). Sociolects show variation at each linguistic level: Figure 1.5 assigns a distinct label to each sub-variety of dialectal variation (second column). If all these dialectal varieties are called *dialect*, then it can no longer be true that dialects are *always* different ways of saying the same thing.

Some three decades ago, Halliday (1972: 871) remarked that the 'possibility of sub-cultural differences at the semantic level' cannot be discounted, and that there was no evidence to suggest that semantic systems must remain identical across sub-cultures. Meaning is what makes language perform the many social acts speakers engage in; it was, therefore, logical to believe that variation in speakers' social conditions would bear some relation to their meaning-making practices. Indeed, research conducted by Hasan (1989, 1991, 1992, 1993, etc.), Cloran (1994, 1999b), and Williams (1995, 2001) supports this claim. Sub-cultures are created through social positioning, which orients one to a specific reading of what the culture is like, how that universe is organized in which one lives, what the legitimate ways of being, doing, and saying are that define the parameters of what may be perceived as possible or impossible. People differently positioned in society develop different orders of relevance. In short, underlying the sub-cultural differences are speakers' ideological stances, i.e. how they orient themselves to certain meanings.[23] From this point of view, Bernstein's coding orientation described as 'culturally determined positioning devices'

(Bernstein 1990: 13) is active in the production of a social subject's *semantic style*; but if so, then obviously this dialectal variety cannot be viewed as different ways of saying the same thing, and variation cannot be seen as always carried by the differences in sound, simply a matter of *accent* variation. If semantic variation realizes speakers' ideological stance which activates the perspective they bring towards making sense of experience, this would imply that semantic style is also active in the recognition of situation – what is or is not legitimate behaviour in it. It would, thus, be concerned with the organization of meaning in discourse. Of course, due to the arbitrary relationship of the level of sound to those of wording and meaning, the description of variation as 'meaningless' is apt at the level of phonology: as a system of signifiers, phonology simply expresses the lexicogrammar; especially, segmental phonology does not make any direct connection with the level of meaning (Hasan 1999b). The upshot is that accent variation becomes entirely indexical of user-type: it signals the identity of the user in terms of *where*, i.e. what location is occupied by the speaker in the physical and/or social space. The significance of variation at the lexicogrammatical level remains ambiguous, but the discussion of whether or not it also necessarily implies variation in meaning will take me too far afield, though it is certainly an area badly in need of careful research. In closing this topic, let me emphasize three things.

First, contra Labov (1972), the relationship of ideology and semantic variation is properly speaking one of the central issues of sociolinguistics; this issue goes much deeper than forms of address (Brown and Gilman 1968), or words for mugs and cups, or the different names for common sense. Second, semo-logically, every dialectal variety, be it accent, social dialect or semantic style, is able to be realized naturally *only* in some discourse, which was defined earlier as the process of language in some recognizable social context. This has two implications: one, discursive variation, in the sense of variation found in discourse, includes dialectal variation; and two, that if, as suggested above, contexts are realizationally related to texts, and semantic styles are active in the perception of context, then dialectal variation would be relevant to the construal of contexts as well. The third point is that the terms *semantic style* and *semantic orientation* are used here interchangeably to refer to variation at the semantic level. They should, however, not be confused with Bernstein's notion of *coding orientation* which has a wider scope, covering all forms of social practice, not just discourse. Also the term *style* in *semantic style*, is not concerned only with 'how'; governing speakers' 'habitual acts of meaning', semantic style is concerned with content. Diatypic variation and dialectal variation come together in the discourse of speaking subjects via their social identity, in the construal of which their semantic style is crucial, because of its role in the formation of speakers' consciousness (Hasan 1992, 2000, 2002). Quite obviously, speakers' ideology, their forms of consciousness, form the foundation of their discourse as pointed out by Mead (1934), Bernstein (1971, 1975, 1990, 1996), Vološinov (1973), and many others.

Semantic Orientation and Discursive Variation

Discourse analysis assumes that a social situation presents itself unambiguously to the speaking subjects. And so it does perhaps, but the same face is not presented to all. Which face of the situation is revealed depends on speakers' identity in terms of their social positioning. The ideological stances, developed in the experiencing of life, inform social subjects what a situation is a situation for: in terms of Bernstein (1990: 17), through this experience we develop recognition rules for reading contexts, and we acquire realization rules for legitimate performance. In other words, social subjects learn how to read a situation, and by the same token, learn what language games can be played in it and what legitimate ways there are of playing them. So the recognition of context and participation in it are both relative to a speaker's semantic orientation. Cloran's research (1994, 1999b) was the first to reveal how the speaker's conception of context impinges on the nature of the complexification of their texts. Cloran examined the conduct of local pedagogy in mother-child interaction in everyday contexts such as eating lunch together, mother bathing the child or both looking at picture books, and so on. The mothers belonged to either a dominating or a dominated group.[24] Cloran found that, typically, in the dominating group, sites for local pedagogy were provided by welcoming a 'diversion' within these quotidian environments. These mothers allowed the discourse to wander; for them, contexts were permeable. The dominated group mothers put their energy into maintaining the ongoing context; for them, contexts had to be kept apart. Technically speaking, the former group displayed a weaker classification of context and a weaker framing of the discourse,[25] while the dominated group protected the existing boundaries and maintained a stronger framing of interaction. Cloran (1994, 1999b) showed that the kind of discourse which centres around some specialized sphere and unmistakably resembles official instruction occurred more frequently and at greater length in the dominating group. These *recontextualizations* of *official pedagogy* in everyday talk form an important aspect of *local pedagogy* in the dominating class; the dominated group did not have such developed episodes of local pedagogy in their interaction.[26]

Note that Cloran's conclusion from her research was not that the dominating group creates complex texts more frequently; the difference lies in what contexts get integrated in the two different groups' discourse. Further, speaking generally, the function of the sub-texts does not vary across the groups. In both cases, at least in our data, the integration tends more often than not to have a tone-setting function. But within this general uniformity of discursive practice, there is a qualitative difference. Hasan (2000, 2002), confirming Cloran's finding, demonstrated that, in the dominating groups, mothers 'package' information in positive tone-setting sub-texts while, in the dominated groups, mothers either 'package' control tactics often in negative tone-setting sub-texts or exercise control in the guise of humour in positive tone-setting sub-texts as in Extract 2 (35–50). In either event, there is, typically, no room for local pedagogy where official pedagogic discourses could be recontextualized: the closest analogue found in the dominated group is a mother 'teaching' the child how everyday life will need to be lived – for example, Helen's mother informing Helen how important it is to learn how to do housework otherwise, when she has her own babies, she would be in trouble. Clearly, these two semantic styles are somewhat incompatible, and this is why the integration of the segments from Extracts 1 and 2 proved problematic (see discussion above). The requirement for the identical interactants can now be reformulated: *integration presupposes homogeneity of semantic style*. Extracts 1 and 2 belong to the same diatypic variety and both represent complex text (fragments), but their speakers have distinct ideologies which do not 'cohere', rendering integration infelicitous. Contra Martin (1985, 1992, etc.), ideology does not so much activate genre, i.e. a diatypic variety's structural shape, as it gives the entire instantiation a certain 'flavour'. The text becomes indicative of the speakers' mode of relating to the classification and framing practices of their own social groups which vary from those of others. This variation is predicted by the co-genesis of language and mind. Talk in society is positioned and positioning; and it is language as social semiotic that personalizes the brain into an individual mind (Greenfield 2000), construing experience through meaning (Halliday and Matthiessen 1999). Herein lies the power of semantic style.

The speaker's semantic style is most evident in the framing practices in negotiating discourse.[27] Our research shows that maternal modes of questioning and responding to questions vary across the dominating and the dominated groups (Hasan 1989; Williams 1995, 1999); similarly, in making children do things with words, mothers' commands and the rationale for the commands as well as their willingness to allow the child discretion vary significantly across the two groups (Hasan 1991, 1992, 1993). And, interestingly, the behaviour in these respects is of one piece so that the correlation in the maternal semantic style between the two contexts is highly positive. When children's modes of questioning and responding to mother's questions are compared with those of their mothers, there is a strong and statistically significant correlation between their behaviour patterns. Extracts 3 and 4 indicate how questions are negotiated across the two social groups while Extracts 5 and 6 reveal forms of reasoning. Lack of space does not permit an analysis[28] of these extracts, but the difference in the 'tone' is so obvious, that one has trouble remembering that Extracts 3 and 4 have a significantly similar context and Extracts 5 and 6 are instances of the social activity of explaining the reason for some command to a small child.

Extract 3:

01 Mother: wait
02   till Daniel comes home or Daddy
03 Pete: he won't come home

04 Mother: yes he is
05 Pete: when?
06 Mother: he's coming home this afternoon
07 Pete: when is it gonna be this afternoon? (PETE HAS BEEN
                   CRYING)
08 Mother: yeah, he'll get it this afternoon
09 Pete: when is it gonna be this afternoon though?
10 Mother: oh a long time
11 Pete: oh no!
12 Mother: oh yes! oh yes!
13   what time is it? (ADDRESSED TO SELF IN A LOW VOICE)
14 Pete: can I play with [?]?
15 Mother: no
16 Pete: oh why not?
17 Mother: no
18 Pete: oh (RESUMES CRYING)

Extract 4:

01 Mother: can you try and remind me to ring Pam this afternoon?
02 Kristy: mm (AFFIRMATIVE)
03   why?
04 Mother: I'm going to ask her if she'll mind you one night next
                   week
05 Kristy: mm
06 Mother: 'cause I'm going out to dinner with some of the ladies from
                   the playgroup
07   because Sue is leaving
08 Kristy: pardon?** pardon?
09 Mother: I'm going out with some of the ladies
10   because Sue is leaving
11 Kristy: mm
12 Mother: did you know they were going to leave?
13 Kristy: no
14 Mother: they've been building a house
15 Kristy: mm
16 Mother: oh they haven't been building it
17   somebody else has been building it for them
18   and it's nearly finished
19   and they're going to move to their house in May
20 Kristy: why in May?
21 Mother: they're going to wait until the end of the school term
22 Kristy: mm
23 Mother: because Cathy goes to school now
24   and then she will change to her new school after *holidays

25	Kristy:	**mm
26	Mother:	if they'd moved earlier
27		she'd only go to the new school for a week or two
28		and then they'd have holidays, you see
29		it would mess it up a bit for her

Extract 5:

01	Mother:	put it up on the stove
02		and leave it there
03	Karen:	why?
04	Mother:	'cause
05	Karen:	that's where it goes?
06	Mother:	yeah

Extract 6:

01	Janet:	that's you
02		because you don't want me playing with marbles
03	Mother:	Chicky I don't like you playing with marbles
04		when Andrew is around, that's all . . .
05		and you know what, yesterday I found a marble right there
06		when Andrew was crawling around
07		now, it was one of those marbles that you were supposed to put back and you forgot
08	Janet:	and —
09	Mother:	and that's why — that's just why I've got to have a rule about it Chicky
10	Janet:	he has — hasn't swallowed it?
11	Mother:	no
12		well, I just happened to find it
13		before he did . . . before he found it
14		because ≪15≫ he would choke
15		if he swallowed it
16		and that's why we have to be very careful
17		and when you have the marbles —
18		I don't mind you having the marbles
19		as long as he is asleep —
20		and then we check
21		and make sure that all the ones that you have gone back into the bowl . . .
22		that's a pretty fierce looking drawing
23	Janet:	it's you
24	Mother:	(LAUGHS) I know

The Production and the Product of Discursive Variation

Let us consider very briefly, the two major questions 'What produces variation?' and 'What does variation produce?' In this paper, I have focused on identifying the kinds of variation found in discourse, because one cannot really address the above questions without establishing the kinds of variation. I believe this is a prerequisite for addressing the above questions. The answer to the two questions is different depending upon which kind of variation we focus on. Let us take a look at diatypic variation first.

What produces this category of variation is the principle of the co-genetic evolution of language and society (Hasan 1999b). Language and society each act as a resource for the other; thus, diatypic varieties evolve and change with change in the social organization while patterns of the growth of social organization differ, depending on what discourses dominate the society. Specific varieties acquire privileging and privileged status by becoming implicated in the promotion of whatever the dominating groups value, which is predicted to a certain extent by a given cultural state (Habermas 1976). For example, science in the Elizabethan era did not have the power it has acquired since. The valuation of the diatypic varieties, as of other categories of language, is always governed by a *socio-logic* (Hasan 1999b) whereby, as Marx put it, ruling ideas come from the ruling class; but the internal semiotic power of the diatypic varieties is entirely governed by *semo-logic*, i.e. by the design of language that makes language a resource for meaning. In a sense, to identify what produces the variety is also to say what the variety produces: access to a wider repertoire of diatypic varieties is, all things being equal, an unmistakable sign of power. There is, in discourse analysis, a curious situation: a substantial number of scholars are focused on the part discourse plays in bringing about social change, but there is scarce research on and, therefore, next to no reliable account of how the 'genres of power' grow, what nurtures some diatypic varieties, how, and with what results. In this environment, the suggestion that greater emphasis on a social critique of discourse in society is relatively more desirable than understanding how and why language works in society does seem somewhat puzzling: certainly, it is always possible to critique the practices of the power group, to denounce the taking of unfair advantage, to unveil acts of conscious or unconscious deception. But in the last resort, critique is at its best and at its most powerful when it is uttered from an understanding of how the states of affairs have come about that one is critiquing.

Turning to dialectal varieties, among these, semantic orientation is a theme that often rouses emotions; it touches a raw nerve by drawing attention to 'inequalities in the distribution of power, and in the principles of control between social groups' (Bernstein 1990: 13). Semantic styles are directly related to the invidious conditions produced by this situation. Figure 1.6, based on Bernstein's insights, shows that, as he puts it, between language and speech lies social structure; the mediating element is the shaping of human minds, specifically the development of ideological

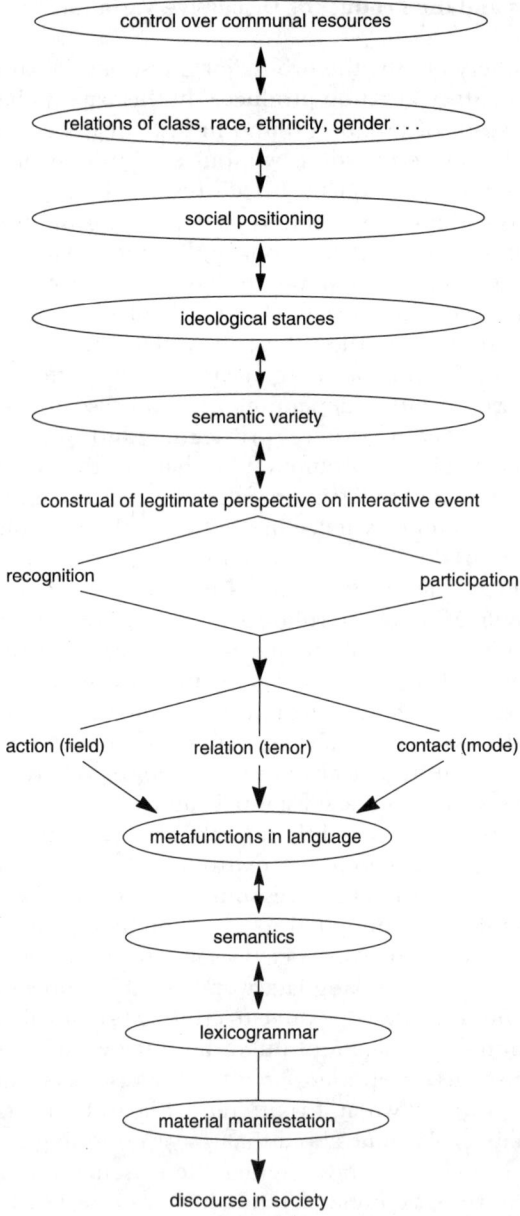

Figure 1.6 Talk in society: from the invisible to the visible

stances which create mental dispositions that regulate the social subjects' relation to all they experience. The organization of the social structure is active in the production of dialectal variation; what it produces is a condition of its own reproduction by acting primarily on the production of forms of consciousness.

Conclusion

There is an assumption that if you talk of language structure, you talk of rigidity; if you talk of system, you devalue the unique, the individual. The discussion of consistency and variation in diatypic varieties presented in this paper throws doubt on these assumptions: uniqueness and individuality need not be, and in the social sphere very often are not, synonymous with serendipity, or chance occurrences. The analysis of randomly selected individual texts can never tell us either about uniqueness or about change; to understand the significance of uniqueness we have to be able to see it side by side with the systematic, the regular. Similarly, focus on the pathology of a system only to point out what 'they', the culpable, are doing is no more useful than becoming aware of how we ourselves contribute most probably unknowingly to this pathology, how our own activities are often in keeping with the ideologies that support the structures of oppression; and this awareness we can achieve only through reflection on how and why systemic stability is maintained. To understand stability is to know what hinders change; to understand system is to understand why process overwhelmingly tends the way it does; and this is surely an important step ahead in producing social change. It has seemed to me for some time now that it is not system or structure that are static; what is static is our ways of looking at them, our mythologies about their nature.

Acknowledgement

I am grateful to Wu Canzhong for helping me with Figures 1.3, 1.5, 1.6.

Notes

1. This is a revised version of the paper presented at the 28th International Systemic Functional Congress, 22–27 July 2000 at Carleton University, Ottawa.
2. On some sources for the uniqueness of instances of discourse types, see Hasan (1985a: 97ff).
3. For some details, see the discussion of dialectal variation in a following section (p. 35).
4. Of course, SF linguists know the story well; if I repeat Halliday here, it is to prepare the ground to show what produces the two kinds of variation, and how and why they interweave in instances of discourse.

5. Social agents seldom, if ever, belong to just one social group since group-defining characteristics typically cut across each other. This implies a complexity in the study of linguistic variation, seldom described with the sensitivity it demands.

6. For some discussion, see Hasan (1995).

7. The interested reader might consult Hasan (1999a) where the network was built step by step with each option and its realization discussed in some detail.

8. See Butt (forthcoming) for an alternative network. It would be useful to compare the two field networks to see which description is preferable and why.

9. Martin (1985, 1992) critiqued this approach to the conceptualization of variable structure in diatypic varieties; for my response to this critique, see Hasan (1995). I take the term *genre* to approximate SFL's *text type* or *register*, but with strong emphasis on its structural aspect as a defining characteristic of the genre. Curiously, though, structure (or, *schematic structure* cf. Martin) remains tied to instance rather than type.

10. It is certainly possible to cite other such crucial identifying properties in the Shakespearean sonnet, but this need not concern us here.

11. This role of semantic options in register studies was suggested in Hasan (1973).

12. For some details about the realization of elements, see Hasan (1984a).

13. For an interesting empirical research on the violation of the genre specific semantic potential, see Cloran (1982). It would appear that even casual conversation, that epitome of hybridity/genre combination, tends to remain within a specified range; the trick is to know how to identify that range. See, however, the next section.

14. Readers not only read the same context from a text, but it is also evident, from the popularity of published materials, that considerable regularities exist in such readings. In the discussion on dialectal varieties I will draw attention to variation in recognition of con/texts.

15. See, in this connection, Halliday (1982) on similarities between clause and text; I should add that a register is an entity at a higher order of abstraction than text.

16. I am not talking here of borrowing expressions from one variety of talk into another, something that is often talked of in discourse analysis under the name of intertextuality, interdiscursivity or hybridity. These notions could be explanatory but, in my view, remain theoretically unanchored so it is not very clear on what ground the presence of these attributes can be claimed. In the description of diatypic varieties, we must move away from single 'words and vocables' for these announce their 'original home' only if they have become ritualized as, for example, have *denture* or *inflation*.

17. Extracts 1 and 2 are taken from data of naturally occurring everyday talk between mothers and their 3;6 to 4;0 year-old children which was

collected for a sociolinguistic research project at Macquarie University by Hasan and Cloran. For accounts of this research see Cloran (1989, 1994) and Hasan (1989, 1992). The transcription conventions are as follows:

[?]	= item unintelligible
[?abc]	= item identified by reference to context/co-text
. . .	= pause in dialogue
(ABC)	= contextual commentary based on recorded material
paired **abc	= overlap in speaking
abc?*	= speaker does not allow time for the other's answer
abc —	= interrupted or discontinued speech

18. The functions performed by the sub-texts in the organization of the primary text are discussed in some detail in Hasan (1999a: 246–70).
19. Precisely for this reason, it is very likely that the system will need to be revised. It is possible that the system of iteration is generally applicable to all three parameters. Here is another area in need of research: How far do two contextual configurations have to differ before they become two distinct identities – two different spheres of communication?
20. Of course, the infelicity of integration becomes obvious more easily if segments have a tangible extent. A line or so of one discourse can be grafted relatively easily into another without causing problems; verbal art, especially poetry, has done this with great effect for generations. But integration is not based on the borrowing of vocabulary or crucial markers of a register. A sub-text must meet the conditions that a simple text does and, at the same time, it should contribute to the organization of another text ongoing within the same spatio-temporally located interaction.
21. Cf. T. S. Eliot's in/famous critique of the prince lacking an objective correlative for his behaviour and the play as 'almost certainly an artistic failure'.
22. For an interesting discussion from a related point of view on the significance of societal organization, see Habermas (1976).
23. See Bernstein (1990: 13) on ideology and social positioning.
24. For some indication of how dominating-dominated groups were established in this research, see Hasan (1989) and Cloran (1989).
25. For classification and framing, see Bernstein (1990, 1996); for the consequences of forms of classification and framing in the context of home discourse, see Cloran (1994, 1999b) and Hasan (2000, 2001b).
26. For official/local pedagogy and recontextualization, see Bernstein (1990).
27. Bernstein presents an elaborate account of framing (1996); it seems to me that all of the parameters might quite possibly not apply in non-pedagogic environments, but this remains to be researched.
28. Detailed discussion of the semantic make-up of questions, answers,

commands, their reasons, etc. has been presented in the work already cited by Hasan, Cloran, and Williams.

References

Bakhtin, M. (1986) 'The Problem of Speech Genre', in *Speech Genre and Other Late Essays*, ed. by C. Emerson and M. Holquist, trans. by V. W. McGee. Austin, TX: University of Texas Press, 60–106.

Bernstein, B. (1996) *Pedagogy, Symbolic Control and Identity: Theory Research Critique.* London: Taylor and Francis.

Bernstein, B. (1990) *Class, Codes and Control, Volume 4: The Structuring of Pedagogic Discourse.* London: Routledge.

Bernstein, B. (1975) *Class, Codes and Control, Volume 3: Towards a Theory of Educational Transmission.* London: Routledge and Kegan Paul.

Bernstein, B. (1971) *Class, Codes and Control, Volume 1: Theoretical Studies towards a Sociology of Language.* London: Routledge and Kegan Paul.

Brown, R. and Gilman, A. (1968) 'The Pronouns of Power and Solidarity', in *Readings in the Sociology of Language*, ed. by J. A. Fishman. The Hague: Mouton, 252–75.

Bühler, K. (1934/1990) *Sprachtheorie*, trans. by D. F. Goodwin. Amsterdam: John Benjamins.

Butt, D. (forthcoming) 'On Establishing the Similarities and Differences between Contexts: A Systemic Functional Approach', in *The Meaning Potential of Language: Mapping Meaning Systemically*, ed. by D. Butt and C. M. I. M. Matthiessen. North Ryde: Macquarie University, Department of Linguistics.

Butt, D. (2001) 'Firth, Halliday and the Development of Systemic Functional Theory: Volume 2', in *History of the Language Sciences*, ed. by E. F. K. Koerner. Berlin: Walter de Gruyter, 1806–36.

Butt, D. (1987) 'Randomness, Order Latent Patterning of Text', in *Functions of Style*, ed. by D. Birch and M. O'Toole. London: Pinter, 74–97.

Cloran, C. (1999a) 'Context, Material Situation and Text', in *Text and Context in Functional Linguistics*, ed. by M. Ghadessy. Amsterdam: John Benjamins, 177–218.

Cloran, C. (1999b) 'Contexts for Learning', in *Pedagogy and the Shaping of Consciousness: Linguistic and Social Processes*, ed. by F. Christie. London: Cassell, 31–65.

Cloran, C. (1994) *Rhetorical Units and Decontextualisation: An Enquiry into Some Relations of Context, Meaning and Grammar.* Monographs in Systemic Linguistics, 6. Nottingham: Nottingham University, Department of English Studies.

Cloran, C. (1989) 'Learning through Language: The Social Construction of Gender', in *Language Development: Learning Language, Learning Culture*, ed. by R. Hasan and J. F. Martin. Norwood, NJ: Ablex, 111–51.

Cloran, C. (1987) 'Negotiating New Contexts in Conversation'. Occasional Papers in Systemic Linguistics, Vol. 1:111–34.

Cloran, C. (1982) 'The Role of Language in Negotiating New Contexts', unpublished B.A. (Hons) Dissertation. North Ryde: Macquarie University, Department of Linguistics.

Eggins, S. and Slade, D. (1997) *Analysing Casual Conversation.* London: Cassell.

Engeström, Y., Miettinen, R., and Punamäki, R. (eds) (1999) *Perspectives on Activity Theory.* Cambridge: Cambridge University Press.

Fairclough, N. (1992) *Discourse and Social Change.* Cambridge: Polity Press.

Firth, J. R. (1957) *Papers in Linguistics 1934–1951.* London: Oxford University Press.

Goffman, I. (1981) *Forms of Talk.* Philadelphia, PA: University of Pennsylvania Press.

Greenfield, S. (2000) *The Human Brain: A Guided Tour.* New York: HarperCollins.

Gregory, M. (1988) 'Generic Situation and Discourse: A Functional View of Communication', in *Linguistics in a Systemic Perspective*, ed. by J. D. Benson, M. Cummings, and W. S. Greaves. Amsterdam: John Benjamins, 301–30.

Gregory, M. (1967) 'Aspects of Varieties Differentiation', *Journal of Linguistics*, 3: 177–98.

Gregory, M. and Carroll, S. (1978) *Language and Situation: Language Varieties and their Social Contexts.* London: Routledge and Kegan Paul.

Habermas, J. (1976) *Legitimation Crisis.* London: Heinemann.

Halliday, M. A. K. (1999) 'The Notion of "Context" in Language Education', in *Text and Context in Functional Linguistics*, ed. by M. Ghadessy. Amsterdam: John Benjamins, 1–24.

Halliday, M. A. K. (1992) 'How Do You Mean?', in *Recent Advances in Systemic Linguistics*, ed. by M. Davies and L. Ravelli. London: Pinter, 20–35.

Halliday, M. A. K. (1988) 'On the Ineffability of Grammatical Categories', in *Linguistics in a Systemic Perspective*, ed. by J. D. Benson, M. Cummings, and W. S. Greaves. Amsterdam: John Benjamins, 27–51.

Halliday, M. A. K. (1985) *Language, Context and Text: Aspects of Language in a Social-semiotic Perspective, Part A.* Geelong, Victoria: Deakin University Press.

Halliday, M. A. K. (1982) 'How is a Text like a Clause?', in *Text Processing: Proceedings of Nobel Symposium 51*, ed. by S. Allén. Stockholm: Almquist and Wicksel International, 209–47.

Halliday, M. A. K. (1979) 'Modes of Meaning and Modes of Expression: Types of Grammatical Structure and their Determination by Different Semantic Features', in *Function and Context in Linguistic Analysis*, ed. by D. J. Allerton, E. Carney, and D. Holdcroft. Cambridge: Cambridge University Press, 57–79.

Halliday, M. A. K. (1978) *Language as Social Semiotic: The Social Interpretation of Language and Meaning.* London: Edward Arnold.

Halliday, M. A. K. (1977) 'Text as Semantic Choice in Social Contexts', in

Grammars and Descriptions, ed. by T. A. van Dijk and J. S. Petöfi. Berlin: Walter de Gruyter, 176–225.

Halliday, M. A. K. (1974) *Language and Social Man: Schools Council Programme in Linguistics and English Teaching: Papers Series II, Volume 3.* London: Longman.

Halliday, M. A. K. (1973) *Explorations in the Functions of Language.* London: Edward Arnold.

Halliday, M. A. K. (1972) 'Sociological Aspects of Semantic Change', in *Proceedings of the Eleventh International Congress of Linguists*, ed. by L. Heilmann. Bologna: il Mulino, 853–79.

Halliday, M. A. K. (1966) 'Lexis as a Linguistic Level', in *In Memory of J. R. Firth*, ed. by C. E. Bazell, J. C. Catford, M. A. K. Halliday, and R. H. Robins. London: Longman, 148–92.

Halliday, M. A. K. (1961) 'Categories of the Theory of Grammar', *Word*, 17: 241–92.

Halliday, M. A. K., McIntosh, A., and Strevens, P. (1964) *The Linguistic Sciences and Language Teaching.* London: Longman.

Halliday, M. A. K. and Hasan, R. (1976) *Cohesion in English.* London: Longman.

Halliday, M. A. K. and Matthiessen, C. M. I. M. (1999) *Construing Experience through Meaning: A Language Based Approach to Cognition.* London: Cassell.

Hasan, R. (2002) 'Semiotic Mediation and Mental Development in Pluralistic Societies: Some Implications for Tomorrow's Schooling', in *Learning for Life in the 21st Century*, ed. by G. Wells and G. Claxton. Oxford: Blackwell, 112–26.

Hasan, R. (2001a) 'Wherefore Context? The Place of Context in the System and Process of Language', in *Grammar and Discourse: International Conference on Discourse Analysis*, ed. by S. Ren, W. Gutherie, and I. W. Ronald Fong. Macau: Universidad de Macau, 1–22.

Hasan, R. (2001b) 'The Ontogenesis of Decontextualized Language: Some Achievements of Classification and Framing', in *Towards a Sociology of Pedagogy: The Contribution of Basil Bernstein to Research*, ed. by A. Morais, I. Neves, B. Davies, and H. Daniels. New York: Peter Lang, 47–80.

Hasan, R. (2000) 'The Uses of Talk', in *Discourse and Social Life*, ed. by S. Sarangi and M. Coulthard. London: Longman, 28–47.

Hasan, R. (1999a) 'Speaking with Reference to Context', in *Text and Context in Functional Linguistics*, ed. by M. Ghadessy. Amsterdam: John Benjamins, 219–328.

Hasan, R. (1999b) 'The Disempowerment Game: Bourdieu and Language in Literacy', *Linguistics and Education*, 10(1): 25–87.

Hasan, R. (1996) 'Semantic Networks: A Tool for the Analysis of Meaning', in *Ways of Saying: Ways of Meaning: Selected Papers of Ruqaiya Hasan*, ed. by C. Cloran, D. Butt, and G. Williams. London: Cassell, 73–103.

Hasan, R. (1995) 'The Conception of Context in Text', in *Discourse in Society: Systemic Functional Perspectives*, ed. by P. H. Fries and M. Gregory. Norwood, NJ: Ablex, 183–283.

Hasan, R. (1993) 'Contexts for Meaning', in *Georgetown Round Table on Language, Communication and Social Meaning*, ed. by J. E. Elatis. Washington, DC: Georgetown University Press, 79–103.

Hasan, R. (1992) 'Rationality in Everyday Talk: From Process to System', in *Direction in Corpus Linguistics*, ed. by J. Svartvik. Berlin: Mouton de Gruyter, 257–307.

Hasan, R. (1991) 'Questions as a Mode of Learning in Everyday Talk', in *Language Education: Interaction and Development*, ed. by T. Le and M. McCausland. Launceston: University of Tasmania, 70–119.

Hasan, R. (1989) 'Semantic Variation and Sociolinguistics', *Australian Journal of Linguistics*, 9(2): 221–75.

Hasan, R. (1987) 'The Grammarian's Dream: Lexis as Most Delicate Grammar', in *New Developments in Systemic Linguistics, Volume 1*, ed. by M. A. K. Halliday and R. Fawcett. London: Pinter, 184–211.

Hasan, R. (1985a) *Language, Context and Text: Aspects of Language in a Social-semiotic Perspective, Part B*. Geelong, Victoria: Deakin University Press.

Hasan, R. (1985b) 'Lending and Borrowing: From Grammar to Lexis', in *The Cultivated Australian: Festschrift in Honour of Arthur Delbridge*, ed. by J. E. Clark. Amsterdam: Helmut Buske, 55–67.

Hasan, R. (1984a) 'The Nursery Tale as a Genre', *Nottingham Linguistic Circular*, 13: 35–70.

Hasan, R. (1984b) 'Coherence and Cohesive Harmony', in *Understanding Reading Comprehension: Cognition, Language and the Structure of Prose*, ed. by J. Flood. Newark, DE: International Reading Association, 181–219.

Hasan, R. (1980) 'What's Going On? A Dynamic View of Context in Language', in *The Seventh LACUS Forum*, ed. by J. E. Copeland and P. W. Davis. Columbia, SC: Hornbeam Press, 106–21.

Hasan, R. (1978) 'Text in the Systemic Functional Model', in *Current Trends in Text Linguistics*, ed. by W. U. Dressler. Berlin: Walter de Gruyter, 228–46.

Hasan, R. (1973) 'Code, Register and Social Dialect', in *Class, Codes and Control, Vol 2: Applied Studies towards a Sociology of Language*, ed. by B. Bernstein. London: Routledge and Kegan Paul, 253–92.

Hasan, R. (1964) 'A Linguistic Study of Contrasting Features in the Style of Two Contemporary English Prose Writers', unpublished Ph.D. Dissertation. Edinburgh: Edinburgh University Department of English and General Linguistics.

Hymes, D. (1986) 'Models of the Interaction of Language and Social Life', in *Directions in Sociolinguistics: The Ethnography of Communication* (2nd edn), ed. by J. J. Gumperz and D. Hymes. Oxford: Basil Blackwell, 35–71.

Labov, W. (1972) *Sociolinguistic Patterns*. Oxford: Basil Blackwell.

Labov, W. (1966) *The Social Stratification of English in New York City*. Washington, DC: Center for Applied Linguistics.

Lemke, J. L. (1995) *Textual Politics: Discourse and Social Dynamics*. London: Taylor and Francis.

Lukin, A. (2002) 'Examining Poetry: A Corpus Based Enquiry into Literary

Criticism', unpublished Ph.D. Dissertation. North Ryde: Macquarie University, Department of Linguistics.

Malinowski, B. (1935) 'An Ethnographic Theory of Language', in *Coral Gardens and Their Magic, Volume II: Part IV*. London: Allen and Unwin, 3–74.

Malinowski, B. (1923) 'The Problem of Meaning in Primitive Languages: Supplement I', in *The Meaning of Meaning*, ed. by C. K. Ogden and I. A. Richards. New York: Harcourt Brace, 296–336.

Martin, J. R. (1992) *English Text: System and Structure*. Amsterdam: John Benjamins.

Martin, J. R. (1985) 'Process and Text: Two Modes of Human Semiosis', in *Systemic Perspectives on Discourse*, ed. by J. D. Benson and W. S. Greaves. Norwood, NJ: Ablex, 248–76.

Matthiessen, C. M. I. M. (1993) 'Register in the Round: Diversity in a Unified Theory of Register Analysis', in *Register Analysis: Theory and Practice*, ed. by M. Ghadessy. London: Pinter, 221–92.

Mead, G. H. (1934) *Mind, Self and Society*, ed. by C. W. Morris. Chicago, IL: Chicago University Press.

Milroy, L. (1980) *Language and Social Networks*. London: Basil Blackwell.

Tucker, G. H. (1998) *The Lexicogrammar of Adjectives: A Systemic Functional Approach to Lexis*. London: Cassell.

Tucker, G. H. (1996) 'So Grammarians Haven't the Faintest Idea: Reconciling Lexis-oriented and Grammar-oriented Approaches to Language', in *Functional Descriptions: Language Form and Linguistic Theory*, ed. by R. Hasan, C. Cloran, and D. Butt. Amsterdam: John Benjamins, 145–78.

Vološinov, V. N. (1973) *Marxism and the Philosophy of Language*, trans. by L. Matejka and I. R. Titunik. Cambridge, MA: Harvard University Press.

Widdowson, H. (1995) 'Discourse Analysis: Critical View', *Language and Literature*, 4(3): 157–72.

Williams, G. (2001) 'Literacy Pedagogy prior to Schooling: Relations between Social Positioning and Semantic Variation', in *Towards a Sociology of Pedagogy: The Contribution of Basil Bernstein to Research*, ed. by A. Morais, I. Neves, B. Davies, and H. Daniels. New York: Peter Lang, 17–45.

Williams, G. (1999) 'Preparing for School. Developing a Semantic Style for Educational Knowledge', in *Pedagogy and the Shaping of Consciousness: Linguistic and Social Processes*, ed. by F. Christie. London: Cassell, 88–122.

Williams, G. (1995) 'Joint Book-Reading and Literacy Pedagogy: A Socio-semantic Examination', unpublished Ph.D. Dissertation. North Ryde: Macquarie University, Department of Linguistics.

2 Predication, Propagation, and Mediation: SFL, CDA, and the Inculcation of Evaluative-Meaning Systems

Phil Graham

In this paper, I propose a theoretical framework for understanding the role of mediation processes in the inculcation, maintenance, and change of evaluative-meaning systems, or axiologies, *and how such a perspective can provide a useful and complementary dimension to analysis for Systemic Functional Linguistics (SFL) and Critical Discourse Analysis (CDA). I argue that an understanding of mediation – the movement of meaning across time and space – is essential for the analysis of meaning. Using two related texts as examples, I show how an understanding of mediation can aid SFL and CDA practitioners in the analysis of social change.*

Introduction: Medium, Media, and Mediation

Much research has been done in Systemic Functional Linguistics (SFL) and Critical Discourse Analysis (CDA) on media texts, which is to say texts *in* the media, or what is commonly termed media 'content'. However, much of this work has been done without an explicit theory of media. The purpose of this paper is to provide a theoretical framework for understanding the role that mediation processes play in the inculcation, maintenance, and change of evaluative-meaning systems, and how a mediation perspective can provide a useful and complementary dimension to analysis for SFL and CDA.

I assume that the most significant commonalities, complementarities, and differences between SFL and CDA are addressed elsewhere in this volume. Also, while providing a brief outline here of what a predication-and-propagation approach means, I refer the reader to Graham (2002) for a fuller account of the analytical method and how it might be deployed. The most basic assumption I make in emphasizing the evaluative dimension of meaning is that it is the prime dimension of meaning for motivating human action, that is, within a given social milieu, I assume people will pursue that which is construed as being of most value, whether that be happiness, holiness, wealth or whatever. There is ample evidence for such an assumption in psychology, anthropology, sociolinguistics, political economy, and many other fields of social science (cf. Firth 1953; Graham 2001a, 2001b). Like Innis (1951) and McLuhan (1964), I also assume that new media forms disrupt and change evalu-ative-meaning systems (hereafter, *axiologies*) both within and between social systems.

First, I will define what I mean by the term 'media', and how techno-logical changes in media environments figure as important *social* forces. In its most common contemporary sense, media refers to technological and institutional systems through which people produce, store, distribute, and 'consume' symbolic material on a mass scale: television, radio, the press, the Internet, and so on. That view tends towards seeing media as techno-logical forms. Another sense of the term refers to various media texts and text types: news stories, reality TV, action movies, editorials, and so on. That view tends towards seeing media as forms of content. A third, less common view incorporates both these perspectives. It also accommodates a proces-sual view of media and allows for multiple perspectives on media in terms of production, consumption, distribution, and transformation of meanings. That view is described by Silverstone (1999) as *mediation.*

Mediation includes the production, movement, and transformation of meanings within and between social contexts, across space and time. It is a perspective that sees 'the movement of meaning from one text to another, from one discourse to another, from one event to another' and 'the con-stant transformation of meanings, both large-scale and small, significant and insignificant' in 'writing, in speech and audiovisual forms' (Silverstone 1999:13). It includes technological, social, institutional, and content pers-pectives on media without confounding them.

Technology, Medium, Genre, and Mode

The technological characteristics of specific mediation systems have effects on *how* meanings are moved, but not necessarily *which* meanings can get moved (whether at lexical, semantic, grammatical or discoursal levels). Television, for instance, can just as easily be used to move pornographic meanings as it can to move evangelical ones, just as print or radio can. In distinction to the concept of media, and more broadly, 'technology is *how* we do things' (White 1940: 141). It is the technological character of a medium that makes, for example, political debates in print or on the radio appear to be entirely different forms of meaning than televised versions of the 'same' debates. Put differently, seen from a technological perspective, there are hierarchies of media, genres, and modes expressed in whichever instance of meaning discourse analysts may care to identify (see Figure 2.1). The particulars of these arrangements and hierarchies change when new technological forms are introduced into a media environment (Innis 1951; McLuhan 1964).

Despite the technological character of a medium exerting its most direct and apparent constraints upon the kinds of modes it will accommodate –

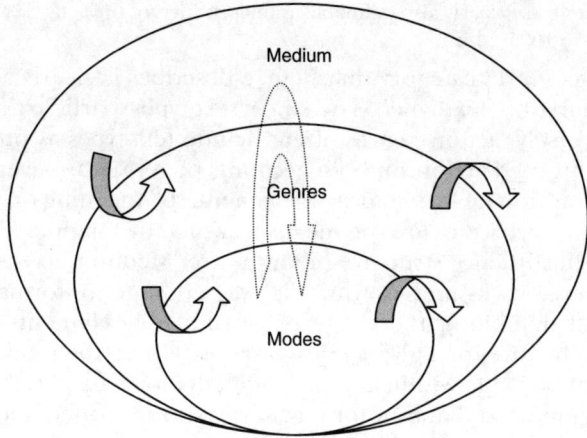

Figure 2.1 Arrangement of medium, genres, and modes from a techno-logical perspective

for example, one can neither transmit photographs through the medium of radio nor sound waves through print media – mode is a far more con-crete analytical category than genre. A given medium will accommodate a theoretically infinite number of genres while accommodating a definite and finite number of modes. A given genre is constituted by multiple modes, and all meanings are multi-modal. Genre, then, at least in the per-spective presented in Figure 2.1, has technological, media-logical, and multi-modal dimensions. Genres are never formally independent of technologies or mediation processes; therefore, any account of genre must also include an account of its technological aspects, how it is mediated, and of the modes which typically constitute a given genre. Modes are the means by which genres are textured, or *formed,* whereas genres express historical inculcations of patterned interactions within and across cultures. Genres *are* patterns of interaction, not merely classes of artefacts. A genre, according to the artefact view of genre, is

> a text-type specified by identifying a common structure of functional units (obligatory and optional) that is repeated again and again from text to text . . . A genre has a constituency structure in which each constituent plays a functional role in the whole and has specific functional meaning relations to the other constituents on its own level. (Lemke 1998b: 1182–3).

Seen as patterned action, genres can also be described as

> *activity formations,* the typical doings of a community which are repeatable, repeated, and recognized as being of the same type from one instance or occurrence to another. A baseball game, a train ride, writing a check, making a phone call. We could also call these *action genres.* Among the special cases of action genres are *speech genres* and *written*

genres, but these are clearly also definable as the products of the activities that produce them. (Lemke 1995: 31–2).

The 'action genre' category that Lemke describes is clearly a more general one than the 'text-type' view since text-types participate in action genres; conversely, action genres often include text-types as products and devices in patterned action. In both accounts of genre, however, we see an explicit assumption of typological movements of meanings from text to text. Mediation processes are the means by which this happens. Modes are part of the constituency structure of any genre. Medium, in the view I am proposing here, works in a 'downwards' way upon genre formations, constraining and delimiting the range of constituency elements which can comprise the features of a given genre by constraining the modes by which meanings can be made within any class of mediations. In fact, the *movement* of similar elements so that they form generic patterns – mediation itself – is the essence of evaluative inculcation, and genres appear to be necessary functions of mediation.

Insofar as a genre 'arouses expectations' that people 'never quite expect to see met' (Lindenberger 1990: xv); insofar as the primary function of genres is to elicit and solicit expectations (Graham 2001a); and insofar as institutions are the sites of genre production and of the source of expectations associated with those genres, analysts can assume that institutional axiologies necessarily pervade genres. It also follows that genres are closely linked to the *irrealis* life of social systems (Graham 2001b). Because they are patterned ways of producing expectations, genres link social pasts with the present, and with possible futures. We can see, in our contemporary context, how certain genres such as those associated with the production of news or policy or advertising shape and delimit future potentials for social change by consistently producing and reproducing expectations about future courses of action. Given that there is much in the SFL and CDA literature about genres and modes, the addition of a mediation perspective may seem trivial or unnecessary, if not irrelevant. Yet, SFL and CDA both place a great deal of emphasis on various notions of context. Included in these notions are such concepts as 'heteroglossia', various forms of 'semogenesis', 'genealogy', 'diachronic change', 'agnation', 'genre hybridity', and 'syntagmatic' change (cf. Fairclough 1992; Halliday 1978; Lemke 1995; Luke 2003; Martin 1999). All of these terms presuppose a theory of mediation, a theory of the historical movement and transformation of meanings across times and spaces.

Halliday (1978: 139), for instance, is explicit about the historical character of the relationship between text and context. It is 'a continuous process', and there is 'a constantly shifting relationship between the text and its environment, both paradigmatic and syntagmatic'. However, in both SFL and CDA, the entire class of context-related historical phenomena goes largely unexplained in terms of theory or analysis in respect of mediation – they are assumed as historical phenomena without any mediating infrastructure. People most certainly make, move, change, and conserve meanings over time, but the differences in *how* this happens, within and between social groups, has very important ramifications for the character of a group, its modes and forms of knowledge, and its modes of relatedness (Innis 1951; McLuhan 1964; Postman 1985).

The primarily evaluative impacts that changes in the media environment have are functions of the technical biases of newly dominant media forms. The visual bias of print, for example, both appeals to and emphasizes an entirely different realm of human experience than does the aural bias of radio – visual distinctions are of a very different order than aural ones (McLuhan 1964). The social memory of a group that relies solely upon oral and aural media will have a very different suite of mnemonic devices and social strategies for conserving various meanings than one that relies, for instance, on writing, television, computer technologies or various ratios of these. I contend that discourse analysts cannot understand the character of meaning systems in social systems without understanding the totality of means by which societies store and move meanings.

If analysts are to claim knowledge of a community's heteroglossic inheritances, its semogenetic changes, changes in its generic forms, and so on, they need to understand precisely how systematic ways of apprehending and evaluating the world are inculcated within social systems. Inculcation is a function of mediation. Mediation processes are primarily evaluative because they are processes 'of classification: the making of distinctions and judgements'; they are the means by which valued meanings are carried over historically and propagated, and by which other meanings are devalued and 'filtered out'. That is because mediations are 'central to this process of making distinctions and judgements' and, 'insofar as they do, precisely, mediate the dialectic between the classification that shapes experience and the experience which colours classification, then we must enquire into the consequences of such mediation. We *must* study the media' (Silverstone 1999: 12). Silverstone's words are an important exhortation for SFL and CDA, especially at a time when cultural, political, and economic activities have merged in an almost seamless manner within globally interconnected systems of mediation. In fact, what is currently called the 'global context' could not exist without its systems of mediation (Silverstone 1999: 144).

A Brief Note on Predication and Propagation

The approach to axiological analysis which I have called 'predication and propagation' is a synthesis of Martin's (2000) work on appraisal and Lemke's (1998a) work on attitudinal meaning (Graham 2001b, 2002). The main difference between analysing the axiological aspect of meaning from predication and propagation perspectives is, firstly, the level of abstraction at which analyses are conducted. Lexical resources deployed in evaluative *predication* inscribe or attribute an element of the text with particular attributes. From the perspective of evaluative *propagation*, axiologies can be seen to propagate across the whole course of a text and beyond (Lemke 1998a: 49–53). Beyond specific acts of meaning, which I understand merely as instances of social dynamics, axiologies can be seen to give coherence to practically every act of meaning-making, both large- and small-scale. These axiologies are inculcated – repeated and, by means of repetition, to some degree imposed and to some degree changed – over long periods of time. That includes the neo-liberal axiology that underpins most (if not all) currently dominant political and economic thought. It is a function of repetition, a process of 'permanent, insidious imposition, which produces, through impregnation, a real belief' (Bourdieu 1998: 29).

Implications for Analysis

The following two related texts are useful for seeing the implications of a mediation perspective for the analysis of axiologies in SFL and CDA. I leave aside an analytical focus on predication and propagation to focus specifically on the medialogical relations expressed in the two texts.

Text 1:

Well, there has been some real news this week. The DNC* announced it will hold the 2000 Democratic Convention in Los Angeles. But what you may not know is that the Los Angeles Planning Committee insisted on some minor changes in the convention format. For example, the Democratic candidate must start his acceptance speech by thanking the Academy, and saying what an honor it is just to be nominated. (Laughter.) In addition to the red-meat rhetoric, as usual there will be a fabulous vegetarian plate prepared by Wolfgang Puck. Tough questions will now be handled by stunt doubles. There'll be a fundraiser at Grauman's Chinese Theater. And, basically – even after it's over – in Hollywood, Oscars will still be bigger than the convention. (Clinton 1999).

(*Democratic National Convention)

Text 2:

So with the value of humor so great, it's no wonder that occupants of the Oval Office have added 'humor consultants' to their arsenal of experts. The modern collection of wise men and wise women has been expanded to include a wise-ass. Personally, I think it's only fair that the political world has raided the world of humor. Because America's opinion of its President is shaped more by the one-liners crafted for late-night comics than through the press releases issued by staffers. Which explains why most politicians have come to fear laughter; more often than not, it comes at their expense.

My job is to remind them that humor can be their friend. The trick is not just to steal the format but co-opt the target as well (Katz 2000).

Text 1 is an annual address to the United States Radio and Television Correspondents Association annual dinner by former US President Bill Clinton. Text 2 is a lecture to a University President's Forum by Mark Katz, the person who wrote Text 1, and numerous other humorous scripts for Clinton.

To understand these two texts from a mediation perspective, analysts need to see the institutional relationships established and expressed within and between them. Clinton's address comes immediately after he was acquitted in his impeachment over events surrounding his affair with Monica Lewinsky. His audience is the same group of journalists who pursued him for a full year in public in a most humiliating manner. Katz's address is for an audience of academics. His purpose is to explain the role comedy has come to play in politics.

In Text 1, Clinton actively blurs the borders between the institutions of entertainment and politics by identifying their functional convergence and changes in their relative political importance. The institutions, conventions, and genres of the Hollywood movie industry are, Clinton jokes, to be appropriated by the DNC. Humour derives from Clinton's implicit admission that politics is, in effect, little more than genre-scripted performance ('the Democratic candidate must start his acceptance speech by thanking the Academy, and saying what an honor it is just to be nominated'). The 'red-meat rhetoric' of power politics converges with the fashionably 'fabulous vegetarian plate' served by celebrity fast-food magnate, 'Wolfgang Puck'. Clinton compares the political danger of interacting with his audience when they are being journalists (asking 'tough questions') with the perils of an action movie 'stunt double'. But regardless of how closely the political machinations of the DNC align with the institutions of mass-mediated culture, the genres of entertainment have the upper hand. So, at least 'in Hollywood, Oscars will still be bigger than the convention'. Clinton deploys humour to exercise and negotiate institutional relations of power between entertainment and power politics. The Oscars may remain impervious to partisan appropriations of Hollywood award genres, but the US President is still the Commander-in-Chief of the world's most powerful army. In Text 1, Clinton acknowledges a symbiosis of power – a barely implicit statement of the power-sharing 'deal' – between the institutions of mass entertainment and mass governance, and the movement of genres between these domains.

In Text 2, Katz provides a framework for understanding how such a speech can be made at all. The institutions of humour have been moved from the lowest ranks in the 'hierarchy of genres' (Bakhtin 1936/1984: 65) to having immense political value and power. The 'value of humor' is now so 'great', says Katz, that a US President's 'arsenal' must now include 'humor consultants'. Here, Katz articulates the historical conflation of military, academic, management, entertainment, and political domains. Humour consultants have become necessary in politics because 'one-liners crafted for late-night comics' are a more powerful political force than official statements 'issued by staffers'. Katz identifies two formerly distinct evaluative domains, or social 'worlds' – the 'political world' and the 'world of humor' – claiming the latter has recently been 'raided' by the former for its increased value and power. At the functional level of mediation, the motives for moving meanings between military, academic, management, entertainment, and political institutions can be seen to have overtly axiological underpinnings. The presidential machine has raided humour on the basis of its perceived symbolic value in respect of creating public value for political figures (Bourdieu 1991). To conduct a successful 'raid' upon 'the world of humor', Katz understands that a raid of comedy genres and techniques is necessary but insufficient. Success requires not only the appropriation of the 'format': the 'target' of political satire (in this case, the President's integrity) must also be co-opted. Katz describes an institutional occupation of an entire media space, including its key participants, processes, and circumstances. He is quite explicit on this point, particularly as regards its historical, political, and social significance.

Text 2a:

It was under the license of humor that for eight years I was granted the immunity to walk into the White House and tell the man widely acknowledged as the most powerful person on earth a bunch of jokes with punchlines premised upon his faults and foul-ups.

To his face, I told the kind of jokes most often spread behind backs. Then I recommended he say them himself, out loud, in front of the entire Washington establishment and the White House press corps. It's how I came to find myself standing in the Oval Office, surrounded by high-level aides, looking directly in the eyes of the leader of the free world and listening to myself say: 'Mr President, I urge you to make the "cheeseburger" joke.'

The strategic value of humour and presidential self-denigration draws attention to a substantial shift in public values, one which is directly premised upon the kinds of media environments in which contemporary politics are enacted, and hence upon the axiologies peculiar to that environment. The 'most powerful person on earth' gains political value by being able to successfully perform political satire with the primary target of his jokes being his own 'faults and foul-ups'. In other words, what would be a political expense for Clinton in the hands of another comedian becomes a strategic value because of his own skill as a comedian. Clinton's understanding of this recapitalizing process is evidenced in the opening lines of his address.

Text 1a:

I want to thank you for your invitation to come have dinner with 2,000 members of the Washington press corps. Amazingly enough, I accepted. If this isn't contrition, I don't know what is.

I know you can't really laugh about this. I mean, the events of the last year have been quite serious. If the Senate vote had gone the other way, I wouldn't be here.

I demand a recount.

To reiterate: this is one of Clinton's first public appearances after being acquitted in an impeachment hearing. In five short sentences, Clinton deploys humour to increase his political capital among a hostile press corps by recapitalizing a process that might well have produced his political demise, if not a jail term. After saying how 'amazing' it is that he accepted the invitation, Clinton apologizes for the events of the past year (his appearance is an act of 'contrition'); notes how 'serious' the process of impeachment has been; that it is *not* funny ('you can't really laugh about this'); and then turns a humorous blowtorch upon himself as well as 2,000 Washington reporters by saying 'I demand a recount'. The basis for humour here is that had his impeachment been successful, he would not have had to perform his act of 'contrition' in front of the people who were largely responsible for one of the most intimately personal, sustained, and thoroughly aired assaults on a US President in history.

Katz describes the historical significance of the 'I demand a recount' joke.

Text 2b:

Even today, I find that joke absolutely breathtaking in its courage – audacity really – and in the incredible set of circumstances that made it relevant in the first place. I don't think you'll find another joke like it in the annals of presidential history and I hope you never will. This past month marked the swansong humor season of the Clinton administration and while we lacked the compelling backdrop of impeachment, we managed to find a few topics that proved fruitful.

The role mediation plays in institutional change becomes quite overt when Katz bemoans the loss of the 'compelling backdrop of impeachment'. Rather than seeing the impeachment process as a political liability, Katz recognizes its potential for generating political value in the form of humour. By deploying the theatrical terminology of 'backdrop' to describe an enabling circumstance for historically unique humour, Katz indicates that the field of presidential politics, even at its most serious, has self-consciously shifted itself to the centre of the entertainment field – the stage. The audience's expected engagement – a prerequisite for humour – derives from the seriousness of the circumstances in which Clinton found himself. That seriousness also performs an amplifying function for the audience – not just the audience Clinton is addressing, but the global audience for the impeachment process with all its relatively sordid details. The engagement resources that Katz leverages are cultural expectations about the potential outcomes of an impeachment. The whole situation is amplified by its worldwide propagation along the lines of entertainment values, the situation literally intensifying as the size of the impeachment audience grows. Clinton's impeachment, after being appropriated by humorists, becomes a medium, a technology, and a macro-circumstance – quite literally, a theatrical backdrop against which humour can successfully be performed. Moved from the sphere of politics to the sphere of entertainment, impeachment, thus, becomes a situation for situation comedy.

Institutional Values, Genre Hybridity, and Inculcation

While power politics adapts itself to the generic values of the sitcom, global media corporations are adjusting themselves to the power bestowed upon them by the political 'sanctification' of their generic forms. Gerald Levin, Time-Warner CEO and co-architect of the world's largest media merger (with America On Line), is clearly aware of shifting generic, institutional, and functional boundaries between power politics and mass media institutions:

> We're going to need to have these corporations redefined as instruments of public service because they have the resources, they have the reach, they have the skill base, and maybe there's a new generation coming up that wants to achieve meaning in that context and have an impact, and that may be a more efficient way to deal with society's problems than governments. (Levin 2000, quoted in Solomon 2000).

In Levin's assertion we see that mediation processes, particularly inter-generic instabilities, give us a window on social change, especially major institutional shifts in the locus of legitimate power. Nowhere is this clearer than in the vaudeville-cum-soap-opera of a globally entertainmentized politics on the one hand, and the sentiments expressed by Levin on the other.

Cross-cut: Media, Genres, and Modes; Discourses, Genres, and Texts

Media, genres, and modes are fundamental and interrelated aspects of meaning-making processes, and there are many levels of redundancy across these analytical domains. The level of genre is where institutional ructions are first expressed because it is at the level of genre that the intersection of textual and discoursal categories with those of mediation can best be seen (see Figure 2.2). It is here, at the level of genre, that analysts can begin to make sense of how mediation processes affect axiological hybridities, including their relationship to modes, the most fundamental resources making meaning.

Figure 2.2 is meant to show that any number of discourses can be articulated through a given medium, and that specific texts draw on the entire pool of modal resources permitted by a given medium without ever exhausting the entire range of modal possibilities. Also in this view, genre as defined from 'below', i.e. as a textually constituted category, appears more as a text type than a media form. Genre is seen to be constituted textually in a formal sense and constrained ideationally (from 'above') by discoursal boundaries.

The intersection between discoursal and media-logical perspectives on genre foregrounds the role of social *function*. That is to say, as analysts approach a text (regardless of its modal composition), moving 'inwards' from the category of mediation, they begin to see what kinds of social 'work' the text is part of. By moving inwards towards a text from the 'longer' and more abstract categories of mediation, discourse, and genre,

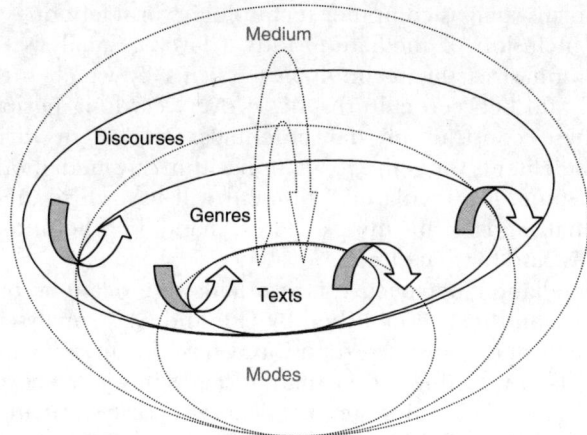

Figure 2.2 Intersection of discourses, genres, and texts with a mediation perspective

the text's history, its institutional inheritances, and, consequently, its axiological underpinnings remain apparent. By maintaining a mediation perspective which merely means approaching the text firstly from this direction, i.e. from outside-in, analysts can maintain a sense of the scale on which the text is produced and distributed, and the various scales from which it draws coherence (Lemke 2000). Once discourse and interdiscursive activity come into view, the functional aspects of the text become apparent. At the level of inter-institutional activity, during which genres are hybridized (Fairclough 2000), the first functional aspect of the text to come into focus is its axiological dimension.

Reiteration and Elaboration

The 'contextual' part of SFL and the 'critical' part of CDA are perhaps their most mutual and complementary aspects. Both emphasize the cultural and historical aspects of meaning. Both set out to comprehend meanings with reference to the coherence-generating function of social context, history, and culture. Yet, neither approach provides a sufficient account of how mediation impacts upon meaning systems or, more importantly, of the role mediation plays as the very means by which meanings are produced, preserved, moved, distributed, and changed over time and across social boundaries. Mediation is a *perspective*, not merely a reference to technological systems, although the latter are important characteristics of any given system of mediations. It may well be that bureaucratic systems are the oldest and, as Max Weber (1913/1991: 228) claims, 'the hardest to destroy' of all media forms. Yet, even the day-to-day operations and axiological principles of any bureaucracy are dramatically changed with the introduction of new media forms such as computer technologies or telephones (McLuhan 1964). The inclusion of mediation adds a layer of analysis to SFL and CDA that emphasizes the technological means by which meanings are *moved* within and between cultures, often over very long periods of time, and how these constrain modal potentials. Modes, in turn, are the constituency elements for genre formation within any mediation system. At any point in time, the media environment will have deep and sustained effects on what kinds of meanings can be made, by whom, under which circumstances, and to what effect.

When a mediation perspective is overlaid with relations between discourse, genres, and texts established by SFL and CDA, analysts can begin to see why texts and genres *appear* as, and have been *widely understood* as being, artefacts of meaning rather than as stages in wider networks of patterned social action, or action genres. Seen as activity formations, genres are revealed as dynamic sites of inter-institutional hybridities. Institutions are largely recognizable as such precisely because of the genres that constitute them. People *do* institutions; they produce and reproduce them through recognizable patterns of action. A university has a suite of action genres such as lectures, exams, and research processes – all loaded with specific expectations that pertain and adhere to the university as a social institution. Similarly, the values of divinity adhere to sermons and other genres of religious ritual; the values of expertise, including accuracy and objectivity, adhere to scientific reports and other overtly technical forms such as architects' drawings, engineers' schematics, and academic articles; and the values of legality and justice adhere (ideally) to the institutions of law.

Yet, institutional axiologies change through institutional hybridities. Certain classes of institutional action get hybridized with others and are subsequently revalued. In the examples I have used above, I have suggested that the genres of power politics have significantly changed because of their situation within a wider media environment in which many people spend a lot of time: the environment of sitcoms, advertisements, action movies, docutainments, soap operas, and advertorials. The movement of power politics into the domain of entertainment, and of the axiological shift that such a movement entails, is self-conscious and uncontentious. It has progressed throughout the twentieth century, its effects felt everywhere (Graham and Luke in press). Baird (2002) describes an instance from Australian politics.

> Peter Beattie [Premier of Queensland] was honest when he admitted in 2000 that, for better or for worse, being a media tart was part of the job of being a politician. It was a bit rich that his colleagues in opposition should make a song and dance about the fact that he admitted it, he said. 'It's like two prostitutes standing on the corner talking about virginity.'

Just as the axiologies of power politics have changed to accommodate new mediations so have many others such as management and high finance.

To understand these changes, researchers need to look beyond the social domain with which they are primarily concerned to see the movement of one set of institutional axiologies into another, and the types of contradictory axiological results such moves inevitably entail.

The presidential humorist, Katz, sees himself as having moved 'from the principal's office to the Oval Office' via the fields of advertising, journalism, party politics, public relations, and academia. He participated in producing a very unstable but remarkable form of political communication – presidential sitcom. The transient form developed by Katz and his colleagues – pre-generic because it never reached a recognizable or stable form (which would ruin its effect in any case) – is remarkable for the way it highlights the relationships among mediation, genre, discourse, and text, and for how it highlights the subtle ways in which the axiological 'ground' must be prepared by one institution before being successfully co-opted and occupied by other institutions which are rivals for power.

Conclusion

The existence of globally dispersed, fast-moving, fast-changing meaning systems is, undoubtedly, a function of new mediation processes which include and depend upon new communication technologies and new institutional relations. The predominant role of this system – its effects felt at every level throughout humanity – makes mediation a central object for the analysis of meaning. And while Clinton and Katz's self-conscious foray into the world of sitcom may present dilemmas in assessing the role and place of power politics in the current environment, it provides an excellent example of the kinds of axiological contradictions that new mediations entail, and which will continue to as disparate social domains are brought into contact on a global scale by new, faster, more chaotic mediations. Approached from a mediation perspective, the first functional dimension of the strange and unfamiliar forms of meaning that will present itself is the axiological dimension as overt reorderings of evaluative priorities become apparent. As it stands, post-September 11, 2001, the realm of power politics has shifted its axiological biases from the institutions of show business to the institutions of war. Terror and violence, not humour, have become the organizing axiological standards for mass mediations. The instability of presidential levity could not last. It has, once again, given way to the 'grand narrative' of good versus evil – a simple, definite, and, one might say, almost comfortable myth by dint of its seemingly eternal recurrence.

References

Baird, J. (2002) 'The Barbs Aimed at a Media Doll', *Sydney Morning Herald* (22 August) at: http://www.smh.com.au/articles/2002/08/21/1029114137192.html (consulted October 2002).

Bakhtin, M. (1936/1984) *Rabelais and His World*, trans. by H. Iswolsky. Bloomington, IN: University of Indiana Press.

Bourdieu, P. (1998) *Acts of Resistance: Against the New Myths of Our Time.* London: Polity Press.

Bourdieu, P. (1991) *Language and Symbolic Power*, trans. by G. Raymond and M. Adamson. London: Polity Press.

Clinton, W. J. (1999) 'Remarks by the President at the Radio and Television Correspondents Association Dinner at The Washington Hilton (18 March)'. Washington, DC. [Whitehouse publications] at: http://www.pub.whitehouse.gov/uri-res/I2R?urn:pdi://oma.eop.gov.us/1999/3/22/3.text.1 (consulted October 1999).

Fairclough, N. (2000) 'Discourse, Social Theory, and Social Research: The Discourse of Welfare Reform', *Journal of Sociolinguistics*, 4(2): 163–95.

Fairclough, N. (1992) *Discourse and Social Change.* Cambridge: Polity Press.

Firth, R. (1953) 'The Study of Values by Social Anthropologists: The Marrett Lecture, 1953', *Man*, 53: 146–53.

Graham, P. (2002) 'Predication and Propagation: A Method for Analysing Evaluative Meanings in Technology Policy', *TEXT*, 22(2): 227–68.

Graham, P. (2001a) 'Contradictions and Institutional Convergences: Genre as Method', *Journal of Future Studies*, 5(4): 1–30.

Graham, P. (2001b) 'Space: Irrealis Objects in Technology Policy and Their Role in the Creation of a New Political Economy', *Discourse and Society*, 12(6): 761–88.

Graham, P. and Luke, A. (in press) 'Militarizing the Body Politic: New Media as Weapons of Mass Instruction', *Body & Society*.

Halliday, M. A. K. (1978) *Language as a Social Semiotic.* Victoria: Edward Arnold.

Innis, H. A. (1951) *The Bias of Communication.* Toronto: Toronto University Press.

Katz, M. (2000) *From the Principal's Office to the Oval Office.* President's Forum Lecture Series. New York: Hobart and William Smith Colleges at: http://www.soundbiteinstitute.com/home/flashout_m_ghost.html (consulted October 2002).

Lemke, J. L. (2000) 'Across the Scales of Time: Artifacts, Activities, and Meanings in Ecosocial Systems', *Mind, Culture, and Activity*, 7(4): 273–290.

Lemke, J. L. (1998a) 'Resources for Attitudinal Meaning: Evaluative Orientations in Text Semantics', *Functions of Language*, 5(1): 33–56.

Lemke, J. L. (1998b) 'Analysing Verbal Data: Principles, Methods, and Problems', in *International Handbook of Science Education*, ed. by K. Tobin and B. Fraser. New York: Kluwer, 1175–89.

Lemke, J. L. (1995) *Textual Politics: Discourse and Social Dynamics.* London: Taylor and Francis.

Lindenberger, H. (1990) *The History in Literature: On Value, Genre, Institutions.* New York: Columbia University Press.

Luke, A. (2003) *The Trouble with Context.* Graduate School of Education Working Paper Series. Brisbane: University of Queensland.

Martin, J. R. (2000) 'Beyond Exchange: APPRAISAL Systems in English', in *Evaluation in Text*, ed. by S. Hunston and G. Thompson. Oxford: Oxford University Press, 142–75.

Martin, J. R. (1999) 'Grace: the Logogenesis of Freedom', *Discourse Studies*, 1(1): 29–56.

McLuhan, M. (1964) *Understanding Media: The Extensions of Man*. London: Routledge.

Postman, N. (1985) *Amusing Ourselves to Death*. London: Methuen.

Silverstone, R. (1999) *Why Study the Media?* London: Sage Publications.

Solomon, N. (2000) 'AOL Time Warner: Calling the Faithful to Their Knees', *Earth Beat* (13 January) at: http://www.fair.org/media-beat/000113.html (consulted November 2000).

Weber, M. (1913/1991) 'Bureaucracy', in *From Max Weber: Essays in Sociology*, ed. by H. H. Gerth and C. Wright Mills. London: Routledge, 196–244.

White, L. Jr (1940) 'Technology and Invention in the Middle Ages', *Speculum*, 15(2): 141–59.

3 Mapping Distinction: Towards a Systemic Representation of Power in Language

Tom Bartlett

This paper looks at criticism levelled at Critical Discourse Analysis (CDA) in terms of its perceived failure to combine a contextually sensitive reading of texts and the scale of analysis necessary to draw more generalized conclusions about the instantiation of power relations in discourse. While accepting the thrust of these arguments, the paper argues that the failings identified should not be used to deny the potential of CDA as a whole, as they represent not an imbalanced notion of the relationship between language and power but the methodological 'teething' problems of a young discipline. This paper, therefore, focuses on developing CDA methodology so that it is both sensitive to the local production of speech and appropriate to large-scale quantitative analysis within a sociological framework.

Introduction

This paper attempts to refine methodology in Critical Discourse Analysis (CDA) in view of criticisms concerning the tensions between micro- and macro-analysis. On the one hand, CDA has been criticized by conversation analysts, Hutchby and Wooffitt (1998: 164), for

> policies of simply counting the number of questions, or coding the type of question asked [. . . while . . .] not being sensitive enough to the more basic sense of context . . . the local . . . sequential context of talk in which utterances are produced.

Similarly, from the field of applied linguistics, Widdowson (2000: 166) complains that

> [t]he procedure is to fix on some particular linguistic feature . . . and assign it ideological significance without regard to how it might be understood in the normal indexical process of reading.

On the other hand, micro-analysis within CDA has been criticized for extrapolating sociological conclusions from small quantities of minutely scrutinized data or for providing 'no more than a commentary on the text' (Eggins 1994: 313) – that is, for a failure to provide an analysis in terms that can be quantified and contrasted with other texts and so be given a *value*.

Of particular concern is the fact that both the indelicate analysis of large amounts of data and the micro-analysis of a limited range of data leave too much space for subjectivity.

The conflict between micro- and macro-analysis has not been lost on the critical discourse analysts themselves, and in a major work, Chouliaraki and Fairclough (1999: 152) explicitly recognize that

> [l]inguists have to be convinced that the social concerns of CDA do not deflect from the detailed and careful linguistic (and semiotic) analysis of texts . . .

while calling for

> . . . the sort of systematic analysis of large, representative bodies of text, including the use of quantitative and computational methods, which could actually give a firmer linguistic grounding to its social claims about discourse.

This paper, then, presents a methodology that attempts to quantify contextually sensitive samples of language as instantiations of social stance.

Increasing Delicacy

It is necessary before undertaking any statistical analysis to ensure that the units being quantified are meaningful in themselves. In terms of CDA, this means relating relations of power in discourse as accurately as possible to linguistic features. A frequently analysed feature in this respect is modality, as this is a rich resource for speakers to *construe* the nature of reality and to *construct* participant roles through discourse. If features such as modality are to be used in macro-analysis, however, the categorizations employed must be sufficiently delicate. As the critics cited above claim, early CDA researchers and those of its precursor Critical Language Studies (CLS) were often guilty of simply counting the modals within texts at the bludgeon level of delicacy and drawing social conclusions from such low-level linguistic analysis, as in Table 3.1.

In these terms there would be no statistical difference between the emphatic offer: *You must stay and have a bite to eat!* and the command *You must obey my every word.* What is needed to produce more meaningful analysis of the social value of speakers' linguistic behaviour is a more delicate representation of the *lexemic meaning potential* of the modals within speech acts, along the lines of that presented for MUST in Figure 3.1

Similarly, the content of the modalized clause should be taken into consideration so as to capture who is asking what of whom, in what way, and for what reason. At the very least, the modal object (the person responsible for carrying out the event or not) needs to be listed, otherwise the commissive *I must, I must, improve my bust* is in danger of counting alongside commands in analyses of language and power.

Table 3.1. Indelicate modality analysis

Modalization probability	[Speaker 1]	[Speaker 2]	[Speaker 3]
high			
median	1 (subjective; explicit)		
low	1 (subjective; implicit)		1 (objective; imp.)
Modulation			
(i) obligation			
high:directive	3	1	2
median:advice		1	
low:permission	1	1	
(ii) capability	5		2
total no. of modalities	11	3	5

Source: Eggins and Slade (1997: 110)

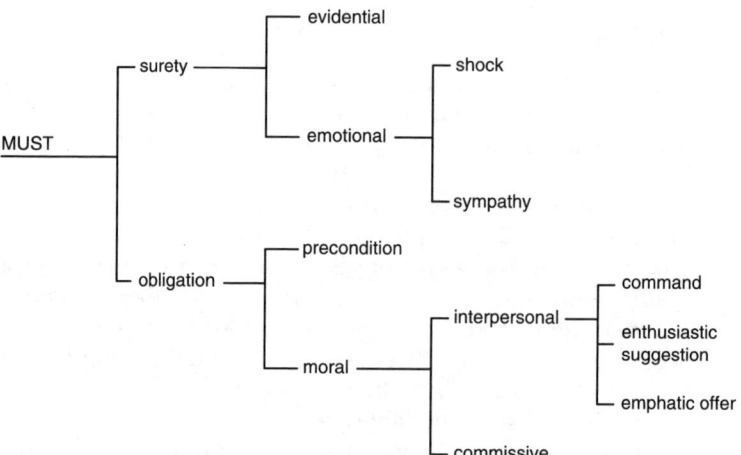

Figure 3.1 Lexemic meaning potential of MUST

Resituating Whorf: Constellations of Instantiation

Once the linguistic units of analysis have been refined, it is necessary to quantify these items in sufficient numbers and in terms appropriate to meaningful sociological analysis. To achieve this, it is possible to turn to Whorf's claim (1956: 158) that the linguistic representation of concepts

> do not depend so much upon ANY ONE SYSTEM within the grammar as upon the ways of analysing and reporting experience which may have become fixed in the language as integrated 'fashions of speaking' and which cut across the typical grammatical classifications, so that such a 'fashion' may include lexical, morphological,

syntactical, and otherwise systematically diverse means coordinated in a certain frame of consistency. (Original emphasis)

However, where Whorf saw these fashions of speaking as institutionalized ways of seeing the world through language, a CDA perspective might reinterpret his primarily anthropological hypothesis sociologically in terms of the fashions of speaking that social actors display in their personal discourse. For if language is the map of speakers' phenomenal worlds, and of their experience of process (Halliday and Matthiessen 1999: ix), then mapping a speaker's representations of the world through language should allow us insight into 'what goes on in the realms of their own consciousness'. For Hasan (1996: 148–9), if a specific configurative rapport – a constellation of linguistic patterns – is perceived as criterial in the context of some ideology, it is not because the system of language has forced the patterns together, but because the speakers' *fashions of speaking* are bearers of their ideology.

These ideas would suggest that approaching the same research question through different areas of the grammar should provide results that *resonate* with each other in their social meaning and so reveal the underlying ideologies of texts. However, while each linguistic item is a star in the constellation of usage, individual instances, unlike DNA, cannot be used to recreate the system as a whole. On the contrary, the description of the system of use, of ways of speaking, is built up slowly from the analysis of large numbers of instances, and these instances will at times appear contradictory. To take a musical analogy, rather than sounding in unison, various features may create complex harmonies, variations on a theme, or downright discord, as shown in Figure 3.2.

In the case of harmonies and variation, it is up to the analyst to identify the deeper common meaning that unites these strands, while irreconcilable discords would seem to be an occupational hazard of dealing with people with pulses and not machines.

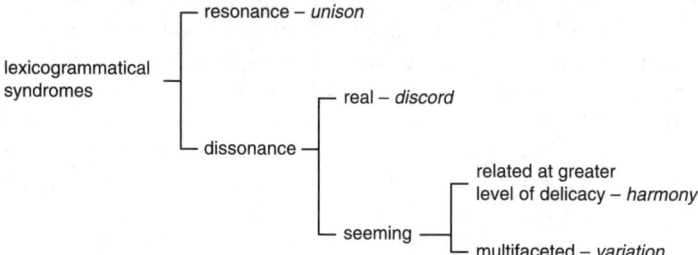

Figure 3.2 Relations between lexicogrammatical syndromes

Mapping Distinction

This paper attempts to produce systems networks of the constellations of lexicogrammatical features employed by different speakers, along with their relative frequencies, as representations of their *ways of speaking* in the sociologically recontextualized terms described above. Such presentations should capture a truth about participants' ways of speaking in the same way as a nominalization might reformulate a clause, as a sort of concretization of the essential elements of a far more complex process. Alternatively, they can be viewed in the same way as sports statistics in that they should reson-ate with a spectator's impressions of a game, losing the detail that makes an event more than mere numbers but offering as compensation insights not available as the process unfolds, including one or two genuine surprises. And as language – as expression and action – is simultaneously the con-strual and construction of reality, these systems networks reflect, in their limited way, the conception of reality of each interlocutor and the system of social values that motivate their speech behaviour. Compiling and correlat-ing relations of power as manifest through ways of speaking, therefore, is a means of depicting social difference, of *mapping distinction*.

The Data

The quantitative-qualitative analyses that follow are taken from my field-work in Guyana, South America, where I am studying communication strategies between the Iwokrama International Rainforest Conservation Programme, a multinational non-governmental organization (NGO), and local Amerindian communities (Bartlett 2001). The two groups possess complementary knowledge(s) regarding the natural resources of the area and, as part of their mutual drive towards the sustainable development of these resources, Iwokrama and the local leaders are committed to combin-ing their knowledge bases. As part of my research, I undertook several interviews with leading members of each group to look at perceptions of who was directing this theoretically mutually beneficial development pro-cess and who were perceived as the chief beneficiaries. These texts are clearly instances of the same genre, and the interlocutors, as interviewer and interviewees, are playing the same participant roles in each instance. Comparisons between the texts are thus viable. However, variables necessar-ily exist that affect the nature of the interview, in particular the status and social relationship between the interviewee and myself. These differences could be seen as a hindrance to the research; alternatively, they could be seen as adding another level of analysis in that they depend on the very relationship of language to power that the methodology has been developed to investigate.

   The original goal of this research was to look at the content of the inter-views, but it soon became clear that the ways of speaking of the protagonists were of equal interest to the research question, and the following linguistic analyses represent some preliminary steps in examining those areas of the language 'at risk' in the construal and construction of participant roles in the development process. The first analysis covers two of the interviews on perceptions of development: one with Steve, a village leader, and the second with Graham, an Iwokrama scientist also responsible for the promotion of collaborative developmental practices. Both speakers have symbolic capital in their own spheres and in relation to each other given the mutuality of their interests, yet Graham could be considered as the more powerful in mainstream terms through his role as salaried representative of an international organization with funds to distribute as well as through his formal certification as a doctor of biology.

The areas of the lexicogrammar to be analysed are the interpersonal realm of modality as a linguistic means of *constructing* social relations, and the transitivity structure of projection as a means of *construing* social reality through hopes, expectations, fears, and so forth. Analysis of features of modality and projection, although they represent different metafunctions of language, can bring out the resonances and dissonances that these features combine to produce as modality is also used to construe reality through the expression of usuality and appropriateness, while projection frequently constructs interpersonal roles through indirect speech acts such as the implication of obligation through expressions of expectation.

Compilation

The first step in the analysis was to extrapolate from the data qualitatively meaningful systems networks as bases for quantifying the data. This means that only those modals and projections that were used by the interviewees and the speech acts they perform in these texts are included in the network. WOULD has not been included in the analysis, as it seems to provide a separate and complementary angle for analysis, while HAVE TO and NEED TO are included although they are not prototypical modals. Presentation of the items used is at a greater level of delicacy than usual, both in terms of the division into speech acts and the inclusion of the modalized or projected clause, i.e. the event clause, in the analysis. In categorizing speech acts, I was largely relying on my status as a veteran of perception, which leaves me open to accusations of subjectivity, although I was also the interlocutor and, therefore, assumedly, intended to understand the implications of each speech act, and this is an area where more work can be done to establish an objective standard for categorization. However, it is precisely through studies such as these that an increased understanding of the social meaning of speech acts might be attained.

The modal source is included in the systems networks as this source is not always the speaker – as in reported speech acts, for example. This point is often overlooked in number crunching. The event clause is represented by the process itself and the participant roles of agent/initiator (the modal object) and (implied) beneficiary. I write these roles without capitals as

they are not identical to those of Functional Grammar but are vaguer categories with a more *ad hoc* relevance appropriate to the immediate research
question. While I have stressed above the need for greater delicacy in the
analysis of features such as modality and projection clauses as the key to the
social meaning of speech acts, the level of delicacy needed to label processes and participants within event clauses depends on the system of contrasts relevant to the research question. In this case, the meanings 'at risk'
were reduced in delicacy to the simple dichotomy of 'work' and 'development' for the processes, and 'local', 'Iwokrama' or 'joint' for the agent/
initiator and beneficiary of the event clause as well as for the modal source.
This seems to be a level of delicacy that can overcome conflict between
micro- and macro-analysis as it is qualitatively adequate to the research
question and quantitatively manageable. The category 'development'
covers both the intransitive meaning and the transitive, while 'work'
represents the activities necessary to bring this development about.

The analysis of modal use by the two interviewees produced the systems
network in Figure 3.3.

Results and Basic Analysis

Only some of the possible sequences that can be generated from this network were used and not all the elements were used by each interviewee;
therefore, the network in Figure 3.3 is not a representation of the ways of
speaking of those involved but an etic framework that allows individuals'
ways of speaking to be analysed and contrasted. Figure 3.4 illustrates the
mapping of choices from the system fragment for obligation as realized in
practice by Steve. In this figure the labelling of speech acts increases in
delicacy from left to right, e.g. with 'objective', and 'subjective' being more
delicate expressions of 'obligation', and 'essential repair', 'external force'
and 'assumed' more delicate still. The lexical realization of each category is
as given in Figure 3.3. The original source of each modality is given as a
further level of delicacy, as are the process types and participant roles
within the event clause. The figures in brackets represent the number of
tokens at each level of delicacy so that less delicate categorizations give the
total number of tokens of all the more delicate speech acts they comprise.
The speech acts carried out can thus be analysed in isolation or as agnate
clusters, as shown in Figure 3.4.

More Delicate Data as More Accurate Representation

The inclusion of the modalized clause within the analysis highlights an
analytical shortcoming with existing CDA work. Within Graham's use of
NEED TO and SHOULD, the deontic object of the modality is either Iwokrama or Joint in 26 out of 31 uses and 23 out of 30 uses, respectively. This
aspect, lost in less delicate analysis, calls into question the standard interpretation of the use of deontic modals as showing power or authority or

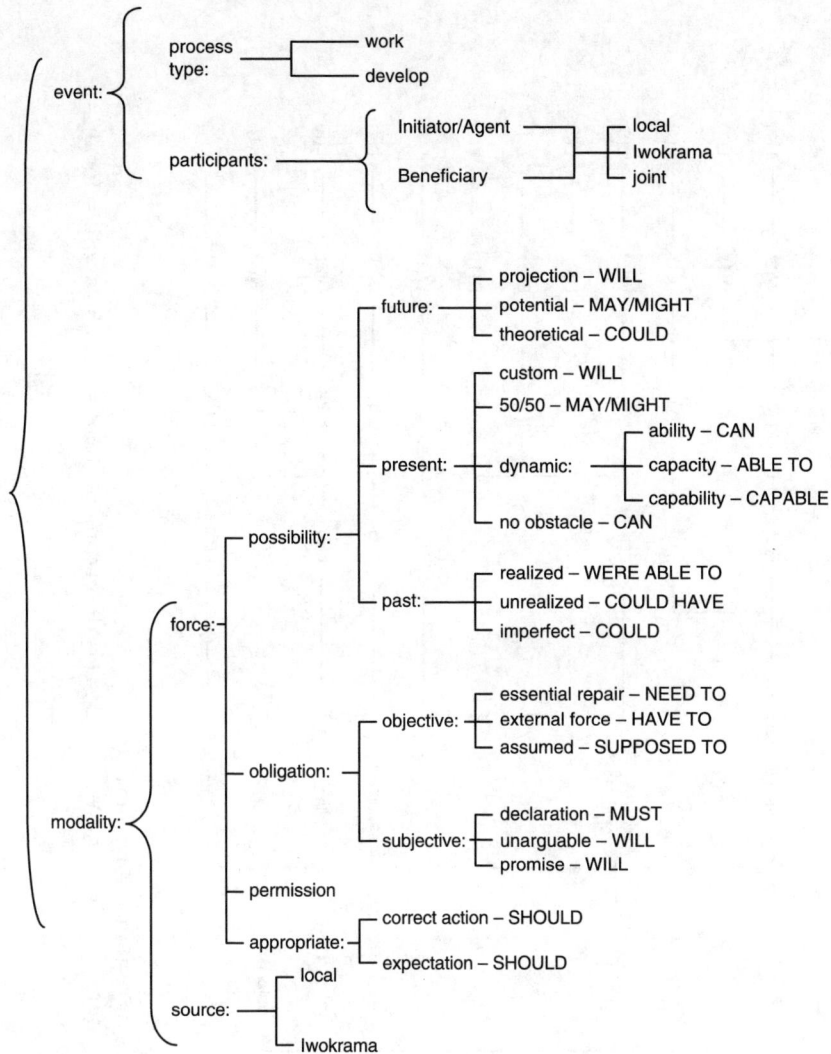

Figure 3.3 Semantic systems network for the construal of the development process

control. Combining the overwhelming inclusion of Iwokrama within the deontic object with a more accurate interpretation of SHOULD as 'appropriate' rather than median obligation, the overriding meaning of Graham's use of these modals would appear to be self-criticism, cataloguing those areas where Iwokrama has not performed as appropriate. However, the question of how and why Graham has the right and the power to define what is appropriate for his own group's behaviour is still of interest.

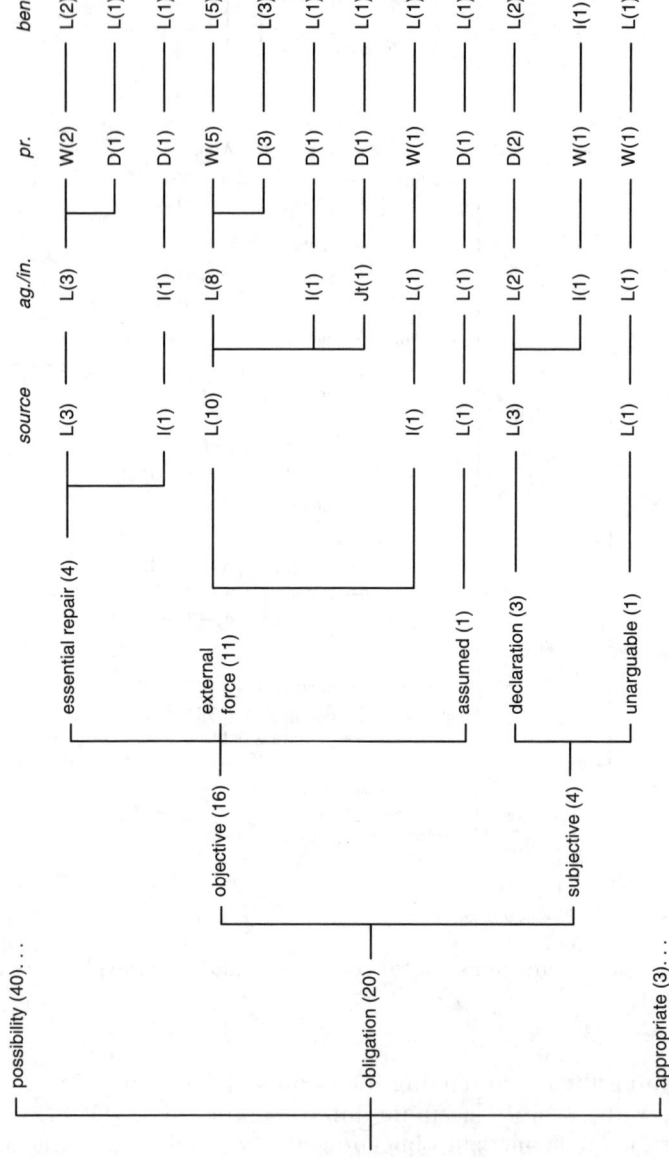

Figure 3.4 Construal of responsibility: Steve

ag./in. = agent/initiator; pr. = process; D = development; ben. = beneficiary; L = local; W = work;
I = Iwokrama; Jt = joint

Multidelicacy

The presentation of the data above, quantified at each level of delicacy within a systems network, allows for analysis at more or less delicate levels, and, in this respect, the data may be called *multidelicate*. This multidelicacy also works in another related way: as the order of presentation of elements in the mapping of expressions of obligation does not represent a psychologically real sequence of options, i.e. the network is simply a means of illustrating all the speaker choices made, alternative orderings are possible which may reveal clusters lost in the original presentation. Within Graham's use of NEED TO, for example, the chain of choices ending at the bold italicized *Jt* in Table 3.2b reveals a pattern, lost in the original ordering of Table 3.2a yet surely worthy of further analysis, that *12%* of Graham's uses of NEED TO occur at this *sixth level of delicacy*, i.e. coinciding in six systematic choices: obligation, objective, essential repair, Iwokrama as deontic source, Iwokrama as agent/initiator, and Iwokrama and locals as joint beneficiaries.

Table 3.2 Reordering of partial systems network for Graham

3.2a

	ag./in.	*pr.*	ben.
obligation:objective:essential repair:source I (30):	L(4)	W(1)	L(1)
		D(3)	L(2)
			Jt(1)
	I(25)	W(12)	L(1)
			I(2)
			Jt(9)
		D(13)	L(2)
			I(2)
			Jt(9)
	Jt(1)	D(1)	Jt(1)

3.2b

	ag./in.	*ben.*	pr.
obligation:objective:essential repair:source I(30):	L(4)	L(3)	W(1)
			D(2)
		Jt(1)	D(1)
	I(25)	L(3)	W(1)
			D(2)
		I(4)	W(2)
			D(2)
		Jt(18)	W(9)
			D(9)
	Jt(1)	Jt(1)	D(1)

Comparisons Between Speakers: Expressions of Obligation

Table 3.3 compares certain aspects of the expression of 'obligation' between Steve and Graham.

This comparison of the modal realization of obligation by Steve and Graham throws up some interesting points lost in a less delicate analysis. Whereas the two speakers are very close in the ratio of obligation to total modal use, in a traditional CDA analysis Steve would be considered the more forceful of the two speakers as 20 per cent of his modals of obligation are subjective (realized by MUST and WILL), as opposed to a tiny 2 per cent (one instance, and that as a 'promise') of Graham's. This is a conclusion that does not resonate with my social analysis of the situation and so should be examined in greater detail. A more delicate look at the modals in the texts and a deeper analysis of the objective expression of obligation demonstrate that the weighting of HAVE TO and NEED TO is reversed between the two speakers. This creates a seeming dissonance as HAVE TO, the classic expression of 'external force', is strongly contrasted with subjective modality in this regard, yet Steve uses both HAVE TO and MUST considerably more than Graham, who has a clear preference for the 'essential repair' statement realized by NEED TO. When harmonizing the two results, however, Steve can be said to be dealing with absolutes, irrespective of the source of the obligation. Graham, on the other hand, could be construed as reluctant to impose his symbolic capital through subjective modality while simultaneously avoiding attributing obligation to external forces. NEED TO as 'essential repair' allows for a greater degree of human agency in accepting or rejecting the proposition, and this is meaningful in two ways: in allowing for choice, it is closer to a suggestion form than HAVE TO, and it reflects a belief in the surmountability of external restrictions. These features are both relevant to Graham's role within Iwokrama as an advocate of collaborative development and as a scientist. At the same time, however, it can be interpreted as a reflection of Graham's greater symbolic capital in that it represents the ability to direct human endeavour through suggestion as opposed to either direct command or on appeal to external force. Importantly, this enhanced analysis of Graham's modality resonates with his extensive use of SHOULD to suggest 'appropriate action' (29 out of 151, or 19 per cent of all modal uses).

Table 3.3 Comparison of Steve and Graham's modal expression of 'obligation'

Speaker	Total modals	Total obligation	As % of modals	Total objective/ subjective	As % of obligation	Total essential/ external	As % of objective
Steve	63	20	32%	16/4	80/20%	4/11	25/69%
Graham	151	52	34%	51/1	98/2%	31/18	61/35%

Refinement of CDA Practice

Four major challenges to current CDA practice arise from this analysis. First, while the subjective/objective split in deontic modality is meaningful in itself, it is not necessarily so in terms of a black-and-white powerful/non-powerful dichotomy. Second, increased delicacy of analysis throws up results that are seemingly dissonant with the less delicate analysis and that must be harmonized through a more complex interpretation of power relations. Third, as in the contrast in agentive capacity implicit between HAVE TO and NEED TO, the social meanings of the linguistic items themselves are in need of greater analysis, an analysis that can begin with the data to hand. Fourth, the above analyses seem to point to *different modes of power differently realized*, necessitating more complex analysis both of language use and the social context in which it is embedded. This point will be taken up in the conclusion.

Comparisons Between Speakers: Expressions of Possibility

Table 3.4 compares certain aspects of the expression of 'possibility' between Steve, Graham, and a third interviewee, Uncle Fred, a local elder.

The contrast between Steve and Graham's modalization of possibility, on the one hand, and Uncle Fred's, on the other, is interesting, not so much for what it demonstrates about the relative status and power of the different participants, but because it points to dimensions of power that could be researched further through both linguistic and other sociological means.

For all the speakers, possibility is primarily situated in the present; yet, whereas Steve and Graham also make extensive reference to future possibility – theoretical, potential, and projected—Uncle Fred largely avoids such reference. Certainly, the mixing of present and future possibility by Steve and Graham makes sense in terms of their roles as instigators of development, and their emphasis on dynamic notions of ability and capacity in the present are in unison with their future usage. Uncle Fred's overwhelming expression of present possibility begins to make sense, however, within a more delicate analysis. This reveals that by far his most

Table 3.4 Comparison of Steve, Graham, and Uncle Fred's modal expression of 'possibility'

Speaker	Total possibility	As % of modals	Total future/ present/ past	As % of possibility	Total dynamic/ no obstacle	As % of present
Steve	40	63%	13/23/4	33/58/10%	11/9	48/39%
Graham	68	45%	26/39/3	38/57/4%	20/15	51/38%
Uncle Fred	34	53%	3/29/2	9/85/6%	6/19	21/66%

frequent modalization of possibility is through CAN to express 'no obstacle'. At the risk of overstating the case, this use of CAN functions as a judgement in both the physical and moral order, it is the *nihil obstat* that simultaneously validates ideational and interpersonal truth. The following example (in bold) seems to capture this duality of possibility and permission, but I must stress that not all instances are as clear and that to rely on quantitative linguistic analysis of such tokens alone is an exercise fraught with danger.

> And, er, I think one of the things that we should encourage is to allow them to put it over in Makushi. Even, I mean, they can't read and write, but they have very good memory collection. They **can** put it over in Makushi and people would take notes, we have scribes who take notes and these things.

'Permitting' processes to go ahead on the grounds that they are theoretically possible, therefore, simultaneously establishes and manifests Uncle Fred's credentials as an expert voice in matters practical and moral as befits a community elder. While I would hate to make such a claim anything more than tentatively without further analysis, it once again suggests the existence of different modes of power that manifest themselves in different forms, both verbally and non-verbally.

Projections of Development: Resonances and Dissonances

Figure 3.5 represents the network of choices from the system of mental projections as realized by either Steve or Graham, and Table 3.5 summarizes the most striking contrasts between the two speakers.

The most obvious point of contrast between the two speakers with regard to the projections themselves is the ratio of affective to cognitive constructions. Twenty-nine per cent of Steve's projections are affective as compared with Graham's 17 per cent, and the figures here are quite possibly revealing of a disequilibrium in the roles of petitioner and provider in what is supposed to be mutual development.

An examination of cognitive projections shows that Graham, rather than projecting concepts as known, overwhelmingly gives opinions, the great majority of which are 'median' in force. In fact, 40 per cent of all Graham's mental projections express median opinions. It might be expected that Graham, from his position of relative power, would deal in facts rather than opinions and in firm opinions rather than weak ones; however, recalling Graham's extensive use of SHOULD to construe appropriate action, it seems likely that the ability to give opinions – of median rather than strong force – is related to a particular mode of power and authority. In this sense, suggestions of appropriateness and opinions of states of affairs are very similar speech acts in that they show an expectation of control both in the construction of reality where the appropriate is decided, and in the construal of reality where Graham seems to be at greater liberty to put forward his personal opinions even when they are no stronger than matters of

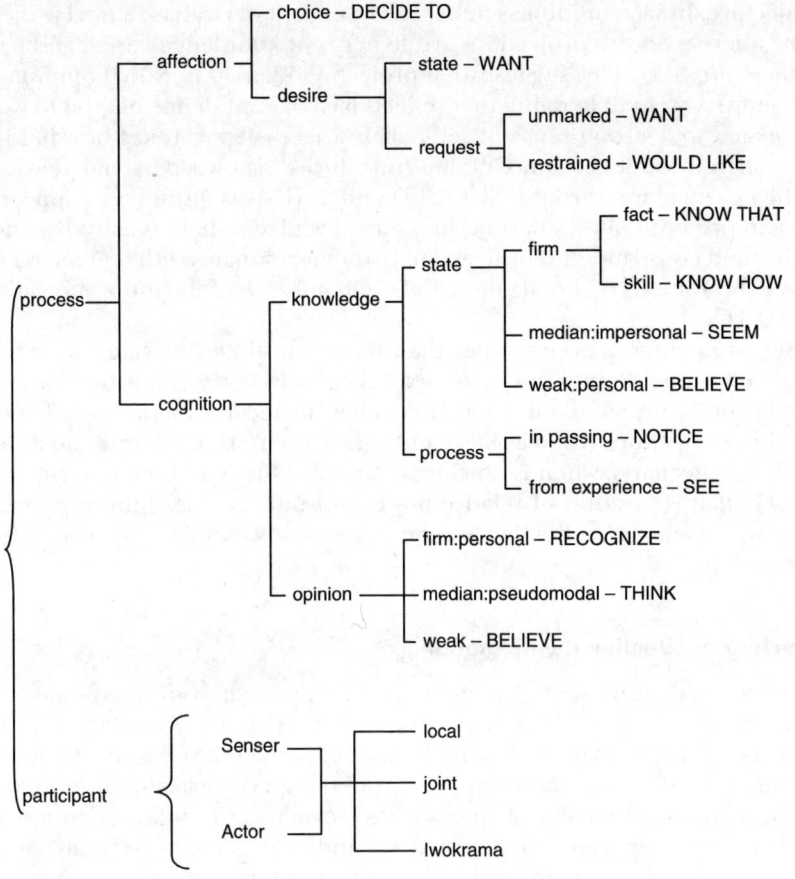

Figure 3.5 Choices made from the systems network for mental projections

Table 3.5 Comparison of Steve and Graham's mental projections

Speaker	Total projections	Total affect/ cognition	As % of projections	Total opinions	As % of cognition	As % of projections	Median opinions	As % of projections
Steve	24	7/17	29/71%	5	29%	21%	3	13%
Graham	92	16/76	17/83%	47	62%	51%	37	40%

conjecture. In fact, opinions count for 51 per cent of Graham's total projections whereas Steve's projections are 48 per cent knowledge-based, and half
of these are firm. This suggests that projecting ideas as personal opinion is
not always a form of hedging that reflects lack of confidence but might well
be related to a strong sense of self-belief: whereas Steve relies on what he
has concrete evidence for, Graham introduces his own personal views of
reality, particularly through SHOULD and THINK clauses. Steve appears,
thus, to present realities beyond his control while Graham is actively negotiating and construing his own, an analysis that resonates with Steve's use of
HAVE TO for external obligation and Graham's use of the more subjective
NEED TO.

But Graham goes even further than this: eight times, he states what the
local community wants to do, compared to only seven times for his own
NGO community. Graham also regularly has the local community as Senser
in other projections whereas Steve only once attempts to get into the mind
of his counterparts, when reporting a request. This would seem to suggest
that Graham's position of relative power not only enables him to present
his own version of reality, but to construct and present reality as it is for
others.

Conclusion: Situating the Methodology

The brief analysis presented above is meant only as a flavour of how ways-of-
speaking networks can be represented and interpreted. The scope of the
networks could be extended by increasing the range of speakers, the number and type of lexical items employed, and the speech acts they instantiate,
or through a comparison of speakers' performance in different contexts.
Similarly, the linguistic behaviour of key individuals could be analysed at
the level of delicacy proposed above with their use of specific features
measured against the baseline data for a particular social group, and the
variations observed related back to co-textual and contextual factors that
take 'on board' both the dynamics of the 'sequential context of talk in
which utterances are produced' (Hutchby and Wooffitt 1998: 164) and the
pre-existing power relations between speakers that conversation analysts
disallow. Such analysis should provide personalized portraits of individual
interactants as opposed to the sort of statistics criticized by Giles and
Coupland (1991: 194).

> [T]he attention paid by discourse analysts and others to idiosyncrasy and interindi-
> vidual variability in the qualitative use of language forms is sadly neglected – most
> clearly in studies which aggregate numerical means and merely provide statements of
> standard deviation.

This approach could be extended beyond the dynamics of linguistic
development within individual texts, or *logogenesis*, and incorporated into
longer-term studies of *phylogenetic* shifts in norms of linguistic usage. A
combination of process and product analysis would deal, therefore, with

both individual socialization within the group and group socialization as the sum of individual behaviours.

A method for the thorough analysis of the relations between social groups and cultural artefacts is outlined in Bourdieu's (1990) 'Programme for a Sociology of Sport'. For Bourdieu, dealing with the cultural links between rugby and beer-drinkers and tennis and wine-drinkers, it is necessary to look at the social history of drinking wine and of drinking beer both in their own terms and as values within a system. Then synchronic pictures of their values relative to each other can be drawn, and diachronic shifts noted. The same diachronic and synchronic analyses are then repeated for tennis and rugby. These analyses are then situated within a diachronic study of the broader relationship between sports and alcohol, and only then can conclusions be drawn regarding the synchronic relationship between rugby and beer and tennis and wine. The agenda for a genuine sociolinguistic study of how social change is realized through, and reflected in, groups' ways of speaking would, therefore, include staged synchronic analyses of the power relations between the two groups and simultaneous and separate analyses of their ways of interrelating through discourse. The results of these synchronic studies would then feed into diachronic studies of both phenomena separately, and these would then be interrelated to map how shifts in power are realized and reflected through shifts in discourse patterns. Such an early separation of sociological and linguistic analysis and their ultimate marriage only under strict conditions should go some way towards eliminating the unconscious effects of researchers' ideology in the interpretation of their data.

References

Bartlett, T. (2001) 'Use the Road: The Appropriacy of Appropriation', *Language and Intercultural Communication*, 1(1): 21–39.

Bourdieu, P. (1990) 'Programme for a Sociology of Sport', in *In Other Words*. Cambridge: Polity Press.

Chouliaraki, L. and Fairclough, N. (1999) *Discourse in Late Modernity: Rethinking Critical Discourse Analysis*. Edinburgh: Edinburgh University Press.

Eggins, S. (1994) *An Introduction to Systemic Functional Linguistics*. London: Cassell.

Eggins, S. and Slade, D. (1997) *Analysing Casual Conversation*. London and Washington, DC: Cassell.

Giles, H. and Coupland, N. (1991) *Language: Contexts and Consequences*. Buckingham: Open University Press.

Halliday, M. A. K. and Matthiessen, C. M. I. M. (1999) *Construing Experience through Meaning: A Language-based Approach to Cognition*. London and New York: Continuum.

Hasan, R. (1996) 'Ways of Saying: Ways of Meaning', in *Ways of Saying: Ways of Meaning: Selected Papers of Ruqaiya Hasan,* ed. by C. Cloran, D. Butt, and G. Williams. London: Cassell, 133–51.

Hutchby, I. and Wooffitt, R. (1998) *Conversation Analysis: Principles, Practices and Applications.* Cambridge: Polity Press.

Whorf, B. L. (1956) 'The Relation of Habitual Thought and Behavior to Language', in *Language, Thought and Reality: Selected Writings of Benjamin Lee Whorf,* ed. by J. B. Carroll. Cambridge, MA: MIT Press, 134–59.

Widdowson, H. G. (2000) 'Critical Practices: On Representation and the Interpretation of Text', in *Discourse and Social Life,* ed. by S. Sarangi and M. Coulthard. London: Longman, 155–69.

4 Role Prescriptions, Social Practices, and Social Structures: A Sociological Basis for the Contextualization of Analysis in SFL and CDA

José Luiz Meurer

Despite all the advances achieved by both Systemic Functional Linguistics (SFL) and Critical Discourse Analysis (CDA) in the description of the pervasive relationship between language and social context, there is still a need to pursue further theorizing on the issue. Thus, in this paper I explore aspects of Giddens' structuration theory as tools for the contextualization of discourse analysis endeavours. Concentrating on rules and resources as structuring properties of social life, I illustrate how they may be used to supplement analyses in SFL and CDA by discussing aspects of national identities as instantiated in a text by Noam Chomsky, 'On the Bombings', of September 11, 2001. The relevance of the paper lies in its attempt to expand the body of knowledge on the interrelationship between language and society.

Introduction

Every text reflects complex social routines and, both within Systemic Functional Linguistics (SFL) and Critical Discourse Analysis (CDA), important advances have been made regarding the interconnections between texts and the context where they occur. For example, within SFL, the Context of Situation with its sub-variables Field, Tenor, and Mode, and the Context of Culture with its link to larger sociocultural aspects of human activity have successfully been used to discuss important ramifications of language and context as they relate to register (Halliday 1978), genre (Eggins 1994; Butt *et al.* 2001), and the notion of contextual configuration (Halliday and Hasan 1989; Hasan 1996). Within CDA, Fairclough and Wodak (1997: 271–9), for instance, have tackled the relationship between language and context by elaborating on socially based topics such as: 'CDA addresses social problems'; 'power relations are discursive'; 'discourse constitutes society and culture'; 'the link between text and society is mediated'; and 'discourse is a form of social action' (also, e.g. Fairclough 1989, 1992, 1993, 1995; Wodak 1996).

There is a consensus in both SFL and CDA that context has crucial bearings on the analysis of language use and language change. In 1978, in his classic sociolinguistic proposal *Language as Social Semiotic*, for instance,

Halliday (1978: 35) emphasizes that the criteria for describing context should be sociological, i.e. 'based on some theory of social structure and social change'. Accordingly, he cautions,

> If we describe the context of situation in terms of *ad hoc* observations about the settings in which language is used, this could be said to be a 'social' account of language but hardly a 'sociological' one, since the concepts on which we are drawing are not referred to any kind of general social theory (Halliday 1978: 34–5).

Despite Halliday's call for sociologically based descriptions of context and a resulting consensus on the issue, there is a need to further problematize sociological notions in relation to discourse, as also observed, for instance, by Chouliaraki and Fairclough (1999), Meurer (1999, 2000), and Lemke (2001). Thus, in this paper I discuss Giddens' structuration theory as a broad sociological foundation to account for context in analysis of texts and their impact on social change, and to complement frameworks provided by SFL and CDA. In my endeavour to further develop the notion of context, I suggest the term *intercontextuality*, in an analogy to *intertextuality* and *interdiscursivity*, to refer to the various contexts that intermesh to influence or determine, and be influenced or determined by, texts, discourses, and other social practices.[1] The theoretical notions presented are proposed as a potential tool for broader contextualization in discourse analysis. Their linguistic realization will be evidenced by an SFL-based analysis of selected aspects of a text by Chomsky, 'On the Bombings', widely circulated on the Internet on September 11, 2001.

> The terrorist attacks were major atrocities. In scale they may not reach the level of many others, for example, Clinton's bombing of the Sudan with no credible pretext, destroying half its pharmaceutical supplies and killing unknown numbers of people (no one knows, because the US blocked an inquiry at the UN and no one cares to pursue it). Not to speak of much worse cases, which easily come to mind. But that this was a horrendous crime is not in doubt. The primary victims, as usual, were working people: janitors, secretaries, firemen, etc. It is likely to prove to be a crushing blow to Palestinians and other poor and oppressed people. It is also likely to lead to harsh security controls, with many possible ramifications for undermining civil liberties and internal freedom.
>
> The events reveal, dramatically, the foolishness of the project of 'missile defense.' As has been obvious all along, and pointed out repeatedly by strategic analysts, if anyone wants to cause immense damage in the US, including weapons of mass destruction, they are highly unlikely to launch a missile attack, thus guaranteeing their immediate destruction. There are innumerable easier ways that are basically unstoppable. But today's events will, very likely, be exploited to increase the pressure to develop these systems and put them into place. 'Defense' is a thin cover for plans for militarization of space, and with good PR, even the flimsiest arguments will carry some weight among a frightened public.
>
> In short, the crime is a gift to the hard jingoist right, those who hope to use force to control their domains. That is even putting aside the likely US actions, and what they will trigger – possibly more attacks like this one, or worse. The prospects ahead are even more ominous than they appeared to be before the latest atrocities.

As to how to react, we have a choice. We can express justified horror; we can seek to understand what may have led to the crimes, which means making an effort to enter the minds of the likely perpetrators. If we choose the latter course, we can do no better, I think, than to listen to the words of Robert Fisk, whose direct knowledge and insight into affairs of the region is unmatched after many years of distinguished reporting. Describing 'The wickedness and awesome cruelty of a crushed and humiliated people,' he writes that 'this is not the war of democracy versus terror that the world will be asked to believe in the coming days. It is also about American missiles smashing into Palestinian homes and US helicopters firing missiles into a Lebanese ambulance in 1996 and American shells crashing into a village called Qana and about a Lebanese militia paid and uniformed by America's Israeli ally hacking and raping and murdering their way through refugee camps.' And much more. Again, we have a choice: we may try to understand, or refuse to do so, contributing to the likelihood that much worse lies ahead.

The main dimensions from *structuration theory* to be explored in this paper are: 'role prescriptions', 'social practices', and 'social structures' as rules/resources. Notions related to these dimensions are intended to provide sociological theorizing on the constitution of 'the active flow of social life' (Giddens and Pierson 1998: 76) and, thus, on interconnections between texts and contexts. Structuration theory is relevant due to its attempt to capture social life as dynamically organized in a flux of interconnected practices which, at one and the same time, can either (a) reproduce previous identities, relations, and forms of conceptualizing the world (Fairclough 1992) which are thus recognized as similar or 'the same', or (b) challenge and change those identities, relations, and conceptualizations, thereby leading to new flows of social life. I will first deal with role prescriptions and social practices and then with rules and resources, illustrating their use in Chomsky's text.

Role Prescriptions and Social Practices

The notion of role prescriptions is necessary to conceptualize social positions and social identities. According to Giddens (1979/1994: 117), a social position is

> a social identity that carries with it a certain range (however diffusely specified) of prerogatives and obligations that an actor who is accorded that identity (or is an 'incumbent' of that position) may activate or carry out: these prerogatives and obligations constitute the role prescriptions associated with that position.

Role prescriptions are, thus, privileges or rights and duties or responsibilities associated with specific social identities, that is, categories or typifications 'made on the bases of some definite social criterion or criteria: occupation, kin relation, age-grade' (Giddens 1979/1994: 118), level of education, religious or political affiliation, income, nationality, and so on.

In SFL, roles and identities have been analysed in numerous ways, one of which is through the exploration of Tenor and its interconnections with the interpersonal metafunction of language realized by the lexicogrammatical systems of mood. For example, Fairclough (1989, 1992, 1995), Heberle (1997, 2001), Reichmann (2001), and Silva (2002) have used this aspect of systemic functional analysis as a tool to explore identities and relations in CDA. The point to emphasize is that because texts arise within intercontexts characterized by the tripartite social framework represented in Figure 4.1, the analysis carried out in SFL and CDA may be enriched by incorporating theoretical principles related to identities, social practices, and especially rule/resources (see next section) as developed in structuration theory.

In Chomsky's text, the most significant identities and associated role prescriptions include those of Chomsky himself, the UN, and several nations, namely, the US, the Sudan, Palestine, Lebanon, and Israel. Furthermore, the lexical references to 'other poor and oppressed people', 'a crushed and humiliated people', and 'refugee camps' also hint at different nationalities. A thorough analysis of such identities/roles would reveal unresolved tensions and even contradictions and, therefore, characterize them as dynamic, controversial, and fluid.[2] Some of these perspectives will be illustrated in the next sections because privileges, rights, duties, and responsibilities, or lack of them, associated with any facet of individual or national identity, will depend on their intermeshing with rules and resources bearing on different social practices.

Social practices are what people actually do, i.e. the activities they engage in as they conduct social life, including the launching of missiles or the use of texts as, for instance, Chomsky's text – a social practice which is a mixture of the genres 'discussion' and 'hortatory exposition' (Martin 1989; Butt *et al.* 2001). Even though social practices may include unexpected actions such as the ones evaluated by Chomsky (2001), Chouliaraki and Fairclough (1999: 21) note that they would most typically be defined as 'habitualized ways, tied to particular time and places, in which people apply resources (material or symbolic) to act together in the world' and that 'practices are constituted throughout social life – in the specialized

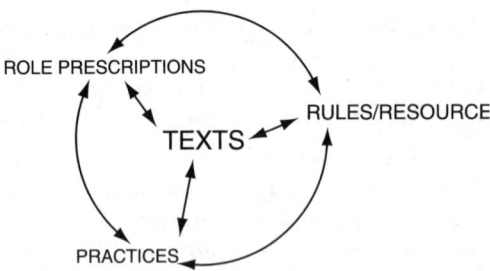

Figure 4.1 Map of the interplay among role prescriptions, rules/resources, and social practices, and the dialectical relationship between texts and these social dimensions (based on Giddens 1979/1994: 117)

domains of the economy and politics, for instance, but also in the domain of culture, including everyday life'. In company with Giddens (1984), I share Chouliaraki and Fairclough's (1999: 21) understanding that it is important to consider social practices in the analysis of human action, including the use of texts, because 'practices constitute a point of connection between abstract structures and their mechanisms, and concrete events – between "society" and people living their lives'.

Thus, as represented in Figure 4.1, no social practice is independent of role prescriptions and larger social structures. In an analogy to Bakhtin's (1986) notion of 'chains of texts', I suggest that SFL and CDA may incorporate the term *chains of practices* and explore the way every social practice interrelates with other social practices within larger social structures. This interdependence may be captured by the notion of inter-contextuality; as different practices are carried out, interdependent social structures and, thus, contexts, may be implicated. To illustrate, some of the interconnected practices in Chomsky's discussion include the appalling: 'Clinton's bombing of the Sudan', 'killing unknown numbers of people', 'harsh security controls', the carrying out of 'the project of "missile defense" ', 'cause immense damage in the US', 'launch a missile attack', 'develop [weapon] systems', 'militarization of space', 'use force to control their domains', 'American missiles smashing into Palestinian homes', 'US helicopters firing missiles', 'American shells crashing into a village', 'America's Israeli ally hacking and raping and murdering their way through refugee camps', as well as those that are less dramatic, more ordinary or mundane: 'blocked an inquiry at the UN', 'good PR', 'express justified horror', 'seek to understand what may have led to the crimes', 'choose [a] course', 'listen to the words of . . .', 'he writes that . . .', 'try to understand', and 'refuse to do so'. The analysis that I propose would also examine the rules and resources involved in such practices, as illustrated below. Notice that most of these actions as portrayed in Chomsky's text involve the US as a nation with its national identity depicted as that of a country attacked by terrorism but also as a consequence of its own even more violent incursions on other countries and its pursuit of control by means of military power.

Social Structures: Rules and Resources

In structuration theory, 'structure is primarily expressed in the things that people do in a regularized and institutionalized way' (Giddens and Pierson 1998: 78).[3] As Giddens (1984: 16, xxxi) points out, rather than resembling fixed patterns or visual configurations such as 'the skeleton or morphology of an organism or the girders of a building', a structure is conceptualized as 'rules and resources recursively implicated in social reproduction'. He (1984: 17) also notes that rules and resources, thus, constitute 'structuring properties', i.e. 'the properties which make it possible for discernibly similar social practices to exist across varying spans of time and space', and accordingly, 'institutionalized features of social systems have structural properties in the sense that relationships are stabilized across time and space'. Stabilization results from individuals' instantiating specific roles/ identities in specific social practices as demonstrated in Figure 4.1.

Rules: Normative Elements and Codes of Signification

In structuration theory, 'any given practice involves an overlapping and loosely connected set of rules' (Cohen 1989: 239) which have two aspects to them: normative elements and codes of signification. The normative elements of rules relate to 'the *sanctioning* of modes of social conduct' or 'techniques or generalizable procedures applied in the enactment/ reproduction of social life', while codes of signification relate to 'the constitution of *meaning*' (Giddens 1984: 21). In other words, the normative or regulative aspect of rules has to do with 'the appropriate or legitimate manner in which activities may be carried out, as well as . . . the positive and negative sanctions which are tacitly or self-consciously applicable to the activities' (Cohen 1989: 236). To know a rule means to 'know how to go on' (Giddens 1979/1994: 67, mentioning Wittgenstein). The signification aspect of rules, on the other hand, refers to the 'discursive and tacit meanings agents ascribe to their own activities as well as to the activities of others, and to the socially constituted contexts generated as meaningful to agents when activities are established and maintained' (Cohen 1989: 236). Several characteristics of rules concerning social structures, Giddens (1984: 18) notes, should be heeded: social rules are 'subject to a far greater diversity of contestation than the rules of games' – for example, 'rules cannot be conceptualized apart from resources'; and rules are always associated to practices.

The instantiation of the two aspects of rules, together with resources (see next section), gives rise to the *duality of structure*, i.e. rules and resources constitute the means and the outcome of social practices. In other words, as individuals act in the world through texts or otherwise, they make use of and, at the same time, recreate specific social structures. Existing structures are, thus, reconstructed anew through individual agency so that structural properties of social systems both constrain and enable human action, engendering potential changes every time a social practice is instantiated.[4] Hence, stabilization is only temporary.

How does the regulative side of rules constitute structuring properties? Take the normative force of a missile defence project such as the one mentioned in Chomsky's text. In the event that it is approved by the US Congress, it will lead to a large number of regulations and consequent practices – for instance, contracts to be signed and agreed on by engineering companies, specification of manufacturing sites, rules for the construction of effective weapon launching platforms, and so forth. Thus, this aspect of rules plays the role of structuring properties because it is deeply embedded in the (re)production of human practices. Individual and institutional actions and identities are to a great extent oriented by regulations, i.e. they greatly depend on what human agents are expected to do, how they are expected to carry out specific activities, and ensuing positive and/or negative sanctions.

Furthermore, how does signification, the semantic side of rules, constitute structuring properties? An examination of processes in Chomsky's text from an SFL perspective demonstrates that 46.27 per cent of the processes are material; 29.85 per cent are relational; 19.40 per cent are mental; and 4.48 per cent are verbal. This means that most of the significations conveyed by these processes have to do with actions, followed by specific attributes, mental operations, and verbal activity, respectively. Within the totality of the material processes in the text, 72.73 per cent relate to actions of the US government and its allies. The processes by themselves paint an ominous picture. They are: 'block', 'control', 'crash', 'develop', 'exploit', 'fire', 'hack', 'increase', 'murder', 'pay', 'put', 'rape', 'smash', 'trigger', 'be uniformed', and 'use'. On the other hand, there is only one occurrence of a mental process attributed to the US, namely, 'hope', in an embedded clause following Chomsky's classifying the attacks as 'a gift to the hard jingoist right, those who <u>hope</u> to use force to control their domains'. In terms of these material and mental processes, the overall signification created in this text is one of a national government that primarily takes action, that is, all brawn and no brain.

Regarding the use of relational processes, two different aspects of national identity and consequent potential practices emerge depending on whether the significations attributed to the attacks are the ones that – according to Chomsky – the US government proposes or Chomsky himself envisages. The relational process 'were', used after the topical theme 'the terrorist attacks' of the first clause, points towards the attributes that Chomsky will attach to the topic discussed. Although he starts by negatively evaluating the events as 'major atrocities', his evaluation is only a concession because his second clause restricts that signification: 'In scale they [the attacks] may not reach the level of many others, for example, Clinton's bombing of the Sudan . . .' The use of denial is notable as it is a seminal linguistic element in the creation of new significations. Through further relational processes in the final paragraph, Chomsky explicitly denies, i.e. rejects the signification, that this is 'the war of democracy versus terror that the world will be asked to believe in the coming days'. And as denials regularly predict correction (Winter 1977), Chomsky accordingly adds a new complement to the relational 'is', thus, correcting the previous statement by citing Robert Fisk:

> It is also about American missiles smashing into Palestinian homes and US helicopters firing missiles into a Lebanese ambulance in 1996 and American shells crashing into a village called Qana and about a Lebanese militia paid and uniformed by America's Israeli ally hacking and raping and murdering their way through refugee camps.

He then emphasizes this negative side of the US government by adding a loaded phrase to the above correction, namely, 'And much more'. Still other significations pinpointed by Chomsky by means of relational processes are: 'The events <u>reveal</u>, dramatically, the foolishness of the project of "missile defense" '; ' "Defense" <u>is</u> a thin cover for plans for militarization of space'; and 'the crime <u>is</u> a gift to the hard jingoist right'.

In the analysis that I propose, the point is not so much to look at signification itself but how signification – in its sense within structuration theory – constitutes structuring properties and intermeshes with individual and institutional identities and ensuing actions. Thus, in their function as structuring properties of human action, the conflicting sets of meanings in the text have the potential to lead to markedly different facets of social identities and practices. Consequently, should the US government implement practices based on the significations favoured by Chomsky in his text, those practices would dramatically differ from those based on the significations he explicitly rejects. They would, too, ameliorate a facet of the country's identity.

Resources: Allocation and Authorization

Like rules, resources are properties of structures implicated in how individuals recursively produce and reproduce social life, and as such, they, too, are both medium and outcome of structuration processes. Resources also subdivide into two types: allocative resources, 'which stem from control of material products or aspects of the material world', and authoritative resources, 'which derive from the co-ordination of the activity of human agents' (Giddens 1984: 17). In other words, allocation refers to 'capabilities – or, more accurately, to forms of transformative capacity – generating command over objects, goods or material phenomena', and authorization to 'types of transformative capacity generating command over persons or actors' (Giddens 1984: 33).

More specifically, allocation (Giddens 1984: 258) encompasses capacities that generate control over:

1. Material features of the environment (raw materials, material power sources);
2. Means of material production/reproduction (instruments of production, technology); and
3. Produced goods (artefacts created by the interaction of 1 and 2).

and authorization (Giddens 1984: 258) which includes capacities that generate control over:

- Organization of social time-space (temporal-spatial constitution of paths and regions);
- Production/reproduction of the body (organization and relation of human beings in mutual association); and

- Organization of life chances (constitution of chances of self-development and self-expression).

Like rules, resources are not isolated structuring processes. Instead, the mobilization of resources implicates the mobilization of rules as well; the same way as rules cannot be conceptualized apart from resources, resources are also impinged upon by rules. Resources, therefore, are not just additional to rules but are the means whereby rules are realized in specific social practices (Giddens 1979/1994).

Without resources, there can be no action. As a consequence, resources are directly implicated in the generation and maintenance of power. As Giddens (1979/1994: 69) states, 'resources are the "bases" or the "vehicles" of power, comprising structures of domination, drawn upon by parties to interaction and reproduced through the duality of structure'. Individuals and institutions draw upon such 'bases' to engage in social practices, to carry out different roles, and to 'control' the course of action and interaction with other individuals or institutions (Cohen 1989). Resulting from an intercontextual interplay of resources and rules, 'power is generated by definite forms of domination in a parallel way to the involvement of rules with social practices; and, indeed, as an integral element of those practices' (Giddens 1979/1994: 69).[5]

Every individual and every institution holds diverse forms of power, but obviously some are more powerful than others. Both individual and national identities will be closely interconnected with resources and it makes no sense to ignore such facets of identities. For instance, although no epithet or classifier is added to Chomsky's name following the title of the text, 'On the Bombings', since his text was circulated on September 11, it would be an anticipated critical analysis of the context surrounding the attacks on the World Trade Center because Chomsky is a well-known US intellectual and critic of North American government policies. As such, he has authoritative resources and legitimation to air his views and challenge significations related to the involvement of the US and its national projects and policies.

I think CDA and SFL researchers should put more explicit effort into investigating textual elements and their intermeshing with human practices to evidence who, in the increasing globalized world at large, holds more power, why, and how. In the case of Chomsky's text, both allocative and authoritative resources may be explored regarding their involvement in the implementation of the actions specified by the material processes mentioned above such as 'block', 'control', 'crash', 'develop', and 'exploit'. The textualization of these happenings should be discussed regarding, for example, what kinds of resources are mobilized for the US to '[block] an inquiry at the UN', for the 'hard jingoist right . . . to control their domains' or for the government '[to exploit events] to increase the pressure to develop weapon systems and put them into place'.

Structures of Legitimation: Signification and Domination

As structuring properties of social systems, rules and resources are implemented simultaneously in different social realms and at different levels of
social life. Rules/resources are being constantly activated within and across
nations, at home, in the church, and in friendly or antagonistic gatherings.
Depending on the complex interrelations between norms/significations
and allocation/authorization implicated in social environments or contexts, different identities/role prescriptions are instantiated, different
relations are established, and different representations of 'reality' and,
thus, different significations are created. These aspects of social life mutually influence one another leading to socially created, interconnected
structures of legitimation, structures of signification, and structures of
domination as shown in Figure 4.2.

As represented in Figure 4.2, structures of legitimation such as legal
institutions and structures of signification such as discourses are associated
to, i.e. they shape and are shaped by normative elements and codes of
signification, respectively, as implemented by individuals playing roles
within different social practices. Along the same lines, structures of domination – political, economic, theoretical, intellectual, and so on – are associated with allocative and authoritative resources as utilized by individuals
invested in specific roles and identities within social practices.

As also suggested by the bi-directional arrows at the bottom of Figure 4.2,
there is an intimate interdependence between structures of legitimation,

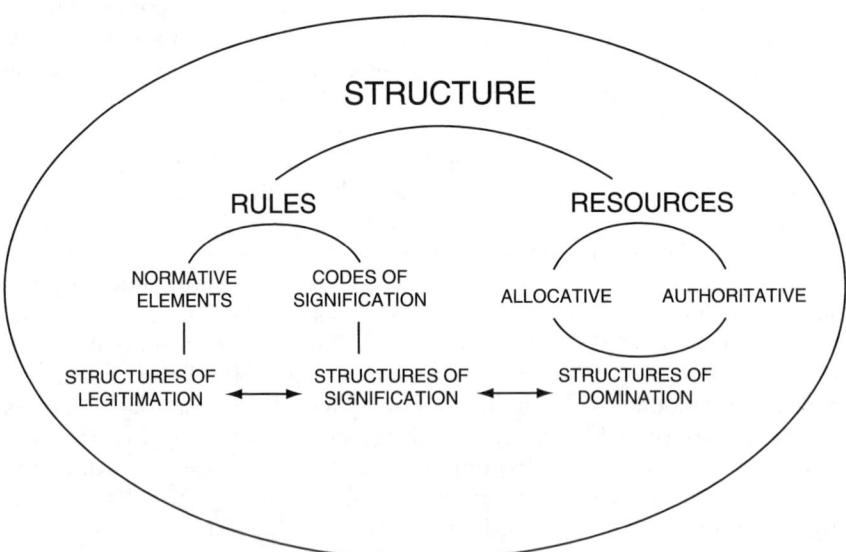

Figure 4.2 Rules/resources: generating legitimation, signification, and
domination

signification, and domination, and a series of events are operative as any given structuration is instantiated via the duality of structure. Intercontexts are involved and, thus, regulations and significations originating in different social environments may be legitimated in a given practice by means of allocative and authoritative resources at the same time that resources may be legitimated by means of norms and significations. As structures of domination are mobilized, structures of legitimation and signification may arise or may be reproduced in a constant interaction between rules and resources, implemented in specific social practices. The same way as structures of domination lead to the (re)production and legitimation of different rules, structures of legitimation and signification affect structures of domination by either reproducing or challenging them and, thus, establishing the potential for social change.

As pointed out by Giddens (1984: 31) (and suggested by the bi-directional arrows in Figure 4.2), 'structures of signification always have to be grasped in connection with domination and legitimation'. Looking at different significations attributed to identical 'facts' such as those depicted in Chomsky's text is crucial for the comprehension of what domination and legitimation structures are at play, what motivates human action, and, most importantly, how the world is structured and how one might perhaps resist or verbally oppose such structurings. The world, in many senses, is characterized by perverse sets of practices unopposedly supported by obscure structures of legitimation, signification, and domination. By looking at wider contexts in terms of the instantiation of sets of rules and resources, language investigation within SFL or CDA may have a bigger impact on the way human agents understand and act upon the different dimensions of such structures.

Because such structures are socially created and recreated, what is considered legitimate or not, and the meanings attributed to things, events or phenomena vary depending on the domination, legitimation, and signification structures involved. Thus, even an identical event may be seen quite differently in terms of appropriateness and may have quite different bearings and meanings.

Conclusion

One of the important concerns in both SFL and CDA is to establish clear relationships between language and context. Important advances have been accomplished in this respect as encapsulated in the notions of Context of Situation (related to register) and Context of Culture (related to genre). While the level of delicacy is quite high in terms of relating the variables of the Context of Situation (Field, Tenor, Mode) to specific metafunctions of language (Ideational, Interpersonal, Textual) and corresponding systems of options in the lexicogrammar (Transitivity, Mood, Theme/Rheme), no such delicate level of analysis exists regarding the Context of Culture. We cannot just say that language use is also related to

the Context of Culture, which realizes genre, and leave it at that. Thus, I
believe the framework I have introduced above may be an initial route
towards a more delicate analysis of the interconnections between the
broader Context of Culture and language use.

The sociological notions from structuration theory I have presented here
may help analysts see how, across chains of practices, different social contexts may impinge upon other contexts, giving rise to what I have referred
to as *intercontextuality*. Rules (norms and significations) together with
resources (allocation and authorization) may be seen to materialize in texts
as they enmesh with social practices and role prescriptions, being both
condition and outcome of such practices and roles via the duality of structure. Discourse analysis endeavours both in CDA and SFL need to focus
greater attention on contexts and intercontexts of domination, signification, and legitimation, ranging from social practices represented in everyday texts up to complexities such as the ones alluded to in Chomsky's text.
Even though human actors do have an impressive amount of knowledge
which allows them 'to go on' in the world, knowledge is always restricted
because it is limited to certain texts and social contexts that directly or
indirectly come into human agents' reach. Because all significations are
socially constructed and because strategies of domination as well as norms
(forms of legitimation) and significations are sometimes quite obscure, it
should be one of the aims of SFL and CDA to construct further explicit
knowledge about the sets of significations as well as norms and resources by
means of which individuals are motivated to attribute or create different
meanings through texts or their actions.

Every social practice as well as every role prescription is related to structures of legitimation, signification, and domination. Contradictorily, however, many times such structures are made opaque or invisible especially by
means of language itself. As both CDA and SFL investigate how language
reflects and reproduces social structure, they may benefit from incorporating principles of structuration theory that attempt to make sense of how
social reproduction happens. The world is, in some contexts, characterized
by quite perverse structures. Sociological principles, as the ones I have
discussed, may foster clearer understanding of how structures of signification get legitimatized for the benefit of what forms of allocation and
authorization. My hope is that language practices, as developed within
SFL and CDA, will have the potential to impact on how individuals
understand and react to such structures, helping them to see relationships
between language and the larger context of culture, leading to changes
where individuals reflect on their roles, on significations and forms of domination in a way that may legitimately lead to better 'life politics' (Giddens
1991: 209–33) both at the immediate context and at larger intercontexts of
human practices. Language is the weapon.

Acknowledgement

I would like to thank Anderson de Souza for the valuable help with the computational analysis of processes and participants in Chomsky's text.

Notes

1. With the complexities of late modernity, practically all contexts are somehow intercontextually based and might thus be referred to as *intercontexts*. They are characterized by the instantiation of rules and resources that cut across specific contexts. An intercontext thus shares features of different contexts. For example, national economies share, increasingly, features of international environments, leading to higher levels of globalization. Or actions such as the ones portrayed in Chomsky's text are intercontextually based because they depend on a number of different contexts – religious, political, economic, military – instantiated by different people invested with different identities in different countries. There is a need to develop the notion of intercontextual systems of practices to better understand human motivation and agency in the present world.
2. Work on discursive construction of national identities has been carried out by Wodak *et al.* (1999: 187) and shows that these 'identities should not be perceived as static, but rather as dynamic, vulnerable and rather ambivalent entities'.
3. Of course, structure may be disrupted by events such as those of September 11, 2001.
4. Along these lines, Chouliaraki and Fairclough (1999: 32) appropriately observe: 'Social systems are both the precondition of social action and the products of social action.'
5. In an insightful chapter on social life and critical research, Chouliaraki and Fairclough (1999: 19) elaborate on the idea that 'life (natural and social) is an "open system", in which any event is governed by simultaneously operative "mechanisms" (or "generative powers")' and they add, 'the various dimensions and levels of life – including physical, chemical, biological, economic, social psychological, semiological (and linguistic) – have their own distinctive structures, which have distinctive generative effects on events via their particular *mechanisms*' (emphasis added). The latter term, however, remains undefined by these authors, and I believe that in talking about the social world, it would be instructive to associate the concept of 'mechanism' (or generating powers) to both the notions of norms/significations (rules) and allocation/authorization (resources). In this sense, operative 'mechanisms' and power itself would be understood as processes 'deriving' from rules and resources and as both medium and outcome of specific social practices, thus, contributing to the activation of specific role prescriptions and consequent actions.

References

Bakhtin, M. M. (1986) *Speech Genres and Other Late Essays*, trans. by Vern W. McGee. Austin, TX: University of Texas Press.

Butt, D., Fahey, R., Spinks, S. and Yallop, C. (2001) *Using Functional Grammar: An Explorer's Guide*. Sydney: Macquarie University.

Chomsky, N. (2001) 'On the Bombings' at: http://www.zmag.org (consulted September 23, 2001).

Chouliaraki, L. and Fairclough, N. (1999) *Discourse in Late Modernity: Rethinking Critical Discourse Analysis*. Edinburgh: Edinburgh University Press.

Cohen, I. J. (1989) *Structuration Theory – Anthony Giddens and the Constitution of Social Life*. New York: St Martin's Press.

Eggins, S. (1994) *An Introduction to Systemic Functional Linguistics*. London: Pinter.

Fairclough, N. (1995) *Critical Discourse Analysis: The Critical Study of Language*. London: Longman.

Fairclough, N. (1993) 'Critical Discourse Analysis and the Marketization of Public Discourse: The Universities', *Discourse and Society*, 4(2): 133–68.

Fairclough, N. (1992) *Discourse and Social Change*. Cambridge: Polity Press.

Fairclough, N. (1989) *Language and Power*. London: Longman.

Fairclough, N. and Wodak, R. (1997) 'Critical Discourse Analysis', in *Discourse and Social Interaction: Volume 2*, ed. by T. A. van Dijk. London: Sage Publications, 258–84.

Giddens, A. (1991) *Modernity and Self-Identity*. Cambridge: Polity Press.

Giddens, A. (1984) *The Constitution of Society*. Cambridge: Polity Press.

Giddens, A. (1979/1994) *Central Problems in Sociological Theory*. Berkeley, CA: University of California Press.

Giddens, A. and Pierson, C. (1998) *Conversations with Anthony Giddens. Making Sense of Modernity*. Stanford, CA: Stanford University Press.

Halliday, M. A. K. (1978) *Language as Social Semiotic*. London: Edward Arnold.

Halliday, M. A. K. and Hasan, R. (1989) *Language, Context, and Text: Aspects of Language in a Social-Semiotic Perspective*. Oxford: Oxford University Press.

Hasan, R. (1996) 'What's Going On: A Dynamic View of Context in Language', in *Ways of Saying: Ways of Meaning: Selected Papers of Ruqaiya Hasan*, ed. by C. Cloran, D. Butt, and G. Williams. London: Cassell, 37–50.

Heberle, V. M. (2001) 'Questões de Gênero e Identidade no Discurso da Mídia', in *Inglês como Língua Estrangeira: Identidades, Práticas e Textualidade [English as a Foreign Language: Identity, Practices and Textuality]*, ed. by M. Grigoletto and A. M. G. Carmagnani. São Paulo: Humanitas/USP, 91–110.

Heberle, V. M. (1997) 'An Investigation of Textual and Contextual Parameters in Editorials of Women's Magazines', unpublished Ph.D.

Dissertation. Florianópolis/Brazil: Universidade Federal de Santa Catarina.

Lemke, J. L. (2001) 'Textuality and Mediation of Social Control', in *The 28th International Systemic Functional Congress – Interfaces: Systemic Functional Grammar and Critical Discourse Analysis*. Abstract Book. ISFC28, Ottawa: Carleton University, 26–7.

Martin, J. R. (1989) *Factual Writing: Exploring and Challenging Social Reality*. Oxford: Oxford University Press.

Meurer, J. L. (2000) 'O Conhecimento de Gêneros Textuais e a Formação do Profissional da Linguagem', in *Aspectos da Lingüística Aplicada: Estudos em Homenagem ao Prof. Hilário I. Bohn*, ed. by M. B. M. Fortkamp and L. M. B. Tomitch. Florianópolis: Editora Insular, 149–66.

Meurer, J. L. (1999) 'O Conhecimento de Gêneros Textuais e a Formação do Profissional da Linguagem', *Intercâmbio*, 8: 129–34.

Reichmann, C. L. (2001) 'Reflection as Social Practice: An In-Depth Linguistic Study of Teacher Discourse in a Dialogue Journal', unpublished Ph.D. Dissertation. Florianópolis/Brazil: Universidade Federal de Santa Catarina.

Silva, F. A. R. da (2002) 'A Linguistic Investigation into the Representation of the Landless Movement (MST) in the Press', unpublished Ph.D. Dissertation. Florianópolis/Brazil: Universidade Federal de Santa Catarina.

Winter, E. O. (1977) 'A Clause Relational Approach to English Texts: A Study of Some Predictive Lexical Items in Written Discourse', *Instructional Science*, 6: 1–93.

Wodak, R. (1996) *Disorders of Discourse*. New York: Addison Wesley Longman.

Wodak, R., de Cillia, R., Reisigl, M. and Liebhert, K. (1999) *The Discourse Construction of Austrian National Identity*. Edinburgh: Edinburgh University Press.

Applied Section: National Identity

5 Critical Discourse Analysis in Researching Language in the New Capitalism: Overdetermination, Transdisciplinarity, and Textual Analysis[1]

Norman Fairclough

I use the term 'new capitalism' to refer to the most recent of a historical series of radical restructurings through which capitalism has maintained its fundamental continuity (Jessop 2000). A great deal of contemporary social research is concerned with the nature and consequences of these changes. The study of language aspects of new capitalism is now developing into a significant area of research for critical discourse analysts. There is a website devoted to it (http://www.cddc.vt.edu/host/lnc/) and the journal Discourse and Society *has recently devoted a special issue to the theme (13(2) 2002). However, using the term 'new capitalism' does not imply an exclusive focus on economic issues: transformations in capitalism have ramifications throughout social life; and 'new capitalism' as a research theme should be interpreted broadly as a concern with how these transformations impact on politics, education, artistic production, and many other areas of social life.*

Introduction

Capitalism has the capacity to overcome crises by radically transforming itself periodically so that economic expansion can continue. Such a transformation towards 'new capitalism' is taking place now in response to a crisis in the post-Second World War model ('Fordism'). This transformation involves both 'restructuring' of relations among the economic, political, and social domains (including the commodification and marketization of fields such as education which become subject to the economic logic of the market), and the 're-scaling' of relations among different scales of social life – the global, the regional (e.g. the European Union), the national, and the local. Governments on different scales, social democratic as well as conservative, have embraced 'neo-liberalism': a political project for facilitating restructuring and re-scaling of social relations in accordance with the demands of an unrestrained global capitalism (Bourdieu 1998). It has been imposed on the post-socialist economies as allegedly the best means of rapid-system transformation, economic renewal, and reintegration into the global economy. It has led to radical attacks on universal social welfare and the reduction of the protections that welfare states provided for people against the effects of markets. It has also led to an increasing division between rich and poor, increasing economic insecurity and stress even for the 'new middle' classes, and an intensification of the exploitation of labour. The unrestrained emphasis on growth also poses major threats to the environment. It has also produced a new imperialism in which international financial agencies under the tutelage of the US and its rich allies indiscriminately impose restructuring, sometimes with disastrous consequences, e.g. Russia and Argentina – an imperialism which has recently begun to take a military form in the 'war on terrorism'. It is not the impetus to increasing international economic integration that is the problem but the particular form in which this is being imposed, and the particular consequences, e.g. in terms of unequal distribution of wealth, which are being made to follow. All this has resulted in the disorientation and disarming of economic, political, and social forces committed to radical alternatives, and has contributed to a closure of public debate and a weakening of democracy. (This summary is based upon the programme for the Language in New Capitalism research network at http://www.cddc.vt.edu/host/lnc/)

Language in New Capitalism

The common idea of new capitalism as a 'knowledge-based' or 'knowledge-driven' socioeconomic order implies that it is also 'discourse-driven', suggesting that language may have a more significant role in contemporary socioeconomic changes than it has had in the past. If this is so, discourse analysis has an important contribution to make to research on the transformations of capitalism. The significance of language in these transformations has not gone unnoticed by social researchers. For instance, Bourdieu and Wacquant (2001: 3) point to a 'new planetary vulgate', which they characterize as a vocabulary ('globalization', 'flexibility', 'governance', 'employability', 'exclusion', and so forth), which 'is endowed with the performative power to bring into being the very realities it claims to describe'. That is, the neo-liberal political project of removing obstacles to the new economic order is discourse-driven.

But, as well as indicating the significance of language in these socioeconomic transformations, Bourdieu and Wacquant (2001) show that social research needs the contribution of discourse analysts. It is not enough to characterize the 'new planetary vulgate' as a list of words, a vocabulary; rather, texts and interactions need to be analysed to show how some of the effects that Bourdieu and Wacquant identify are brought off, e.g. making the socioeconomic transformations of new capitalism and the policies of governments to facilitate them seem inevitable; representing desires as facts; and representing the imaginaries of interested policies – the interested possible realities they project – as the way the world actually is (Fairclough 2000a). Bourdieu and Wacquant's (2001) account of the effectivity of neo-liberal discourse exceeds the capacity of their sociological research methods.

But it is not only text and interactional analysis that discourse analysts can bring to social research on the new capitalism, it is also a satisfactory theorization of the dialectics of discourse (elaborated further below). If analysts think of the restructuring and re-scaling which Jessop (2000) refers to as changes in the networking of social practices, they are also a restructuring and re-scaling of discourse, of 'orders of discourse' (the term is explained below). The restructuring of orders of discourse is a matter of shifting relations, i.e. changes in networking, between the discourse elements of different (networks of) social practices. A prime example is the way in which the language of management has colonized public institutions and organizations such as universities, although I need to add at once that this process is a colonization/appropriation dialectic, i.e. not only a matter of the entry of discourses into new domains, but the diverse ways in which they are received, appropriated, and recontextualized in different locales, and the ultimately unpredictable outcomes of this process. The re-scaling of orders of discourse is a matter of changes in the networking of the discourse elements of social practices on different scales of social organization – global, regional, national, and local – for instance, the enhanced and accelerated permeability of local social practices (local government, small-scale industry, local media) in countries across the world to discourses which are globally disseminated through organizations such as the International Monetary Fund (IMF) and the World Bank. Working the above account of the transformation of capitalism into a dialectical theory of discourse provides a theoretical framework for researching the global penetrative power of the 'new planetary vulgate' which Bourdieu and Wacquant (2001) allude to, as well as its limits.

This theoretical framework is also needed to research what Bourdieu and Wacquant (2001: 4) call the 'performative power' of the 'new planetary vulgate', i.e. its power to 'bring into being the very realities it describes'. How does this discourse come to be internalized (Harvey 1996) in social practices, and under what conditions does it construct and reconstruct (rather than merely construe) social practices including their nondiscoursal elements? How does it come to be enacted in ways of acting and interacting, e.g. organizational routines and procedures including genres, and inculcated in the ways of being, i.e. the identities of social agents? How does it come to be materialized in the 'hardware' of institutions and organizations? Researching this crucial issue requires detailed investigation of organizational and institutional change on a comparative basis, such as the study by Salskov-Iversen *et al.* (2000) of the contrasting colonization/appropriation of the new 'public management' discourse by local authorities in Britain and Mexico, but working with the sort of dialectical theory of discourse I sketch out below (also Iedema 1999).

An Example: The Blair Text

Having given above a general account of the transformations of new capitalism and a general rationale for a language focus in researching new capitalism, I now want to focus on specific issues which arise from a single text. Table 5.1 is the 'Foreword' to a UK Department of Trade and Industry White Paper, 'Our Competitive Future: Building the Knowledge Economy', written by (or at least signed by) the Prime Minister, Tony Blair.

One thing I find striking about this text (and many other contemporary texts in politics and government but also other fields such as education) is the texturing of a relationship between the 'global'[2] and the national. The relevance of this feature of the text to the concerns of this paper is that this way of constructing the global and the national as well as the relationship between them is, as I shall argue in more detail later, characteristically neo-liberal – using that term as above for the dominant political position within current transformations of capitalism. In using the term 'texturing', I am focusing on the 'work' that is done textually, i.e. the textual 'working up' of that relationship. Blair is writing about, and texturing, a relationship between 'the modern world' (more specifically the 'new global economy', an expression he uses often although not in this text) and Britain. Let me refer to these as different 'space-times': the global space-time and the national space-time. I shall come back to that term later. For instance, Paragraph 1 represents the global space-time of the 'modern world'. The first sentence of Paragraph 2 can be seen as combining representations of global and national space-times. The relation between 'success' and exploitation of 'assets' is global (it applies anywhere in the 'new global economy'), but the relational process verb ('depends on') links a nominalization ('our success') and an embedded clause ('how well we exploit . . .'), which represent processes in British national space-time. The second and third sentences of Paragraph 2 represent the global space-time. I shall comment first on how these space-times are constructed, and then on how they are textured together.

The Global Space-time

Global space is represented as an entity, a place, 'the modern world', 'this new world'. It is a participant in processes rather than a circumstance as it would be in, for example, 'new markets are opening up *on an international level*'. It is the passive subject (and 'logical object') in the first sentence of Paragraph 1 and the active subject in the first sentence of Paragraph 3: 'This new world challenges . . .' It is also the Theme of the text's opening sentence and, one might say, of the first paragraph.

Global time is represented as present although what that means needs some clarification. The verbs are present tense, either simple present or present continuous ('are opening up'). In most cases, the simple present is 'timeless present', representing an indeterminate stretch of time which

Table 5.1 Text by Tony Blair (1998)

Paragraph	Text
1	The modern world is swept by change. New technologies emerge constantly, new markets are opening up. There are new competitors but also great new opportunities.
2	Our success depends on how well we exploit our most valuable assets: our knowledge, skills and creativity. These are the key to designing high-value goods and services and advanced business practices. They are at the heart of a modern, knowledge-driven economy.
3	This new world challenges business to be innovative and creative, to improve performance continuously, to build new alliances and ventures. But it also challenges Government: to create and execute a new approach to industrial policy.
4	That is the purpose of this White Paper. Old-fashioned state intervention did not and cannot work. But neither does naïve reliance on markets.
5	The Government must promote competition, stimulating enterprise, flexibility and innovation by opening markets. But we must also invest in British capabilities when companies alone cannot: in education, in science and in the creation of a culture of enterprise. And we must promote creative partnerships which help companies: to collaborate for competitive advantage; to promote a long-term vision in a world of short-term pressures; to benchmark their performance against the best in the world; and to forge alliances with other businesses and employees. All this is the DTI's role.
6	We will not meet our objectives overnight. The White Paper creates a policy framework for the next ten years. We must compete more effectively in today's tough markets if we are to prosper in the markets of tomorrow.
7	In Government, in business, in our universities and throughout society we must do much more to foster a new entrepreneurial spirit: equipping ourselves for the long term, prepared to seize opportunities, committed to constant innovation and enhanced performance. That is the route to commercial success and prosperity for all. We must put the future on Britain's side.
	Tony Blair (signature) The Rt Hon Tony Blair MP, Prime Minister

includes but pre-dates and post-dates the present. The present continuous
with the event verb 'open up' has both the meaning of inception and
incompletion ('are beginning to open up') and an iterative meaning
('keep opening up'), as it does when the simple present 'emerge' combines
with the adverb 'constantly'.

The modality of representations of the processes and relations of the
global space-time is epistemic and categorically assertive: positive statements without modal markers which represent processes as real and
actual. These statements of some of the truisms of the age are of a somewhat gnomic character. Yet, 'are opening up' and 'emerge constantly'
bring covert predictions ('will carry on emerging and opening up') of an
irrealis future into the representation of global space-time as *realis* present (Iedema 1998; Graham 2001). So too does the contrast in Paragraph 6
between 'today's tough markets' and 'the markets of tomorrow'; there is
an implicit prediction of the competitive character of these future
markets.

The processes of the global space-time are material (the three processes
in the first two sentences of Paragraph 1), existential (the third sentence of
Paragraph 1), relational (Paragraph 2), and verbal (Paragraph 3). The
actors in the material processes are non-human, inanimate ('new technologies', 'new markets') or nominalized ('change'), and the actor in the
verbal process is 'this new world'. The global space-time is represented as
processes without human agency.

The representation of relations between processes is also worth noting,
especially in Paragraph 1. Semantically, the relationship between the first
sentence and the rest of the paragraph is elaboration; the relationship
between the second and third sentences as well as between the two clauses
of the second is addition; and the relationship between the two phrases of
the third can be seen as both additive ('also') and contrastive ('but')
(Halliday 1994). Grammatically, there are three sentences: the second and
third containing paratactically related clauses and phrases, respectively.
The global space-time is represented as a list of processes. But there is also a
nominalized process ('change') and two inanimate nouns ('markets',
'opportunities') which, like the nominalization, represent processes, i.e.
people trading in new ways and people being able to do new things as
entities, two of which ('change', 'new markets') are actors in material
processes.

The National Space-time

National space is also represented as a place, Britain, although it is implicitly evoked through some of its attributes ('we', 'the Government', etc.)
rather than directly represented, e.g. 'Britain' does not appear until Paragraph 7, and 'British' appears just once in Paragraph 5. It is also differenti-
ated (see the final paragraph) in terms of fields ('Government', 'business',
'our universities') in which, as 'throughout society', 'a new entrepreneurial

spirit' is to be 'fostered', bringing all domains of social life under the sign of business.

In contrast to the predominant timeless present of the global space-time, the temporality of the national space-time is predominantly future – for instance, in Paragraph 5. Notice also that the future is to be put 'on Britain's side' (Paragraph 7). The verbs of the main clauses of the first three sentences are deontically modalized ('must'), and the meanings are 'present necessity of future action'. The implicit normative framework is not, for instance, ethical but pragmatic and circumstantial, i.e. we are forced by circumstances. On the other hand, in using 'must' rather than 'have to', Blair commits himself to these necessities rather than locating their source elsewhere. Whereas statements about the global space-time are descriptive, statements about the national space-time are predominantly prescriptive. Paragraph 6 begins with a sentence which is epistemically modalized, i.e. a prediction ('We will not meet our objectives overnight'). The national space-time is represented mainly in terms of *irrealis* processes: what things should be like and must be made like, rather than what they are like. The processes of subordinate and embedded clauses ('stimulating', 'opening', 'collaborating', 'benchmarking') are also *irrealis* through a process of 'propagation' of the *irrealis* processes of main clauses analogous to the 'value propagation' discussed by Lemke (1998), but so too are the embedded processes of nominalizations ('competition', 'flexibility'). Furthermore, the *irrealis* processes are in (*irrealis*) causal relation with each other, e.g. 'creative partnerships' lead to 'collaboration' which leads to 'competitive advantage'.

The processes of the national space-time are predominantly material and, in contrast to the global space-time, the actors in material processes are human, either represented by the pronoun 'we' or collective nouns ('the Government', 'companies').

I shall just comment on the representation of relationships between processes in Paragraph 5. The semantic relationship between the first sentence and the second and third taken together is both additive ('also') and contrastive ('but'); the relationship between the second and third sentences is addition; and the relationship between the first three sentences and the fourth is elaboration. In terms of relations between sentences, the representation of global space-time in Paragraph 1 and national space-time in Paragraph 5 have a similar list-like quality. But there is a difference in relations within sentences. In the first sentence, the first non-finite clause (from 'stimulating') is subordinate to the preceding finite clause while the second non-finite clause ('by opening') is subordinate to the first non-finite clause. Semantically, the relations are elaboration and means, respectively. In the second sentence, the second finite clause (from 'when') is subordinate to the first, i.e. the semantic relation is apparently temporal but perhaps rather causal ('because companies alone cannot'). There is layered embedding in the third sentence: a restrictive relative clause (beginning 'which help') embedded in a noun phrase and a list of co-ordinated non-finite clauses in a semantic relation of addition (from 'to collaborate') which are embedded in the relative clause as complements of 'help'. There are many nominalized processes ('competition', 'flexibility', 'innovation', etc.) although, in contrast with Paragraph 1, they do not function as actors.

The text as a whole, in the representation of both global and national space-times, is notable for the number of lists: elements in a semantically additive and grammatically paratactic relationship. Using a terminology I shall come back to, these lists texture relations of equivalence among elements. In some cases, equivalent elements are co-hyponyms, for instance 'our assets: knowledge, skills and creativity' in Paragraph 2 where 'knowledge', 'skills', and 'creativity' are co-hyponyms of 'assets' (the superordinate term). 'New technologies emerge constantly', 'new markets are opening up', '[there being] new competitors', and 'new opportunities' are co-hyponyms of 'change' in Paragraph 1; and 'education', 'science', and '[the creation of] a culture of enterprise' are co-hyponyms of 'British capabilities' in Paragraph 5. But 'equipping ourselves for the long term', '[being] prepared to seize opportunities', '[being] committed to constant innovation and enhanced performance' are co-meronyms of 'foster[ing] a new entrepreneurial spirit' – the former are aspects of the latter (Martin 1992). Elsewhere, elements are textured in equivalence relations without being in such hierachies as co-members of a class that is not labelled (what van Leeuwen 1996 calls 'associations') – for instance, in Paragraph 3, 'to be innovative and creative', 'to improve performance continuously', and 'to build new alliances and ventures'. In the last sentence of Paragraph 2, the relation of equivalence between 'modern' and 'knowledge-driven' can be taken as the semantic relation of elaboration (Halliday 1994).

Let me come to how the global space-time is textured into a relationship with the national space-time in the Blair text:

(a) The overall semantic pattern or rhetorical formation of the text can be seen as the 'problem-solution' pattern (Hoey 2001). The problem is the incontrovertible and inevitable reality that people are faced with (the global economy); the solution is what they must do to succeed in this new reality. A relationship is textured between 'is' and 'must', reality and necessity, which precludes real policy options.

(b) A relationship of subordination of national space-time to global space-time (national policy to global economy) is textured through projection in Paragraph 3, in verbal processes in which 'this new world' is addresser (posing 'challenges') while (national) 'business' and 'Government' are addressees.

(c) A relationship of subordination of national space-time to global space-time is textured in Paragraph 2 as the relation between national policy action (the embedded clause in sentence 1) and an implicit global reason (sentences 2 and 3) for this action. Notice the slippage from national to global in the anaphoric reference at the beginning of sentence 2: 'these' refers anaphorically not to '*our* knowledge, skills and creativity', but to 'knowledge, skills and creativity' generally.

(d) Processes on a national level are framed by circumstantial elements ('in a world of short-term pressures', 'in today's tough markets', 'the markets of tomorrow') which embed them within processes on a global level in Paragraphs 5 and 6.

(e) The national space-time is populated, one might say colonized, by the entified and spatialized processes of neo-liberal representations of the 'global economy' ('flexibility', 'enterprise', 'innovation', 'partnerships', etc.) which are positively valued, i.e. verbs such as 'stimulate' and 'promote' can be seen as textual triggers for positive valuation.

Critical Discourse Analysis (CDA) in Research on New Capitalism

Let me come back to relations of equivalence, using 'knowledge, skills and creativity' as an example. There is potentially a negative aspect to texturing elements as equivalent: it can subvert prior differences. What is striking about this example is that it makes equivalent words which come from different discourses that are historically associated with different domains of social life: education and learning ('knowledge'), crafts and trades ('skills'), and art ('creativity'). This subversion of the difference between prior discourses is constitutive in the making of a new discourse. A discourse is a representation of some area of social life from a particular perspective. One might refer rather to 'registers', but 'discourses' implies that all domains of social life (and of language use) are multi-perspectival, i.e. representing artistic production in terms of 'creativity' might be abhorrent from certain perspectives in the artistic field. The new discourse in this case is neo-liberal. That is a way of labelling a particular perspective within the political field, and a characteristic of this labelling is that it makes these words equivalent as co-hyponyms of 'assets'. I should add that there are issues of time-scale here: the equivalence of 'knowledge' and 'skills' is older than their co-equivalence with 'creativity'. Furthermore, some texts are original in texturing new equivalences while others (including this one) are typical of large bodies of texts which characteristically texture particular equivalences. This text is typical, I would suggest, of a body of texts which draws upon the political discourse of New Labour, of the 'Third Way', which one can see as a particular variant of the political discourse of neo-liberalism (Fairclough 2000b).

So, at one level of analysis, the relations textured by texts constitute discourses in relation to (and, potentially, in subversive relation to) other discourses. The particular constructions of global and national space-time can be seen in the same terms. They are characteristic of neo-liberal political discourse and, at the same time, subversive of prior political discourses; in this case, the neo-liberal political discourse of the 'Third Way' is subversive especially of the social democratic discourse of 'old Labour'. The relations of equivalence, in particular, point to what I suggest is a general property of texts: they hybridize discourses in constituting discourses. Actually, that is only one aspect of other, more general processes: they also hybridize genres in constituting genres and hybridize styles (in the sense of ways of being, i.e. identities, in their language aspect) in constituting styles. This is an aspect of the multifunctional character of texts, but I am suggesting that texts not only simultaneously have representational, actional, and identificatory functions in their linguistic features, they also have these functions 'interdiscursively' at the level of discourses, genres, and styles. (The version of multifunctionality I am adopting here is, of course, different from the most familiar version of the ideational, interpersonal, and textual metafunctions in Systemic Functional Linguistics (SFL), but the principle of multifunctionality is the same (Halliday 1994; Fairclough 2003).)

In CDA, interdiscursive analysis of texts is the mediating level of analysis which is crucial to integrating social and linguistic analyses (Fairclough 1992; Chouliaraki and Fairclough 1999). I prefer to use the term 'semiosis' to 'discourse' as an abstract noun. One advantage is that it is a reminder that what is at issue is not just (verbal) language but also other semiotic modalities (Kress and van Leeuwen 2000); another is that it avoids confusion with 'discourses' as a count noun in the sense I have just discussed. Semiosis in an element of social practices which is dialectically interconnected with other elements – in the terminology of dialectical theory, it is a 'moment' of the social. What this means is that, while different elements of social practices, including forms of activity, social relations, and their institutional forms; persons with beliefs, values, emotions, histories, and so on; material objects (including the means or technologies of activities); *and* semiosis, are indeed different, they cannot be reduced to each other, and, therefore, demand different social scientific theories and methodologies, i.e. they are not discrete. They flow to one another, they 'internalize' one another in Harvey's terminology (Harvey 1996; Fairclough 2001, 2003). Discourses, genres, and styles are three main ways in which semiosis figures in social practices as part of the action (genres), in representation (discourses), and in identification (styles).

Social practices are networked. One way of describing a particular social field in the sense of Bourdieu (Bourdieu and Wacquant 1992) or indeed a social order is in terms of the networking of social practices which characterizes it. Social change is change in the networking of social practices; therefore, the transformations of new capitalism can be analysed in terms of changes in network relations, i.e. both structural changes (changes in relations between fields or domains) and scalar changes (changes in relations between global, regional, national, and local), in the terminology I introduced earlier. The semiotic element or moment of a network of social practices is an 'order of discourse' – a particular articulation or configuration of genres, discourses, and styles. Orders of discourse are the social structuring of semiotic difference or variation. Interdiscursive analysis of texts is the mediating link between linguistic analysis and social analysis because, on the one hand, the 'mix' of genres, discourses, and styles in a text is realized in its semantic, lexicogrammatical and phonological features and, on the other hand, that 'mix' constitutes a particular working at the level of the concrete event of the semiotic moment of social practices. A particular text can simultaneously, depending on the 'mix' of genres, discourses, and styles, constitute: a reworking of prior, habitual or familiar constellations of linguistic features, e.g. relations of equivalence; and a reworking of the relatively durable articulations of genres, discourses, and styles which constitute orders of discourse and relations among orders of discourse (and hence, given the dialectical view of semiosis as a moment of the social, relations among social practices). Thus, the equivalences noted in the text not only rework relations among orders of discourse but also among the social practices they are moments of (education, crafts/trades, art). Interdiscursive analysis, thus, enables textual analysis to be properly integrated into social analysis, and, in the case of the particular focus in this paper, to be properly integrated into social analysis of the transformations of new capitalism.

I have focused upon the political discourse of Blair's text. It would also be possible to analyse its genre and its style, i.e. to analyse it as a form of political action (specifying what such 'Forewords' are doing) and as a form of constituting the identity of a political leader. But I want, rather, to comment on relations between discourses, genres, and styles in terms of the historical process within which this text is positioned. I described the temporality of the national space-time as *irrealis*. To put it differently, this sort of political discourse deals in imaginaries: it projects ways of acting and ways of being. Whether it remains merely a construal of possible ways of acting and being, or comes to construct real ways of acting and being, is a contingent matter (Sayer 2000). Discourses can be socially constructive, i.e. social life can be remodelled in their image, but there are no guarantees in that regard. There are conditions of possibility for discourses to have such constructive or performative effects (Fairclough *et al.* 2002). If they do have such effects, then the dialectics of discourse takes effect: discourses may be enacted in ways of acting and interacting; and they may be inculcated in ways of being, i.e. identities. Take, for instance, 'creative partnerships'. For 'creative partnerships' to go beyond the realm of imaginary construal into the realm of actual existence, people would need to start acting, interacting, and being 'differently'. Partly these enactments and inculcations are themselves semiotic, entailing new genres and styles. But partly they are non-semiotic: for instance, the dialectical internalization of discourses in new management systems and forms of embodiment; or their materialization in new architectural forms; or new ways of organizing urban space. Texts such as this one are, of course, precisely in the business of creating imaginaries as a step towards changed realities. One needs a dialectical view of semiosis to grasp that potential process in a way which gives due force to the impact of language in initiating it and in carrying it through.

Blair's text is positioned in complex chains or networks of texts with which it contracts intertextual relations, both 'retrospective' and 'prospect-ive', i.e. both with prior texts, which in one way or other have shaped it, or which it is oriented to, or in dialogue with; and with subsequent texts which report, represent, echo, and so forth the text, and which it may anticipate. The concept of recontextualization helps to grasp the dynamics of these relations (Bernstein 1990). But these relations on the concrete level of relations between specific events and texts are shaped by the more durable relations of networks of social practices and orders of discourse as their semiotic moments. Orders of discourse are characterized by 'chain' relations as well as 'choice' relations. In particular, relations within as well as among orders of discourse are regulated by genre chains, i.e. relatively durable and institutionalized relationships among genres characterized by particular principles of recontextualization and transformation. Thus, the genres of politics and government are chained with the genres of mass media in such a way that the recontextualization of a political document like the Blair text within a press report, and the transformations from the one to the other, have a relatively regular and predictable character. Social change, importantly, includes change in these relations of recontext-ualization and genre chains. For instance, the 'globalizing' character of the transformations of new capitalism includes the emergence of relations of recontextualization and genre chains which enable and regulate more fluid ways of acting across scales (at the limit, from the global to the local). Texts such as this not only represent relations among space-times, they are also positioned within such relations. And any account of the constitutive or performative effects of semiosis in the transformations of new capitalism must include these shifts in relations of recontextualization.

At the same time, however, recontextualization should be seen in terms of a colonizing/appropriating dialectic (Chouliaraki and Fairclough 1999). In this case, for instance, one might refer to recontextualization relations between the economic field and the political field (and their orders of discourse), and between the global scale and the national scale. Blair's representation of global space-time can be seen as a recontextualization of representations of the 'new economic order' and economic 'globalization' which are pervasive in texts, for instance, of the World Bank, IMF and Organization for Economic Co-operation and Development (OECD). One can meaningfully consider how national political discourse is being colon-ized by global economic discourse. But, at the same time, this narrative of economic change can be seen as appropriated into doing particular sorts of ('rhetorical') work in particular sorts of text. Thus, Hay and Rosamund (2002) claim that, by legitimizing national policy change in terms of inexorable and uncontrollable processes, globalization is a rhetorical strat-egy used in domestic political discourse in Britain (although not British political discourse within international agencies such as the United Nations), but not in France where the legitimizing narrative is one of 'European integration'. Textually, one can look at how such a recontextual-ized narrative is transformed – in this case, into a very minimal narrative compared with the elaborated versions one finds, for instance, in World Bank texts (Fairclough 2000a) – and worked into a relation with other elements, for example in this case, elements of policy formulation, in ways which are rhetorically motivated.

Overdetermination and Transdisciplinarity

Above, I have distinguished different levels of concreteness and abstractness: social events and texts on the one hand, social practices and orders of discourse on the other. I assume a realist social ontology in which social structures as well as social events are part of social reality. Social structures are abstract entities which define potentials, i.e. sets of possibilities. However, the relationship between what is structurally possible and what actually happens, i.e. between structures and events, is a very complex one. Events are not, in any simple or direct way, the effects of abstract social structures. Their relationship is mediated: there are intermediate entities between structures and events. I call these 'social practices'. Social practices can be thought of as ways of controlling the selection of certain structural possibilities and the exclusion of others, as well as the retention of these selections over time, in particular areas of social life.

Language is an element of the social at all levels. Schematically:

Social structures: languages
Social practices: orders of discourse
Social events: texts

Languages can be regarded as among the abstract social structures I have just been referring to. A language defines a certain potential and certain possibilities, and excludes others. But texts as elements of social events are not simply the effects of the potentials defined by languages. There also exist intermediate organizational entities of a specifically linguistic sort: the linguistic moments of networks of social practices, i.e. orders of discourse. The elements of orders of discourse are not, for instance, nouns and sentences (elements of linguistic structures), but discourses, genres, and styles. These elements select certain possibilities defined by languages and exclude others; they control linguistic variability for particular areas of social life. So orders of discourse can be seen as the social organization and control of linguistic variation. There is an argument in Chouliaraki and Fairclough (2000) for an extension of Hasan's (1999) account of 'semologic' to include orders of discourse.

When moving from abstract structures towards concrete events, it becomes increasingly difficult to separate language from other social elements. In the terminology of Althusser, language becomes increasingly 'overdetermined' by other social elements (Althusser and Balibar 1970).[3] So, at the level of abstract structures, the analyst can talk more or less exclusively about language – more or less – because 'functional' theories of language view even the grammars of languages as socially shaped (Halliday

1978). The way I have defined orders of discourse makes it clear that, at this intermediate level, there is a much greater 'overdetermination' of language by other social elements. Orders of discourse are the *social* organization and control of linguistic (semiotic) variation, and their elements (discourses, genres, styles) are correspondingly not purely linguistic categories but categories which cut across the division between semiosis and non-semiosis and can act as a bridge between disciplines in transdisciplinary research (see below). When one comes to texts as elements of social events, the 'overdetermination' of language by other social elements becomes massive: texts are not just effects of linguistic structures and orders of discourse, they are also effects of other social practices and structures as well as of the casual powers of social agents. Therefore, it becomes difficult to separate out the factors shaping texts (Fairclough *et al.* 2002).

It follows, I suggest, that researchers should work in a 'transdisciplinary' way (Dubiel 1985; Halliday 1993) in doing discourse analysis and text analysis. 'Interdisciplinarity' covers a multitude of practices, including the coming-together of researchers with different disciplinary backgrounds and training for the purposes of a particular research project, without any implication that the contributing disciplinary theories or methods are affected or changed by the experience. Working in a transdisciplinary way is one method of working in an *interdisciplinary* way, which is distinguished by a commitment to enter a dialogue with other disciplines and theories, and put their logic to work in the development of one's own theory, methods, research objects, and research agendas. It is not simply a matter of adding concepts and categories from other disciplines and theories, but working on and elaborating one's own theoretical and methodological resources so as to be able to address insights or problems captured in other theories and disciplines from the perspective of one's particular concerns. It makes sense to do so in the light of what I said above about 'overdetermination': semiosis is an analytically separate element of social events whose analysis requires its own theories, categories, and methods but, at the same time, one must be seeking to analyse the language element of events – text – in ways which elucidate its dialectical relations with other elements. Disciplinary specialization is simultaneously necessary and insufficient, desirable and dangerous.

The critical realist distinction between the real, the actual, and the empirical is also germane to this issue. I have already, in effect, distinguished between the 'real' and the 'actual': the 'real' for critical realism is structures and their associated 'mechanisms', i.e. the structural delimitation of the possible whereas the 'actual' is the concrete, i.e. what actually happens as opposed to what could happen. (This critical realist sense of 'real' is unfortunate because both the 'real' and the 'actual' are real in any reasonable sense of the term.) The 'empirical' is what is available as knowledge of the real and the actual. However, the real and the actual cannot be reduced to the empirical, i.e. one cannot assume that what is known exhausts what is. When applying this perspective to texts, it implies that analysts should be somewhat cautious about what they know as linguists about texts, avoid any claims for a positive science of texts, and recognize the need to work on the common social opacity of textual analyses by developing their resources for textual analysis through a transdisciplinary way of working.

Space-time and Equivalence/Difference Relations

With these considerations in mind, let me come back to the Blair text and put into focus the incipient transdisciplinary character of the analysis I have done by positioning the text in relation to social scientific theories of space-time on the one hand, and logics of equivalence and difference on the other.

The use of the category of 'space-time' in recent geographical and social theory registers the view that there is an 'indissoluble link' between space and time (Harvey 1996). People in modern societies simultaneously inhabit different space-times: their own localities ('places'); sub-national regions, e.g. 'the North' in the UK; nation-states; and international space-times, e.g. the European Union, the 'global' space-time. Furthermore, these space-times are not externally given but are socially constructed. So, too, are relationships which are established (and negotiated and contested) among them. These relationships can prove to be problematic in different ways for different classes and groups of people. For instance, Harvey (1996) discusses the persisting problem in working-class politics of how to connect the 'militant particularism' (the term is Raymond Williams') of trade-union and political activists in particular places (localities, workplaces) with universalist national and international agendas for social emancipation. At the same time, there are mundane and banal ways in which relationships among different space-times are lived and experienced in people's daily lives.

The transformations of new capitalism include changes in the social construction of space-times and of relations among space-times. The emergent new social order brings new problems in relating and moving among simultaneously occupied space-times and among new social divisions which have been discussed, for instance, by Castells (1996) in terms of the differences between those who primarily occupy global and local networks (also Bauman 1998). It also brings new problems in achieving and legitimizing normalized, banal relations among space-times. The significant points, in terms of my present concerns, are that (a) these processes of establishing, negotiating, and legitimizing space-times and relations among space-times are processes which are omnipresent in texts, and (b) an elucidation of these processes (whether for theoretical purposes of understanding them or for political purposes of contesting them) requires the resources of textual analysis. At the same time, however, those resources need to be enhanced in the transdisciplinary way by exploring methods by which one can 'operationalize', in textual analysis, perspectives on space and time which have been developed in social theory.

My earlier analysis of the Blair text, in which I attempted a transdisciplinary approach, is intended to suggest the significance of the text and texturing in the shifting constructions of global and national space-times and of the relationship among them associated with the new capitalism and neo-liberal political discourse. Global space-time is represented, and described, as a reality of the undelimited ('timeless') present although, as I pointed out in a somewhat contradictory way, the *realis* description disguises some *irrealis* prediction. The processes of global space-time are also represented as spatially universal though 'great new opportunities' might seem rather difficult to see for millions of people in the poorest countries. Its processes are processes without responsible human agents. For instance, technologies simply 'emerge', i.e. they are not developed and promoted by human agents such as corporations or governments in connection with particular purposes and interests. Such processes are described rather than analysed or explained; a sense of their reality is built up through a cumulative list of evidences and appearances rather than through analysis of causes and effects. A relationship is textured between the global space-time and the national space-time which frames the latter within the former: the global space-time is an incontrovertible and inevitable reality; and 'we' must respond to it in ways which allow us to live and succeed within it. This is reminiscent of accounts of 'time-space compression' and its implications in terms of enhanced connectivity among scales of social life, and the inescapability of global processes and events at other scales (Giddens 1990; Harvey 1996). National space-time is *irrealis*, a set of prescriptions for future action to achieve success in the global reality. Its agents are human and collective. Policies and actions which are prescribed are, in some cases, rationalized and legitimized. Ends are associated with means, e.g. 'by opening markets'; reasons are given although generally implicitly, e.g. 'companies alone cannot [invest in British capabilities]' is a reason for 'us' doing so, and being in 'a world of short-term pressures' is a reason for promoting a long-term vision. In contrast with the description of the global in terms of appearances, there is a causal logic at work in these national policy prescriptions.

Heller (1999) characterizes modernity as legitimizing present actions in terms of grand visions of the future. The Blair text has something of this character but without its optimistic or visionary aspects. The national space-time is not envisioned in terms of progress in the modernist sense. The inevitable and imperative global space-time, which broods over the national space-time, enforces a particular direction of change: the grand vision (if such it be) is coloured by an implicit sense of risk and danger from 'new competitors'; 'success' is contingent; and failure to compete effectively now will mean we will not 'prosper in the markets of tomorrow'. Neo-liberalism may, as Gray (1993) suggests, share the 'canonical thinking' of socialism but without its optimistic sense of progress for the betterment of humankind. The prescribed future is more a matter of acting to create reality in accordance with a neo-liberal blueprint so as not to fail.

Let me turn more briefly to relations of equivalence and difference. Laclau and Mouffe (1985) theorize the political process (and 'hegemony') in terms of the simultaneous working of two different 'logics': a logic of 'difference' which creates differences and divisions; and a logic of 'equivalence' which creates equivalences in 'subverting' existing differences and divisions. This can usefully be seen as a general characterization of social processes of classification: people in all social practices are continuously dividing and combining and, thereby, producing (also reproducing) and subverting divisions and differences. Social interaction, as Laclau and Mouffe (1985) suggest, is an ongoing work of articulation and disarticulation. This is true of the textual moment of social events. Elements (words, phrases, etc.) are constantly being textured into relations of equivalence and relations of difference; prior equivalences and differences are constantly being 'subverted'; and these processes are an important part of the textual moment of the social process of classification. By operationalizing this theory in textual analysis, one also strengthens the claims of textual analysis to be able to contribute to social research on classification and processes of articulation and disarticulation. Laclau and Mouffe's (1985) political theory is already a discourse theory in a Foucauldian sense, but what it lacks is a text analytical capacity.

Conclusion

What is at issue on one level in this paper is how we (as systemic linguists or critical discourse analysts) can make a strong case to other social scientists for textual analysis as a significant element in social research on the transformations of new capitalism (or 'globalization'). Traditions of textual analysis in linguistics already have much to offer, and I have, of course, drawn upon SFL in particular in the analysis. But I have also made a case for a transdisciplinary way of working in textual analysis in which one attempts to maintain a dialogue with social theoretical and research perspectives and to develop and enhance textual analysis by seeking to operationalize within it categories and insights from these perspectives. I have also argued that interdiscursive analysis of texts is a crucial mediating link between linguistic analysis and social analysis, a link which is needed, I would argue, if one is to succeed in incorporating textual analysis more substantively within social research. The rationale and clarification of how interdiscursive analysis can act in this mediating way depends upon theoretical categories and perspectives within CDA which I have briefly discussed.

There is much in SFL which is of value in this project, including a long-term concern with socially oriented analysis of text and a linguistic theory which is itself socially oriented and informed. Also, the dynamic, process view of text as 'texturing' echoes thinking within SFL (Lemke 1988). The key difference regards interdiscursivity and the category of 'order of discourse' (Chouliaraki and Fairclough 1999). One can put this in terms of the levels of concreteness and abstractness I have distinguished; just as the general relationship between social structures and social events needs to be seen as mediated by social practices, so too does the relationship between semiotic structures (languages) and texts need to be mediated by orders of discourse, the semiotic moment of social practices. The interdiscursivity of texts is the correlate at the concrete level of social events of orders of discourse at the more abstract level of social practices. Incorporating inter-discursive analysis into textual analysis provides, as I suggested earlier, the way to link linguistic analysis to social analysis and, thus, places us in a stronger position to make a substantive contribution to social research.

Notes

1. I am grateful to Isabela Preoteasa for her helpful comments on a draft of this paper.
2. I shall sometimes put 'global' in scare quotes to indicate the conten-tiousness of claims about 'globalization'. A key issue is the relationship between real processes of increased international trade, international operation of corporations, international cultural flows, etc., and their representation as 'globalization'. Some argue that 'globalization' is more of a partial and interested and ideological way of representing actual changes than a real process (Held *et al.* 1999).
3. Althusser takes the term 'overdetermination' from Freud who uses it to describe the condensation of a number of thoughts in a single image in dreams or the transference of psychic energy from a potent thought to an apparently trivial image. Althusser uses the term to describe the effects of the contradictions of each practice within a social formation on the social formation as a whole, with respect to relations of domin-ation/subordination between contradictions. Althusser (Althusser and Balibar 1970: 188) notes that this was not an arbitrary borrowing from Freud but a necessary one, 'for the same theoretical problem is at stake in both cases: with what concept are we to think the determination of either an element or a structure by a structure?' Similarly, my use of the concept reflects my concern with the same theoretical problem (Fairclough *et al.* 2002).

References

Althusser, L. and Balibar, E. (1970) *Reading Capital.* London: New Left Books.
Bauman, Z. (1998) *Globalization.* Cambridge: Polity Press.
Bernstein, B. (1990) *The Structuring of Pedagogic Discourse.* London: Routledge.
Blair, T. (1998) 'Foreword', in *Our Competitive Future: Building the Knowledge-Driven Economy* (Department of Trade and Industry White Paper). London: Stationery Office.

Bourdieu, P. (1998) 'A Reasoned Utopia and Economic Fatalism', *New Left Review*, 227: 25–30.

Bourdieu, P. and Wacquant, L. (2001) 'New Liberal Speak: Notes on the New Planetary Vulgate', *Radical Philosophy*, 105: 2–5.

Bourdieu, P. and Wacquant, L. (1992) *An Invitation to Reflexive Sociology*. Cambridge: Polity Press.

Castells, M. (1996) *The Rise of the Network Society*. Cambridge: Blackwell.

Chouliaraki, L. and Fairclough, N. (2000) 'Language and Power in Bourdieu: On Hasan's "The Disempowerment Game" ', *Linguistics and Education*, 10(4): 399–409.

Chouliaraki, L. and Fairclough, N. (1999) *Discourse in Late Modernity: Re-Thinking Critical Discourse Analysis*. Edinburgh: Edinburgh University Press.

Dubiel, H. (1985) *Theory and Politics: Studies in the Development of Critical Theory*. Cambridge, MA: MIT Press.

Fairclough, N. (2003) *Analyzing Discourse: Textual Analysis for Social Research*. London: Routledge.

Fairclough, N. (2001) 'The Dialectics of Discourse', *Textus*, 14: 231–42.

Fairclough, N. (2000a) 'Represenciones del cambio en discurso neo-liberal', *Cuadernos de Relaciones Laborales*, 16: 13–36.

Fairclough, N. (2000b) *New Labour, New Language?* London: Routledge.

Fairclough, N. (1992) *Discourse and Social Change*. Cambridge: Polity Press.

Fairclough, N., Jessop, R., and Sayer, A. (2002) 'Critical Realism and Semiosis', *Journal of Critical Realism*, 5(1): 2–10.

Giddens, A. (1990) *Modernity and Self-Identity*. Cambridge: Polity Press.

Graham, P. (2001) 'Space: *Irrealis* Objects in Technology Policy and Their Role in a New Political Economy', *Discourse and Society*, 12(6): 761–88.

Gray, J. (1993) *Beyond the New Right: Markets, Government and the Common Environment*. London: Routledge.

Halliday, M. A. K. (1994) *An Introduction to Functional Grammar* (2nd edn). London: Edward Arnold.

Halliday, M. A. K. (1993) 'Language in a Changing World'. Occasional Papers 13. Sydney: Applied Linguistics Association of Australia.

Halliday, M. A. K. (1978) *Language as Social Semiotic*. London: Edward Arnold.

Harvey, D. (1996) *Justice, Nature and the Geography of Difference*. Oxford: Blackwell.

Hasan, R. (1999) 'The Disempowerment Game: A Critique of Bourdieu's View of Language', *Linguistics and Education*, 10: 441–58.

Hay, C. and Rosamund B. (2002) 'Globalization, European Integration and the Discursive Construction of Economic Imperatives', *Journal of European Public Policy*, 9(2): 147–67.

Held, D., McGrew, A., Goldblatt, D. and Perraton, J. (1999) *Global Transformations*. Cambridge: Polity Press.

Heller, A. (1999) *A Theory of Modernity*. Oxford: Blackwell.

Hoey, M. (2001) *Textual Interaction*. London: Routledge.

Iedema, R. (1999) 'Formalizing Organizational Meaning', *Discourse and Society*, 10(1): 49–66.

Iedema, R. (1998) 'Institutional Responsibility and Hidden Meanings', *Discourse and Society*, 9(4): 481–500.

Jessop, R. (2000) 'The Crisis of the National Spatio-temporal Fix and the Ecological Dominance of Globalizing Capitalism', *International Journal of Urban and Regional Studies*, 24(2): 323–60.

Kress, G. and van Leeuwen, T. (2000) *Multimodal Discourse*. London: Arnold.

Laclau, E. and Mouffe, C. (1985) *Hegemony and Socialist Strategy*. London: Verso.

Lemke, J. (1998) 'Resources for Attitudinal Meaning: Evaluative Orientations in Text Semantics', *Functions of Language*, 5(1): 33–56.

Lemke, J. (1988) 'Text Structure and Text Semantics', in *Pragmatics, Discourse and Text: Systemic Approaches*, ed. by R. Veltman and E. Steiner. London: Pinter, 158–70.

Martin, J. (1992) *English Text*. Amsterdam: John Benjamins.

Salskov-Iversen, D., Hansen, H., and Bislev, S. (2000) 'Governmentality, Globalization and Local Practice: Transformations of a Hegemonic Discourse', *Alternatives*, 25: 183–222.

Sayer, A. (2000) *Realism and Social Science*. London: Sage Publications.

van Leeuwen, T. (1996) 'The Representation of Social Actors', in *Texts and Practices*, ed. by C. R. Caldas-Coulthard and M. Coulthard. London: Routledge, 32–71.

6　Prolegomena to a Discursive Model of Malaysian National Identity

Faiz Sathi Abdullah

Malaysia's geo-political resilience is somewhat enigmatic, particularly in the wake of recent events before and after September 11, 2001. The state continues to forge strategically a sense of nationhood via official decree (common language, education, culture, and ideology). This paper argues, however, that the dynamic concepts of nation, nationality, and identity are less amenable to definition solely within political space. What does it mean to be Malaysian? Very little research has been done with respect to this discursive space and the apparent discursive divide in the identity complex. A preliminary, critical review of selected discourses within a discourse-historical framework showed that macro-constructs such as 'Malaysian', 'nation' (bangsa), and 'we' (kita) were ambivalently represented with a broad grammatical analysis providing initial support for a nationalist/national strategic ideological framing model. Cognizant of the localization/globalization dialectic and the emergent heterogeneity in the socio-discursive space, the paper proposes a comprehensive national research project.

Introduction

The aftermath of the murderous attacks of September 11, 2001 has been punctuated by the invasion of Afghanistan, George W. Bush's 'axis of evil' speech, the tragic events in Palestine, and the 2002 Bali terrorist bomb blasts which effectively brought the 'war on terrorism' to the East. While the geo-political ramifications of these events are bound to be far reaching, to say the least, their impact on nation-centredness and security are already being felt: '. . . for all the talk of a borderless world, states remain significant' (Hall 2001, quoted in Hewison 2002: 4). Hence, 'national security', perceived paramount in terms of aligning the nation with the US, is expected to assume a broader range of values in the sociopolitical discursive space of countries such as Muslim-dominant Malaysia where press freedom is already controlled by laws such as the *Printing Presses and Publications Act*, the *Official Secrets Act*, and the *Sedition Act*. Perhaps it is too early to say to what extent further statist measures will affect the representations of social reality addressed in this paper, but their potential for muddying the waters of the globalization/localization identity dialectic (Chouliaraki and

Fairclough 1999: 94–5) and/or ideological positioning *vis-à-vis* the Other cannot be disputed.

An earlier paper presented in Kuala Lumpur entitled 'The State of Being Malaysian' (Faiz Abdullah 2002) drew what seemed to be a greater-than-expected interest, both among the local and international participants. It was noted that the notion of a collective national disposition inherent in the word 'state' in the title is itself an ambivalent construction. On the one hand, it encapsulates the discursive perceptions of the citizen in relation to creed, community, and country, and on the other, albeit in a slightly convoluted sense, the apparent aspirations of the body politic ('being a Malaysian state') as it strives to forge a strategic sense of resilient nation-hood via official policies on language, education, culture, and ideological development.

'National identity' may be evinced as a fluid, dynamic complex which comprises similar socialized beliefs and/or opinions as well as common emotional attitudes and behavioural dispositions, 'including inclusive, solidarity oriented and exclusive, distinguishing dispositions and also in many cases linguistic dispositions' (Wodak *et al.* 1999: 28). Kaunismaa (1995) cites Giesen (1993) who also defines national identity as a complex, as 'a three-sided phenomenon . . . constituted by contextual everyday-life understanding, historical processes of interaction, and symbolical (discursive) codes'. This type of componential definition, Kaunismaa (1995) adds, lends itself to a 'minimalistic' empirical approach in that 'the researcher does not have to ask what some nation's national identity "really" is . . . [but rather] studies national identity as claims and expressions that people have produced about themselves'. Given that the researcher studies constructions, the concerns of the present paper may be addressed via questions such as: 'What does it mean to be a Malaysian?' and collectively 'What are we as a Malaysian people?' Further, granted the global/anti-global posturing, particularly on the part of the state, another question seems appropriate: 'Whither *Bangsa Malaysia* (lit. "Malaysian Nation") or *homo Malaysiacus*, as it were?'

The final question is probably most salient currently as both political dictate(s) and people's perceptive states are under scrutiny in the face of the twin spectres of 'globalization' and a 'borderless world', sending sovereign states and hitherto supine subjects into a soul-searching spiral: in short, a question of the sovereignty of the 'nation-state' that has been called into question given the scholarly attack on such a geo-political entity via moderate, anti-nationalist theory (Castells 1997: 27). Perhaps it is no accident of history that the post-cold war (or is it the *neo*-cold war?) period continues to be marred by the oft-violent fragmentation of past geo-political entities, not to mention coloured by realignments of regional, politico-economic allegiances in an increasingly bipolar representation of the world. Hence, notwithstanding Huntington's (1993) thesis about a possible 'The West versus the Rest' clash of civilizations, the implications of the tragic events of and following September 11, 2001 are likely to be extensive for a multi-ethnic, and especially multi-religious society such as Malaysia. Indeed, what is the nature of national identity in a world that is already being changed by 'master discourses' of global appropriation (mainly through neo-capitalist language, after Fairclough 2000), and more recently by those of the 'war on terrorism' which leave very little democratic *third* space ('Either you're with us or against us.')?[1]

Problematized as a macro-ideological complex in the Gramscian tradition, national identity in the era of globalization can be approached as 'people's source of meaning and experience' (Castells 1997: 6) that characterizes the tension between the two poles of the imagined communities/ communal images dialectic 'expressed both in the challenge to established nation-states and in the widespread (re)construction of identity on the basis of nationality, always affirmed against the alien' (Castells 1997: 27). It may be argued that in the Malaysian case, and possibly in other similarly structured multicultural contexts, this sourcing of meaning and experience in discourse is framed via principal dichotomic (but not necessarily antithetic) sets of strategies serving a broad meta-narrative of inclusive national ideologies that transcend *inter alia* ethno-cultural, socioeconomic, and gender differences, and a narrower one that celebrates nationalist ideologies to the relative exclusion of identifiable sub-national identities, respectively.

While several international commentators have expressed their views on the Malaysian case within a broad regional perspective (e.g. Derichs 1999; Milne and Mauzy 1999; Hilley 2001), local studies (e.g. Asmah Omar 1995; Abraham 1999; Shakila Manan 2001; Faiz Abdullah 2002) concerning the discursive construction of the multifarious facets of national identity have been far and few. Hence, this paper attempts to address this paucity of investigations by presenting a preliminary theoretical perspective on selected themes, strategies, and the linguistic means of their realization within a discourse-historical framework. This initial orientation towards problematizing national identity theorizes a discursive divide that may be discerned in the national discourse with respect to what might be termed 'nationalist' and 'national' ideologies (see Figure 6.1), drawing in part from van Dijk's (1998) conceptualization of ideology as a tripartite dialectical configuration of discourse, socio-cognition, and society.

A Critical Approach to National Identity Discourse

As Abraham (1999) has aptly pointed out, 'the concept of Malaysian nationhood and nationality is more than a geographically or politically defined space'. Herein lie the *discursive* aspects of the critical, fresh perspective alluded to by Derichs (1999). Put differently, one has to examine language together with other semiotic systems as discourses which not only reflect power relations in society but also play a crucial role in the way citizens construct representations of who they are, which groups they

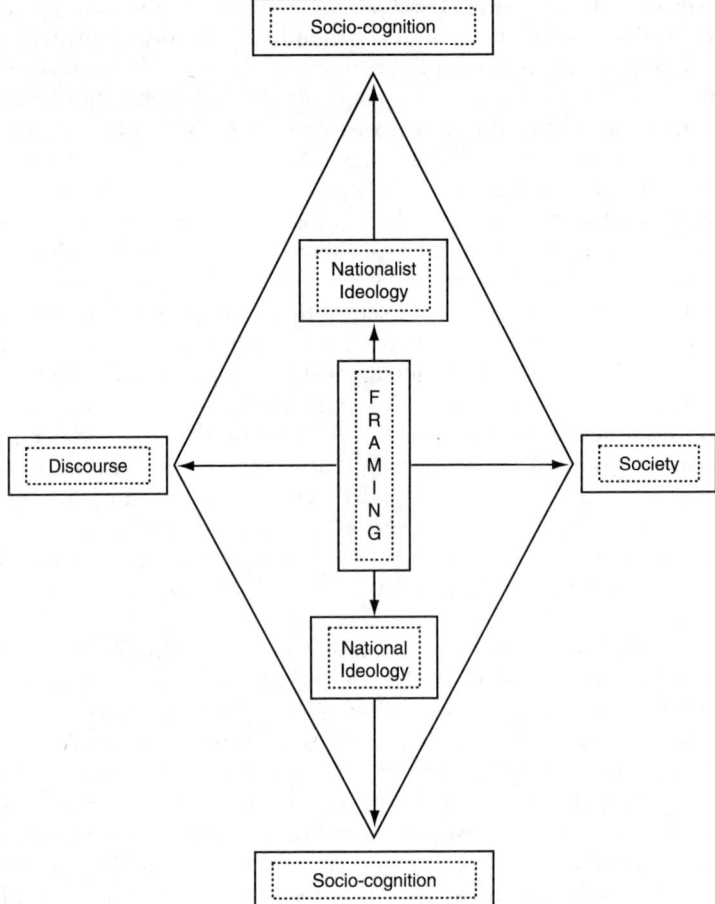

Figure 6.1 A proposed discursive model of Malaysian national identity

identify with in particular contexts, and as somewhat stable, objective selves in a relatively context-free sense (van Dijk 1998: 118). Hence, national 'Discourse' (after Gee 1999: 6–7) is the means, i.e. the site of as well as the 'prize' in sociocultural struggles over ethnic, religious, cultural, and/or political definitions of identity, mainly through heterogeneous discursive practice as the harbinger of social change, be it of the reproducing or transformative kind.

The discourse analyst, then, in adopting an informed, multidisciplinary approach to political, institutional, and mass media discourse as well as everyday speech, attempts to reveal and/or demystify hegemonic, discriminatory, and/or oppressive practices in identity construction. For instance, with respect to media discourse, Fairclough (1995b) employs a Systemic Functional Linguistics (SFL) model to show that 'legitimate language' is used together with intertextual/interdiscursive elements by dominant groups to (re)produce social structures of power, and similarly by the dominated to concede their relative powerlessness. Shakila Manan (2001) shows how lexical and transitivity analyses may be used as systemic functional tools to understand linguistic forms through which ideas and views about Malaysia's Anwar and the *reformasi* movement have been represented in the media.

The above framework of analysis conceptualizes ideological dimensions underlying hegemonic struggles in society as representations of the world that are 'implicitly manifest in art, in law, in economic activity, and in the manifestations of individual and collective life' (Gramsci 1971, quoted in Fairclough 1995a: 76). Dominant ideologies that are invested in discursive practice become 'commonsense' assumptions and/or naturalized beliefs about social reality. For instance, one could reflect on the enduring British colonial ideology of the past (probably *endearing* as well to millions of 'natives') of the 'white man's burden' of bringing civilization and, hence, enlightenment to the uncivilized: 'Ask *any* man what nationality he would prefer to be, and ninety nine out of a hundred will tell you that they would prefer to be Englishmen' (Cecil Rhodes, quoted in Paxman 1999: 1; emphasis added).

However, the goals of Critical Discourse Analysis (CDA) as a means of describing, interpreting, and explaining the socially constituted and constitutive nature of discourse as social practice (Fairclough 1989, 1995a, 1995b; Chouliaraki and Fairclough 1999) crucially include the discursive provision to empower the oppressed and the dominated in that 'discursive practice may be effective in transforming, dismantling or even destroying the status quo' (Wodak *et al.* 1999: 8). CDA is therefore rightly invested with an emancipatory function, and by extension, the possible resolution of social problems largely caused by the manufacture of consent through the strategic deployment of selected orders of discourse and appropriated language. Fairclough's related terms of 'subjects' and 'subject positions' are germane to the present line of reasoning in that the 'subject' as either 'agent' or 'affected' is 'qualified to act through being constrained – "subjected" – to an institutional frame' (Fairclough 1995a: 39; cf. Bourdieu's notion of 'habitus' as identity comprising both agency and structure). Accordingly, Fairclough refers to 'social subjects' and 'institutional subjects', the latter occupying subject positions in various institutional discourse types, and maintains, after Gramsci (1971), that 'It is the hegemonic control of the dominant class over the institutions of civil society (education, family, work, family, leisure, etc.) within the "outer defences" of the repressive state apparatus that makes revolutionary transformation of modern capitalist societies so difficult' (Fairclough 1995a: 93). Needless to say, then, the very concept of national identity may be seen as being largely shaped by the hegemonic structures of the state:

> Through classificational systems (specially according to sex and age) inscribed in law, through bureaucratic procedures, educational structures and social rituals ... the state moulds mental structures and imposes common principles of vision and division ... And it thereby contributes to the construction of what is commonly designated as national identity (or, in a more traditional language, national character)   (Bourdieu 1994: 7f, cited in Wodak *et al.* 1999: 29).

In investigating how identities are constructed in the excerpts of actual Malaysian national/nationalist discourse presented later in this paper, one needs to identify certain recurring themes and/or strategies in the critical analysis of the discourse types in question. With regard to the proposed model in Figure 6.1, these predominantly language-based resources may be hypothesized among possible others as: (1) the rhetoric versus reality divide that characterizes much of the master discourse of the state (Fairclough 2000); (2) 'the unseen hand' that is often realized as the reluctance to speak openly about 'sensitive issues'; and (3) the (classic?) *us* and *them* dichotomy as a discourse of threat rationalization internally within the country *vis-à-vis* the 'in-group' and 'out-group', respectively, and externally as regarding the perceived threat of the forces of globalization to national security and identity.

To help illuminate this further within the context of Malaysia, the next section makes a brief journey into the country's past to see how events have shaped the nation's sociopolitical status quo.

Pre- and Post-colonial Malay/Malaysian Identity

For centuries, Islam as *ad-deen* (roughly glossed here as 'a self-contained way of life') has been quintessential to the whole notion of being *Melayu* to the extent that 'to become Moslem, it was said, was to *masuk Melayu* [lit. "become Malay"]' (Andaya and Andaya 2000: 55). Nevertheless, much of this was to be radically challenged with the incursion and subsequent intervention of Portuguese, Dutch, and particularly British colonialism which helped institute state boundaries and contributed to intra-national provincial identities among the Malays of the peninsula.

Further, British economic considerations in the Malay world resulted in large-scale migration of Chinese and Indian immigrants to the region. Thus, it was only a matter of time before the Malays felt a threat to their identity, a fact further compounded by the British tendency to identify each ethnic group with a particular style of economic activity. Independent Malaysia, thus, inherited an essentially British form of governance juxtaposed on a set of long traditions descending from the Srivijayan-Melakan state. The arrival of Chinese and Indians in relatively large numbers complicated the sociocultural equation and the national unity/identity discourse, which was also compounded by the more recent addition of the East Malaysians. Perhaps the time was ostensibly ripe for an egalitarian, multicultural approach towards addressing the nation-building dilemma, but Malaysia's day of infamy, the 1969 race riots, and the subsequent New Economic Policy (NEP) from 1971 to 1990 changed that.

In the NEP era, a fundamental realignment of state-race-class relations through affirmative discrimination polices sought to achieve national unity through poverty eradication irrespective of race and social restructuring as well as to place Malay/*Bumiputera* (lit. 'Son of the land') interests 'at the core of the political *and* economic agenda' (Hilley 2001: 34) within the extant multi-ethnic consociational framework of race-based politics. Needless to say, this period marked the manifestation of a new dominant Malay middle class and the reaffirmation of nationalism as ethnic ideology that was to influence later national development as a discursively contested site, particularly with respect to language and culture in the Malaysian mosaic, and which contributed to the distinction between *bumiputera* and *non-bumiputera*. While the classification of national subjects in this way has served to effect affirmative action to uplift the lot of the indigenous Malays, Kadazan-dusun, Iban, and the like, the practice also appears to have hardened racial-ethnic lines right up to the Vision era discussed below.

Mahathirism and the Vision Ideal

The last decade saw the emergence of the national project of 'Vision 2020', the brainchild of Dr Mahathir Mohamad,[2] as an overarching ideology of socioeconomic growth which surpasses even the *Rukunegara* (lit. 'National Ideology') (Hilley 2001: 4). As a populist call to more inclusive nationalism, common social community development, and the ideal of a *Bangsa Malaysia* (lit. '[One] Malaysian Nation'), Vision 2020 has been actively promoted in the mass media, promotional discourses (particularly under the theme, 'Malaysia: Truly Asia', Tourism Development Corporation of Malaysia 2002), and other officially mediated discursive practices. These discourses employ constructed symbols of national unity and resilience: *Malaysia Boleh!* (lit. 'Malaysia can do it!') and, correspondingly, the record-breaking Petronas twin towers 'as a celebratory statement of national achievement ... [and] more appropriately, the sense of duality with the West' (Hilley 2001: 3). To understand the significance of the Vision 2020 project for the Malaysian identity complex, one needs to delve a little into aspects of its architect and prime mover, Mahathir the man, and his nationalist ideology, 'Mahathirism' the Vision ideal.

Indeed, Khoo Boo Teik's prominent study, *Paradoxes of Mahathirism*,[3] differentiates between the two constructs mentioned above: a complex political personality often approaching cult status (thanks to spin doctors and the media) that is '[a manifestation of] race *and* class *and* individual' (Khoo Boo Teik 1995: xxi), and a relatively consistent, coherent political ideology comprising the five core components of nationalism, capitalism, Islam, populism, and authoritarianism, respectively (1995: 6–7). Mahathirism succeeded to some extent by providing 'a common "chain of equivalences" ... between progress, development, modernization, economic advancement, self-determination, national sovereignty and modernist Islam' and by eliminating or confronting the counter-values of the 'Constitutive Other' such as 'Western' liberalism, communism, traditionalism, obscurantism, religious fundamentalism, and militancy (Farish Noor 2001). However, the exact 'content' of the evolving all-encompassing identity ideal would at best remain contested, necessitating strategic, discursive means within the context of civil society as opposed to coercive measures such as the *Internal Security Act* (ISA) which, although readily available, are not without limitations as a legitimation strategy option in Vision development (Hilley 2001: 7).

Legitimizing the Vision

In a speech entitled *Transcending the Divide*, delivered at the second World Knowledge Conference in Kuala Lumpur on 8 March 2000 (Mahathir Mohamad 2002a: 60), Dr Mahathir talks about Vision 2020 mainly in the past tense as if to remind the audience of the nation's 'pledge' to honour the ideals therein:

> Malaysia launched its march into the information age with Vision 2020, which was enunciated in 1991, and which struck a responsive chord in the hearts and minds of all Malaysians of all stations, creeds and political affiliations. In our Vision 2020, we set the goal of becoming a fully developed nation by 2020, the end of the second generation of our independent country. We stated our conviction that 'What we have between our ears is much more important than what we have below our feet and around us'. We fully understood that 'our people are our greatest resource'.

The populist tenor is clearly evident in the use of the pronouns 'we' and 'our' to align the Prime Minister as being one with 'all Malaysians of all stations, creeds, and political affiliations' in a consensus-seeking language of active participation as social actors in the material processes of the global information age. In fact, this setting up of a common identity continues over the next two paragraphs of the speech, understandably replete with modernist imagery, as the speaker engages listeners discursively to recontextualize the relevance of Vision 2020 as being equal to the challenge of socioeconomic change towards 'a quantum leap which will remake Malaysian corporations and re-invent Malaysian society'.

However, the rhetoric would seem to stand in stark contrast with the reality, at least insofar as the regional/global identity of young Malaysians are concerned within a comparable time frame. Preliminary survey data about perceived national identities (Faiz Abdullah 2002) show that although some 62.9 per cent of 135 multi-ethnic university undergraduates felt 'very close' to Malaysia, given a pool of competing geo-political entities such as Indonesia, Singapore, China, India, US, and UK, barely 20 per cent of them identified themselves as Malaysians *first* in apposition to their respective ethnic identities. There were no significant differences across racial-ethnic groups for these responses, thus effectively making the Malaysian a minority in his/her own country!

As alluded to earlier in this paper, the discursive legitimation of the Vision project has since been the site of new challenges. The spate of geo-political events of the post-September 11 era, including the many clearly contempt-ible acts of mass destruction either as state-sponsored terror or cloaked as 'trenches of resistance on behalf of God, nation, ethnicity, . . . [and] local-ity' towards legitimizing and/or project identities (Castells 1997: 2), as it were, are almost certainly expected to impinge on people's civil liberties and political freedom *vis-à-vis* 'resistance identities' in Castells' terms, within and outside of national boundaries. Even before the events of September 11, 2001, in the face of sociopolitical upheavals particularly in Eastern Europe and Indonesia, Malaysia's resilience as a multi-ethnic 'nation-of-intent' had apparently surprised European observers as 'the enigma of the East, the adventurism of Empire, the allure of alternative races, religions and cultures' (Hilley 2001: 1). More specifically, Derichs (1999) has ten-dered the explanation that strategic nation-building action on the state's part by way of 'the smart adjustment of strategies to changing conditions of "ideological" framing has at least up to now prevented the Malaysian nation-state from falling apart', and that 'the general typologies of nation and national identity should be reviewed critically and from a fresh perspective'.

Indeed, as was the wont before the September 11 crisis, the Malaysian state continues to forge conservative nationalism as a corollary of its gener-ally anti-globalization stance to create 'a united nation based on common, shared values [and] . . . a common national outlook' (Abraham 1999). However, besides the present need to reconcile the tension between the Islamic/non-Islamic positions, to mediate the perceived extremes of multi-culturalist sentiment, and to save the 'nation' from the vagaries of inter-national capitalism in the post-Asian 'contagion' period (Hewison 2002: 6), the exigencies of the populist politics of the state would appear to dictate strategies of mitigating the 'success' of terrorism from the perspective of peace and non-violence (Chaiwat 2002). And this is realized through the further strengthening of the state security apparatus to pre-empt any form of militant activity with the resultant uncertainty (Karim Raslan 2002) about the extent of democratic rights and civil liberties in an emergent glasnost-like era.

Perhaps the die has already been cast; the five years following the eco-nomic crisis of 1997 and the 'Anwar saga' have witnessed an unprecedented discursive sojourn into the sociopolitical realities of living in an emergent nation, a phenomenon quite patently abetted by the advent of the Internet together with the highly publicized Multimedia Super Corridor (MSC) pro-ject that 'ironically offers promises of wider democratic space for dissenting views, and alternative news and information sources' (Shakila Manan 2001: 34). The validity of this statement would seem to be supported by the heterogeneous nature of the discourse that addresses an array of issues concerning race, ethnicity, religion, and citizenship in conjunction with rights, privileges, and particularly identities as inhabitants of the 'imagined community' in question.

Framing National and Nationalist Identities

The nascent model of Malaysian democratic socialism would appear to be predicated on a theory of race as a sociopolitical categorization[4] and as the common denominator in power relations, and the strategic ideological positioning in almost all spheres of public life (cf. 'We want to become a developed nation in our own mould' in the Vision rhetoric of Dr Mahathir Mohamad 2002a: 154). This has happened to the point that the socio-economic structures as well as the political mantra in which citizens have been socialized over the decades have become rather unwieldy and resistant to change, possibly precipitating yet another Mahathirist paradox of reproducing/empowering discourses. Rehman Rashid, a prominent journalist and the author of *A Malaysian Journey*, succinctly observes this social reality (quoted in 'Malaysia: Special Report on Race and Ethnicity'):

> Malaysians had greeted independence as a nation equally divided between indigene and immigrant, and this had made all the difference . . . There has been this assiduous effort in social engineering to try and eliminate these differences between the races. It has happened to a great extent. There is now a new and burgeoning middle class in this country that didn't exist a generation or two ago. The trouble and difficulty we are facing here is of course that our political process is predicated upon these differences. So in a sense, the mechanisms, the systems and processes that we instituted in order to rise above these distinctions have now become something of a strait jacket.

The first sentence is an assertion of perceived reality (note the material processes in all three clauses), but then the 'unseen hand' takes over to obfuscate agency: 'There has been . . .', and further compounded by the linguistic elements of overwording and Grammatical Metaphor in 'The trouble and difficulty', 'our political process', and 'the systems and processes that we instituted'. Finally, a lexicalization of the pervasive sense of powerlessness inherent in the speaker's representation of reality is realized via the term 'strait jacket'.

One could compare the sensing of some kind of 'permanence' above with the 'separateness' metaphor in the following by K. S. Maniam (1996), a local writer and novelist of international acclaim:

> Is there a tacit recognition behind this philosophy that it would be impossible to produce a common Malaysian identity because of the diversity of cultural attitudes and practices? That only a sense of togetherness could be generated among the multicultural population? What is this sense of togetherness? It is the feeling that the people of the country are living and working for a common objective; that they are seen to be living side-by-side, achieving goals side-by-side. But there still remains the feeling that this side-by-side divide need not be eroded or removed. It becomes an acknowledged frontier, a necessary barrier.

The rhetoric, particularly the questions, is relational but the chain of equivalences is unmistakably that of the metaphorical state of affairs: 'sense of togetherness', 'living side-by-side', 'achieving goals side-by-side', 'side-by-side divide', and 'acknowledged frontier' to end, almost inexorably, in 'a necessary barrier'. This paradox of creating differences to eliminate differences reflects the discursive divide that so often seems to pervade text and talk concerning Malaysian national unity/identity. It highlights the assimilation versus integration divide *vis-à-vis* the socialized subjectivities of unity and diversity based on one ideological frame or the other. Indeed, in ideological terms, assimilation and integration can be equated to forms of social action serving distinct political doctrines that are *nationalist* and *national* in orientation, respectively (Eriksen 1991, after Gellner 1983).[5] Usman Awang (1982, cited in Maniam 1996), the late Malay national poet laureate, rather poignantly voices a similar discontent about the politics of separation in *Sahabatku* (lit. 'My Friend'), dedicated to Dr M. K. Rajakumar, an ethnic Indian:

> Dear Friend
> > The one, free
> > nation we imagined,
> > Remains a distant truth,
> > My anger becomes bitterness,
> > When we are forced apart,
> > The distance ever wider,
> > Now that I am proclaimed 'bumiputra'
> > and you are not.

A survey of the recent public discourse concerning the official line on the assimilation/integration issue reveals a putative policy change, that assimilation could not succeed in plural Malaysia. In a 1996 interview with *TIME* magazine, the Prime Minister responded to a question about his earlier statement that efforts to assimilate races have not been successful and it was time to try something else (quoted in Lim Kit Siang 2000; emphasis added):

> The idea before was that people should become 100% Malay in order to be Malaysian. *We* now accept that this is a multi-racial country. *We* should build bridges instead of trying to remove completely the barriers separating us. *We* do not intend to convert all the Chinese to Islam, and *we* tell *our* people, *the Muslims*, 'you will not try to force people to convert' . . .

The pronoun 'we' in the first half of the excerpt appears to refer exclusively to the Malays as the dominant ethnic group, quite clearly so in the second sentence, ambiguously so in the third sentence, and rather patently so in the clause 'we tell our people, the Muslims'. In fact, the ending quote is an invocation of a basic precept of Islam that exhorts peaceful coexistence with other faiths, but the fact remains that the Prime Minister's use of the collective pronoun in this ambivalent way serves as a 'language of consensus . . . which disguises differences' (Fairclough 2000: 160), and hence projects a populist image. One notes, too, the lack of clear agency in the initial defining sentence of this 'open acknowledgement' in reference to prior official policy.

Lim Kit Siang (2000), a prominent party leader of a Chinese-based opposition party, who has championed the identity leitmotiv of a 'Malaysian Malaysia' since the 1970s, has noted that

> Dr Mahathir has conceded that Malaysians should reduce their strong sense of eth-
> nicity in order to achieve *Bangsa Malaysia* and that while a citizen of a nation may
> associate himself with the country, he would not be readily prepared to give up his
> culture, religion, or language.

One cannot but note the optimism in Lim's attribution of agency and,
hence, responsibility as head of state in constructing Dr Mahathir as 'social
subject' in the act of 'conceding', a position that the Prime Minister
(Mahathir Mohamad 2002b) seems to have taken almost unequivocally on
a discourse addressing all Malaysians.

> We need to make a little sacrifice. We're not likely to lose our racial identity. We'll
> remain Chinese, Indian, Malay, Kadazan, Iban and others. But we'll also become
> more Malaysian, making us different from the communities in our countries of origin.

Then, as is so often the case with similar statements by Dr Mahathir about
the need for the people to stand united, he recontextualizes the above
within the supposed dangers of globalization and recolonization invoking
the spectre of external threat, the national *us*/global *them* divide
underlying the caveat 'The price of freedom is eternal vigilance'.

Perhaps a classic example of Dr Mahathir's anti-globalization rhetoric is
his didactic poem (2002b) entitled 'Facing challenges: Caring for the race'
to commemorate Malaysia's National Day. Rich in interdiscursivity (mainly
invocations of ethno-Islamist images in relation to socioeconomic framing
of 'waves' of globalization, impending doom, recovery, and hope), it is
allegorical in its symbolic representation of the challenges facing the
indigenous Malay and their potential resolution through a united response
to the Prime Minister's visionary call for action. Hence, the entire treatise
may be analysed using Hoey's (1983) problem-response discourse model.
However, due to space constraints, only the poem's major communicative
moves in their original sequence and their corresponding linguistic signals
are presented here:

1. Situation: 'A new age will dawn/ . . .'
2. Problem: 'Where will my race be?/ . . .'
3. Response: 'Stand up, my race/ . . .'
4. Evaluation: 'The skies can be probed with power/ . . .'
5. Conclusion/restatement of thesis: 'To face the challenges/And caring
    for the Race'.

Whether or not Dr Mahathir is addressing the 'Malay agenda' to the
exclusion of the Other in this one instance would appear to be moot since
one generic construction does not make a whole discourse, even if it is
currently dominant in the public domain where other voices for a more
egalitarian approach to nation-building are emergent, both in print as
well as the Internet. Again, whether or not there will be a paradigm shift in
the ideological-framing continuum to a position of some finality as the
Vision project plays itself out, only time can tell.

Conclusion

Without unduly simplifying what is essentially a complex phenomenon, the discourse analyst should be able to hypothesize that the key denominator in a sufficiently representative range of discourse types is that of strategic positioning/framing on a continuum between nationalist and national ideologies (as these terms have been dichotomized in this paper). This is a reasonable postulation taking into account the observation that social actors are predisposed to negotiate specific facets of the national-identity complex as their source of meaning and experience in a variety of contexts. Such a critical understanding of discursive engagement in identity (re)construction has the potential not only to provide insights into the strategic nature of discourse production and interpretation, but also thereby to empirically validate using the framework of language meta-functions at the centre of sociocultural practice.

To outline the proposed ideological-framing model as an initial 'working framework', this paper has necessarily deliberated on issues concerning Malaysian national identity rather selectively with regard to discourse types for a 'quick and dirty' analysis. Clearly, to explore the experiential and relational values inherent in the language of Malaysian national/nationalist identity construction, a more principled analysis of a representative sample of discourses is imperative, taking into account other semiotic modalities for a comprehensive, critical assessment of discursive strategies, their linguistic realization, and underlying ideologies.

Notes

1. See Gomez and Smith (2002: xxx): 'September 11 changed the world or, in some people's eyes, it changed the US and that, in turn, changed the world. Its war in Afghanistan and constant rumblings on wanting to remove Saddam Hussein from Iraq has led to talk of the US as "burdened with empire" (reference).'
2. Vision 2020 was officially announced by Dr Mahathir Mohamad on 28 February 1991 at the inaugural gathering of the Malaysian Business Council.
3. Some of these paradoxes may be summed up as follows: survival of Malays/end of 'Malayness'; 'ultra' Malay nationalist/new Malaysian nationalist; ideologue of state-sponsored protection/advocate of capitalist competition; 'Look East'/catch up with West, work-oriented Islam/Islam-oriented work; and frankness/populism (Khoo Boo Teik 1995: 9–10).
4. Recently, ethnic Chinese who belonged to a ruling National Front component party have been admitted as UMNO (United Malay National Organization) members.
5. Eriksen (1991) defines nationalism within the context of a nation-state as 'a political doctrine which holds that the boundaries of the state

should be coterminous with the boundaries of the [dominant] cultural group' and that most extant nationalisms today can be further defined as *ethnic* nationalisms that insist on homogeneity as a nationalist ideology 'in the attempt to bring about cultural standards for national unity and identity'.

References

Abraham, S. J. (1999) 'National Identity and Ethnicity: Malaysian Perspectives' at: http://phuakl.tripod.com/pssm/conference/Sheila Abraham. htm (consulted March 2001).

Andaya, B. W. and Andaya, L. Y. (2000) *A History of Malaysia.* Hong Kong: Macmillan Press.

Asmah Omar (1995) 'Verbal and Non-verbal Symbols: An Investigation into Their Role in Self and Group Identification in Malaysia' at: http:// hometown.aol.com/wignesh/7asmahomar.htm (consulted March 2000).

Castells, M. (1997) *The Power of Identity.* Cornwall: Blackwell.

Chaiwat Satha-Anand (2002) 'Mitigating the Success of Terrorism with the Politics of Truth and Justice', in *September 11 and Political Freedom: Asian Perspectives,* ed. by U. Johannen, A. Smith, and J. Gomez. Singapore: Select Publishing Pte. Ltd, 30–43.

Chouliaraki, L. and Fairclough, N. (1999) *Discourse in Late Modernity: Rethinking Critical Discourse Analysis.* Edinburgh: Edinburgh University Press.

Derichs, C. (1999) 'Nation Building in Malaysia under Conditions of Globalization' at: http://phuakl.tripod.com/pssm/papers.htm (consulted June 2001).

Eriksen, T. H. (1991) 'Languages at the Margins of Modernity: Linguistic Minorities and the Nation-state' at: http://www.uio.no/~geirthe/ Margins.html (consulted April 2001).

Fairclough, N. (2000) *New Labour, New Language?* London: Routledge.

Fairclough, N. (1995a) *Critical Discourse Analysis. The Critical Study of Language.* London: Longman.

Fairclough, N. (1995b) *Media Discourse.* London: Edward Arnold.

Fairclough, N. (1989) *Language and Power.* London: Longman.

Faiz S. Abdullah (2002) 'The State of Being Malaysian', in *Diverse Voices 2: Readings in Languages, Literatures and Cultures,* ed. by Rosli Talif, Shameem Rafik-Galea, and Chan Swee Hong. Serdang: Faculty of Modern Languages and Communication, Universiti Putra Malaysia Press, 42–55.

Farish A. Noor (2001) 'Mahathir and Mahathirism (Part 1)' at: http:// www.malaysiakini.com (consulted July 2001).

Gee, J. P. (1999) *An Introduction to Discourse Analysis: Theory and Method.* London: Routledge.

Gellner, E. (1983) *Nations and Nationalism.* Ithaca, NY: Cornell University Press.

Gomez, J. and Smith, A. (2002) 'Introduction', in *September 11 and Political*

Freedom: Asian Perspectives, ed. by U. Johannen, A. Smith, and J. Gomez. Singapore: Select Publishing Pte. Ltd, xiii–xxxv.

Hewison, K. (2002) 'Globalization: Post 9/11 Challenges for Liberals', in *September 11 and Political Freedom: Asian Perspectives*, ed. by U. Johannen, A. Smith, and J. Gomez. Singapore: Select Publishing Pte. Ltd, 2–29.

Hilley, J. (2001) *Malaysia: Mahathirism, Hegemony and the New Opposition*. London: Zed Books.

Hoey, M. (1983) *On the Surface of Discourse*. London: George Allen and Unwin.

Huntington, S. P. (1993) 'The Clash of Civilizations?' at http://www.foreignaffairs.org/19930601faessay5188/samuel-p-huntington/the-clash-of-civilizations.html (consulted November 2002).

Karim Raslan (2002) 'So, Are Full Civil Liberties Too Risky?', *Business Times Online*, 16 October at: http://business-times.asia1.com.sg/views/story/0,2276,60614,00.html (consulted October 2002).

Kaunismaa, P. (1995) 'On the Analysis of National Identity' at: http://www.jyu.fi/~rakahu/kaunismaa.html (consulted January 2001).

Khoo Boo Teik (1995) *Paradoxes of Mahathirism: An Intellectual Biography of Mahathir Mohamad*. New York: Oxford University Press.

Lim Kit Siang (2000) 'Chinese or Malaysian Identity? Issues and Challenges', CSCSD Public Lectures, Australian National University at: http://rspas.anu.edu.au/cscsd/lim.html (consulted June 2001).

Mahathir Mohamad (2002a) 'Speeches', in *Mahathir Mohamad: A Visionary and His Vision of Malaysia's K-Economy* with commentaries by D. N. Abdullai, ed. by Ng Tieh Chuan. Kuala Lumpur: Pelanduk Publications, 1–239.

Mahathir Mohamad (2002b) 'Facing Challenges: Caring for the Race', *The Star*, 31 August: 3.

'Malaysia: Special Report on Race and Ethnicity' at: http://www.malaysia.net/lists/sangkancil/2000-03/msg00585.html (consulted April 2001).

Maniam, K. S. (1996) 'The New Diaspora' at: http://www.ucalgary.ca/UofC/eduweb/engl392/492/maniam-dias.html (consulted March 2001).

Milne, R. S. and Mauzy, D. K. (1999) *Malaysian Politics Under Mahathir*. London: Routledge.

Nathan, K. S. (2001) 'Economic Slowdown and Domestic Politics: *Malaysia Boleh?*' at: http://www.iseas.edu.sg (consulted August 2002).

Paxman, J. (1999) *The English: A Portrait of a People*. London: Penguin Books.

Shakila Manan (2001) 'Re-reading the Media: A Stylistic Analysis of Malaysian Media Coverage of Anwar and the Reformasi Movement', *Asia Pacific Media Educator*, July–December: 34–54.

The Star (2000) 'PM: Make a Little Sacrifice for Racial Harmony', 31 August: 23.

Tourism Development Corporation of Malaysia (2002) *Malaysia Truly Asia*. Complimentary Video CD. Kuala Lumpur.

van Dijk, T. A. (1998) *Ideology*. London: Sage Publications.
Wodak, R., de Cillia, R., Reisigl, M., and Liebhart, K. (eds) (1999) *The Discursive Construction of National Identity*. Edinburgh: Edinburgh University Press.

7 Celebrating Singapore's Development: An Analysis of the Millennium Stamps

Chng Huang Hoon

My paper provides a critical reading of the stamp-texts that make up the Millennium Collection *– a collection of stamps issued to commemorate Singapore's developmental milestones from a colony to a nation. Divided broadly into two sets – 'twentieth century stamps' and 'Singapore 2000 stamps' – the* Millennium Collection *comprises 14 minted stamps, each carrying a theme such as 'Housing', 'Government', 'Immigration', 'Colonialism', 'Globalization', and so on. My aim in this analysis is to examine the overt/official construction of Singapore's nation-building with a view to unpacking the ideological messages underlying this construction.*

Introduction

'I want to be proud of Singapore . . . but what about?' – this is the headline of a recent newspaper article that appeared in the Singaporean broadsheet, *The Straits Times* (Teo 2001: H1). In this news article, the question of what it means to be Singaporean is once again raised, as it has been raised many times before. As Teo noted in the article,

> The quest for a Singapore identity is as old as the country. Lacking a long and deep history, Singaporeans have long grappled with the question of just who they are. Now, it seems, the soul-searching has been taken up by a younger, more restless and globalized set eager for answers.

It is in this context that I wish to discuss the official construction of Singaporean identity as manifested (obliquely and not unproblematically) in the *Millennium Collection* (see Figure 7.1).[1] The *Millennium Collection* is a set of 14, minted stamps that mark 'the milestones in Singapore's development' and which are presented in a promotional package. Commissioned by the Singapore Philatelic Museum, this collection was launched at the Istana, the official residence of the President of Singapore, Mr S. R. Nathan, on 20 December 1999. In the Foreword message, President Nathan said,

> The milestones we have travelled are well captured in the series of 10 stamps issued on the last day of this century. . . . These 14 stamp images superbly minted in gold-plated

Celebrating the Milestones in Singapore's Development

20th century stamps

Immigration
*Multicultural immigrants make
Singapore their home*

Colonialism
*Significant figures and majestic
landmarks of colonial government*

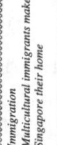

Japanese Occupation
*Memorable moments before and after
Japanese occupation*

Government
Parliament in session

National Service
*A strong defence force to guard our
homeland*

Transportation
*A world class transportation system
for Singapore*

Economic Progress
*From traditional trades to a global
economic centre*

Tourism
Celebrating our multi-ethnic diversity

Housing
*Building world class homes for every
resident*

Education
*A strong workforce and active
citizenry through education*

Singapore 2000 stamps

Information Technology
*An intelligent island
linked by fibre optics*

Arts & Culture
*A renaissance city
through arts and culture*

Heritage
*Preserving Singapore's
vital roots and heritage*

Globalisation
*Linking up through
info-communications*

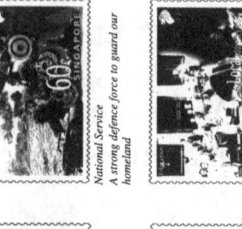

The stamps chosen commemorate the milestones in our past and our aspirations for the future. These stamps are meticulously reproduced into 999 bullion silver ingots layered in 24 carat gold to make up the Millennium Collection.

Figure 7.1 The *Millennium Collection*

silver are a perpetual reminder of our journey through the twentieth century and the next. These stamps serve as a poignant reminder of the road we have made and travelled on, as well as our future focus.

This 'road we have made and travelled on' – from a British colony to an independent nation[2] – is officially equated with the early days of Singapore's immigration and colonial history (1819 to 1942), the three-year period marked by the Japanese occupation of Singapore (February 1942 to August 1945), and various other milestones including the establishment of a local (People's Action Party, 1954) government and the institution of national military service (1967). This phrase also refers to the progress made in areas such as building a transportation system, creating affordable public housing for the masses, and making education accessible to all Singaporeans. What Singapore is said to be aspiring towards is celebrated in the four Singapore 2000 stamps which depict a vision of Singapore as 'an intelligent island' and 'a renaissance city', simultaneously striving to preserve 'vital roots and heritage', yet also actively participating in the world of globalization. In short, Singapore is a nation that is determined to remember its past achievements (hence the act of enshrining each milestone in the development from colony to nation) but, at the same time, it is not a nation that wants to be left behind.

In my analysis of the Millennium stamps,[3] I focus on aspects in the construction of Singaporean history and identity from the perspective of Critical Discourse Analysis (CDA), the classification scheme used in the construction, and the conflicts and gaps in the discourse. In addition, I examine the texts from the point of view of Systemic Functional Linguistics (SFL), a framework that allows analysis of the nature of agency and clause structures. Furthermore, the nature of the visuals – the stamps themselves – also merit consideration. Through this exploration, I discuss the official values promoted via the *Millennium Collection*, thus answering, in part at least, what being a Singaporean means from the institutional point of view.

Classification Schemes

As Fairclough (1989: 115) asserts, a classification scheme is 'a particular way of dividing up some aspect of reality which is built upon a particular ideological representation of that reality'. The verbal text of the *Millennium Collection* exhibits a dual classification scheme that seems to map opposing values. For ease of discussion, I call these opposing schemes 'local' versus 'global'. Table 7.1 indicates the word choices made to index these two opposing realities.

I have placed 'renaissance city', 'world class homes', and 'world class transportation system' in the middle column, because these can arguably be said to fit into both the local and the global networks. This issue aside, however, the local-global contrast above shows the following. On the one hand, there is a distinct effort to retain the aura of the old homeland as

Table 7.1 Classification scheme – local versus global

Local	Local and Global	Global
art	renaissance city	fibre optics
citizenry	world class homes	global economic centre
culture	world class transportation system	globalization
heritage		info-communication
home		information technology
homeland		intelligent island
immigrants		
multicultural		
multi-ethnic		
diversity		
residents		
traditional trades		
vital roots		
workforce		

signalled by word choices like 'heritage' and 'vital roots' as well as to have the 'citizenry' consciously recall Singapore's immigrant background. But even on this point, I note also the overt push towards 'world class homes' and a 'renaissance city' which show obvious global or European influences. On the other hand, there is an equally obvious effort on the part of decision-makers to turn Singapore into an ultra-modern city that is fully connected to the rest of the world. Echoing 'world class homes' is the phrase 'world class transportation system'. This 'homeland', characterized by 'multicultural' and 'multi-ethnic diversity' is expected to coexist with a globalized 'intelligent island' driven by the new world of 'information technology'. The Singaporean reality is thus divided up into both a local culture and a global economy. The underlying ideological motivation seems to stem from twin desires to acknowledge humble immigrant beginnings even as Singapore as an island state admits to the need to go global. This results in a somewhat schizophrenic mentality that is manifested in multiple ways in the local population. The constant questioning about what makes a Singaporean and what constitutes a Singaporean identity are, I argue, the consequence of such opposing tensions operating in the Singaporean psyche.[4]

In Singapore today, we have three kinds of Singaporeans. First, we have Singaporeans who are equally comfortable in both local and global cultures. The young man, named Frederick Wong, featured in the news article cited at the start of this paper was described as follows:

> The Nanyang Technological University (NTU) undergraduate supports English football clubs, eats sushi and steak, watches Taiwanese dramas, and chats on the Web with

friends in Hongkong. There is little in the 25-year-old's life that is intrinsically Singaporean, he laments (Teo 2001: H1).

Unlike Frederick Wong, however, there are other kinds of Singaporeans who identify with only one reality. In the local rhetoric, these are officially described either as 'heartlanders' or 'cosmopolitans', the former being Singaporeans who are more attuned to the local culture while the latter are described as Singaporeans who have more of a global outlook.[5] Though the virtues of 'heartlanders' have been publicly extolled, there is still the nagging feeling among decision-makers that these are the Singaporeans who are not able to negotiate on the international scene due in part to their level of education and, therefore, their competence in the English language. Similarly, while the 'cosmopolitans' can be counted on to represent Singapore in the world outside, they are precisely the ones who have been perceived as lacking a local Singaporean identity, and hence their loyalty to the country has often been the subject of public discussions. In short, many Singaporeans feel the opposing pressures of having to maintain a local identity and the need to respond well to global influences as well as striking a healthy balance between the two.

The *Millennium Collection*, as one official embodiment of local (developmental) history, seems to express, and endorse, this split or dual reality in Singapore: if the ten twentieth-century stamps can be said to emphasize local values, the four Singapore 2000 stamps effectively project a global reality that Singapore has to some extent already achieved, and to a greater extent, is still actively moving towards.

Conflicts and Gaps in the Discourse: Progress versus Heritage

In examining this stamp collection, it is possible to contest some of the verbal claims made. For example, Stamp 7 entitled 'Economic Progress', subtitled 'From traditional trades to a global economic centre' seems to suggest that there is a natural and unproblematic developmental progression in this realm. The reality is that in the 1970s, due to the onslaught of modern life, some of these traditional trades (such as the charcoal dealership and the master storytellers who told their stories to a live audience on the street and, later, over the radio)[6] have been all but wiped out, and currently some of these traditional practices are only actively being rehabilitated in this new heritage revival that seems to have gripped the nation.[7] In this new spirit which places renewed emphasis on heritage, values, and roots, the sentiment depicted in Stamp 13, 'Heritage: Preserving Singapore's vital roots and heritage' comes as no surprise. However, a recent public debate over the fate of a local landmark, the National Library building in Singapore, seems to go against this renewed call to value our heritage as some Singaporeans moan over the decision to have the historic library building torn down to make way for the nation's third university campus (the Singapore Management University). These conflicts in the national/public discourse on issues of heritage and progress once again reinforce the earlier point made about the schizophrenic forces that run through the nation's heartbeat, at one time favouring the old but at other times promoting the new. That 'Economic Progress' and 'Heritage' can be featured in the same collection (though in two different sections) reflects the presence of these twin tensions that so fracture the Singaporean consciousness, resulting in a similarly ill-formed national identity.

In assessing these 14 stamps in the *Millennium Collection*, the question of theme selection immediately comes to mind. In the light of the task to celebrate significant moments in local history, the choice of specific themes is, needless to say, a debate unto itself. Why these 14 moments in history, if these can all be accurately called historical moments at all? But perhaps an even more interesting question is: 'What has been left uncommemorated?' In a system of available choices, what eventually gets actualized – the real-ized elements – are as significant in terms of meaning as those other elem-ents in the system that failed to be realized. In an interrogation about what a particular construction really means in the context it is situated, it is therefore just as important to examine the gaps in the discourse. Within this way of thinking about *what might have been* chosen as a featured theme in the *Millennium Collection*, I venture to suggest at least three potentially equally important themes that *could have been realized* as themes in the *Collection* but are not depicted here.

There is, firstly, a gap in this stamp discourse in relation to the issue of race. Race is, and rightly so, a highly sensitive issue in Singapore – in fact, it is so sensitive that people avoid discussing it. Such an avoidance and absence in rhetoric is not altogether bad, especially given the risks involved in the possible misuse of rhetoric in today's post-September 11 world of heightened security alert. In the stamps featured here, race is euphemized under the terms 'multicultural immigrants' and 'multi-ethnic diversity' which foregrounds the harmonious side of local racial dynamics while ignoring the occasional fissures along racial lines. Given this silence about race issues in Singapore, it is not a surprise that there is no stamp com-memorating 'Racial Harmony' or 'Multi-racial Singapore'. However, given how treasured this racial harmony is in a multi-racial and multi-religious society like Singapore, the fact that there is no overt celebration of this aspect of Singaporean reality is, therefore, curious to a certain extent.

Secondly, there is a gap with respect to gender issues. Singapore prides itself as a meritocracy that rewards deserving individuals based on merit. The idea of discrimination, or more specifically gender discrimination, is quite alien to many Singaporeans. Singapore at the threshold of the twenty-first century is still generally lacking in consciousness on gender issues, and many people, I would say, lack an overall feminist consciousness. Within the Asian ethic that takes for granted the (supporting) role and place of women in society, there is an implicit understanding that there are no gender problems in Singapore, and if there are, they are not sufficiently important to be put on the national agenda. That the *Millennium Collection* does not include a stamp that marks 'Gender Equality' or 'Women's Contribution' is therefore a gap not likely to be felt by too many in the general population.

Thirdly, there is silence with respect to the fateful separation of Singapore from the Malayan Federation in 1964, a significant historical moment in which independence was forced upon a reluctant Singaporean government. Between 1959 and 1964, Singapore was part of the Malayan Federation, having struck an alliance with its most immediate neighbour, Malaya. But in the later years of this partnership, disagreements between leaders from both sides became serious enough for Malaya to decide to exclude Singapore from being a member of the Federation, much to the dismay of the local leadership who hung on to this political alliance. It was under such a tumultuous climate that Singapore's independence in August 1965 came about.[8] This was quite understandably a major historical moment in Singapore's history. But just as clearly, perhaps, this is one historical moment that is surely not worth celebrating by official sentiment.

Agency

For a text celebrating Singapore's development, there is a curious absence of explicit agency that signals overtly who the participants are. In particular, there is no occurrence of the use of 'we' or 'Singaporeans' throughout. For example, in the text, 'Celebrating the Milestones in Singapore's Development' (Figure 7.1), who is celebrating is not named in the clause. In addition, the text accompanying each stamp contains clauses such as 'Celebrating our multi-ethnic diversity', 'Preserving Singapore's vital roots and heritage', and so on. In these clauses, the same elliptical structure is used, thus avoiding the explicit naming of any participants. But since it is 'our past and our aspirations for the future' that is being commemorated, it seems obvious that it is the unnamed 'we' who are celebrating, preserving, building, and so on. What is explicitly named in the text as agents or participants are found in the following two clauses:

Multicultural immigrants make Singapore their home.
A strong defence force to guard our homeland.

Apart from these, some of the other clauses do not have explicit agents realized in noun phrase (NP) structures but instead have a prepositional phrase (PP) with a means function in the clause:

A strong workforce and active citizenry through education.
An intelligent island linked by fibre optics.
A renaissance city through arts and culture.
Linking up through info-communications.

In the above examples, the text focuses on how (for example, through education) a goal, e.g. a strong workforce and active citizenry, is to be achieved as part of national development, but it does not say explicitly who will bring this about. When agency is explicitly named, responsibility is clearly assigned. When participants are known, it becomes clear who is doing what to whom. But when these go largely unnamed, what can be said about their absence? In this context, it seems that the absence of participants and agents within clauses has the effect of spreading out the responsibility and the action. In other words, everyone is implicated in this celebration and this process of nation-building and development. Being unnamed, therefore, does not imply absence; instead, it implicitly assumes that all Singaporeans know and must accept it as their individual and collective responsibility to play their part in nation-building, in preserving our heritage, in defending the country, and so on. Hence, leaving agency and participants vague actually calls to the implicit presence of the most logical of participants in this context – all Singaporeans. This reading resonates well especially when considering the rhetoric in Singapore echoed many times over in political speeches, in news reports, in national songs, and so on that reiterates time and again that 'every Singaporean counts' and 'together, we can make a difference'.[9] Therefore, omitting agency in this text does not leave the reader at a loss. Far from it; any Singaporean reader knows that he/she is being exhorted to participate in the activities of nation-building. It is understood that through active participation in nation-building, a Singaporean identity will over time emerge naturally as Singaporeans increase their personal stakes in the making of the nation.

Clause Structures

Closely linked to the issue of agency is the clause structure itself. The stamp texts show a variety of clause structures.

The Independent Finite Clause

Stamp 1 is the only independent finite clause in which agency and goal are clearly spelled out. The explicitly named agent, 'Multicultural immigrants', acts through a material process to effect the goal of establishing a home in Singapore.

Stamp 1

Multicultural immigrants	make	Singapore	their home
NP actor	Material: finite present	NP goal, location	NP goal, attribution

This is the only clause that contains the complete Subject + Verb + Complement structure. It is hard to determine with any measure of confidence why the stamp-text is inconsistent in not maintaining the clause patterning that is evident throughout the rest of the text. If it *had* maintained this structural consistency, the caption for Stamp 1 could conceivably be

'Making Singapore their home'. But this caption is unsatisfactory, perhaps because it leaves crucial participants ('multicultural immigrants') out of the verbal process, and these participants were key elements in making modern Singapore what it is today. Or, Stamp 1 could have the wording, 'Multicultural immigrants in Singapore', but this is again not satisfactory as it misses out on the very important NP, 'their home' in this context. The description for Stamp 1, the first stamp in the collection, is realized by an independent clause, perhaps because, in this way, the producer of the stamps sets the stage (if only subconsciously) for the rest of the stamp discourse.

NP Structures Accompanied by PP's

Six stamps have NP structures accompanied by PPs. These are:

Stamp 2

Significant figures and majestic landmarks	of colonial government
NP	PP (classifier)

Stamp 3

Memorable moments	before and after Japanese Occupation
NP	PP (time)

Stamp 4

Parliament	in session
NP	PP (range)

Stamp 6

A world class transportation system	for Singapore
NP goal	PP (beneficiary)

Stamp 10

A strong workforce and active citizenry	through education
NP goal	PP (means)

Stamp 12

A renaissance city	through arts and culture
NP goal	PP (means)

The effect of these NP structures is that specific chunks of objective reality or specific targets are first named, then made into crucial parts of factual reality, and within the context of the stamp, identified as landmarks or 'milestones' worthy of celebration.

This line of thought explains why we see included in the *Millennium Collection* a stamp marking the 'Japanese Occupation' as a milestone in Singapore's development since this traumatic period in local history reminds (or more accurately, warns) modern Singaporeans (especially Generation M – the Millennium generation), who have never experienced the traumas associated with an occupying force, to treasure and be grateful for the peace that Singapore now enjoys. According to Neal (1998: 36–7),

> traumas are drawn upon in shaping collective identities, in setting national priorities, and in providing guidelines for what to do or not to do in any given case. We negotiate between the past and the future through our concern about historical repetitions. Serious disruptions of tranquility of everyday life tend to be remembered and to become embedded in collective perceptions of society as moral community. Such perceptions provide a close link between self-identity and national identity.

However, because this stamp celebrates the period before and after the Japanese disruption of peace in Singapore, it is immediately subject to ideological challenge. For many who had to live through the dark days of the Japanese occupation, such a characterization of 'Memorable moments' ignores a significant part of local history. Like the Holocaust, where the sheer magnitude of the trauma does not allow for selective forgetting because its victims are neither ready to forgive nor forget, the Japanese occupation in Singapore remains a crucial part of fresh memory in some Singaporean minds even after a lapse of six decades, especially in the minds of those Singaporeans who are now in their 60s or 70s. And, in many ways, the local authorities encourage this memory as can be seen from the inclusion of this event in local history books, in the prevalence of television programmes that feature this theme, and more recently in a small local war museum exhibition entitled, 'Reflections at Bukit Chandu: A World War II Interpretative Centre'. However, it seems that according to this stamp celebration of Singapore's development, the intentional forgetting of what happened *during* the occupation is promoted, thus giving rise to a very specific attempt to celebrate only certain moments in history. Of course, in official constructions of history, there is a need for institutions to take heed of other sites of ideological struggles. In the interest of diplomacy perhaps, the official construction has glossed over a detail that is highly sensitive in regional politics, and this may explain the silence in this collection with regard to the dark days that characterized the Japanese occupation.

NP Structure with a Non-finite Element

Apart from these PP modified NP structures, there is also one NP structure occurring with a non-finite element.

Stamp 5

A strong defence force	to guard our homeland
NP goal	Infinitive (purpose)

Like the other NP structures above, this stamp-text does not show the fully-fledged clause structure such as 'We need a strong defence force to guard our homeland'. Such omissions suggest that it is clear who the participants are in these structures. In other words, what we get is a series of structured NPs that assumes common goals and desires. In the imagining of the nation as a unified entity, such structures go a long way to promote such a sentiment of a shared harmonious vision and mission.

Text with Only PP Structures

There is just one text (Stamp 7) which has only PP structures.

Stamp 7

From traditional trades	to a global economic centre
PP	PP

This PP structure seems to map out a route in Singapore's development – from past to present, from old to new economy, from local to global and so on. Once again, recall the President's Foreword: 'These stamps serve as a poignant reminder of the road we have made and travelled on, as well as our future focus' within the 2000 promotional package. The above PP structure reflects this progression and aspiration.

Clausal and Verbal Ellipses

Another structure common to a number of stamp-texts is ellipsis, either clausal or verbal. For example, Stamp 11 demonstrates a clausal ellipsis: We want an intelligent island that is linked by fibre optics.

Stamp 11

An intelligent island	linked	by fibre optics
NP goal	Reduced passive	PP (means)

Stamp-texts 8, 9, 11, 13, and 14 all demonstrate verbal ellipsis. In many of these stamp-texts, the words 'We are' are missing before the progressive -ing verb form. The use of this verb form creates various effects. First, there is a rhythm that suggests ongoing action, indicating that in Singapore we are always building (which is true!) and preserving, and ever celebrating, and in the latter, there is a further suggestion that there is always something that is worth celebrating in Singapore. Second, using ellipsis here omits the need for explicit mention of agency. As I noted earlier, this lack of explicit mention means that agency is taken to be understood or obvious, or at least it is constructed as shared knowledge that cannot be challenged, that is, who does what to whom is not textually identified. In the gap between the implicitly assumed knowledge of who's who and what's what and the actions that are textually manifested lies what feels to be an interminable silence that is at once ideologically suggestive and is, for this reason perhaps, left deliberately vague.

Title text

Celebrating	the Milestones in Singapore's Development
-ing verb	NP goal

Stamp 8

Celebrating	our multi-ethnic diversity
-ing verb	NP goal

Stamp 9

Building	world class homes	for every resident
-ing verb	NP goal	PP (beneficiary)

Stamp 13

Preserving	Singapore's vital roots and heritage
-ing verb	NP goal

Stamp 14

Linking up	through info-communications
-ing verb + part.	PP (means)

Visuals

Pictures not only testify to the existence of objects and events, they also place on permanent record how these entities are to be remembered and recalled. Similarly, each of the 14 stamps in the *Millennium Collection* depicts an aspect of reality that can in some future time be referred to as concrete testimony that these events, or scenes or landmarks have indeed been real, and at one point, even considered important.

The first ten stamps are drawn with a clear black-and-white/coloured contrast, reflecting the old/new, past/present, and then/now moments in Singapore's development. For example, in the stamp depicting 'Housing', there is a foregrounded, coloured picture of new government-built, high-rise flats and a backgrounded, black-and-white picture of an old low structure. Within this framing, there is visual coherence as the non-coloured/coloured portions relate to each other in a relationship that suggests continuity and progress. The accompanying caption – 'Building world class homes for every resident' – underscores the government's goal not only to raise the standard of living of Singaporeans, but also to match our housing standard with that of the world. The visual contrast functions to establish what is given information (that which is depicted in black-and-white, and that which is backgrounded) and what is new (the coloured picture in the foreground), thus mapping visually the progressive development of the nation with the suggestion that not only have Singaporeans/Singapore changed through the years, we have changed for the better. In this very specific way, the stamp image conveys its meaning via the technique of colour contrast and foreground/background placement, providing a composite assembly of salient information, framed in a particular way.

Stamps 11 to 14 differ from the first ten stamps in that they are fully coloured, and in visual terms, may be said to have maximum salience. Consistent with 'Singapore 2000', these four stamps seem to prominently represent modern Singapore, concerned with globalization, information technology, heritage, and the arts. As manifested in these four stamps, the old (culture) and the new (IT) are depicted as distinct and separate, unlike the first ten stamps which depict the old/new contrast within the spatial frame of each stamp. In other words, the four Singapore 2000 stamps depict only present realities.

Specific stamps feature well-known icons like the samsui women, the Singapore Girl, a block of government-built flats, a view of the financial district, and so on. The familiarity of these images is reassuring in that they seem to say, 'There is nothing new here; you knew all these before', reinforcing the old in a new context. There is a sense of continuity in this kind of portrayal, and an official construction of national development relies to some extent on such continuity, especially in a world filled with rapid changes. But this same familiarity also has a way of freezing certain images in specific associative frames. When Singaporeans think of immigration in their national context, the samsui woman comes to mind as she provided the quintessential kind of immigrant labourer that built Singapore, literally from the ground up. Her weather-worn face has graced many books whose authors give her due credit for a lifetime of hard labour. When Singaporeans think of economic progress, the banking industry in Singapore comes to mind, and this slick image of concrete, glass, and steel structures in the financial district is often pictured on touristy Singapore postcards. While these visuals are comforting because of their unthreatening familiarity, these specific associations severely limit and restrict the scope of conceptualizing and imagining aspects of Singaporean realities, which though not wrong in themselves, represent only a small fragment of historical truth.

A little less familiar perhaps than what we are used to in Singapore, simply because they are newer images by comparison, are the images pictured in the last four stamps – the computer screen, the globe, and the arts and heritage buildings. However, even these are fast becoming fixtures in people's imagination, especially among the younger generation of Singaporeans who have grown up, literally fed on IT and global culture. In short, the pictorial representation of 'the Milestones in Singapore's Development' succeeds in bringing to the public imagination a reinforcement of the way Singapore was, and the way Singapore is now, all of which are nevertheless selective, frozen, fixed moments in local history that are deemed by officialdom to be worth preserving and commemorating.

Singaporean Values

> The act of commemoration is a formal means of giving recognition to the importance of past events and designating them as worthy of collective remembrance. Symbolic representations of past events are designed to give special recognition to great men and women, to heroic undertakings, and to personal sacrifices for the benefit of the nation. The act of commemoration is essentially a means of rejuvenating cultural values and promoting images of society as a moral community (Neal 1998: 207).

The sentiment expressed in the above quote echoes well the purpose of the *Millennium Collection*. However, the stamp collection discussed here also promotes and perpetuates a number of values that are a constant pre-occupation in the Singaporean mentality at both institutional and grass-roots levels. I identify four such values promoted here: value hard work; remember history; cultivate world-class standards; and develop an appreciation for the finer things in life.

The need for hard work (Stamps 1, 10) is something that Singaporeans are constantly exhorted to adopt as a kind of personal practice. The hard labour of the samsui woman, undertaken in another era, is equivalent to education that today's individual needs to be successful in. Encompassed in the emphasis on education is also the notion of hard work – that nothing can be achieved without individual sacrifice and investment. In fact, in the local rhetoric that repeatedly pronounces that people are our only resource, the need for hard work and (continued) education takes centre stage.

A second type of value that is promoted here is 'remember history'. Stamps 2 and 3 depict our origins as the colonized and the sufferings of our ancestors in war times. The lessons to be learnt from these historical depictions are expressed in Stamps 4 and 5, that is, the appreciation for the efficiency and efficacy of the local government and the need for national defence. The reminder that we are vulnerably positioned is always in the Singaporean consciousness.

A third kind of value is manifested in the national aspiration to be world class in every arena of our lives (Stamps 6, 7, 8, 9, 11, 14). In Singapore, we are obsessed, or we are educated into being obsessed, with being and becoming 'No. 1' and maintaining the 'No. 1' spot in as many aspects of our lives as it is humanly possible to excel. Excellence is commonly defined with overt reference to the outside world, especially the Western countries (cf. the aspiration towards becoming a 'renaissance city', for example). Most recently, the overt use of the term 'benchmarking' in public discourse is evident of this kind of outward-looking attitude as Singaporeans and local institutions are constantly asked to match themselves against well-established institutions in the West. The drive towards world-class standards now rules almost every aspect of Singaporean life.

Finally, this collection also promotes Singapore's most current pre-occupation – the need to develop an appreciation for the finer things in life (Stamps 12, 13). After decades of hard work and intense economic progress, there is a sudden realization that, as a society that has 'arrived' economically on the world stage, we need also to develop a sense of culture. Hence, there is a recent push for preserving local heritage and promoting the arts in Singapore. The Esplanade: Theatres on the Bay in Singapore, opened on 12 October 2002, is a $600-million testament to this current promotion of the arts.

Conclusion

I will end this paper on the philatelic construction of the history of Singapore by returning to the opening headline quote from the newspaper article. The question was asked, 'I want to be proud of Singapore . . . but what about?' Clearly, the official construction is unambiguous about what one should be proud of: the various successes that Singapore has achieved and maintained in its 37 years of independence are what Singaporeans should be proud of. Incidentally, the milestones are all, unsurprisingly perhaps, People's Action Party milestones; the ideological significance of this fact is straightforward, I think. The question remains as to why, at the official level, what Singaporeans should be proud of is so clear-cut, while at the level of the individual, there remains such a problem identifying with a Singaporean identity. I leave this as food for thought and as the subject of future papers on the subject.

Notes

1. Thanks to the Singapore Philatelic Museum for the permission to reproduce the 2000 Millennium Stamps for use in this article.
2. The historical information and dates marking each milestone in the history of Singapore are gathered from the following websites: http://

www.pap.org.sg; http://www.inic.utexas.edu/asnic/countries/singapore/
Singapore-History.html; and from history books such as E. C. T. Chew
and E. Lee (eds), *A History of Singapore* (Singapore: Oxford University
Press, 1991) and C. M. Turnbull, *A History of Singapore, 1819–1988* (Singapore: Oxford University Press, 1989).

3. In another paper tentatively entitled 'The Millennium Collection: History, Memory, and Singaporean Values', I analyse the promotional texts
   that were designed to sell the stamps to the local and international
   audiences.

4. This opposing tension has been variedly characterized across time. In a
   speech by Prime Minister Goh Chok Tong, the terms of 'heartlander'
   versus 'cosmopolitan' were introduced. More recently in his 2002
   National Day speech, PM Goh urged Singaporeans to ask themselves if
   they are 'stayers' or 'quitters'.

5. These are terms used in Prime Minister Goh Chok Tong's National Day
   Rally 1999, 22 August 1999.

6. In a book called *Vanishing Trades of Singapore*, the details of 20 kinds of
   traditional trades are documented by the Oral History Department.

7. The latest cultural development in Singapore is the newly built Esplanade: Theatres on the Bay, a performing arts centre that aims to be the
   venue for both international and local arts events. Annexed to this structure is a library section for the arts; this library hopes to educate the
   visitors on the arts, and houses all kinds of audio, visual and textual
   materials on the subject.

8. A recent account detailing this break from the Federation is the published memoirs of Senior Minister Lee Kuan Yew, entitled *The Singapore
   Story: The Memoirs of Lee Kuan Yew* (Singapore: Times Editions Pte. Ltd,
   1998).

9. 'Every Singaporean counts' is part of a Singapore 21 manifesto where it
   is made clear that every Singaporean has a stake in Singapore; 'Together,
   we can make a difference' is also an often reiterated official line that
   urges Singaporeans to participate actively in making Singapore a better
   place for everyone.

References

Fairclough, N. (1989) *Language and Power*. London: Longman.
Neal, A. G. (1998) *National Trauma & Collective Memory: Major Events in the
American Century*. New York: M. E. Sharpe, Inc.
Teo, L. (2001) 'I want to be proud of Singapore . . . but what about?', *The
Straits Times*, 20 February: H1.

8 The Representation of Social Actors in the *Globe and Mail* during the Break-up of the Former Yugoslavia

Dragana Polovina-Vukovic

This study focuses on the portrayal of different ethnic groups involved in the wars during the disintegration of Yugoslavia (1991 to 1999) as represented by one segment of the Canadian press. Through a Critical Discourse Analysis (CDA) of the articles that appeared on the front pages of the Globe and Mail, *the only Canadian daily national newspaper at the time of the events being examined, this paper identifies and compares the representation of different Balkan participants: the armed forces, politicians, and civilians. The analysis illustrates that different ethnic groups were largely portrayed either as 'villains' or 'victims' and argues that such a portrayal contributed to Western actions in the Balkans and Western acceptance of refugees.*

Introduction

According to Chouliaraki (1999: 38), the media can construct a certain discursive reality for readers as it is within the 'public sphere, that is, social space where people as citizens are drawn into informed debates about contemporary issues of national and international interests . . . which weigh heavily on the formation of public opinion'. The purpose of this paper, therefore, is to examine the portrayal of the parties involved in the wars in Croatia and Kosovo as represented by one segment of the Canadian press – specifically, the *Globe and Mail,* the only Canadian daily national newspaper at the time of the events being examined – in order to determine the discursive reality presented to Canadians during the break-up of the former Yugoslavia.

Through a Critical Discourse Analysis (CDA) of the articles that appeared on its front pages, I identify and compare the representation of different Balkan participants: the armed forces in Croatia and Kosovo (both state and rebel); politicians; and civilians. Because the identified Balkan participants belong to different ethnic groups, this paper discusses the representation of specific sub-groups: Albanians; Croats; and Serbs. These group portrayals prompted the following research questions:

- What are the differences among the portrayals of the different ethnic groups identified above (comparing, for instance, the armed forces in Croatia and the armed forces in Serbia)?
- Is there overt or covert prejudice in relation to different groups by the media, and if so, how is it produced and reproduced linguistically?

If discourse is seen as a form of social practice and if media discourse is an influential medium, investigation of these questions in relation to the media can reveal considerable information about the formation of Canadians' attitude towards different ethnic groups from the former Yugoslavia. The ultimate question is whether the discursive practice of differential representation contributed considerably to the construction of particular mental models for readers and further influenced the 'ways in which Canadian readers called for, and accepted, actions taken in relation to a particular group' (Young 2000: 2).

Because I participated in some of the events that are the object of my investigation, the question of my objectivity in studying and analysing these events must be addressed. Although objectivity in any absolute form is an illusion, I followed Wodak's (in Wodak *et al.* 1999: 12) suggestion to minimize the risk of critical bias by integrating historical, political, and sociological information in my analysis and interpretation.

Overall Corpus and Selected Data

There were 68 front-page stories on the war in Croatia and 98 front-page stories on the war in Serbia/Kosovo published in the seven-year period (January 1992 to December 1999) in the *Globe and Mail*. As well as examining the articles' content, I also analysed the headlines in addition to particular stories from the front pages, assuming that these are considered by editors to be the most important for and of most interest to their readership (Geis 1987; Parenti 1993). For a detailed textual analysis, I randomly selected 17 front-page stories, which make up 10 per cent of front-page articles published in each year of the period under the study. These articles allowed me to identify the dominant discursive roles and voices assigned by reporters and editors to participants in the wars in the former Yugoslavia.

According to van Dijk (1998) and Wodak (1996, 2000), it is impossible to understand the discursive strategies adopted without understanding the social background against which they were formulated. Therefore, my analysis starts with a brief overview of the former Yugoslavia prior to its dissolution in order to 'transcend the pure linguistic dimension and to include more or less systematically the historical, political, and sociological dimension in the analysis, theory and interpretation of a specific discursive occasion' (Wodak 1996: 24).

Brief History of Yugoslavia

The former Socialist Federal Republic of Yugoslavia (SFRY) consisted of six republics: Bosnia and Herzegovina; Croatia; Macedonia; Montenegro; Serbia; and Slovenia, and six founding (constituent) peoples of Yugoslavia: Croats; Macedonians; Montenegrins; Serbs; Slovenes; and, after the 1963 constitution, Muslims. In addition, there were many citizens who had a national homeland elsewhere, and who were referred to as 'nationalities'. These individuals such as Jews, Czechs, Romanians, Bulgarians, Turks, Italians, Roma, and Vlachs, had been guaranteed cultural rights to preserve their sense of community and their heritage. Albanians and Hungarians, the largest of these groups, were also given local self-government in two autonomous regions in the republic of Serbia where they predominated (Kosovo and Vojvodina, respectively). The only legal right, which the Constitution did not give to Yugoslav nationalities, was the right to secede. Hungarians never demanded a change in their status, but the Kosovo Albanians began to demand the status of a republic and, thus, the right to secession in 1968.

The concept of constituent nations required that all federal activities – from appointments to public office such as army generals or the rotation of the prime minister to the distribution of federal investments and represen- tation at cultural festivals – take into account the proportional representa- tion of individuals by constituent nationality and, therefore, use a quota system (Crnobrnja 1996; Woodward 1995). This system aimed to prevent any single national group from gaining political dominance over the state (Parenti 1999; Woodward 1995; Crnobrnja 1996). This arrangement worked, as Parenti (1999: 14) points out, between 1960 and 1980 when Yugoslavia 'had one of the most vigorous growth rates: a decent standard of living, free medical care and education, a guaranteed right to a job, a literacy rate of over 90 per cent, and a life expectancy of 72 years'.

The first problems occurred in Yugoslavia in the early 1980s after Tito's death which coincided with the beginning of an economic depression. Throughout the 1970s, Yugoslavia, like many other countries, had borrowed heavily from the International Monetary Fund (IMF) and com- mercial banks (Woodward 1995). Tensions grew between the Belgrade central government and the republican governments over the manage- ment of the foreign debt. The richest republics, Slovenia and Croatia, started to complain about their 'exploitation' (Crnobrnja 1996: 62). Nationalists praised the Slovenes' and Croats' 'European, civilized, effi- cient' traditions as opposed to the 'Balkan peoples' tradition' (Woodward 1995: 42). Serb nationalism became a powerful force in 1987 when Slobodan Milosevic became the head of the Serbia League of Communists.

The communist regime in Yugoslavia ended in 1990 with the breakdown of the federal Communist party and the multi-party elections held in the republics from April to December of that year. In all republics, nationalist leaders with policies of ethnic intolerance won the first democratic elections (Crnobrnja 1996; Woodward 1995). The conflict among different ethnic groups started in Slovenia in 1991. In 1992, a war ensued in Croatia between Croatian government forces and the country's local Serbian minority from the Krajina and Slavonia regions. By April 1992, the fighting spread to Bosnia and Herzegovina among the region's Muslim, Serb, and Croat factions. By February 1998, Serbia itself was at war when the Kosovo Liberation Army, an Albanian armed group, launched an attack in Serbia's southern region of Kosovo. By March 1999, US-led NATO warplanes launched a bombing campaign over Yugoslavia – the first time in the organization's 50-year history that it attacked a sovereign nation without UN Security Council approval.

The relationship between NATO air strikes and the mass displacement of people from Kosovo remains disputed. Critics of the NATO action argued that the air strikes indirectly caused the humanitarian disaster that followed because they triggered more intensive Serb military activities on the ground and exacerbated violence. NATO officials, in turn, presented the bombing campaign as justified to stop the violence perpetrated against the Kosovo Albanians. NATO also argued that the Serb offensive against the civilians was planned, and that the exodus was a fully organized expulsion, which, of course, strengthened the rationale for air strikes.

During the war(s) in the former Yugoslavia, two of the greatest global refugee tragedies (as per the number of people that had to flee their homes) took place in 1995 and 1999, respectively. The first one was related to the operations that were carried out by the Croatian Army in 1995 when up to 480,000 Serbs were forced out of Croatia. The second one occurred in 1999 when almost all of the Albanian population was forced out of Kosovo, a province of Serbia (UNHCR 1996, 1998, 1999).

There are remarkable parallels between these two events. In each case, a local ethnic minority – according to the 1991 census, just over 12 per cent of Serbs in Croatia and 17.2 per cent of Albanians in Serbia – saw its cultural, civil, and human rights abused by the central government. In each case, members of the minority responded by organizing an armed guerrilla force in their local territories (Krajina and Kosovo, respectively) that acted to achieve secession and independence. And, in each case, the states responded with overwhelming force, cleaning out villages suspected of providing support for the rebels and committing widespread human-rights abuses against civilians – all the while claiming they were merely preventing 'terrorists' from threatening the territorial integrity of their country. In both countries, the human costs were enormous.

Representation of Croats and Serbs in Croatia

In order to examine the portrayal of Croats and Serbs in the *Globe and Mail*, it is first necessary to present, as background, the events that occurred during the war in Croatia.

The War in Croatia

When, on 25 June 1991, Croatia declared independence from the Socialist Federal Republic of Yugoslavia, the goal of the Croatian government was twofold: Croatia wanted not only Western recognition of its independence, but also to solve relations with members of the Serb group in Croatia. Croatia was ethnically mixed with around 12 per cent of Serbs living within its borders.

The problems that occurred in relations between Croats and Croatian Serbs cannot be understood without some reference to the policy of geno-cide against Serbs, Jews, and Roma perpetrated by the Nazi puppet regime of Ante Pavelic's Ustasha during the Second World War. Croatia's Serbs viewed the nationalism that accompanied the new Croatian independence movement with alarm because the Croatian leadership, headed by Franjo Tudjman, restored all the symbols (flag, coat of arms, currency, uniforms, etc.) of the state that had been responsible for the mass murders of Serbs, Jews, Roma, and anti-fascist Croats during the Second World War. Accord-ing to Woodward (1995: 229), President Tudjman also 'imposed a special tax on Serbs from Serbia who had cottages in Croatia (but not on such persons from any other republic)' and the Croatian government 'did little to protect its citizens from terror in mixed communities where Croat nationalists firebombed homes, and harassed or arrested potential Serb leaders'.

The leader of the Serbian Democratic Party in the Krajina, the region of Croatia where the Serbs had a strong majority, announced that, if Croatia seceded from Yugoslavia, the Serbs in Croatia would have a right to decide in a referendum with whom and on whose territory they would live. The day after the Croatian Parliament declared independence of Croatia, its Serb citizens proclaimed their own 'state' and declared Krajina's independence from Croatia (Woodward 1995: 231).

These events led to clashes between Serb rebels and Croatian police (Crnobrnja 1996; Woodward 1995) with the Yugoslav army serving as a buffer between the two warring sides (Crnobrnja 1996). The Croatian war ended in 1995 after Croatian offensives, in just one day, expelled approximately 250,000 Serb citizens from their homeland.

Representation of Participants

The *Globe and Mail* identified the social actors in the Croatian war as follows:

1. **Armed formations**
   - **Croats**: Croatian forces (3×); Croatian militia (2×); Croat soldiers; the republic's militia
   - **Yugoslavs**: Yugoslav army thrust (2×); the army (2×); soldiers and men of the federal army; the armoured thrust; Yugoslav air force; Yugoslav navy; Yugoslav People Army; Yugoslavia army with its

Serbian-dominated officer corps, already purged of elements willing to crack down secessionist republics; Serbian generals; conscripts; pilots and sailors

- **Croatian Serbs**: Serbs; secessionist Serbs; Serb ethnic paramilitary groups; Serbia irregulars

2. **The officials**
   - **Croats**: The country's head of state; the leader of rebel republic; Croatian President Franjo Tudjman (6×); Croatia's leaders; secessionist republic; rebel republic
   - **Yugoslavs**: the Croatian chairman of the federal presidency; the head of Yugoslavia's moribund federal presidency, Stipe Mesic, a Croatian; Prime Minister Ante Markovic, a Croat; Yugoslavia's defence minister General Veljko Kadijevic (2×); Yugoslav leaders; the collective federal presidency; the Yugoslav presidency, now comprising only four pro-Serbian members; Branko Kostic, vice-president of the federal presidency and a Serbian ally; leader of the Yugoslav federal government
   - **Croatian Serbs**: Slavko Dokmanovic, the former Serb mayor of Vukovar

3. **Ordinary people of Croatia**
   - **Croats**: 1,000 people; Croats (3×); many residents of Zagreb [the capital of Croatia]; residents of Osijek
   - **Croatian Serbs**: exhausted and disillusioned Serb refugees; the exodus of Serbs; the Serb refugees; 600,000 Serbs; 40,000 refugees; a Croatian Serb soldier who identified himself only as Neno [he is also a refugee]

What becomes evident in the list of Croat officials is that the only person who is fully titled and nominated is their president: 'Croatian President Franjo Tudjman'. In other words, he is portrayed in terms of his unique identity, which according to van Leeuwen (1996) gives the participant an elite status. All armed formations are *functionalized* in van Leeuwen's (1996) term, that is, described according to the function they perform. They are, thus, seen as a group, not as individuals, and have a non-elite status in the text.

Lexical choices for military formations of the Croats as well as of the Yugoslav army connote legitimate warfare – 'troops', 'forces', 'army', 'conscripts', 'soldiers', 'navy', etc. In contrast, Croatian Serb forces are described as 'irregular', 'paramilitary', and 'secessionist', which places them in the position of the 'out-group', a placement that is reinforced when they are further downgraded to 'Serbs/secessionist Serbs', especially when contrasted with other forces that are referred to as organized forces, for example 'Croatian forces', 'Croatian militia', 'Croatian soldiers', 'Yugoslav army', etc. In addition, the reference to 'Serbia' in the nominal group 'Serbia irregulars' suggests that military personnel of another republic are engaged in the territory of Croatia. The ethnicity of Serbs, members of the Yugoslav army, is foregrounded in order to suggest that the army is biased against the Croats. On the other hand, the ethnicity of Albanian generals who fought as members of Croatian armed formations and that of Slovenian and Croatian Yugoslav army generals who ordered the actions in Croatia were not mentioned at all. This, coupled with the omission of the modifier 'Croatian' with nominal groups referring to Serbs, who were citizens of Croatia, likely suggested to Canadian readers that Serbs were 'invaders' who came from outside of Croatia.

Yugoslav officials are represented by a combination of referential strategies of nomination and explicit ethnicization – '*Croatian* chairman of the federal presidency', '*Stipe Mesiç*', 'Prime Minister Ante Markovic, *a Croat*'. Foregrounding of the ethnicity of Croat participants such as this as well as Serbian participants in the federal presidency – 'four *pro-Serbian* members', 'Branko Kostic . . . *a Serbian ally*' – suggests that the conflict is a result of only different ethnic backgrounds of the participants. In this way, complex political, historical, territorial, and economic causes of the war are reduced or eliminated, and the war is perceived as 'consequences of qualities inherent in the character of the communities involved' (Allen and Seaton 1999: 44).

Processes

Further, differential representation is evident in 44 per cent of cases where Croats are sayers in mental verbal processes. As agents of direct action processes they appear only in four per cent of cases such as:

> *The republic's militia had thwarted* the army's attack.

> *Croatia's offensive to regain Serb-held land forced* Serbs to flee.

> . . . military garrisons *had been besieged by Croatian militia* . . .

This contrasts with the Yugoslav army, which in 55 per cent of the cases is placed in the position of the agent in direct action processes. Also, the army is either the grammatical or logical subject in clauses with transactive predicates, for example:

> *Yugoslav assault pushes* Croats *back.*

> *The offensive had broken* Croatian lines . . . *Gunboats of the Yugoslav navy continued to blockade* Croat ports . . . *The Yugoslav air force attacked* Zagreb . . . *Yugoslav army makes major push* into Croatia.

In trying to stop Croatia's secession and defending the Croatian Serbs, the Yugoslav army, as Crnobrnja (1996) points out, lost impartiality and became involved on the Serb side of the conflict so that this social actor became the 'out-group', and it is not surprising, therefore, that the army's violent actions are foregrounded as we have seen in the examples above. By contrast, negative violent actions of Croat participants are backgrounded, more in line with the 'in-group' role. This is achieved both by passive constructions with deletion of agent and through nominalization. For example,

> Three officials *were reported shot to death* in one town and other *shootings were reported* . . .
>
> . . . a police chief, deputy major and city councilman *were shot dead* in one town . . .
>
> *there are reports of shooting* in other Serb-dominated parts of Croatia . . .
>
> the three deaths bring to 41 the number of peoples *killed* in Serb-Croatian *violence* in the republic . . .

Readers are also not told either who killed whom (Did Croat forces kill Serbs? Did Serb irregulars kill Croats? Is the Yugoslav army shooting at Croats?) or who the source for information is. Readers do not even know the name of the place where the shooting happened. The article that reported 'officials were reported shot to death in one town' was published on 2 July 1992. The day before, in the Croatian town of Osijek, Croat paramilitary formations of Branislav Glavas killed the mayor of Osijek and two other policemen (all Croats) because they maintained good relations with Serbs living there (Tanjug News Agency 1992: 1).

To reinforce this picture of the Serbs, the paper never presents them as 'patients' with Croats acting upon them. Even in the article that reported the expulsion of 250,000 Serbs from the territory of Croatia ('Refugees columns flood Bosnia/Refugee exodus "humanitarian catastrophe" '), the agency of Croats is backgrounded. This is grammatically achieved by removing Croats from the topical subject position.

> . . . Serb refugees *trekked* into northern Bosnia after *fleeing* Croatia's offensive.

Croatian Serb refugees also appeared as agents in the actions that affected innocent Bosnian Croat civilians:

> *Refugee exodus affected* ethnic Croats living in Banja Luka and an unknown number of them *was evicted* from their homes.

Furthermore, Croatian action seems to be justified from the choice of action processes such as 'Croatia had *retaken* its territory', implying that Croatian Serbs were the occupier force; suppressing the fact that this was the land held by Croatian Serbs for more than three centuries was in line with the general portrayal of the participants. Atrocities committed against Croatian Serbs (Taylor 2000: 4) are excluded from the texts.

In this manner, the portrayal of Serb civilians, victims of war in Croatia, is in sharp contrast with the portrayal of Albanian victims.

Representation of Albanians and Serbs in Serbia/Kosovo

Before examining the representation of Kosovo Albanians and their victimizers in terms of naming and actions, it is once again important to understand the background of events in which they were involved.

The War over Kosovo

Kosovo, a province of Serbia, had a population of about two million in 1998, 200,000 of whom were ethnic Serbs, Montenegrins, Roma, and members of other minorities, and 1.8 million (90 per cent) of whom were ethnic Albanians (Crnobrnja 1996). At the same time, Albanians made up 17 per cent of the total population of Serbia.

In 1980, immediately after Tito's death, Albanian demonstrators voiced calls for Kosovo to be made a full republic. Their demonstrations were broken up and the federal government declared that the situation in the province had become a threat to the constitution, integrity, and sovereignty of the country. The government imposed 'special measures' which assigned responsibility for public security to the federal government instead of the government of Serbia. This was followed in 1989 by constitutional changes that limited the autonomy of the province.

Tension in Kosovo rose when the Kosovo Liberation Army (KLA) emerged in 1996 with its declared aim of achieving the Kosovo Albanians' political aspirations for independence through armed struggle (OSCE 1999). As the KLA escalated its armed attacks on Serbian police stations and stepped up assassinations of Serbian politicians and sympathizers among the Albanian population, the Serbian security forces retaliated with very strong anti-insurgency tactics.

In 1998, the UN Security Council called for an end to the fighting, a withdrawal of the Yugoslav army to barracks, and the introduction of Organization for Security and Co-operation in Europe (OSCE) observers into Kosovo as monitors to ensure that both parties kept the peace. Initially, the army and security forces complied, but the KLA did not stop its attacks and the army once again reacted with force. Villages suspected of harbouring KLA activists were burned and their inhabitants dispersed. According to the UNHCR Reports, by October 1998, approximately 2,000 Albanians and Serbs had been killed and some 200,000 people, mainly Albanians, had been displaced within the province.

In February, the US brought both sides to the negotiating table at Rambouillet, France. Under the terms of this agreement, or the 'ultimatum' in Chomsky's (2000: 3) terms, a NATO-led international force was to be given access to operate in all of Yugoslavia, not only in Kosovo. It also included a provision for a referendum to be held in Kosovo after three years to determine the province's future political status. When the Serbs refused to sign, NATO started bombing Yugoslavia on 24 March 1999. (NATO action was not approved by the UN Security Council.) The bombing campaign lasted 78 days. It devastated the Yugoslav economy by destroying bridges, factories, oil refineries, government buildings, the environment, and Yugoslav military equipment. During the air strikes, thousands of refugees fled into Albania and Macedonia from Kosovo. According to the OSCE (1999) Report, an estimated 862,979 Albanians (or 48 per cent of the Albanian population) and 'more than 100,000' Serbs (or 50 per cent of the Serb population) fled Kosovo during the period of bombing from March to June 1999. The number of refugees belonging to other ethnic groups who fled the province during the bombings is not mentioned in the OSCE Report.

Representation of Participants

It is, once again, very informative to see how these events and participants were represented in the *Globe and Mail*. The *Globe and Mail* identified the social actors in the Kosovo war as follows.

1. **Armed formations**
   - **Albanian**: Kosovo Liberation Army guerillas; guerillas; Kosovo Liberation Army fighters; Kosovo separatists; Shaban Mehmeti, a Kosovo Liberation Army fighter; Hashim Thachi, KLA commander
   - **Serbian**: the Serbs (6×); Serbians; police (3×); Serbian nationalists; angry Serb mobs; the gang (2×); gang of police; police officers; paramilitary forces (3×); security forces and their dogs; Milosevic's police (2×); soldiers; the Yugoslav army; military
2. **Albanian and Serb officials**
   - **Albanian**: No terms referring to Albanian officials were found in the analysed sample.
   - **Serbian**: Yugoslav officials; the Serbs leadership; Serbian leaders; Mr Milosevic and his government; Serbian president Slobodan Milosevic (2×); Mr Milosevic, 50, a nationalist and former Communist; the pro-Milosevic politicians, hard-line nationalists all; Mirjana Markovic, Milosevic's wife, nicknamed Red Witch; Vojislav Seselj, leader of the Radical party and their brutal militia; Milan Panic, the Serb-born US businessman; Mr Draskovic, opposition leader; Patriarch Pavle of the Serbian Orthodox Church; Bogoljub Karic, ex-Milosevic ally/ Serbia's richest tycoon/and his four siblings/accordion-player billionaire and now Serbian presidential candidate-in-waiting/ Milosevic's former comrade; Crown prince Alexander Karadjordjevic; Goran Svilanovic, head of the Civic Alliance of Serbia; Ljubomir Madzar, an economist at Belgrade University; Ognjen Pribicevic, a research fellow at Belgrade University; Radomir Diklic, director of the independent BETA news agency; Milan Protic, director of the Centre for Serbian studies
3. **Ordinary Albanians and Serbs**
   - **Albanians**: Ethnic Albanian refugees; bewildered refugees; Professor from Pristina; 22-year-old Leonore Lutolli; a well-dressed 26-year-old man; a young woman Irijana Zhubi, 31, with two sons; 80-year-old M. Boni; sound technician Mr Doda; Dren Caka, who is 10 years old; his mother and two-year-old sister; 105-year-old man; one elderly man; 14-year-old niece; Milan Bellanica; Mr Popoj; a tearful Hajrije Maksutaj, the 26-year-old mother of an eight-month-old boy; her husband; a two-year-old child in his mother's hand; senior cleric [in

tekke]; 60–100 people; 4 brothers; 13 members of family; more than a million ethnic Albanians; Fatmira Berisha, a slim woman, the 19-year-old student and her mother; Dr Flori Bakalli; refugee Emun Mujaremi; Mr Krasniqui; local/ethnic Albanians (5×); refugees from Kosovo; a journalist at the Pristina daily Bujku; ethnic Albanian majority (2×); 50,000 ethnic Albanians; a million ethnic Albanians; 100,000 refugees; Ahmed Beka, a locksmith; one old woman; the victims; surviving villagers; 500 bodies; 4,256 bodies; 11,334 victims; shattered refugees; refugee women and infants; slaughtered sons; her husband Muhamet, a 41-year-old jeweler; two sons, Granit, 5, and Gramen, 3; Kosovo Albanians (5×); Albanians (7×)

- **Serbs**: Mitrovica's Serbs; Serbs

As the examples above demonstrate, the overwhelming focus of reporters was on Albanian civilian victims of the war. There are only six terms that refer to Albanian armed formations and none refers to Kosovo Albanian officials. What is immediately evident is a high level of personalization of social actors – participants are portrayed in terms of their unique identity, which, as noted earlier, gives them an elite person status. Civilians are further classified by age ('14-year-old', 'elderly', 'infants'), gender ('women', 'men', 'boy'), and kinship relations ('mother', 'children', 'sons', 'husband', 'family'). Nomination combined with classifications according to kinship relations, gender, and age serve to individualize Kosovo Albanians and, thus, make it easier for readers to identify with them, i.e. they are not portrayed as a group but as persons with names, families, jobs – in a word, people like us.

Processes

The helplessness of the mothers with children and elderly people is highlighted in the roles they play (as noted above) and the processes in which they are involved. Albanians are patients in more than 90 per cent of transactive clauses while Serbs are agents of negative violent action. For instance,

> *The refugees were forced* out of their homes by Serbian police.

> . . . *her* [Irijana Zhubi's] *14-year-old niece was burned to death* . . .

> *13 members of Kosovo Albanian family were shot to death* . . .

> '[. . .] they [Serbian police] *killed my husband and the brother of my husband*'

In addition to the patient role, Albanians are subjects of particular kinds of actions such as fleeing, hiding, taking shelter, and dying in 25 per cent of non-transactive clauses.

Representation of the Serbs, on the other hand, had all the basic 'portrayal of the enemy' features (Kress and Hodge 1993; van Dijk 1998). Lexical choices describing their actions and participant roles have only negative connotations such as 'gangs', 'captors', 'security police units with their dogs', and 'paramilitary forces'. The Serb leader Slobodan Milosevic is described as 'imperial', 'aloof', 'authoritarian', 'a shrewd dictator', 'communist', and 'a hard-line nationalist'. The Serbian state is portrayed as the last bastion of Communism in Europe. For example,

> The *Communist nomenclature* rules the country.
>
> The *Communist autocracy* supports Milosevic.
>
> The *Communist style of governing* has not disappeared.
>
> Serbia has never renounced its *50 years of socialism.*
>
> The Serbian *economy* is still *state-controlled.*

The picture of the 'Serb enemy' is completed by descriptions of action processes in which the Serbs, in 83 per cent of transactive clauses, are direct agents of negative, violent actions. Grammatically, they are placed in subject position and are agents who '*kill*', '*lined up* men', '*cut off* hands', '*separated* men and women', '*shell*', '*engage in systemic massacres and summary executions*', as well as in '*ethnic cleansing*'.

The only time the Serbs are placed in the position of affected participants, that is, 12 per cent of transactive clauses where something is done to them, the NATO forces are portrayed as the agents of these actions.

Conclusion

Although this study is limited in terms of its sample size, it nevertheless allows for some generalizations to be made regarding the questions I initially posed:

- What are the differences among the portrayals of the different ethnic groups identified above (comparing, for instance, the armed forces in Croatia and the armed forces in Serbia)?
- Is there overt or covert prejudice in relation to different groups by the media, and if so, how is it produced and reproduced linguistically?

The analysis revealed that there was a difference in the portrayal of armed formations. The Yugoslav army, Croatian forces, and Kosovo Albanian forces were presented as legitimate ('soldiers', 'army', 'fighters'). On the other hand, Croatian Serb forces and Serb forces in Serbia were portrayed as acting in lawless ways and were, thus, 'illegitimate'. Such a portrayal was achieved through foregrounding of Serbs as the agents of violent actions and through the lexical choices used for the description of Serbian armed formations. While Croatian forces were described as fighting for the 'liberation' of the 'fatherland' against 'aggressors', the lawless armies were characterized as the attackers of an unarmed population. Moreover, the nature of the violent actions in which they were engaged was such ('raping', 'cutting off parts of bodies', 'ethnic cleansing', and 'murdering in concentration camps') that readers' emotions could not help but be outraged. In each action, Serbs were portrayed not as an army but as criminals who perpetuate unspeakable brutal acts; this, combined with the portrayal of the innocent and weak Albanian victims ('bewildered refugees', 'a tearful ... 26-year-old mother of an eight-month-old boy', '105-year-old man', 'women', 'infants'), adds to the sense of anger and disgust of readers towards the Serbs. There is little doubt that an average reader of the newspaper would feel sympathetic about the destiny of Kosovo Albanians, who are 'fleeing', 'dying', 'hiding', and 'had been tortured' by 'security police units with their dogs'. Thus, the actions of the Serb forces excluded them from the 'discourse of Western morality' (Chouliaraki 1999). This was all the more frightening to readers because, at the same time, the Yugoslav army and Serb forces were described as very powerful; as a result, none of the armed Balkan formation or the UN peacekeeping forces could confront them. The only actor capable of dealing with such a military power was NATO, which provided the necessary rationale for its actions in the Balkans as being natural, lawful, necessary, and guided by moral principles. The newspaper did not explore alternative possibilities for actions. Instead, it was taken for granted that peace could be achieved only by war. According to Bissett (2001), 'herein lies a new danger, because the protection of human rights may be the cloak for a new type of imperialist military intervention worldwide'.

A similar dichotomy was evident in the portrayal of victims of the war. Serbs from Croatia and Kosovo were represented in the analysed sample as groups consisting only of armed males without women, old people, and children. If mentioned at all, the victims – members of these groups – were portrayed as faceless groups of people, aggregated and assimilated without names, gender or age. Readers, thus, saw them as a group, not as individuals with unique characteristics. The journalists never mentioned that some of them were killed or tortured. Thus, there is no possibility for readers to feel the same compassion for this group of victims, as was the case previously, in the portrayal of Kosovo Albanians.

The exodus of Croatian Serbs was one of the largest flights of refugees during all the wars in the former Yugoslavia. Also, Croatian Serbs lived in so-called protected UN areas, which made their situation very similar to those of Kosovo Albanians. Despite these similarities in their status and in the number of killed and people forcibly removed from their homes, reporters chose to portray only Kosovo Albanians as victims, and when they did so, with sympathy.

Results of the analysis suggest that the *Globe and Mail* discursively reproduced the ideological framework that echoed ethnic inequality among various groups from the Balkans. While Serb atrocities were widely condemned, Serb suffering was minimized or, worse yet, overlooked. In this simplified story about the struggle between good and evil, NATO played the role of rescuer of innocent victims. Galtung (Galtung and Jacobsen 2000: 10) argues that seeing reality only as black-and-white reflects, in general, the Western approach to covering international affairs. He also argues that such a dichotomy reinforces the mythology of war-making because the 'cosmic battle between good and evil serves to justify the revenge for an imagined wrong, tyrannical centralization of power, and the belief that the West stands as God's trustee of civilization'.

Through critical analysis of one segment of the media, it has been possible to make the underlying rationale for these different ideologies transparent. As Fairclough and Chouliaraki (1999: 3) point out, we live in times of changes, which cause 'considerable disruptions and suffering for societies, communities and individuals' and CDA seeks to open the dialogue across the public sphere, with the aim to 'bring into democratic control aspects of social use of language and to advocate a critical awareness of language as a fundamental element in contemporary social lives'.

What I have presented here as an academic discussion of media discourse had, in fact, consequences on the lives of people in the Balkans. Some of them received no humanitarian aid, some of them were bombed, some of them were not granted visas in different developed countries, and some of them are still waiting to return to their homes. Uncovering inequality in discourse has implications not only for media coverage, but also can lead to the changes in non-discursive practices, which affect the lives of those represented.

References

Allen, T. and Seaton, J. (eds) (1999) *The Media of Conflict.* London and New York: Zed Books.

Bissett, J. (2001) 'NATO's Balkan Blunder' at: http://www.deltax.net/bissett.htm (consulted October 2001).

Chomsky, N. (2000) 'In Retrospect: A Review of NATO's War over Kosovo' at: http://www.zmag.org/Zmag/articles/chomskyapril2000.htm (consulted June 2001).

Chouliaraki, L. (1999) 'Media Discourse and National Identity: Death and Myth in a News Broadcast', in *Challenges in a Changing World – Issues in Critical Discourse Analysis,* ed. by R. Wodak and C. Ludwig. Vienna: Passagen Verlag, 37–62.

Crnobrnja, M. (1996) *The Yugoslav Drama* (2nd edn). Montreal and Kingston: McGill-Queen's University Press.

Fairclough, N. and Chouliaraki, L. (1999) *Discourse in Late Modernity: Rethinking Critical Discourse Analysis.* Edinburgh: Edinburgh University Press.

Galtung, J. and Jacobsen, G. C. (2000), with contributions by Brand-Jacobsen, F. K. and Tschudi, F., *Searching for Peace: The Road to Transcend.* London: Pluto Press in association with Transcend.

Geis, M. (1987) *The Language of Politics.* New York: Springer-Verlag.

Kress, G. and Hodge, R. (eds) (1993) *Language as Ideology.* London: Routledge.

OSCE (Organization for Security and Co-operation in Europe) (1999) 'Kosovo/Kosova: As Seen, As Told' at: http://www.osce.org/kosovo/reports/hr/part1/index.htm (consulted May 2000).

Parenti, M. (1999) 'The Rational Destruction of Yugoslavia' at: http://www.michaelparenti.org/yugoslavia.html (consulted September 2000).

Parenti, M. (1993) *Inventing Reality: The Politics of News Media.* New York: St Martin's Press.

Tanjug News Agency (1992) at: www.tanjug.co.yu (consulted March 1999).

Taylor, S. (2000) *INAT: Images of Serbia and the Kosovo Conflict.* Ottawa: Esprit de Corps Books.

UNHCR (United Nations High Commission for Refugees) (1999) Reports at: http://www.unhcr.ch (consulted May 2001).

UNHCR (United Nations High Commission for Refugees) (1998) Reports at: http://www.unhcr.ch (consulted May 2001).

UNHCR (United Nations High Commission for Refugees) (1996) Reports at: http://www.unhcr.ch (consulted May 2001).

van Dijk, A. T. (1998) 'Opinions and Ideologies in the Press', in *Approaches to Media Discourse,* ed. by A. Bell and P. Garrett. Oxford: Blackwell Publishers, 21–63.

van Leeuwen, T. (1996) 'Representation of Social Actors in English Language', in *Texts and Practice Readings in Critical Discourse Analysis,* ed. by R. C. Caldas-Coulthard and M. Coulthard. London: Routledge, 32–69.

Wodak, R. (2000) 'Discourse on Unemployment in the EU: The Conflict and Consensus between Diverging Ideologies', plenary lecture: *Language and Ideology,* May, Vienna: University of Vienna.

Wodak, R. (1996) *Disorders of Discourse.* London and New York: Longman.

Wodak, R., de Gilia, R., Reisigl, M., and Liebhart, K. (eds) (1999) *The Discursive Construction of National Identity.* Edinburgh: Edinburgh University Press.

Woodward, S. (1995) *Balkan Tragedy: Chaos and Dissolution After the Cold War.* Washington, DC: The Brookings Institute.

Young, L. (2000) 'Differential Representation of Minorities in the Canadian Print Media', paper delivered at the 27th International Systemic Functional Linguistics Conference, 10 July, Melbourne, Australia.

Applied Section: Institutional Identity

9   Authority and Its Role in the Pedagogic Relationship of Schooling

Frances Christie

The twentieth century was notable for many matters, among them the spread of mass education and the growth in a great deal of educational theory. Major themes that emerged in much educational theory were given a variety of names: 'progressivism', 'constructivism', 'inquiry learning', to name some. All such trends in educational theory tended to identify and foreground the learner, at the expense of a concern for the nature of the knowledge the student should learn. Among the many problems created by such models of the learner, the curriculum and of knowledge was a tendency to confuse the authority of the teacher, leaving a great deal of uncertainty about its significance in educational process. Using a model of classroom discourse that draws on systemic functional (SF) theory and Bernstein's theory of pedagogic discourse, this paper argues the need for a reinstatement of knowledge and a reassessment of the nature of teacher authority in apprenticing students in their learning.

Introduction

What constitutes the nature of authority in the pedagogic relationship of schooling? How is it recognized, and what is its significance in an educational enterprise? How is it related to the various models of curriculum and of knowledge that apply in different classrooms? Strangely, given the considerable volumes of educational theory and research that have appeared in the English-speaking world for many years now, such questions are very rarely addressed directly. Sometimes, it is true, one finds discussion of appropriate 'teacher roles' expressed, for example, in terms of 'facilitation of students' learning'. Elsewhere, as in much of the literature on classroom discourse analysis, teachers are enjoined, in assuming their roles, to avoid dominating classroom talk and, instead, to create opportunities for students to pursue their own talk and learning. In the latter cases, in fact, a degree of confusion can emerge about the nature of any authority the teacher may exercise, for it would seem that the teacher is often held to be most successful when being generally silent and even invisible. Yet, important questions to do with the authority the teacher might employ in guiding students' learning remain largely unexplored, their significance left out of much educational theorizing.

How authority is conceived is, of course, intimately part of the manner in which knowledge and the curriculum are conceived, and any attempt to address the former will necessarily draw us into some consideration of the other two, while reflection on all three will inevitably have consequences for the models of the learner adopted. Over the last century or so, powerful ideologies have been at work in forging particular notions of knowledge, the learner, and the curriculum whose effect, as I shall argue below, has been to compromise both the nature of knowledge and the nature of the authority it is suggested that teachers should exercise in its pursuit.

In this paper, I shall argue the need to develop critical perspectives on a great deal of educational theory and research of the last half century or more, the better to articulate useful models of knowledge and the curriculum and, hence, of the nature of the authority exercised by the teacher in the pedagogic relationship of schooling. In developing the discussion, I shall draw on a model of classroom discourse analysis (see Christie 2002b for a longer discussion) which uses systemic functional (SF) linguistic theory (e.g. Halliday 1994; Halliday and Matthiessen 1999; Martin 1992) and aspects of Bernstein's discussion (1990, 2000) of pedagogic discourse. Using some classroom texts, I shall suggest that a close study of classroom discourse can provide a useful basis on which to test both the processes of knowledge construction and the nature of the teacher-student relationship in those processes. On the basis of the discussion, I shall argue the values of a respect for the importance and significance of authority in schooling and for the values of knowledge which teacher authority helps to construct. Among other matters, I shall, like Bernstein, argue that a form of 'moral regulation' applies in the functioning of a pedagogic discourse in schooling, and I shall also suggest that its successful operation requires the presence of a teacher who is *in authority*. I am not the first person, by the way, to draw attention to the fact that while the English language has the one noun 'authority', it has two associated adjectives – 'authoritative' and 'authoritarian'. I hope it requires no explanation that my interest is in authority in the authoritative, rather than the authoritarian, sense.

In order to develop the discussion, I shall need initially to consider some recent and contemporary themes in educational theory and curriculum research and design which have accounted for the models of pedagogy, knowledge, and teacher authority which I wish to critique. I shall then go on to consider Bernstein's discussion of pedagogic discourse before turning to some discussion of classroom texts.

Some Significant Movements in Educational Theory of the Twentieth Century

While theorizing about education is in many senses quite old, the fact remains that it was in the twentieth century that it gained particular significance, for its growth matched both the spread of mass education in the Western world and the associated expansion of teacher education. By the end of the century, all developed countries had witnessed a significant growth in the resources devoted to education and to the preparation of teachers, and the bodies of theory about education were considerable. It is no part of my brief to offer a comprehensive account of the educational theory that emerged, for space would not permit it. I shall, instead, take up some selected themes in educational theory which have had an impact on notions of the nature of knowledge, the design of curricula, and notions of the authority of the teacher and professional preparation of teachers. I should note, as I proceed with this discussion, that while I have said the developments in educational theory to be critiqued have been extensively found in the Western world, their manifestations have, no doubt, differed from country to country. Hence, the brief review of relevant themes in the literature will draw upon work in various parts of the English-speaking world. However, subsequent instances of classroom activities considered in later sections will necessarily reflect experience in Australian classrooms.

One of the most pervasive of the themes to which I allude in educational theory has, over the years, gone by a variety of names: an interest in 'inquiry learning' or 'learner empowerment' and, sometimes, 'pupil-centredness' or 'learner-centredness'; a concern for 'process approaches' to teaching and learning, sometimes also referred to as 'activity-based' or 'inquiry learning'; an interest in 'constructivist approaches' to teaching and learning; and, relatedly in recent years, a concern for 'Problem Based Learning' (known as PBL for short), an interest in developing and building on 'personal experience' in learning and expression of 'personal voice' as essential characteristics of the desired learner. While theorists differ considerably in what they say, all, I would suggest, have this much in common: a preoccupation with foregrounding the role of the learner as actively engaged in the pursuit of information; an associated tendency to see the nature of knowledge as something constructed in activity and a related tendency to dismiss the claims of knowledge as ordered and constructed in the light of extensive scholarship, often over years; and, correspondingly, a tendency to see the teacher's role in terms of 'facilitation' of the process of learning in which students engage as they become, ideally at least, autonomous and independent learners possessed of their 'own' understandings.

Such theories, sometimes referred to loosely as 'progressivist', derive in part from a movement in educational thinking in Europe and North America dating from the last years of the nineteenth century and into the first half of the twentieth. Various writers contributed to the movement, including the physician Maria Montessori and the psychologist William James as well as educators such as Francis Wayland Parker and, later, John Dewey whose work (1902, 1916) was particularly influential. Progressive education is itself rather difficult to define because its proponents were many and their interpretations varied. (A useful review of the history of progressive education is offered by Röhrs and Lenhart 1995.) However, at least one authority (Röhrs 1995: 11–12) has stated that, among its 'basic criteria' were a commitment to 'pupil-centredness' and a view of the teacher-educator as one who 'relinquishes the role of instructor and becomes instead an initiator, observer and adviser of the activities of the pupils'. Progressivism, while always contested by some, was nonetheless influential in educational theorizing until the Second World War at least. In the post-war period, especially in the 1960s and 1970s, progressive ideas remained, but they were often expressed in other kinds of discourses.

Thus, 'constructivism', a term taken from Piaget originally, emerged as a theme in educational theory from the 1950s, having greatest influence in discussions of mathematics and science education although its influence was felt in other areas. Just as was true of the progressivist movement, con-structivism has claimed many theorists, and its proponents differ over many matters although the commitment to the notion of the constructedness of knowledge is central, as is the corresponding view of the learner as one who actively constructs what he or she knows. (See Larochelle *et al.* 1998 for detailed discussions of the theory, and Wilson 1996 for various accounts of case studies using constructivism.) The most radical form of constructivism, according to von Glasersfeld, who invented the term 'radical constructiv-ism', would state that 'knowledge cannot be transmitted, but must instead be constructed by each student individually'. Such a view, among other matters, would give a rather diminished significance to the function of the teacher. Meanings, according to von Glasersfeld, whether expressed in lan-guage or any other signing system, are not to be 'tacitly assumed to be the same' for different users. On the contrary, each person constructs meanings individually on the basis of 'subjective experience'. Thus, for von Glasersfeld, language is not to be thought of as something used for taking ideas and wrapping them in 'little packages' to be passed on to the 'receiver'. Instead, since learners must always construct their own knowledge, says von Glasersfeld (1998: 26–7), teachers should speak 'in such a way as to "orient" students' efforts at construction', but that is apparently all they can do.

The particular conception of language and of the nature of experience involved here (while it would attract linguists in formalist traditions) is remarkable nonetheless, denying as it does so much scholarly work of the twentieth century on language and learning that would affirm the nature of language as a semiotic system, fundamentally involved in the construction and negotiation of experience, ideas, and identity (e.g. Halliday 1975; Painter 1999; Halliday and Matthiessen 1999; Wells 1999). Latter-day dis-cussions of constructivism, incidentally, have often taken a less 'radical' view of learning and of knowledge than von Glasersfeld, and, somewhat surprisingly given its historical antecedents, the work of Vygotsky has been invoked (e.g. Baker and Piburn 1997: 101–19) to justify those aspects of constructivism that (for some constructivists, at least) stress the socio-cultural and collective nature of knowledge-building. This seems, however, to rest on a significant misreading of Vygotsky, as Bernstein (2000: 62) has suggested, and in many ways his ideas sit very uneasily in a constructivist model, not least because of his commitment to the mentoring role of the adult/teacher.

Turning to related movements in educational theory since the 1960s and 1970s, one can also identify 'process models of the curriculum' and 'process models' of learning. According to Stenhouse (1975: 91), for example, who provided one influential account of a process model, teachers should focus on 'discovery or inquiry methods rather than . . . instruction'. The official report on *Children and their Primary Schools* (1967) in England, known as 'The Plowden Report' after its chair, provided what became an influential account of the primary school curriculum. The collective effect of its recommendations was to endorse a model of schooling in 'process' terms: where the 'processes' of learning were seen as more significant than the 'products' or the outcomes; where the child was to be understood as 'the agent in his own learning' (The Plowden Report 1967: 194); and where the role of the teacher appeared to be that of a facilitator of the child's learning. Although the Plowden Report reported on primary schooling, its thinking, no doubt supported by advice from many other associated sources, was in time (in Australia, at least) to extend up into the years of the junior secondary school, thereby having consequences for the ways the curricula of most school subjects were conceived.

Nowhere was the influence of process more apparent than in the case of the subject English although moves in that area of the curriculum had their origins in developments apart from Plowden and had to do with interests in the nature of language and its role in personal development. After the appearance of Dixon's *Growth through English* (1967), English was defined increasingly in 'process terms'. For Dixon, the role of the English programme, as the title of his book suggested, was to promote the growth of the child in learning and using language while the function of the teacher was that of 'trusted adult' facilitating such growth. The child should grow in self-expressive ways, developing what has often been termed 'personal voice' in learning. In such a model of the English programme, individual learning is everything while considerations of what might be the 'content' of the English programme take a much diminished significance. Knowledge becomes a rather relativistic phenomenon, and this is, in fact, a more general trend in much educational theory, well beyond the English curriculum, and certainly clearly argued in constructivist models of knowledge. (See Muller 2000 for a useful critique of constructivism.)

While there is much in the literature about the concern for learning in activity and, indeed, about an acknowledgement that knowledge is socially constructed that one can endorse, the progressivist/constructivist position is nonetheless unacceptable, as it stands, for at least two related reasons: the first of which relates to the notion of the learner that is involved; and the second to the notion of knowledge. I would suggest that the particular model of curriculum proposed involves a very idealized notion of the unique individual, making and shaping his or her 'own' world through private and independent ways. Such a model shows no respect for, or understanding of, the nature of the social processes in which individuals forge and shape their identity and in which they also learn. Furthermore, while an interest in knowledge is claimed, there is in practice often very little respect shown for the manner in which the different areas of knowledge are constructed and ordered, their bases built up, and their various methods of identifying and addressing questions established. Finally, and given these problems, it is notable that, in the progressivist/constructivist position critiqued here, there is insufficient respect for the kind of authority a teacher will need in order to apprentice students into an understanding of such areas of knowledge.

Examining authority in a different sense from that intended here – to do with the language of administration and bureaucracy – Iedema (1997: 73) has written that administrative and bureaucratic practices 'constrain' but also 'enable'. I shall propose that the pedagogic relationship in the classroom should be seen as both constraining and enabling. I want to turn to some examination of how teacher authority both constrains and enables. I shall begin with a brief discussion of Bernstein's observations about a pedagogic discourse, and I will use these to turn to some classroom texts.

Pedagogic Discourse

According to Bernstein (1990: 183), a pedagogic discourse 'is a principle for appropriating other discourses and bringing them into a special relation with each other for the purposes of their selective transmission and acquisition'. The pedagogic relationship is not unique to education. On the contrary, pedagogic discourses and their relations are very widespread in contemporary societies, and teachers are only some of the agents of symbolic control familiarly found. A few of the other possible agents Bernstein identifies include psychiatrists, social workers, and even government officials. Varied though their relations are with their 'clients', all have a role in using specialist discursive codes which they dominate and manipulate, shaping habits of thinking and of reasoning as well as shaping forms of consciousness and their distribution in a society (Bernstein 1990: 134–47).

Two matters are of particular interest for the purposes of this discussion: the first to do with the claim that a discourse is taken from its original source and relocated; and the other to do with the claim that habits of thinking and forms of consciousness are at issue in the pedagogic relationship. The latter is to be understood as critical to the 'moral regulation' said to be a feature of a pedagogic discourse. About that, Bernstein (1990: 184) wrote,

> It is of course obvious that all pedagogic discourse creates a moral regulation of the social relations of transmission/acquisition, that is, rules of order, relation, and identity, and that such a moral order is prior to, and a condition for, the transmission of competences.

With respect to the 'relocation' of discourses, Bernstein (1990: 184–5) illustrated the point by giving the instance of physics which, he said, is taken from some primary context(s) in which it is generated (universities, for the most part) and 'relocated' for its teaching and learning. In the process, the physics is transformed, and 'the rules of relation, selection, sequencing, and pacing' that are involved in transmitting the knowledge derive, not from the logic of physics, but from the logic of the pedagogic discourse itself. The pedagogic discourse involves two discourses – regulative and instructional – where in Bernstein's terms, the former 'embeds' the latter. Adapting Bernstein's terms, I propose that there are two registers – a first order or regulative register, and a second order or instructional register. The former, in my terms, 'projects' the latter, where the metaphor of projection is taken from Halliday's (1994) description of clauses that project.[1] In the operation of a pedagogic discourse, it is the first order or regulative register that is of primary importance because it is responsible for the sequencing and pacing of activity as well as the evaluation of what is taught and learned. But remembering the principle of 'appropriation' to which Bernstein alluded, the theory also argues that the regulative discourse – or register – appropriates or 'speaks through' the instructional register.

The 'regulation' that applies in working through the pedagogic discourse has two dimensions, both to do with organization and shaping of behaviour: (a) establishing what constitutes acceptable behaviour for the work at hand; and (b) establishing those principles to be adopted for addressing questions and organizing information that constitute the particular abilities or skills associated with the instructional field. Both come into play in different ways in classroom texts for their manifestations differ, depending partly on the age of the students, partly on the instructional field being taught, and partly on the ideology of schooling that applies. Just as the two registers actually constitute the one pedagogic discourse, so too are the two dimensions of behavioural regulation merely manifestations of the one thing: the apprenticeship of the students into various pedagogic subject positions.

Thus, to put the point in less abstract terms, classroom discourse serves to 'regulate' student behaviours in some ways, and it does this by selection and appropriation of some instructional field through which the regulation is effected. Hence, in an early childhood literacy classroom, for example, the object, as part of the regulative register, may be to regulate behaviour by teaching and developing capacities in writing. An instructional field needs to be selected as well, however, for it will be through engagement with this that the eventual piece of writing will be produced. As the classroom activity unfolds, the voice of the regulative register becomes silent although it remains tacitly expressed in the discourse, shaping the realization of the instructional field in the written text that emerges.

In Bernstein's terms, it is the teacher who is the agent of symbolic control. In exercising that agency, I shall suggest, the teacher is the authority who mediates the processes by which the regulative register works to institute the pacing, sequencing, and eventual evaluation of activity, and that makes possible the mastery of the skills and knowledge associated with the instructional field.

Whatever the manifestations of the two registers, these both help shape, and are shaped by, the spatial and temporal conditions that apply in the classroom which the teacher has a significant role in determining. Teachers define tasks both in terms of the times devoted to them and in terms of the spaces occupied while doing them. Physical dispositions of pedagogic subjects are, in many ways, as important as their mental dispositions in establishing the bases of pedagogic relationships.

How are these things realized in classroom texts? I want to illustrate some of the issues here by reference to, and in extracts from, two classroom texts. Both are drawn from much longer instances of classroom texts whose nature I have elsewhere discussed in terms of curriculum genres and/or macro-genres (Christie 2002b). No attempt will be made to justify the claim that these are drawn from curriculum macro-genres. Furthermore, I shall not try to explore all that happens in each text. Instead, because my focus is on the pedagogic discourse and the particular ways in which authority is realized in it, I shall use selections only from the two classroom texts to illustrate what I want to say.

An Instance of Early Childhood Literacy Teaching and Learning

I have said, following Bernstein's observations, that teachers define both spatial and temporal dimensions of classroom activity, and I have suggested that this is itself an aspect of the regulative activity that is intended to predispose students to engage in learning. It is also, therefore, an aspect of the manner in which teacher authority works both to constrain and to enable behaviours. Thus, for example, most teachers of students at any age tend to invoke references to time, building connectedness to earlier activities or perhaps defining the periods of time to be devoted to tasks. Early childhood teachers, in particular, appear to devote some effort to establishing the physical dispositions to be taken up by students preparatory to going on to teaching and learning. Once these matters are established, references to them tend to disappear from the text. However, their tacit operation as part of the overall functioning of the regulative register remains, and this is apparent in the fact that the children will, over time, take up the appropriate dispositions without being asked to do so.[2]

The example of early childhood literacy learning I shall use here is taken from Gray (1999) involving a teacher working with young Australian Aboriginal children. The class was involved with a unit of work that explored the life-cycle of chickens. Over a few weeks of activity, the children watched chickens hatch in an incubator in the classroom while the teacher read several stories about hens and chickens. The students also had read, and reread, to them a factual book, *Egg to Chick*, which traced the stages of chicken development in the egg in some detail. At one point, they even cooked and ate eggs in the classroom. At various points through the unit of work, they also engaged in joint-writing activities with the teacher. The instructional register, then, concerned hens and chickens, while the regulative register concerned development of reading and writing skills as part of the ongoing curriculum goal for teaching literacy. The skills in reading and writing, it should perhaps be noted, relied very heavily on the role of the teacher and the joint activities she generated. The children were themselves not yet independent readers or writers.

The text extract used here occurred some days into the unit of work, and having taken up her position in front of the children holding the book *Egg to Chick*, the teacher (T) commenced the activity. (It should be noted that a row of three dots indicates a slight pause in the talk.)

T:	Right. Now we'll have a look at our . . . Naomi, would you like to come over here please. (addressed to Naomi who had been moving a chair to sit on) We don't need another chair thank you. Pop the chair down. That's right. Come and sit over here.
Naomi:	Look. Jenny's on a chair, Mrs Price.
T:	Yeah, Jenny can sit on the floor too.
David:	Jenny you gotta sit on the floor too.
T:	Come and sit on the floor too please Jenny. That's right.

Having arranged the children in a group around her (a common practice in early childhood education), the teacher then went on.

T:	OK, so day nineteen. Now let's have a look at our little science book (holds it up) and find out where we're up to. Now that was on Friday (shows a page with 'day 16' written on it) because that was day sixteen. This one (points to the number '16'). Now we've got seventeen, eighteen (turns the pages). What's the next day?
Naomi:	Nineteen.
T:	Day nineteen, and that's today isn't it? And have a look at our little chick now.
Naomi:	It's getting bigger.
T:	It's getting really big and (overlap)
Naomi:	with long feathers
T:	With long feathers. Good girl!

Initially, the regulative register was foregrounded in several ways. Note, for example, in terms of the experiential metafunction, the process types that realized aspects of desired behaviour such as

Come (material) and *sit* (material) over here.
Jenny *can sit* on the floor too.

and, interpersonally, the use of one interpersonal metaphor to soften a command:

would you like to come over here (meaning congruently: 'you must come'),

as well as the more overt and congruent expressions of command in imperative mood choices:

Pop the chair down.
Come and sit on the floor.

Teacher direction towards the adoption of appropriate physical dispositions was a necessary part of preparing the children for entry to the instructional field. Desired dispositions being generally established, teacher talk again realized an aspect of the regulative register, this time moving more specifically to the task in hand: 'Now let's have a look at our little science book'. Here, the inclusive imperative ('let's') and the behavioural process ('have a look at') were involved in building collective behaviour. It was within the participant role of range that an aspect of the instructional field was realized, albeit fairly generally, establishing its status as 'scientific': 'our little *science book*'. This points to a general tendency when the regulative register is foregounded: while the latter is realized typically in transitivity process and associated participant (be that actor, behaver or perhaps senser), the instructional field will be realized either in a second participant as here (range, goal or phenomenon, for example) or in a circumstance. A subsequent foregrounding of the instructional register will be realized more comprehensively in the grammar of the clauses. One further matter I should mention before moving on from this extract is the significance of the use of the first person plural in '*our* little science book' and, by implication, in the inclusive imperative 'let's'. Teachers make very selective uses of the range of the personal pronouns, and the first person plural will typically occur, as here, when the aim is to build solidarity in a shared endeavour.

The instructional field rapidly found more overt expression in the talk as children and teacher turned the pages of the book and identified the days ('sixteen', 'seventeen', 'nineteen') of development of the chicken while still in the egg. From then on, aided by display and use of the textbook, the discourse realized the instructional field, a good deal of it expressed by children, as in the instance of a clause involving an attributive process produced by Naomi: 'It's getting bigger with long feathers.'

A few seconds later, the teacher used a verbal process ('can tell') to realize an aspect of the children's behaviour, participant choices ('you' and 'me') to realize class members, and an interrogative mood choice to invoke the regulative register in order to guide talk about the instructional field (where the latter was realized in the circumstance of matter: 'about the yolk').

T: And what can you tell me . . . what can you tell me about the yolk?

And the talk proceeded, once again foregrounding the instructional field,

Naomi:	It's all gone.
David:	It's gone.
Naomi:	It's all gone.
David:	And he's in a water sac.
T:	And he's in a water sac.
Naomi:	If he tried to peck that . . . that egg the water would burst like a balloon.
T:	That's right. The water bursts, right . . . The water bursts like a balloon.
Naomi:	I know what he's getting when he's hatched.
T:	What?
Naomi:	He's getting a little tooth.
T:	Yes, he's getting a little egg tooth. Good girl.
David:	Here . . . (points to picture) Here's a little egg tooth.
Jenny:	And that helps him
T:	That helps him to . . . That's right. That helps him to peck out of the . . .
Naomi:	Egg. (overlap)
David:	Shell.
Jenny:	Egg.
T:	Yes. Good girl.

For the last few seconds, the discourse plainly realized the instructional field, as already stated, and this was present either in attributive processes ('he's in a water sac') or in material processes ('it's – the yolk – gone') and in the complete absence, for the most part, of any matters realizing the regulative register. But what is also notable is the very dialogic nature of the field construction and the confidence with which the children contributed items of field knowledge which the teacher accepted ('I know what he's getting when he's hatched'; 'He's getting a little tooth'; and 'that helps him'). Teacher authority remained clearly acknowledged, and this was apparent not least in the teacher's praise – 'Good girl!' – although its presence was apparent in more profound ways. In that she accepted, and herself contributed to, the talk, the teacher helped expand the range of instructional field matters expressed in the discourse. Such will be the effect of a successful instance of any instructional register: as the registerial opportunities are opened so, by implication, other registerial possibilities are closed. The course the discourse is to take has, thus, been defined by the teacher, acting with authority to pursue certain opportunities in meaning-making.

One further point needs to be made about the joint construction of the instructional field in the extract just considered: its construction was dependent upon successful mastery of some well-established scientific knowledge, which was expressed most powerfully in the textbook and whose authority had been mediated by the teacher in assisting the children to master the necessary language and its meaning over several lessons. It was the teacher's expertise in interpreting that knowledge that had made its successful mastery possible. The knowledge, furthermore, was in no sense her 'own' construct, nor was it 'owned' by the students, in the sense that at least some of the process proponents have suggested. Knowledge is not, on the whole, the private preserve of individuals, but rather the preserve of the communities of scholars who create it and of the students who are apprenticed into an understanding of it.

Overall, like some at least of the constructivists, we can indeed argue that knowledge was in construction in this text. However, as I have tried to demonstrate, it was the presence of the teacher and the role she took that made possible that construction. She did indeed 'instruct' the children in their learning (to use a word which, as noted earlier, was rejected by those in progressive education). In addition, in her manner of initiating and orchestrating the talk, she both constrained the directions the talk took and enabled the children to talk as they did. Through her efforts, the pedagogic discourse did its work in apprenticing the young into an aspect of important scientific knowledge – knowledge that had been taken from the contexts in which it was originally generated and 'relocated' for the purposes of the children's learning. The process of teaching and learning was clearly one of apprenticeship.[3] The latter point is worth making since I suggest that most discussions of 'inquiry' teaching and learning, or of various constructivist positions of the kind alluded to earlier, have not acknowledged the importance and the relevance of teacher authority or the notion of apprenticeship proposed here.

The talk led shortly to discussion of the role of the incubator in the classroom, compared with that of the mother hen, and here the instructional field was very successfully negotiated, and it was notable that the children manipulated the necessary lexis of that field ('incubator', 'water sac', 'mother hen') as they once again engaged in dialogue.

T:	'Cause the little chick has to be kept moving in the egg so he doesn't get all like . . . (overlap)
Children:	Yeah.
T:	He needs a bit of exercise in there.
Jenny:	An he don't die 'cause the mother hen . . .
Sylvia:	We don't have a mother hen. We have an incubator (overlap)
Jenny:	An he's not hurt in the . . . inside . . . inside the egg.
T:	That's right. We have an incubator. That's right. That's the water (points to picture in the book). That's the water sac. The water sac stops the little chick from getting hurt if it gets knocked.
Sylvia:	We don't have mother hen.
T:	Yeah we don't have.
Sylvia:	If mother hen kicks it, it's going . . . the little chick can't feel it.
T:	Yeah. Why?

Children: Yeah because they're* in the water sac.
T: Yes, because they're in the water sac.

(* The switch from singular to plural here with the use of 'they' was unremarked, and there was no sense of discontinuity in the talk.)

One of the notable aspects of the functioning of the dialogue here – a characteristic found elsewhere in the discourse – was the degree of redundancy as children and teacher repeated words and phrases.

> We don't have a mother hen. We have an incubator.
> That's right. We have an incubator.
> The water sac stops the little chick from getting hurt.
> Yeah because they're in the water sac.
> Yes, because they're in the water sac.

Similar redundancy, it will be noted, occurred in the earlier extract, as in these examples.

> It's all gone (said three times).

> And he's in a water sac.
> And he's in a water sac.
> He's getting a little tooth.
> Yes, he's getting a little egg tooth.

Redundancy of this kind is a feature of a great deal of successful classroom talk, and it functions cumulatively to build the growing sense of shared understandings created by teacher and students. (See Lemke 1995: 166–75 for a related discussion.) In this case, redundancy helped to develop a strong sense of the language of the instructional field and, thus, also helped lay the basis for the creation of the jointly written text.

The written text was developed over three lessons. It was produced by the teacher on large sheets of paper that the students could see, and that, with her assistance, they learned to read. The text produced on the first day read:

> We didn't have a mother hen so we used an incubator to keep the eggs warm. The incubator has a thermometer that tells how hot the eggs are. The orange light comes on every time the eggs start to get cold. When the arm* turns over it moves the eggs around to give the little chicks exercise.

> (*The reference is to the arm of the incubator.)

The teacher and children returned to the text some time later, and at one point the teacher invited the children to read what they had written.

> First, we switched on the electricity and put the eggs in. The little chick looked like a dot. It stays in the egg for twenty-one days.

In rereading this, the teacher stopped the reading to say

T: Right then we put a little mark there because we wanted to say
                something else there. So let's find the little mark (a reference

to a mark she had made on the sheet to remind themselves when they resumed the activity).

Naomi: There's another little mark (points to another spot on the sheet).

T: Yeah.

Jenny: What's this?

T: We're going to say this next: 'His food is the

T/children: 'Yolk'.

T: All right, so we're going to put that little piece . . . we're going to put that little piece in . . . in here. All right so we'll write it in. Shall we write it in?

T: 'His food' (writes as she says this)

Naomi: 'is'

T: 'is the . . .'

T/children: 'Yolk'.

T: All right now when we write up our book we'll put that in. That goes in there like that, all right? OK? (a reference to the planned final typed production of the text) Right now what do we say next?

And on the talk went, the teacher drawing the children into helping her compose what should be written. In passages of the kind just cited, the two registers were both involved as teacher and children talked of their writing. Thus, the regulative register appeared in: 'we're going to say this'; 'we're going to put that little piece in here'; and so on. The instructional register was, of course, realized in the 'content' for writing: 'his food is the yolk'. The complete text for this section of the writing read:

> First, we switched on the electricity and put the eggs in. The little chick looked like a dot. It stays in the egg for twenty-one days. His food is the yolk. The little chick grows a little bit bigger. He grows a tiny head, a tiny heart, tiny eyes and tiny blood vessels. Then he grows tiny ears, tiny wings and tiny legs. Next he grows a tiny tail and a tiny beak. Then he grows tiny feathers and an egg tooth.

The last stage of the text read:

> While the little chick is in the egg it is floating in a water sac. When it is twenty-one days the little chick cracks open the egg with his egg tooth. It's hard work. At last the chick is out. He is all wet and weak and wobbly. When he dries out he is soft and fluffy.

In the writing of it, it will be apparent, the teacher and children relied a great deal on what they had rehearsed in reading the class textbook, in observation of the class incubator, and in talk. The written text displayed some features that reflected the nature of the talk and the class experience with the incubator, including most notably the tendency to refer to the class at several points ('We didn't have a mother hen so we used an incubator to keep the eggs warm') as well as a tendency to shift between past and present tense (e.g. 'The little chick looked like a dot', followed by 'It stays in the egg for twenty-one days').

Overall, apart from the references to 'we' (drawn strictly from the regulative register), the text successfully foregrounded the instructional register. However, as the theory being pursued in this paper suggests, in that the instructional register was successfully foregrounded in the written text, this itself was a measure of the fact that the regulative register had done its work in shaping the nature of the children's tasks.

Space will not permit that I reproduce much more from the text. It was notable that the teacher moved between involving the children in creating whole clauses or phrases for writing (e.g. 'His food is the yolk' and 'It stays in the egg for twenty-one days') and seeking advice about how to spell words.

T:	Who can help me with egg? Egg. How do we write that?
David:	I know.
T:	Can you help me?
David:	I know.
T:	What's the first letter?
David:	I know.
Naomi:	I want to help. I want to help.
T:	You see if you can write the word 'egg' (hands the pen to Naomi).
T:	What's tooth start with?
Jenny:	To (an attempt to sound the letter).
Melissa/David:	/t/ (T writes 't').
Naomi:	A /t/.
T:	Two /o/s together, a /t/ and a /h/.

The approach to writing was essentially discourse-driven in that the emphasis was primarily upon shaping the written text, but frequent opportunity was also provided for learning the spelling of words. In addition, frequent opportunity was also provided to read and reread the passages the class had written.

Finally, as a result of the class endeavours, the text as reproduced above appeared in a class book, which was then displayed in the classroom and available for frequent rereading throughout the rest of the year. The book was the major written outcome of the unit of work on chickens. As such, in terms of the evaluative principles that applied in the overall operation of the pedagogic discourse, it was judged by both teacher and students as visible evidence of the fact that the students had been apprenticed into knowledge about chickens – their life cycle, in particular.

An Instance of Junior Secondary English Teaching and Learning

Much earlier, in briefly reviewing aspects of educational theory that I wished to critique, I alluded to developments in English teaching, the effects of which remain in many places today. I referred to 'process' approaches to teaching English and an associated tendency to see the teacher as facilitating 'personal growth' (sometimes referred to as 'personal voice') and identity at the expense of an interest in teaching any 'content' about English. The goal in the English programme, I would suggest, should be to teach knowledge about language as well as skills in its use. It should involve, among other matters: teaching about the discourse patterns, text types or genres that students need to read and write; knowledge of grammatical features in which these are realized; and an associated range of skills in handling the various text types as well as manipulating their language features. Such teaching and the skills developed, ironically enough, lead to the very capacities in self-expression that the process proponents have often loudly proclaimed they want to see emerge. The teaching of language knowledge and skills, however, has been often resisted by members of the English-teaching profession – process proponents especially – normally for one of two reasons.

The first reason is that teaching knowledge about language (sometimes called 'KAL') has not been shown to make any difference to students' capacities in using language (literacy, in particular) since students will learn best in situations in which they are 'immersed' in using various forms of literacy. Exposure to the models of literacy usage is sufficient. Freedman (1993) has argued such a position while in Australia, with respect to young children in particular, Cambourne (Cambourne *et al.* 1988) has even articulated what he terms a 'natural learning theory' (some of which has been reworked more recently in Turbill and Cambourne 1997). Thus, Cambourne says, children learn the mother tongue 'naturally' in contexts of use and without overt instruction; so too, he goes on, literate skills are learned 'naturally' and in exposure to models in use. (Goodman 1982 has argued similar positions.) The argument, incidentally, is a very unsatisfactory one in at least three ways. In the first place, early language learning is, in fact, quite effortful, requiring the mentoring and scaffolding of many caregivers; therefore, the claims to some kind of 'natural' process without instruction are spurious. In the second place, the natural language learning theory is quite naïve about the considerable differences between the grammars of speech and writing, discussed in detail, for example, in Halliday (1985). It takes some years of schooling for students to master the grammatical features of writing, and the best evidence suggests that it is not until late childhood to adolescence that control of the grammar of written language emerges (Derewianka 1995, in press; Aidman 1999; Christie 2002a). A third sense in which the 'natural learning theory' is unsatisfactory is that even if we concede that a lot of oral language is learned in interaction and without conscious effort on the part of the mentor to teach it (as is true), children are never exposed to the models of literate language as systematically and frequently as they are to those of the oral language. For that reason alone, the learning of literacy has to be understood differently from the learning of oral language, and it does require overt intervention.

The other reason given by some educational theorists for rejecting teaching KAL is that it compromises the independence and capacity for self-expression of students, imposing formulae for use in literacy, rather than encouraging them to express themselves in independent, even critical ways. The issues have been hotly discussed and have led to a considerable debate about so-called 'genre-based' pedagogy (e.g. Reid 1987; Freedman and Medway 1994; Lee 1996; Cope and Kalantzis 1993). Such a pedagogy seeks to identify genres or text types needed for successful mastery of the various areas of school learning and to teach them, making overt use of a functional grammar to do so. Accounts of genre theory may be found in Derewianka (1990), Christie *et al.* (1990a, 1990b, 1990c), Christie and Martin (1997), Macken-Horarik (1998), Christie, in Christie and Misson (1998), Martin (1999), Unsworth (2000, 2001), and Butt *et al.* (2000).

No detailed discussion of the theory will be offered here as the issues have been extensively canvassed elsewhere. However, I shall note that, in my view, the arguments for the values of 'independently developed self-expression' and for the role of the English teacher as 'facilitator' of language learning, rather than as authority teaching knowledge about language, are very inadequate. Such arguments regularly trivialize the claims of teaching and learning important knowledge about language; they fail to recognize the grammatical differences between speech and writing alluded to above and, thus, have nothing to offer students experiencing difficulties in handling literacy; and, finally, they fail to recognize that in order to operate in independently critical ways in using oral language and literacy, one needs to understand how language is used to shape and organize meanings. Language is a tool or a resource, and like any other tool, the better one understands it, the better one can manipulate and use it, a point made by Macken-Horarik (1998) when discussing what she terms 'the requirements of critical school literacy'. Teachers of English need knowledge about language and literacy themselves and a skilled capacity to teach such knowledge to their students.

In order to demonstrate the point, I shall use some extracts from a classroom text in which the teacher was teaching students KAL as aspects of teaching them how to read and write in a unit of work in English. The students, aged 12–13 years, were in Year 7 – the first year of the Australian secondary school. The class had been pursuing a study of animals and animal welfare, which had included, among other things, discussions of treatment of animals and the propriety of keeping animals in circuses and zoos. They had read a number of books and newspaper articles, and after several lessons exploring such matters, the teacher prepared the students to do some research and writing. Some minutes into the lesson, with the students sitting in groups of four at tables, she distributed some articles that set out arguments to do with whether animals should be kept in captivity and told the students they were to research and eventually write about the question, 'Should we use animals for entertainment?' She proceeded thus, reminding the students (as teachers so often do) at one point of a previous related writing activity, and foregrounding the regulative register as part of the business of setting pedagogic goals.

> T: Now you're going to be working with your partners on this essay together but you're each going to write your own. So you can write and share these articles together, but you're going to write it on your own. (some text is left out) Alright, so what I want you to do is . . . what we're going to do today is read through these articles. We're going to highlight for and against, just as we did when we did our other essay, where we did looking at whether the government should say sorry to the Aboriginal community, and what we did was we wrote down all the things why the government should say sorry, all the things why the government shouldn't say sorry, and we wrote an essay.[4] And we called it an argumentative essay. Why did we call it an argumentative essay?
>
> Jessica: Because you're arguing about it.
>
> T: Good, you're arguing a point of view, you're looking at both sides, and remember when you're looking at two sides of an argument, Michael, you need to support your arguments with reference to the different parts of these articles.

The regulative register was apparent in several linguistic features. For example, it was apparent in the teacher's textual Theme choices, helping to point directions.

> *now* you're going to be working . . .
> *but* you're each going . . .
> *so* you can write and share these articles together,
> *but* you're going . . .
> *alright*, so what I want you to . . .

Textual Themes, realized in particular in continuatives such as 'now' and 'alright' (or 'OK', or 'well') are very characteristic of teacher talk and much less commonly found in student talk although, as I have shown elsewhere (Christie 1998), when students work together on shared tasks, as in some science lessons, such linguistic features will appear in their talk.[5] This is evidence of the fact that even linguistic features as simple as continuatives have functional significance so that here the teacher used them because of her responsibility in determining the directions class activity would take. Elsewhere, when it is functionally relevant, students will use such expressions as they determine the directions of their learning activities.

The regulative register was also apparent in several process types which realized aspects of student behaviours appropriate to the task in hand.

> you *'re going to be working* with your partners (material)
> you *can write* (and later) we *wrote* an essay (behavioural)
> we *'re going to highlight* for and against (material)

Participants' roles in these processes were realized initially in the second person pronoun, '*you*'re going to work'. But later the teacher adopted the first person plural, '*we*'re going to highlight', establishing solidarity in undertaking the task, much as the early childhood teacher did above.

At two points the teacher used an identifying process, and both instances are significant for what they reveal of the way the regulative register was foregrounded, and of the ways the teacher's authority was expressed. The first, very characteristic of teacher talk, involved two participant roles realized in embedded clauses.

[[what we're going to do today]]	is	[[read though these articles]].
Value	Process: identifying	Token

The clause embeddings here are notable for they serve to 'pack in' a deal of relevant information. After many years of reading and analysing teacher talk, I can say that such expressions are very characteristic in teacher talk at certain points in classroom discourse, and, as such, they have functional significance. Such expressions occur, as here, at points where directions are being pointed pedagogically, at certain summarizing stages in a lesson, and finally at points of closure. Of course, such expressions can appear elsewhere in the overall pattern of a classroom text, but they are much less common (and they are not common in student talk). That is because it is the teacher's responsibility to establish goals and/or summarize what has been achieved. The function of such an identifying process is to establish, in reasonably forceful terms, what is to be done, and here Halliday's (1994) terms for the two participant roles are enlightening: the Value is so-called because it defines a value of some kind while the Token identifies that which is to stand for the Value. 'Reading through the articles,' thus, represents the activity defined as particularly valuable by the teacher. Such an identifying process has a categorical status in teacher talk, and it is because such processes are categorical that they appear somewhat sparingly in an overall passage of teacher talk.

The other identifying process found in the teacher talk occurred when the teacher said, 'We called it an argumentative essay. Why did we call it an argumentative essay?' In terms of the analysis, we can lay out the process in this way:

we	called	it	an argumentative essay
Assigner	Process: identifying	Value	Token

Here the identifying process has another significance, this time in terms of building a technical language ('essay') to do with the regulative register and the pedagogic goals with respect to learning aspects of literacy. The students in the class had not long been in the secondary school; therefore, learning to write 'essays' was a new aspect of their schooling.

One further aspect of the teacher talk and its function in realizing the regulative register can be mentioned: its consistent use of positive polarity. Teachers use positive polarity in particular when pointing directions. Like the absence of teacher modality (apart from one point when reference was made to the topic of a previous essay written by the students – 'the government should say sorry'), the positive polarity serves to indicate directions and, by implication, to deny the possibility of others.

Overall, then, the process types that realized student behaviours; the uses of the first person plural pronouns in participant roles; the two identifying processes that defined, respectively, a task and a technical term; the use of textual themes that helped to define directions; and the consistent use of positive polarity – all served to offer a strongly assertive sense of directions being defined for the pedagogic activity. Thus, the regulative register serves to identify pedagogic directions: regulative registerial directions are foregounded and opened up. Thus, is the teacher's authority also expressed.

A few minutes later, the teacher moved the students on to consideration of the instructional field. She asked the students to take out a piece of paper, put the date on it, and then create two columns to do with whether animals should be used for entertainment. She advised the students, working in pairs, to read through the articles she had given them and, using highlighters, to identify arguments for and against use of animals for entertainment.

> T: Just take out these (the articles) and a highlighter and a pen. You might want to use a red pen so it stands out. A highlighter and red pen. . . . For the first articles I'm going to go through with you and highlight for you the arguments against. Alright? The second article you're going to do by yourselves . . .

Here, once again, the regulative register was at issue as the teacher established behaviours in which the students should engage to undertake the intended learning. Process types realized student behaviours.

> just *take out* these . . . (material process)
> I *'m going to go* through . . . (material process)
> you *'re going to do* by yourselves . . . (material process)

while participant roles of actor were realized in either the first person ('I') when the teacher spoke of what she would do or the second person ('you') when identifying class members.

What was at issue here was that the teacher directed the students' reading in order to develop habits of reading for information, a necessary part of learning to research for the purposes of writing on many matters. Reading and research skills of the kind involved, while they can be taught in all school subjects, have a particular relevance for the purposes of the pedagogic goal in this case, i.e. learning to research for the purposes of writing an essay. Yet, such matters are not typically foregrounded in many process accounts of the English classroom, preoccupied as they have tended to be with developing personally expressive information, rather than information or opinion based on research. Yet, such skills are among the many undervalued, often invisible, skills that competent users of written English will display, and it was of interest that the teacher chose to foreground them as part of the regulative register she developed in preparing the students for an eventual writing task. In fact, since she distributed several articles, she allowed the students a couple of lessons to read them, to highlight the main arguments, and then to write summaries of points.

Reading and class discussions led to such exchanges as the following:

T: (having just read a paragraph about how humans are more concerned for themselves than for animals) What's that paragraph saying, Anthony?
Anthony: We worry about ourselves, we don't worry about animals. They suffer as well.
T: Um . . . they suffer as well.

Several minutes later:

T: Do you remember what happened to the elephant? (a reference to a class visit to the zoo)
James: Its foot was hurting because it was always on concrete.
T: . . . And what else was it doing?
Steven: It was resting on one foot.
Jessica: It was swaying from side to side.
T: Why was it swaying from side to side?
Jessica: I don't know.
George: So he could put his whole weight on the back leg.
T: Maybe, that's a good point. But also because he's so used to being confined at times . . . the man in charge of the zoo said they rock from side to side because of stress, and it's a way of comforting themselves.

In these exchanges, it will be clear that it was the instructional register that was in construction in the dialogue, apparent in most aspects of the grammar, and realizing, for example, aspects of animal behaviour: 'its foot was hurting because it was always on concrete' and 'it was swaying from side to side'. The regulative register was apparent in the dialogic nature of the talk and, in particular, in the regular adoption of the interrogative mood as the teacher elicited information from the students about the instructional field.

Class research and note making in pairs eventually led to a joint construction of points on the board, taken from materials read, and indicating arguments for and against keeping animals for entertainment:

For	Against
1. In order to save species, you have to let the public see the animals and then they will take action.	1. Abnormal behaviour, e.g. elephants moving from side to side, bear staying in one spot for long time, rocking.
2. Human circuses do not meet public demand because people want to see animals.	2. Travelling, confined space affects animals.
3. Animals are a core element of traditional circuses.	3. Environment causes stress because they are not in their natural habitat.
4. Educational to meet the animals because people learn about their habitat, food, habits, and have the experience of meeting them.	4. Having to perform causes stress due to travel and noisy audience.
	5. Natural behaviours, e.g. hunting, territorial patrolling, nesting, etc. no longer used to same extent.
	6. Should use humans in circuses.

Most students had similar sets of points on their sheets of paper although the teacher apparently thought it useful to engage the students in joint construction of arguments that could be advanced and which had been arrived at from the class reading. I suggest, at least, two advantages to the activity of joint construction and display of a list of points like this. First, it involves the redundancy alluded to above in looking at the early childhood text for a great deal of the lexis relevant to the instructional field being examined was displayed. Second, and relatedly, it helped build a shared knowledge of the arguments relevant to the eventual essay to be written. I earlier noted that critics of genre theory often argue that students need to be encouraged to develop and express their own opinions, implying that genre theorists constrain their capacity to do this. In fact, genre theorists would agree that students need to develop personal opinions, noting, however, that students need assistance in researching and collecting information relevant to expression of opinion. Thus, for the writing of both factual and opinionated texts, students need help in identifying the necessary language and information, and in developing the skills to manipulate these for the task of writing.

The essay the students were to write was one normally identified as a discussion genre in Australian genre theory in order to distinguish it from the conventional exposition. A discussion genre or 'essay' requires the writer to review the arguments for and against an issue and then to arrive at a recommendation for oneself. As the teacher had noted, the students had had some experience in writing one earlier instance of such an essay. She, nonetheless, returned to the essay structure she had taught the students before, introducing the major elements in such a genre and reviewing their functions. These were displayed on a handout and on the board.

Element of structure	*Function*
Preview of Issue	States issue to be discussed
Argument for (recursive)	Point for: expansion Point for: expansion
Argument against (recursive)	Point against: expansion Point against: expansion
Recommendation	

However, well before the students moved to write their own essays, the teacher involved them in reviewing the arguments they had collected and which were displayed above. One student, Lauren, had been reading an article that supported the use of animals in circuses when the teacher stopped her to ask,

T: This report was written by whom, who's written this report?
Peter: Barry Nixon.
T: OK, who does he work for?
Steven: The National Conference of Circus people.

A few seconds later a student asked,

Lauren: Who wrote the first article? It says at the end. The RSPCA.*

(*Royal Society for the Prevention of Cruelty to Animals.)

The exchanges led to considerable talk about whether writers could be said to show *bias* in their writing, or whether they were *objective*, because different points of view were expressed. The need for reviewing both sides of the issue before arriving at a recommendation was discussed at length, and again the regulative register was at issue here because students were being inducted into some time-honoured expectations in a Western tradition – reviewing evidence and arriving at views that are *based on evidence* (the teacher's words).

I shall reproduce here just one of the essays, written by a student called Lauren. I have indicated the elements of structure although the student did not actually write these on her page.

Should we use animals in the circus?

Preview of issues

'Should we use animals for entertainment' is the name of the topic we're talking about in this essay. Below, I have stated the positive and negative points for the issue.

Arguments for

In the report we read it said that in order to let a particular species survive we need to at least capture a few to show to the public, to let them learn about the animal and then maybe the public would do something to help the endangered animals. It also said the animals are never hurt or tortured during training or their performances and they are kept very clean, and in natural yards while not performing. At one stage it said that animals are the core element of circuses and the statistics proved that people like the animals best at the circus. Therefore human circuses would not meet the pubic demand. Most people judge circuses on the old ways, not on the current, improved ways.

Arguments against

But then on the other hand, animals like the elephants and bears are very prone to stress so they make a habit of standing in one place and rocking or swaying, which is bad for their joints and feet. Things like constant travelling and performing in front of very large audiences nearly every day affect this. They're nearly always in confined spaces and the biggest places they are ever in are the circus arena or tent, which is also really small. The animals are not usually kept in the natural habitat, which stops their basic instincts like fighting for mates, building nests, hunting etc. from being used to the same extent they do in the wild. An alternative is to use humans in circuses because they can't exactly force people to join; they have to be voluntary.

Recommendation

After looking at all these facts, I believe that it's wrong for us to keep animals in circuses for our entertainment. We should be able to entertain ourselves, not rely on animals. For this reason, and the ones I have mentioned before, I believe it is wrong for us to train and force animals to perform in circuses.

I shall say very little about the text here, since space does not permit it. However, let me note these matters: the fact that the text was well organized, following the structure the students had been given; each stage clearly signalled by changes in the language used, mostly in the theme choices (e.g. 'In the report we read'; 'But then on the other hand, animals like the elephants and bears'; and 'After looking at all these facts'); and the fact that the student had clearly adopted a great deal of the lexis relevant to the instructional field ('particular species'; 'endangered animals'; 'prone to stress').

In all, the text revealed an understanding both of the pedagogic goals of the activity as clearly realized in the regulative register and of the instructional field to be written about. In an evaluative sense, the text was judged a good one by the teacher who wrote the comment: 'A good argumentative essay, Lauren. You have seen both sides of the argument.'

Teacher authority had been important: in guiding discussion of the text types to be written; and in guiding reading and summarizing of information. While the students were clear that they expressed their own views (at one point, Lauren insisted to the teacher that she wanted 'to express my views'), it will be apparent that the manner of information selection, like the manner of shaping opinions and writing the essays, had been very much constrained by the actions of the teacher in directing the course of activities as she did. Yet, in constraining the choices available to the students in their research and writing, I would argue that the teacher also enabled the students: to develop research skills with respect to an instructional field of interest and use; and to practise writing a useful genre involving thought about the need to marshal evidence in support of positions. The pedagogic discourse had served its purpose in apprenticing the young into some important knowledge and skills valued in an English-speaking society. The regulative register, mediated as it was by the authority of the teacher, had served its purpose.

Conclusion

I began this paper with some observations about a great deal of educational theorizing of the twentieth century, much of which I argued has harmed the cause of education and of knowledge. It has also compromised and confused understandings of the authority of the teacher in the pedagogic processes of schooling. I referred to various progressivist/constructivist positions and, relatedly, to various 'inquiry' and/or 'process' approaches to models of the curriculum and of the learner. The various approaches and models identified, I suggested, all had in common a tendency to foreground the nature of the learner conceived in some idealized, even private way, and to diminish the significance of the knowledge the learner should learn. In fact, in the curriculum models referred to, I suggested, knowledge itself has been given a very equivocal status while the particular claims of the different areas of knowledge, and their methods of addressing questions and of dealing with experience, have been accorded little respect in the apparent drive to create individuals possessed of their 'own' understandings in uniquely independent ways. Among the many difficulties created by such models of the curriculum, of knowledge, and of the learner, is the confused and ambiguous status it accords the authority of the teacher. Using a method of classroom discourse analysis, I have sought to demonstrate how successful teacher authority is essential to the processes of teaching and learning in schools. Educational theory is in need of a major review and reassessment, such that a renewed understanding is achieved both of the nature of knowledge offered students in schools, and of the authority teachers must use in teaching such knowledge to their students.

Notes

1. The metaphor of projection is preferred rather than that of embedding because, in the functional grammar, the notion of embedding already has another significance to do with notions of constituent structure and items of rank which have others that are 'down-ranked' within them. The metaphor of projection is a useful one: according to Halliday (1994: 219) where projection occurs, 'the secondary clause is projected through the primary clause, which instates it as (a) a locution or (b) an idea'. In the terms discussed here, the regulative register is said to project the instructional register.
2. Teachers of older students tend to devote less overt attention to such matters, mainly because students will have recognized the required behaviour patterns, including the appropriate physical dispositions; although, of course, at any age, such matters can be expressed directly in the regulative register.
3. Apprenticeship is a metaphorical term taken here from Bernstein (1990) although it is also found in much other contemporary educational writing. This metaphor is a useful one for it implies that, just as a person was initiated or 'apprenticed' into some craft or skill in the traditional sense, so too the student in an educational setting can be thought of as initiated or apprenticed into knowledge, skills, and attitudes.
4. This is a reference to the debate in Australia about whether the Aboriginal people should be given a formal apology for the ways in which they were treated in the past.
5. Continuatives were not a notable feature in the teacher's talk in the extracts from the early childhood text examined although they were, as it happens, apparent in her talk at other points in the text not cited.

References

Aidman, M. (1999) 'Biliteracy Development through Early and Mid-primary years. A Longitudinal Case Study of Bilingual Writing', unpublished Ph.D. Dissertation. Melbourne: University of Melbourne.

Baker, D. R. and Piburn, M. D. (1997) *Constructing Science in Middle and Secondary School Classrooms.* Boston: Allyn and Bacon.

Bernstein, B. (2000) *Pedagogy, Symbolic Control and Identity. Theory, Research, Critique* (Revised edn). Maryland: Rowman and Littlefield.

Bernstein, B. (1990) *Class, Codes and Control, Volume 4: The Structuring of Pedagogic Discourse.* London: Routledge.

Butt, D., Fahey, R., Feez, S., Spinks, S., and Yallop, C. (2000) *Using Functional Grammar. An Explorer's Guide* (2nd edn). Sydney: National Centre for English Language Teaching and Research.

Cambourne, B., Handy, L., and Scown, P. (1988) *The Whole Story: Natural Learning and the Acquisition of Literacy in the Classroom.* Auckland, NZ: Ashton Scholastic.

Christie, F. (2002a) 'The Development of Abstraction in Adolescence in Subject English', in *Developing Advanced Literacy in First and Second Languages. Meaning with Power*, ed. by M. Schleppegrell and C. Colombi. Mahwah, NJ: Erlbaum, 45–66.

Christie, F. (2002b) *Classroom Discourse Analysis. A Functional Perspective.* London: Continuum.

Christie, F. (1998) 'Science and Apprenticeship: The Pedagogic Discourse', in *The Language of Science*, ed. by J. R. Martin and R. Veel. London: Routledge, 152–77.

Christie, F., Gray, P., Gray, B., Macken, M., Martin, J. R., and Rothery, J. (1990a) *Exploring Procedures* (Student Books 1–4 and Teachers' Book). Sydney: Harcourt Brace Jovanovich.

Christie, F., Gray, P., Gray, B., Macken, M., Martin, J. R., and Rothery, J. (1990b) *Exploring Reports* (Student Books 1–4 and Teachers' Book). Sydney: Harcourt Brace Jovanovich.

Christie, F., Gray, P., Gray, B., Macken, M., Martin, J. R., and Rothery, J. (1990c) *Exploring Explanations* (Student Books 1–4 and Teachers' Book). Sydney: Harcourt Brace Jovanovich.

Christie, F. and Martin, J. R. (eds) (1997) *Genre and Institutions. Social Processes in the Workplace and School.* London: Cassell.

Christie, F. and Misson, R. (1998) *Literacy and Schooling.* London: Routledge.

Cope, B. and Kalantzis, M. (eds) (1993) *The Powers of Literacy. A Genre Approach to Teaching Writing.* London: Falmer Press.

Derewianka, B. (in press) 'Grammatical Metaphor in the Transition to Adolescence', in *Lexicogrammatical Metaphor: Systemic and Functional Perspectives*, ed. by A. M. Simon Vandenbergen, M. Taverniers, and L. Ravelli. Amsterdam: John Benjamins.

Derewianka, B. (1995) 'Language Development in the Transition from Childhood to Adolescence: The Role of Grammatical Metaphor', unpublished Ph.D. Dissertation. NSW: Macquarie University.

Derewianka, B. (1990) *Exploring How Texts Work.* Sydney: Primary English Teachers' Association.

Dewey, J. (1916) *Democracy and Education: An Introduction to the Philosophy of Education.* New York: Macmillan.

Dewey, J. (1902) *The Child and the Curriculum.* Chicago, IL: University of Chicago Press (reprinted by University Chicago Press, 1966).

Dixon, J. (1967) *Growth through English.* London: National Association for the Teaching of English and Oxford University Press.

Freedman, A. (1993) 'Show and Tell? The Role of Explicit Teaching in the Learning of New Genres', *Research in the Teaching of English*, 27(3): 222–51.

Freedman, A. and Medway, P. (eds) (1994) *Genre and the New Rhetoric*. London: Taylor and Francis.

Goodman, K. S. (1982) *Language and Literacy: The Selected Writings of Kenneth S. Goodman*, ed. by F. V. Gollasch. London: Routledge and Kegan Paul.

Gray, B. (1999) 'Accessing the Discourses of Schooling. English Language and Literacy Development with Aboriginal Children in Mainstream Schools', unpublished Ph.D. Dissertation. Melbourne: University of Melbourne.

Halliday, M. A. K. (1994) *An Introduction to Functional Grammar* (2nd edn). London: Edward Arnold.

Halliday, M. A. K. (1985) *Spoken and Written Language*. Geelong, Victoria: Deakin University Press.

Halliday, M. A. K. (1975) *Learning How to Mean. Explorations in the Development of Language*. London: Arnold.

Halliday, M. A. K. and Matthiessen, C. (1999) *Construing Experience through Language. A Language-based Approach to Cognition*. London: Cassell.

Iedema, R. (1997) 'The Language of Administration: Organizing Human Activity in Formal Institutions', in *Genre and Institutions. Social Processes in the Workplace and School*, ed. by F. Christie and J. R. Martin. London: Cassell, 73–100.

Larochelle, M., Bednarz, N. and Garrison, J. (eds) (1998) *Constructivism and Education*. Cambridge: Cambridge University Press.

Lee, A. (1996) *Gender, Literacy, Curriculum: Re-writing School Geography*. London: Taylor and Francis.

Lemke, J. L. (1995) *Textual Politics. Discourse and Social Dynamics*. London: Taylor and Francis.

Macken-Horarik, M. (1998) 'Exploring the Requirements of Critical School Literacy: A View from Two Classrooms', in *Literacy and Schooling*, ed. by F. Christie and R. Misson. London: Routledge, 74–103.

Martin, J. R. (1999) 'Mentoring Semogenesis: "Genre-based" Literacy Pedagogy', in *Pedagogy and the Shaping of Consciousness: Linguistic and Social Processes*, ed. by F. Christie. London: Continuum, 123–55.

Martin, J. R. (1992) *English Text. System and Structure*. Philadelphia: John Benjamins.

Muller, J. (2000) *Reclaiming Knowledge. Social Theory, Curriculum and Education Policy*. London: Routledge Falmer.

Painter, C. (1999) *Learning through Language in Early Childhood*. London and New York: Cassell.

The Plowden Report (1967), in *Children and their Primary Schools*. Nottingham (Monographs in Systemic Linguistics, No. 10). London: Her Majesty's Stationery Office.

Reid, I. (ed.) (1987) *The Place of Genre in Learning: Current Debates.* Geelong, Victoria: Typereader Publications No. 1. Centre for Studies in Literary Education.

Röhrs, H. (1995) 'Internationalism in Progressive Education and Initial Steps towards a World Education Movement', in *Progressive Education Across the Continents. A Handbook,* ed. by H. Röhrs and V. Lenhart. Frankfurt: Peter Lang, 11–27.

Rörhs, H. and Lenhart, V. (eds) (1995) *Progressive Education Across the Continents. A Handbook.* Frankfurt: Peter Lang.

Stenhouse, L. (1975) *An Introduction to Curriculum Research and Development.* London: Heinemann Educational Books.

Turbill, J. and Cambourne, B. (eds) (1997) *The Changing Face of Whole Language.* Newark, DE: International Reading Association.

Unsworth, L. (2001) *Teaching Multiliteracies Across the Curriculum. Changing Contexts of Text and Image in Classroom Practice.* Buckingham: Open University Press.

Unsworth, L. (2000) *Researching Language in Schools and Communities. Functional Linguistic Perspectives.* London: Cassell.

von Glasersfeld, E. (1998) 'Why Constructivism must be Radical', in *Constructivism and Education,* ed. by M. Larochelle, N. Bednarz, and J. Garrison. Cambridge: Cambridge University Press, 23–8.

Wells, G. (1999) *Dialogic Inquiry. Toward a Sociocultural Practice and Theory of Education.* Cambridge: Cambridge University Press.

Wilson, B. G. (ed) (1996) *Constructivist Learning Environments. Case Studies in Instructional Design.* Englewood Cliffs, NJ: Educational Technology Publications.

10 The Principal's *Book*: Discursively Reconstructing a Culture of Teaching and Learning in an Umlazi High School

Ralph Adendorff

This paper reports on an investigation, using the Appraisal framework, of a ritualized discursive practice introduced by the new principal of a school in Umlazi, South Africa, namely, The Book. *This appears to be an attempt at mobilizing the teaching corps and of reconstructing a culture of teaching and learning in an institution which, until recently, eschewed any serious commitment to education and could not rely on community support. The entries in* The Book *themselves as well as evidence from interviews with the principal and staff members suggest that a struggle is currently taking place over acceptance of the discursive practices mentioned. This struggle appears to relate to the legitimacy of power in the school and to the kind of community of practice that teachers at the school envisage for themselves. It is clear, too, that the meanings that the principal seeks to express, themselves struggle with one another in his texts.*

Introduction and Overview

This paper provides a close study of situated pedagogic discursive practice in an educational site, Thukeleni High School (a pseudonym), in South Africa. Very much like the studies in Sarangi and Baynham (1996), it is concerned with identity construction, more particularly, the constitutive effect of discourse (*The Book*) on identities (those of the teachers and principal) in the context of post-apartheid South Africa. At the heart of this study, as well, is an attempt to show that a dialectical relationship exists between the micro-level practices associated with *The Book* and the macro-level sociopolitical forces that prevail (May 1995). In the situation described, these macro-forces are, on the one hand, by-products of apartheid and its legacies, and, on the other, attempts within the 'new' South Africa, to reconstruct a culture of teaching and learning, stimulated by various mechanisms set in place by Kader Asmal, the Minister of Education (1999). This dialectical relationship between text and macro-context is captured at a relatively early point in the reconstruction process at Thukeleni High School, the discursive practices underlying *The Book* and the teachers' reaction – being in microcosm, a barometer of change within a significant sector of the education system and also tangible evidence of that change. As Fairclough (1995: 15) remarks,

> Texts provide usually temporary and short-lived ways of resolving the dilemmas into which people are put by the tensions and contradictions which frame those texts. Textual analysis can give access to the detailed mechanisms through which social contradictions evolve and are lived out, and the sometimes subtle shifts they undergo.

What further characterizes the uniqueness of this study is the nature of the situated pedagogic discourse examined, namely the interaction between a principal and his staff. As such, it adds to the range of research in interactional discourses in the educational domain – for instance, Sarangi and Baynham (1996) who discuss classroom interaction, i.e. teacher-pupil interactions of various kinds; Keogh (1996) and McKenzie (1992), who study institution-parent, parent-teacher, and peer relationships; and Watters (1996) who investigates communicative practices within the service departments of a school, including some involving the principal and other authority figures, but not those between the principal and teaching staff.

After a section that briefly sketches the pertinent contextual features, I deal, at first separately, with what are effectively the two main foci of the struggle associated with identity in the data: *power* and *community*. As I show, the struggle associated with each derives from *The Book*'s broad purpose, which is to help reconstruct a culture of teaching and learning which the principal seeks to accomplish in two ways: (a) through using *The Book* as a means simply of conveying information to his staff – which is its overt and accepted function; and (b) by mobilizing the staff and seeking to imbue them with a new sense of identity and purpose – a much more covert, but also more contested function. Because of its twin functions, *The Book* realizes two distinct discourses which themselves struggle to coexist: a discourse of Authority (oriented towards the exercise of power); and a discourse of Exhortation (oriented towards the building of a community of teachers and learners of a particular kind).

Contextual Information

Thukeleni High School is located in the heart of Umlazi, near Durban. It has a pupil enrolment of 1,100 and a teaching complement, including the principal, of 39. With few exceptions, Zulu is everyone's mother tongue although English is the medium of instruction. The average class size at the school is 54, which is high, while the senior certificate pass rate is low and cause for concern, having dropped from 46 per cent in 1997 to 18 per cent in 1999.

Thukeleni High is dilapidated and troubled school, located close to a very large shopping centre and noisy bus/taxi rank, in an area, generally, where unemployment is very high. It is adjacent, too, to a large squatter/shack settlement from which the school draws up to 80 per cent of its pupils and from which it gets many loiterers and trouble-makers. Criminal activity in the area is high and, because parents and guardians of the children are largely jobless, the school cannot rely on their support, e.g. to pay school fees or to protect the school's property. The facilities at the school are meagre and in a very poor state: the principal, for example, has never had administrative support; the home economics room has no ovens; there is no science laboratory; and the only computer in the school was recently stolen.

There are also problems with teaching staff. First, Thukeleni High School was originally a primary school, and a number of the teachers have not yet upgraded their professional qualifications. Second, unstable governance in the recent past has resulted in irresponsibility and a lack of commitment on the part of some teachers. And, finally, older teachers drew attention in interviews to what they call 'the new kind of teachers' on the staff, who 'don't want to work and don't want to go into classes', who 'come at ten o'clock and leave at two o'clock'.

It is against this background that one must place Mr Mzinyati (a pseudonym), the school's new principal. Faced with the severe and pressing problems and challenges associated with inculcating a culture of teaching and learning; ensuring delivery of educational services in the form, for example, of acceptable senior certificate, i.e. matric results; protecting school property; and ensuring greater safety in the institution he agreed to lead, Mr Mzinyati explained that he has tried to return to first principles: 'I just said to myself, the only way in which I'm going to put things right was just to . . . make people follow the descriptions of themselves. If you are a learner, you've got to become what a learner is; if you are an educator, you've got to become what an educator is.' In addition, he has taken various steps towards building community support and responsibility, enhancing safety, and promoting better communication and, therefore, cohesion in the teaching corps, at the same time attempting to nurture and develop a value system commensurate with a genuine culture of teaching and learning. With these issues in mind, Mr Mzinyati has instituted, modified or else resuscitated various communication mechanisms and procedures/ literacies. All are handwritten and include: a time book in which teachers are expected to record their daily times of arrival and departure; a log book in which the principal records daily events and details such as financial transactions, absenteeism, and school visitors; and focal to this study, *The Book*, also referred to as the instruction or circular book – both of which, as will become apparent later, are misnomers.

The Book, a series of hardcover, A4 exercise books, is not an innovation. It pre-dated Mr Mzinyati but has been reshaped by him in order to accomplish more than simply informing teachers. Rather, it has become the means by which the principal communicates with staff and seeks to imbue them with a sense of mission. *The Book*, with Mr Mzinyati's remarks, makes its daily rounds, conveyed from one teacher to the next by a pupil designated by the principal. This pupil hands *The Book* to each teacher who is expected to read each entry and enclosures, sign in a designated place to acknowledge having read its contents, and return it to the waiting pupil who, ultimately, returns *The Book* to the principal. It is, clearly, a ritualized discursive practice in the sense, for example, of Magolda (2000).

While the staff interviewed believe *The Book* has an important place in the school, they all resist it. Among the major criticisms of *The Book* in its current form are the following: it is intrusive and ways need to be found to ensure that *The Book* is not so disruptive; entries are often too long; and it is used to disseminate information and direct staff in ways that are unilateral and non-negotiable. As a consequence, staff members choose sometimes not to 'endorse' or sign the entry while some sign without reading the message. Staff have, on one occasion, erased part of what the principal has written and replaced it 'with something in a more polite manner'.

Methods of Data Collection and Analysis

The main data sources on which I have drawn are: 99 entries in four copies of *The Book*, spanning the period from July 1997 to August 2000, and prior to my contact with the principal or staff; interviews with the principal and members of his staff; and, where relevant, contextual information of various kinds.[1]

A colleague and I conducted six semi-structured interviews with an equal number of Arts and Science subject teachers of varying periods of service at the school: some pre-Mzinyati appointees; others appointed after Mr Mzinyati became principal. The interviews were each roughly 40 minutes long and sought information on: the teachers' backgrounds; experience of teaching at the school; sense of the kinds of community influence on the school, and vice versa; the leadership styles of the principals under which they have taught; information on how *The Book* circulates; their understanding of the nature and function as well as insights into the sorts of entries that comprise it; and their own and their colleagues' reactions to *The Book*.

Data analysis relied on the methods of Critical Discourse Analysis (CDA) and involved: *describing* the formal features of selected, representative *Book* entries as texts; *interpreting* the interaction process by which the *Book* exchanges are constructed and construed, i.e. specifying what conventions are drawn on and how; and *explaining* the properties of the *Book* entries as a form(s) of social action. This means 'placing the interaction within the matrix of social action it is a part of' (Fairclough 1992: 11); assessing the extent to which the interaction associated with the *Book* entries confirms or challenges social relations of power; and specifying the ideological and political content implicit in *The Book*. For the purposes of the first two dimensions of the analysis, I have relied on the Appraisal framework within Systemic Functional Linguistics (SFL).

Originally developed by Martin (1997) and White (1997), Appraisal Theory is concerned with exploring the discourse semantics and lexico-grammar of the language of evaluation, attitude, and intersubjective positioning. In particular, it seeks to provide an account of how language construes the interpersonal relationships of solidarity and power. It encompasses aspects of the grammar which, in other contexts, have been grouped variously under headings such as modality, hedging, evidentiality, attitude, and stance. Appraisal is mainly realized lexically although it can also be realized by whole clauses. Because lexis is the most fluid area of language and the meanings of words are constantly under renegotiation and change, it is often not possible to state whether a lexical item has attitudinal colouring, and which value is being realized, until it is considered in context. Additionally, the interpretation of interpersonal meanings 'is not only dependent on the co-text but also on the sociocultural background and positionings of the interactants' (Eggins and Slade 1997: 126).

The two Appraisal categories that seemed most pertinent to the aim of considering the principal's construction of identities and relationships in the discourses of AUTHORITY and EXHORTATION evident in *The Book* are those of ATTITUDE and ENGAGEMENT. ATTITUDE includes those meanings by which writers attach an intersubjective value or assessment to participants and processes by reference to emotional responses (AFFECT), or to the evaluation of human behaviour (JUDGEMENT), or of objects and products (APPRECIATION) evaluated against culturally determined value systems. For instance, AFFECT is the main value attached to the following extract, when the principal reports the death of a pupil: 'We *loved* her just like we do to all other learners . . . she will be *sadly missed* by the school.' The system of JUDGEMENT encompasses meanings which serve to evaluate human behaviour positively or negatively by reference to a set of institutionalized norms concerning rules and regulations (SOCIAL SANCTION) or social expectations (SOCIAL ESTEEM). Thus, the phrase 'we *indulge* ourselves and our times in *useless, directionless thinking*' carries overt values of negative social esteem judgement. APPRECIATION, too, involves positive or negative evaluation, but this time of objects, plans or policies, as in: 'We have just written the March test, I am sure we know the *importance and impact* of the above in the lives of the learners.'

The system of ENGAGEMENT covers all those resources by which writers negotiate positions for themselves and readers. White (1997: 4–5) argues that such stance values as 'I believe that', 'perhaps', and 'it seems that', which are traditionally construed as indicating certainty/commitment or uncertainty/lack of commitment to truth values, alternatively or additionally signal willingness to 'engage with' one's audience. Authors take on a position and simultaneously leave open the possibility of alternatives or contradictions or, alternatively, they 'close' off the interaction by limiting or even eliminating altogether the expression of any alternative viewpoints. The textual analysis which follows will show, for example, that in the previously quoted extract, 'We have just written the March test, *I am sure we know* the importance and impact of the above in the lives of the learners', the principal is overtly suppressing any divergent opinions, any other voices than his own.

I first analysed the overt format features, e.g. dating and numbering, greetings and salutations, acknowledgement grids, of all 99 entries. Then, I coded the textual features of 20 entries between 22 May 1998 and 10 August 2000 in terms of the framework outlined above. This coding enabled me to establish the general patterns of meanings in what I have subsequently labelled the discourses of Authority and Exhortation evident in these entries. Finally, I selected three highly representative entries for exemplification purposes. Because space in this paper is limited, I provide only two of these in reproduced and coded format in the Appendix: Text 1 (T1) from 22 May 1998 and Text 2 (T2) from 10 August 2000, but I also refer in the following discussion to the third text from 6 April 2000.[2]

The Discourse of AUTHORITY

The first major interpersonal orientation in *The Book* is one of authority and power. The principal positions himself unambiguously as 'the boss': he is the person with the authority to write entries in *The Book* and to insist that they be read and acknowledged; he is the one who gives information that others do not possess and calls meetings; in the troubled context of the school, he is also the one who castigates teachers for not doing their job. In this section, I consider first the format features, then the textual features that index AUTHORITY in *The Book*.

Format Features of AUTHORITY

The most obvious format features of this role give the principal's entries a strong bureaucratic flavour and remind one of the kinds of close management associated, for instance, with stock control because careful attention is given to numbering and dating each entry, of passport control because stamping and signing is a prominent feature, and of routinized forms of institutionalized correspondence, hence the principal's reliance on standardized (impersonal) greetings and salutation formats. Elements of the attendance register and roll-call are also represented because teachers are expected to supply overt evidence of their having read each entry, and the principal initials entries after having checked that all staff have signed each entry.

Closer investigation reveals the following conventions and preferences, their ubiquity and redundancy, the principal's obvious 'busy-ness' in maintaining them, and, cumulatively, their 'weight'. Readers are typically greeted as 'Colleagues' (65 entries) or else as 'Staff personnel'. 'Thank you' and 'Yours in the Office' are the most prominent salutations, each used 39 times. The principal concludes 90 of the 99 entries by signing his message. He then stamps the end of the entry (42×) (the school stamp also precedes 92 of the entries), after which he lists by hand the names of his staff (35×) or draws a grid in which he lists their names or numbers (54×). He tallies the number of staff who sign the Acknowledgement list or grid five times,

and either signs it and records 'seen' or 'Your presence has been acknowledged'; for those not present, he writes 'Absentees. Your absence has
been acknowledged', or asterisks the absentees and writes 'acknowledged',
signing and dating the grid.

The above features (and, especially, their statistical 'weight') testify to the
principal's 'ownership' of each entry in the data, the extent of his surveillance over his staff's behaviour, and, therefore, his authority. The most
obvious tokens of that authority are, of course, his use of the school stamp,
the number of times he signs and/or initials his name, and the manner in
which he prescribes (and circumscribes) the staff's response options. As
Iedema (1999: 50–1) notes, the formality of such features 'is a limiting or
closing off of possibilities' which brings about 'interactive closure'.

A final formatting feature of note is the principal's inclusion within
entries of aphorisms. These occur many times at the start of entries, as
headings, and sometimes inside entries. Exhortatory in tone, they are further evidence of the principal's discourse of AUTHORITY. At the same time,
however, they are part of the discourse of community-building that coexists
in *The Book* with the discourse of power and appear to promote a sense of
common goals, common understandings, and a common 'language'
among the staff. Some of the aphorisms used are: 'Lead by example';
'There's no such thing as failure. There are results'; 'Where there's a will
there's a way'; 'The more I change the less I blame'; and 'Just in time
Principle' (T1).

Textual Features of AUTHORITY

Perhaps the most salient of the textual features of *The Book* that index
authority and power is the use of 'proclamation', whereby authors inter-
polate themselves directly into the text 'as the explicit source of the utterance' (White 1997: 22). Examples of proclamation in T1 are: 'I therefore
do not think that', 'I therefore urge', 'As far as I observed', 'As far as I am
concerned', and 'there is'. White (1998: 12) argues that, in addition to the
clear assertion of authority, proclamation options 'close' dialogue, because
they 'act in some way to limit the range of possibility of interaction with the
diversity' of voices. Furthermore, proclamation implies that any rejection
or doubt on the part of the readers becomes a direct challenge to the
authority of the writer.

Another feature of the discourse of AUTHORITY is the high number,
throughout *The Book*, of imperative forms, often linked with old-fashioned
businessese – for example, in the 6 April 2000 text alone: 'be advised',
'think of . . .', 'make', 'be informed', 'be reminded that', 'Kindly be advised
and informed', 'kindly submit as requested', 'kindly report', and 'kindly
bear with me'. While the inclusion of 'kindly' might be interpreted as a
softening of the commands, it is more likely to be a remnant of some old-
fashioned type of routine, formulaic business writing that emphasizes form
over meaning and reinforces the bureaucratic flavour of these phrases.

The use of proclamation and imperative forms functions to assert authority and close interaction. The same function is carried by many of the interrogative forms the principal uses, particularly those that carry meanings of reprimands, accusations, and commands. T1 is especially representative of the use of these forms: 'Why can't we follow the simple procedures that I have laid?', 'Why do we destroy that which we have started?', 'Why do we allow the demolishing spirit that separate us?', 'Have you seen the time book off-late?', 'Why do we ignore the signing of it?' Tellingly, one of the teachers interviewed commented: 'Sometimes he's poetic, you know. Perhaps giving an instruction through a question, you see. "Do you think you're doing enough?", "Do you think those kids came here for the purpose of doing . . .?" You see the way in which he is asking questions. It's not a straightforward thing.' Asked what he would do instead, the teacher responded: 'I would be clear with my instructions . . . clear and very much simple and straightforward: "This is what I want, this is what I don't want." Not in the form of questions because who is going to get the people . . . I mean, are they going to respond in writing – no.'

The principal's concern for the poor performance of both teachers and pupils at the school is evident in the high-value, negative social-esteem judgements made in many entries. Through these, teachers are positioned as delinquents who need castigating, as the cumulative effect of these forms makes clear in the following excerpt from T1:

> The setting of Question Papers does not necessitate one to abandon the classes. This work was supposed to have been done long time ago. I therefore do not think that we should suffer because of that. If one of us is not performing or rather is not attending a class as expected, result to a number of cases that come forth to the office. I therefore urge the personnel to see to it that classes are attended to.

These judgements are usually coupled with high-value engagement signals such as '*It is high time*', 'We *cannot* allow things to continue like this', 'Our efforts *should not* aim at lowering our standards', and '*It is imperative that* we all attend' (6 April 2000), which serve to foreground the sense of urgency the principal wishes to convey and the seriousness of the situation. Not surprisingly, teachers react against such forms. As one teacher put it, 'sometimes he can be so harsh', and another teacher commented, 'If he used something a little bit politely maybe it will have more effect.'

An important function of *The Book* is, thus, to control and exercise power over teachers, whether through its distribution system, formatting features or through the language of proclamation. It is not surprising, therefore, that the teachers resisted the intrusion of *The Book* into their daily routine, thus confirming Foucault's (1977: 142) observation that 'there are no relations of power without resistances: the latter are all the more real and effective because they are formed right at the point where relations of power are exercised'.

The Discourse of EXHORTATION

At the same time, though, as the principal uses *The Book* for the purposes of authority, he also has a very different purpose – that of (re)building a sound community of learning and teaching in a school and an educational system beleaguered by difficulties. In order to combat the lack of purpose and discipline in his school as well as teacher demoralization – what Asmal (1999) called 'a real malaise in the teaching corps' – the principal uses *The Book* to try and mobilize his staff towards greater commitment.

The principal's use of identification forms and the pronoun system in English conveys most emphatically the desire to unite staff and to help them focus on their role as teachers. Throughout *The Book*, the pronouns 'we', 'our', 'us' (and variants such as 'all of us', 'us all', 'everyone') predominate. Naming practices foreground people's institutional role, as the principal refers to his readers as: 'colleagues', 'the personnel', 'teachers', 'staff', 'staff members', 'the executive Committee', 'educators', 'educationists', 'team', and 'professionals'. In one entry on 2 July 1998, he mentions 'our family'. Pupils at the school are *always* referred to as 'the learners', thus similarly highlighting their specific institutional role in the school. The following extract from 6 April 2000 shows the cumulative effect of such choices:

> Schools are there to develop and promote the potential talents that lie idle in the learners. Can we think of any person who can do this? The answer is YES! WHO? THUKELENI EDUCATORS. When I see each one of us, I see a potential talent that is hidden, deliberately. Our learners need us. In our school we lack that eye, a visionary one, that can give smiles in our faces, joy in our hearts and success in our efforts. The reason is, we indulge ourselves and our times in useless, directionless thinking when the direction is there for us to take. C'mon be positive. I am just thankful for the few Sports Committee members whose efforts are looked down upon. What do you have to offer? We are waiting for your input. The learners are waiting for you.

In contrast, when the principal is castigating teachers, he uses more neutral forms such as 'one', 'person' or 'people', as the following examples from T1 show:

> The setting of Question Papers does not necessitate one to abandon the classes. [. . .] There is again an increasing number of people who do not see it fit to report to the office when they are to absent themselves.

While he does use the pronoun 'I' frequently, his use of 'the office' is ambiguous. Sometimes it refers to an administrative locum, the place where documents are filed or where meetings are held, as in the following examples:

> I would appreciate if all the members of this team assemble/report at the office on Friday immediately after prayers in the morning 07/04/2000. (6 April 2000)

> The first Quarterly class schedules as well as the Y/M schedules need to be filed in the office. (2 May 2000)

Kindly forward to <u>the office</u> your class list as requested. (2 February 2000)

At other times, however, 'the office' appears to refer to himself, as in:

(if uncertain, <u>the office</u> is prepared to explain) (6 April 2000)

Kindly excuse <u>the office</u> for causing this inconvenience. (T2)

The Grade 12s are excused/excluded in this exercise, for they are the responsibility of <u>the office</u> this week. (24 July 2000)

The two meanings are united in his regular salutation, 'Yours in the office'. While one needs to remember that Mr Mzinyati does not have any administrative help, and 'the office', quite literally, means himself in a room, such slippages of meaning as the ones exemplified above also point to his retaining a leadership role in the discourse of EXHORTATION.

Proclamation forms appear to play a dual role in *The Book*; identified earlier as constituting a prominent feature of the discourse of AUTHORITY, they play an equally important role in the discourse of EXHORTATION. Forms such as 'I believe', 'I am sure', 'I want it to be known', and many others, seem to do much more than assert the writer's authority and contribute to interactive closure. They also help promote the identity of the principal as a committed, passionate leader of the school community who tries to draw his readers into his vision of it as a more successful and congenial place for teachers and pupils.

Having looked at the role of interrogation in the textual features of AUTHORITY, some of these features also contribute to the sense of EXHORT-ATION in *The Book*. Firstly, some questions function as pleas or supplications, particularly when they are coupled with high-value positive or negative social-esteem judgements, as in:

Why do we <u>destroy</u> that which we have started? Why do we allow <u>the demolishing spirit that separate us?</u> (T1)

What <u>contribution</u> have you made in as far as <u>the upliftment</u> of this school? (31 August 1998)

In your own observation, do our classrooms represent areas where people's (learners') <u>futures are being carved</u>? (2 May 2000)

What <u>indicators</u> are there for your <u>success</u>? (8 March 2000)

Then, there are a number of SOCIAL-ESTEEM judgements, positive or negative, which are used to help readers focus on the issues and make the right decisions, as exemplified in this extract from 6 April 2000:

Schools are there <u>to develop and promote the potential talents</u> that lie <u>idle</u> in the learners. Can we think of any person who can do this? The <u>answer</u> is <u>YES!</u> WHO? THUKELENI EDUCATORS. When I see each one of us, I see a <u>potential talent</u> that is hidden, deliberately. Our <u>learners need us</u>. In our school we <u>lack that eye</u>, <u>a visionary</u> one, that can give <u>smiles in our faces, joy in our hearts and success in our efforts</u>. The reason is, <u>we indulge</u> ourselves and our times <u>in useless, directionless thinking</u> when the direction is there for us to take. C'mon be positive. I am just thankful for the few Sports Committee members whose efforts are looked down upon. What do you have to offer? We are waiting for your input. The learners are waiting for you.

The two discourses of AUTHORITY and EXHORTATION coexist in *The Book*, sometimes awkwardly, as the principal's attempts to energize his staff and imbue them with a new sense of responsibility become enmeshed in the heavy bureaucratic surveillance system he has established, and which staff resist. A teacher who commented on some of her colleagues' lack of qualifications seems to be aware of the dual role Mr Mzinyati is playing when she says: 'Then sometimes he's forced by circumstances to be harsh . . . he has to work with them [teachers who have not upgraded themselves], encourage them on all cost. On the other hand, show them that they are expected to work because the department needs something. He is frank, he tells us. He can't keep hiding things.'

Conclusion

'The school principal', Asmal (1999) asserted, 'has the crucial role of professional and administrative leadership, and is responsible for the standard of learning and teaching in the school.' This study has investigated one of the steps taken by a principal to fulfil this role through a particular form of communication with his staff. Through the analysis of selected entries in *The Book*, I have shown how the principal attempts both to exercise power over teachers and, at the same time, to redefine their role in the school. The complex mix and ambiguities of meanings created by his dual role of 'boss' and 'leader' reflect the complex and unstable sociopolitical context in post-apartheid South Africa. As Fairclough (1995: 61) notes:

> In very general terms, a conventional discourse practice is realised in a text which is relatively homogeneous in its forms and meanings, whereas a creative discourse practice is realised in a text which is relatively heterogeneous in its forms and meanings. . . . Also in general terms, one would expect a complex and creative discourse practice where the sociocultural practice is fluid, unstable and shifting, and a conventional discourse practice where the sociocultural practice is relatively fixed and stable.

In this particular 'community of practice' (Holmes and Meyerhoff 1999), *The Book* defines simultaneously one struggle over membership identities (of the principal and his staff) and another over preferred practices, in ways that both reflect the troubled situation of the school, and perhaps contribute towards the maintenance of some of its troubled aspects. Mr Mzinyati's overt imposition of power, actively resisted by staff, may be reinforcing many of the latter's inappropriate behaviours, hence severely diminishing the impact of his rallying call. That *The Book*'s entries are remarkably similar over the three-year period would appear to show that, up until mid-August

2000, Mr Mzinyati was less than successful in his attempts at reconstructing a culture of teaching and learning in his school.

Acknowledgements

I am extremely grateful to the principal for allowing me access to copies of *The Book* and thank him and those members on the staff of Thukeleni High School for agreeing to be interviewed. I am indebted to the informant mentioned in note 1 and am especially indebted to Nicole Geslin. A former colleague, she has had a major influence on the conception, form, and content of this work.

Appendix

The texts are coded according to the Appraisal categories outlined in the paper; however, in order not to clutter the texts more than is strictly necessary, I do not show the distinction between ESTEEM and SANCTION JUDGEMENTS, nor that between positive and negative values. For the same reason, interrogative forms which function as commands, reprimands, and so on are indicated with a large, bold interrogation mark (**?**).

Bold: Engagement signals, including proclamation and imperative forms.

Dotted underline: ATTITUDE values of JUDGEMENT.

Italics: Identification forms.

Text 1

22 MAY 1998

Re: *Staff Personnel*   [Stamp]

Colleagues

May *I* bring the following to the attention of *us all*:

(a) The setting of Question Papers does not necessitate *one* to abandon the classes. This work was **supposed to** have been done long time ago. *I* **therefore do not think** that *we* should suffer because of that. If *one of us* is not performing or rather is not attending a class as expected, result to a number of cases that come forth to the office. *I* **therefore urge** *the personnel* to see to it that classes are attended to.

(b) There is again an increasing number of *people* who do not see it fit to report to the office when they are to absent *themselves*. Is this right**?** Is this what *we* **should** all be doing**?** Why can't *we* follow the simple procedures that *I* have laid**?** What **could** be the cause of this**?** Why is this done **after all?**

(c) In the past few weeks *I* **had thought** *we* have achieved one significant step i.e. teamwork. **As far as *I* observed** this had also bore good results that which *we* like. **Seemingly**, there are now other development which are opposite to what *I* have been thinking. Why do *we* destroy that which *we* have started? Why do *we* allow the demolishing spirit that separate *us*?

(d) Next week, *I* **shall be** excusing / chasing away all *learners* that (having) up to this far, [they still] owe the school fund. *I* **therefore urge** / **plead** for *your* support and co-operation on this regard.

(e) The verb 'to submit' is not an offending / oppressing Thank you word, only if *you* do not apply the 'just in time' principle will it changes and oppresses *one*.

Thank you.
BNMzinyati

[Stamp]

PS

1. Have *you* seen the time book off-late? **Should *I*** make entries like *I* have done? Why do *we* ignore the signing of it? Why? **As far as *I* am concerned**, there is no workplace without it.

2. *I* am **still** waiting for the 1st Quarter Results analysis as well as the class schedule. When are they forthcoming?

[Acknowledgement Grid] [Stamp]

Text 2

10 AUG 2000   [Stamp]

Staff Personnel

Be informed that there will be a meeting ('urgent') meeting at 11h45 am. **Kindly excuse** the office for causing this inconvenience. These are matters that require *our* immediate intervention.
Your prompt response **will be greatly appreciated.**
Thank you.

Yours in the office
BNMzinyati

PS: **Bring** along a piece of paper and a calculator if *you* have one.
[Acknowledgement Grid]

Notes

1. What greatly facilitated access to the data and to personnel at the school is the 'insider' status of an informant, he being a graduate student in the Linguistics Programme on which I was teaching at the time. Through his association with the school it was possible to approach the Principal, whose co-operation ensured access to copies of *The Book*, and whose willingness to be interviewed paved the way for the interviews with other members of the staff.

References

Asmal, K. (1999) 'Call to Action: Mobilising Citizens to Build a South African Education and Training System for the 21st Century' at: http://www.education.pwv.gov.za/Tirisano_Folder.htm (consulted July 1999).

Eggins, S. and Slade, D. (1997) *Analysing Casual Conversation*. London: Cassell.

Fairclough, N. (1995) *Media Discourse*. London: Edward Arnold.

Fairclough, N. (ed.) (1992) *Critical Language Awareness*. London: Longman.

Foucault, M. (1977) *Power/Knowledge: Selected Interviews and Other Writings 1972–1977*. New York: Pantheon.

Holmes, J. and Meyerhoff, M. (1999) 'The Community of Practice: Theories and Methodologies in Language and Gender Research', *Language in Society*, 28: 173–83.

Iedema, R. (1999) 'Formalizing Organizational Meaning', *Discourse and Society*, 10(1): 49–65.

Keogh, J. (1996) 'Governmentality in Parent-teacher Communications', *Language and Education*, 10(2, 3): 119–31.

Magolda, P. M. (2000) 'The Campus Tour: Ritual and Community in Higher Education', *Anthropology and Education Quarterly*, 31(1): 24–46.

Martin, J. R. (1997) 'Analysing Genre: Functional Parameters', in *Genre and Institutions: Social Processes in the Workplace and School*, ed. by F. Christie and J. R. Martin. London: Cassell, 3–39.

May, S. A. (1995) 'Deconstructing Traditional Discourses of Schooling: An Example of School Reform', *Language and Education*, 9(1): 1–29.

McKenzie, M. (1992) ' "What I've always known but never been told": Euphemisms, School Discourse and Empowerment', in *Critical Language Awareness*, ed. by N. Fairclough. London: Longman, 223–37.

Sarangi, S. and Baynham, M. (eds) (1996) 'Discursive Construction of Educational Identities: Alternative Readings', *Language and Education*, 10(2, 3): 77–81.

Watters, K. (1996) 'Communicative Practices of the Service Staff of a School', in *The Social Uses of Literacy*, ed. by M. Prinsloo and M. Breier. Cape Town: Sached Books and John Benjamins, 85–102.

White, P. R. R. (1998) 'Towards a Grammar of Power and Solidarity –
    Developments in the Linguistics of Evaluation, Inter-subjectivity and
    Ideological Position', paper presented at the 10th Euro-international
    Systemic Functional Workshop, Liverpool.
White, P. R. R. (1997) 'The Grammar of Fact and Opinion: Authorial
    Stance and the Construction of Media Objectivity', paper presented at
    the 24th International Systemic Functional Conference, Toronto.

11 Representations of Rape in the Discourse of Legal Decisions

Débora de Carvalho Figueiredo

Much has been said, investigated, and discussed about the tough handling of rape victims by the court system during a rape trial. My work explores a specific dimension of the rape trial: from the perspective of Critical Discourse Analysis (CDA), I investigate the vocabulary used in British reported appeal decisions on rape cases to depict sexual assaults. The data analysis indicates that appellate decisions on rape cases present the event in different lights, depending on how the assault has been labelled and categorized. This categorization system reflects and recreates a body of sexual myths and ideological presuppositions about how men and women behave and relate to each other, and it is this ideological frame that will determine how blame, discipline, and punishment is judicially apportioned, and who will be cast in the roles of 'victim' and 'villain'.

Introduction

The tough handling of rape victims by the court system during a rape trial has been widely commented on. Nowadays, it is fairly well established that the victim suffers what is sometimes called a 'double rape': she is first raped by her assailant, and she is then 'raped' again by the court system, in the sense that in both instances she loses her privacy and, during the trial, her sexual and social lives are scrutinized.[1] This paper explores yet another dimension of this 'double rape': the judicial discourse used by the British criminal justice system to construct the legal responses to appeals on rape cases. My aim is to add to this well-established line of inquiry (Liebes-Plesner 1984; Adler 1987; Smart 1989; Coates *et al.* 1994; Edwards 1981, 1996; Conley and O'Barr 1998; Lees 1997; etc.) by investigating how the linguistic and discursive structure of reported appellate decisions (RADs) contribute to the gender-biased treatment given to victims of rape.

In this paper, I investigate, from the perspectives of Critical Discourse Analysis (CDA) and gender and feminist legal studies, how judicial discourse constructed by legal decisions represents the event 'rape'. To do so, I examine and then analyse the vocabulary used in legal decisions to depict the sexual assaults, i.e. the event.

Vocabulary

In analysing legal decisions on cases of rape, it is possible to see that certain images are very constant throughout the texts. These images, or myths, correspond to and express commonsensical beliefs about men, women, and sexuality. The sexual mythology that surrounds rape starts with the victim specificity: until recently, British law stated that only women could be raped by penile penetration of the vagina, and the majority of rape trials today involve a female victim (McLean 1988).[2] Since, until recently, the law stated that only women could be raped, it leads to the conclusion that perhaps there is something about women that leads them to be raped. Feminist scholars also contend that the 'female-ness' of the victim leads to harsh official treatment because official institutions entertain preconceived and prejudiced notions about gender (McLean 1988).

My interest in analysing the vocabulary of RADs is not to investigate a specific professional lexicon or jargon, but to suggest how the lexical choices made by the producers of RADs indicate a system of classification, or categorization, of the events involved in these texts, and indirectly of their participants, especially the appellant and the complainant. This vocabulary, which is not specific to legal discourse, is nevertheless an indication of how the criminal justice system separates people and events into groups or classes, and which world-views are expressed by this system of categorization.

Words can only be interpreted and understood in context. It is important to remember that contexts are socially, culturally, and politically constituted. So, to understand a word used in the context of a legal decision on a rape case, the reader has to take into account the judicial discourse on rape as a whole, with all its ideological overtones. The lexis of a discourse represents its conceptual repertoire. Although there are different terms to refer to the same object, event or experience, the term chosen expresses a point of view. The vocabulary used by writers is a strong indicator of, and an influence on, the scope and the structure of their experience and their world-view (Halliday 1985). Fowler (1996: 215), for instance, calls for a dynamic view of vocabulary or lexis as 'the encoding of ideas or experience'.

Due to the fact that it is not possible to say everything about something in a text (Winter 1994), text producers have to rely on implicit propositions, which allow the text consumer to establish links between the clauses and sentences of the text. However, text writers can also structure their texts in order to predispose their readers to establish certain links and not others, creating predominant readings which rest on specific taken-for-granted propositions that are part of the implicit meaning of the text. Thus, a text addresses an 'ideal reader', who will bring to bear on the text the propositions which will lead to its 'preferred reading' (Fairclough 1995). The ideological function of a 'preferred reading' is to lead text consumers to accept as 'natural' the framework of common sense in which the text and the reader are positioned. As any other texts, legal decisions on rape cases also express and rely on a wealth of implicit commonsensical assumptions about gender roles, gender relations, and sexuality. As many of these assumptions are part of implicit meanings present in RADs, they are difficult to bring to a level of awareness, and equally difficult to deconstruct and combat.

Interpretative Repertoires and Prototypes

I suggested earlier that the judicial discourse on rape rests on a system of categorization of men, women, and sexuality. The purpose of this categorization is to assist people in making sense of the large number of things and events they encounter in their daily lives. The use of categorization as a cognitive device allows people to simplify infinite variation, and ignore irrelevant features (Fowler 1996). Vocabulary choices rest on sets of pre-constructed categories, and the process of representation involves deciding how to 'place' people and events within these sets of categories (Fairclough 1995).

It could be argued that the need to categorize is a natural cognitive strategy used by human beings. However, what CDA challenges is the notion that the world has an intrinsic, natural structure, divided into equally natural categories, from which language passively draws its meanings (Fowler 1996). Language does not simply provide words for existing concepts; it crystallizes and stabilizes ideas. Words make ideas palpable through the signs they provide, which can then be spoken or written. In addition, words enable the storage of ideas into systems, which, in turn, enables the expression of distinctions and relationships.

By selecting a particular category to describe someone or something, speakers and writers are establishing a link between the person or thing categorized and other members of the same group. To describe something by using categorization devices is revealing not only of what is being described, but also of who is describing: speakers and writers try to make themselves understood by fitting people and events into categories, and the categories they select to construct their descriptions, and thus clarify the world, indicate how they understand and interpret reality (Jalbert 1983; Meurer 1998).

Categories include both prototypical and marginal examples. Fowler (1996) argues that categories and prototypes allow people to concentrate on essentials and be able to identify rapidly what a thing or event is. A prototype is a word (or representation) that is perceived as a 'classic' example of its field, springing more immediately to mind in terms of its class. This phenomenon indicates that, for cultural and social reasons, people tend to perceive (or construct) certain words (or representations) as more central or more salient within a semantic field, while others shade away from these prototypical examples until the class merges in a fuzzy boundary with its less typical examples.

The danger of prototypical definitions is that they may turn into stereo-types, 'oversimplified, automatic interpretations – [which] inhibit under-standing; thought becomes routine, uncritical, and discourse becomes prejudicial' (Fowler 1996: 26). Discourse does not represent a rendering of the objective world, but rather a way of relating to, constructing, and sim-plifying objective phenomena, making them manageable and economical for thoughts and actions. However, systems of categorizing and classifying phenomena frequently seem so natural that they become 'common sense', thereby corresponding to an objective 'reality' instead of a 'world-view', 'theory', 'hypothesis' or 'ideology'.

Another illuminating concept that can be used to understand systems of categorization is that of 'interpretative repertoires'. Interpretative repertoires are

> building blocks speakers use for constructing versions of actions, cognitive processes and other phenomena. Any particular repertoire is constituted out of a restricted range of terms used in a specific stylistic and grammatical fashion. Commonly these terms are derived from one or more key metaphors and the presence of a repertoire will often be signalled by certain tropes or figures of speech. (Wetherell and Potter 1988, quoted in Coates *et al.* 1994: 197).

In this paper, I use the notions of 'prototypes' and 'interpretative reper-toires' to investigate the process of categorization of the event 'rape' in the vocabulary of reported appellate decisions on cases of rape. In the follow-ing sections, I will discuss and illustrate with examples from reported appeal decisions how judicial discourse seeks to define the event 'rape'. To do so, I will divide the examples into two groups, corresponding to the categorization system used by appeal judges to classify, systematize, and simplify the complex phenomenon of sexual violence against women: 'real'/prototypical rapes and non-typical rapes.

The data used in this work consist of excerpts taken from a corpus of RADs published in the Criminal Appeal Reports (Sweet and Maxwell) and the All England Law Reports (Butterworths) between 1987 and 1998. The delimitation of this time-span was due to the fact that I wished to collect a reasonable number of appeals on rape cases, and to investigate if there had been many changes in the judicial treatment of rape over a ten-year period. Within this time period, I randomly collected RADs on rape trials involving adult women. The excerpts are individually numbered, each number rep-resenting one RAD. If the same number is repeated in two or more excerpts, this indicates that all of them come from the same RAD. The words or sentences highlighted within each excerpt are the ones I wish to focus on, because it is mainly through them that the categories or prototypes being discussed are constructed.

The Legal View of Rape

According to the English legal definition, rape consists of vaginal penetration by the penis, when the man knows the woman is not consenting to sex or does not care whether she is consenting or not (Section 1 of *Criminal Offences Act 1956* – Temkin 1987).[3]

From a woman's point of view, however, rape may be a life-threatening event where sex (of any kind) is used to control and humiliate her, during which her only concern is to survive (thus, so many women offer no resistance to rape). The definitions of consent, consensual, and forced sex traded in the legal discourse of rape all rest on male rather than on female experiences, e.g. if a woman shows no verbal and/or physical resistance, she is considered to be consenting; rape without physical violence is considered less serious; and rape by a known man is considered less traumatic. At the restricted level of the specific case, one of the main functions of a rape trial is to define the meaning of the act to the parties – the defendant and the complainant, i.e. to establish if the sexual acts that took place were consensual or not and, thus, if they constitute the crime of 'rape' or not. At the broader level of the legal system and of society, the trial and its legal decisions also help to define the meaning of the act, this time to a larger audience: legal practitioners (lawyers, judges, etc.) and members of the public (witnesses, newspaper readers, etc.).

The discourse of rape trials, along with other discourses, helps to establish what constitutes consensual versus forced sex and 'normal' versus 'abnormal' sex. However, rape laws and legal practitioners alike do not take into consideration that men and women have different perspectives of sexuality and, therefore, might have different definitions of rape. Women's experiences of heterosexual sex are not either consensual sex or rape; rather, they exist along a continuum that goes from choice, to pressure, to coercion, to force.

The 'Real'/Prototypical Rape (Standard Rape Episode)

From the legal point of view, rape is defined as a 'serious legal offence' when: it involves the penetration of the vagina by the penis; the victim is very young or very old; intercourse is achieved through the use of physical force; the rapist is a stranger, particularly a stranger who broke into the victim's home. If brought to trial, this kind of rape is severely punished because it represents not just an attack against an individual woman, but a threat to social values to do with youth and old age, the home, virginity, and the good name of women. In constructing their legal decisions, many judges still try to match the particular case they are analysing against this stereotypical standard episode; a mismatch makes conviction unlikely or sentence length shorter.

Below are a number of examples of how a 'real' rape is seen from the judicial viewpoint. The excerpts selected represent examples of prototypical rapes. Inside each excerpt, the particular lexicalizations chosen by appellate judges to evaluate the cases under analysis have been highlighted.

1. On October 26, 1993, he was released on parole. Four days later he committed this terrible offence . . . He accepts that this was a terrible case. [**Albert Thomas (1995) 16 Cr App R (S) 686 – elderly widow raped by a burglar – 15-year sentence**]

2. Over a period of three years the appellant committed offences against five men-tally deficient women, some of whom were resident in a hospital where the appel-lant had been employed for many years as a nursing assistant . . . The offences were grave and despicable, involving preying on mentally ill, vulnerable women, sexu-ally abusing them and leaving them helpless and lost. [**Michael Fox (1995) 16 Cr App R (S) 688 – stranger rape – life imprisonment**]

3. On three subsequent occasions he [the appellant] gained access to flats occupied by women, and raped them, using violence and threats to kill . . . these horrendous rapes . . . the terrifying nature of the rapes which were committed . . . [**Paul Brandy (1997) 1 Cr App R (S) 38 – stranger rape – life imprisonment**]

4. The appellant was convicted of attempted rape, robbery and indecent assault. The appellant attacked a young woman who was six months pregnant as she walked home from a friend's flat. The appellant threatened her with a knife, made her remove her clothes and attempted to rape her and then indecently assaulted her . . . This was undoubtedly a very serious attack on a total stranger at night who was simply wending her way home . . . [**Roy Low (1998) 1 Cr App R (S) 68 – standard 'stranger rape' episode – life imprisonment**]

All these cases fit the criteria of a standard rape episode: rape by a strange man, frequently aggravated by the use of threats or a weapon and the victim's age. The lexical choices construct the events as 'real' crimes: the offences are described as 'terrible', 'grave', 'despicable', 'horrendous', 'ter-rifying', and 'very serious'. It is clear that the judges felt shocked and dis-gusted by the crimes and that their sympathies lay with the victims. This severe judicial attitude was reflected in the long sentences handed down to these rapists.

A frequent lexical choice made by appellate judges to fit certain rapes into the 'real' rape slot is the use of the noun 'ordeal' to evaluate the event. When the event is interpreted as an 'ordeal', there is no doubt that it is indeed rape, and that the corresponding sentence will be severe. Below is an example of a case categorized as an 'ordeal'.

5. The case had to be slotted into its appropriate place in the overall spectrum of sentencing for the range of appalling cases that come before the Court . . . Aston-ishingly, despite the appalling ordeal to which the appellant had subjected her, in her very full statement she felt able to say this: 'Although this man seemed horrible by the things he did, I feel he wasn't a bad man underneath' . . . One's first reaction to the case is inevitably one of outrage and revulsion. The thought of invading an old woman's home and subjecting her to this dreadful ordeal is almost unthinkable. [**Laurence McIntosh (1994) 15 Cr App R (S) 163 – rape of a 100-year-old widow by a stranger – nine-year sentence**]

The 'real' or prototypical rape is often connected to the presence of aggravating features in the case. According to the *Dictionary of Law* (Collin 1992: 8), 'aggravation' is 'something which makes a crime more serious'. In a rape trial, the features which aggravate the crime and, therefore, result in a longer sentence to the offender, are: use of a weapon; attempt to frighten or wound the victim; subject the victim to sexual indignities; the victim's virginity; the victim's very young or very old age; burglary followed by rape; and the after-effects of the rape on the victim.

The following excerpt illustrates some of the aggravating factors found in the corpus, i.e. the victim's youth, her virginity, her subsequent trauma, and the fact that she was attacked in her own house.

6. In the early hours of the morning he entered a house occupied by two sisters, one of who was six months pregnant. The offender threatened to kill both of them, and then raped the younger of the two sisters and indecently assaulted her by pushing his penis into her mouth and his fingers into her vagina . . . For the Attorney-General it was submitted that the offence was aggravated by the fact that the offender had broken into the victim's home at night, that the victim had no previous sexual experience of sexual intercourse, and that the offence had caused her long-lasting psychological damage. [**Attorney-General's Reference No. 16 1993 (1994) 15 Cr App R (S) 811 – stranger rape – nine-year sentence**]

Non-Typical Rapes

Forced sex, especially with a known man, is often described within the sexual discourse of pain and pleasure, of masochism and sadism (Edwards 1996) or of duty and obligation, and as such it can easily come to be seen as part of the 'normal' sexual life of couples. For instance, the fact that many women do not always want or enjoy sex but frequently participate is still considered, in many circles, as part and parcel of a woman's sexual life. The naturalization of these supposedly non-violent forms of coercive sex helps to explain why law-and-order officials have difficulty in labelling episodes of forced sex between partners as rape.[4]

In spite of the legal belief that the existence of a previous relationship between assailant and victim renders the rape less traumatic, rape by a known man is devastating for women because, besides the usual pain, guilt, and shame linked to any sexual offence, this act involves feelings of betrayal of trust, confusion, and uncertainty. The difficulty in formulating coercive sex as rape also has the effect of keeping women silent (it is probably linked to the low reporting rate of rape), and of letting many abusive men go undetected.[5] Much of this is due to the power of language, i.e. to the power to categorize and label events and experiences.

In this section, I discuss how many rapes brought to the legal fore are named otherwise than 'real' rape. As I will illustrate, the judicial definition of 'real' rape found in RADs is still restricted to the prototypical 'stranger' rape, thus either leaving a great number of sexual assaults out of the punitive reach of the criminal justice system (and a great number of women unprotected), or treating the most common type of rape, i.e. rape by a known man, as a less serious sexual offence. The examples in this section have been divided into two categories of 'non-typical' rapes: marital rape and ex-partner rape.

Marital Rape

Cases of forced sex within the context of an established relationship are usually seen as 'non-typical' rapes, a kind of sexual assault which is endemic and difficult to detect (Hall 1985; Lees 1997). The first example in this section comes from a case tried in 1988 when the English legal system did not contemplate the existence of marital rape as a crime. Curiously, other kinds of forced sexual acts within marriage (fellatio, buggery, etc.) could be tried as 'indecent assault', as is the case here. The event is not described as an 'ordeal' or as 'appalling', nor is the act of fellatio depicted as an 'indignity', as it frequently is in cases of stranger rape.

7. The appellant and his wife were married in January 1985. By September 1986 sexual intercourse between them had ceased, and the wife had served a divorce petition on the appellant. On September 14 the appellant forced his wife, at knife-point, to undergo an act of fellatio, and then went on, still at knifepoint, to have intercourse with him. The act of fellatio formed the basis of a count of indecent assault to which the appellant pleaded guilty, after a ruling by the trial judge that it was capable of being an indecent assault. He appealed against conviction.

– **Held**, dismissing the appeal, that although an act of fellatio was not unlawful, it was not, like the act of intercourse per vaginum, an act to which the parties gave consent by their marriage. If the act was performed without actual consent, it was capable of being an indecent assault. [**Roy Kowalski (1988) 86 Cr App R (S) 338 – four-year sentence reduced to two years**]

The following excerpt is less gender-biased than the previous ones. It acknowledges the seriousness of marital rape, and the previous relation between the parties is not used as a mitigating factor for sentencing purposes. However, the five-year sentence in this case is lower than the average sentence for stranger rape aggravated by violence.

8. The appellant's wife told him she wished to separate from him. Some time later, the appellant grabbed her by the throat, pushed her face into a cushion, took off her clothing and made her put on a pair of stockings which he had bought. The appellant then forced her to have intercourse against her will several times and forced his penis into her mouth twice.

– **Held**: . . . the appellant's conduct was gross and involved threats of violence . . . The ordeal had lasted something of the order of one-and-a-half hours.

– There can be no doubt at all that this was the most dreadful ordeal for this woman and, equally, there can be no doubt that she has suffered very considerably as a result of it. This Court must never overlook what has happened so far as the victim of a sexual crime such as this is concerned. [**Michael H. (1997) 2 Cr App R (S) 338 – marital rape – five-year sentence**]

The use of the word 'ordeal' is interesting because not every rape is described as such. This term conjures up an image of a real victim, a woman who resisted her attacker and really suffered both physically and psychologically as a result of the rape. Prior to 1991, married women who were raped by their partners found no protection under the British law. Since then some married victims have achieved the real victim status, and their attacks are now sometimes defined as 'ordeals'.

Since the event was an 'ordeal', the complainant had the status of genuine victim, thus deserving the consideration of the courts. This approach to rape victims represents a positive change in judicial attitudes if compared with cases from the late 1980s (when marital rape was not even seen as a crime), and even with many recent appellate decisions.

Ex-partner Rape

Some women suffer abuse even after separation (Lees 1997; Campbell 1993). Judicial treatment is always more lenient towards husbands who attack their wives than men who attack strange women. Sentence reduction is a trend for ex-partner rape. In the corpus, more sentences for partner/ex-partner rape cases were reduced than for stranger rape cases. The following example illustrates the judicial treatment of cases of ex-partner rape.

9. The appellant broke into the house at about midnight, prevented the victim from calling the police, and tied her hands behind her. The appellant then removed her underwear, put a pillow case over her head and raped her. He then put his penis into her mouth and raped her again. He later put his hands round her throat and squeezed until she became unconscious.

–   It is apparent from the recital of the facts of this case that this was a very serious offence of rape . . . On the other hand, it is a striking and unusual feature of this case that not only was the victim of this appalling offence one who had had a long-standing and intimate relationship with the appellant, but she has not suffered the degree of mental trauma which is sometimes associated with offences of this kind. Furthermore, to put it no higher, she has gone a long way along the road towards forgiving the attacker. Those are clearly material matters when the question of what is the appropriate sentence is considered. [**Derek John Hind (1994) 15 Cr App R (S) 114 – marital rape – ten-year sentence reduced to six years**]

Here the judges admitted that the offence was a serious one. This is not surprising since a husband's immunity to rape prosecution was abolished in England in 1991 in precedent, and in 1994 in statute (Lees 1997). However, the previous intimate relationship between the parties was presented as a mitigating factor because, from the judicial point of view, women sexually attacked by present or former partners are less traumatized than women attacked by strangers. Even though the original ten-year sentence was high, the four-year reduction was also considerable, amounting to 40 per cent of the original sentence. The judges refrained from using a cause-and-effect connector to indicate that the victim was not deeply traumatized due to her previous intimacy with the offender, but opted for the neutral pair 'not only

– but', which merely indicated addition. One of the possible reasons for this rape to be considered 'appalling'[6] was the fact that the victim forgave her assailant, which was seen as a mitigating feature in the case, and which led to a sympathetic judicial attitude towards the victim. As the complainant was seen positively by the court, the event was equally labelled 'an appalling offence'.

> 10. The appellant had lived with the complainant for some years and later married her; they had two children. The relationship deteriorated and the appellant left the matrimonial home . . . the appellant was seen by a psychiatrist who found him very depressed. On two occasions the appellant assaulted the complainant.
> – **Held**: courts are now far more aware of the sort of cruelty that can be inflicted by a man on his wife. The Court had come to the conclusion that some reduction in the sentence was appropriate, and would substitute a sentence of two years for the original sentence. [**Wayne B (1996) 2 Cr App R (S) 305 – marital rape – two-and-a-half-year sentence reduced to two years**]

Here it is interesting to observe the contradiction in the appeal judges' basis for their decision. First, they indicated that the courts had evolved with the times and now recognized the existence of domestic violence and cruelty, which implied that they consider this particular appellant guilty of assaulting his ex-wife. However, following this statement they reduced the original sentence without explaining why, i.e. the absence of a logical connector indicating contrast such as 'however'. Apparently, the legal writers did not wish to establish any contrast (or indicate a contradiction) between the first and the second sentences. It is as if the second statement: 'The Court had come to the conclusion that some reduction was appropriate . . .' followed the first: 'courts are now far more aware of the sort of cruelty that can be inflicted by a man on his wife' naturally with no incongruities. The impression is that the appeal judges were paying 'lip service' to the notion that women should be protected from domestic violence. It is also interesting to consider why they abstained from giving reasons for reducing the original sentence. A possible inference is that, in spite of apparently condemning domestic violence, they did not find the case serious enough or the appellant guilty enough.

Conclusion

A closer observation of social and legal practices indicates that there is a disparity between the way sexual violence is treated in theory and in praxis. At the level of legislation, sexual abuse is defined as illegal and as liable to punishment; at the level of everyday life, most forms of coercive sex are unknown, unreported, unacknowledged, and unpunished (Rhode 1989). At the trial level and at the level of legal decisions, sexual abuse is dealt with in a similar contradictory way. Although officially all cases of rape are strongly combated, in practice some cases are subjected to harsh punishment, while others are either presented as 'normal' and thus go unpunished or are treated as less serious and consequently subjected to lighter forms of discipline. The degree of punishment is directly linked to how the event is legally constructed.

A more detailed analysis of the data used in this work indicates that appellate decisions on rape cases present the event in very different lights, depending on how the assault has been labelled and categorized. This categorization system reflects and recreates a body of sexual myths and ideological presuppositions about how men and women behave and relate to each other, and it is this ideological frame that will determine how blame, discipline, and punishment are judicially apportioned, and who will be cast in the roles of 'victim' and 'villain'.

Judicial discourse makes use of several prototypes to help categorize rape cases and their participants, such as the 'real' rape, the 'true victim', and the 'typical rapist'. The prototypical cases are seen as serious and as deserving severe punishment. Events and participants that shade away from these central, core examples, e.g. marital rape, date rape, and rape of sexually experienced women, are viewed with disbelief and suspicion and, frequently, end up in acquittals or short sentences.

Some feminist scholars propose that rape be inserted into a broader context of crimes of violence against the person (Temkin 1987). However, to expand the definition of rape to include all kinds of coercive sex, i.e. whether the woman fought vigorously back or just said 'no', and that of 'rapist' to include all kinds of men, e.g. strangers from the streets, maniacs, and drug addicts as well as husbands, boyfriends, neighbours, relatives, men of previously good character, nice college boys, and so forth, would make many people uncomfortable. As Wood and Rennie (1994: 145) point out, 'men want rape to stay in the realm of the reprehensible, a realm peopled by the deranged and the sick'. Within a certain set of gender and sexual assumptions: that men have a greater sexual appetite than women; that men are sexually active and women sexually passive; that male sexual drive, once aroused, is very difficult to control; and that sexual violence provoked by the pain of rejection and separation is less grave, rape is made into something reprehensible yet understandable, and certain types of forced sex are seen as something excusable.

Notes

1. Although many countries today have rape shield laws that technically do not permit the rape victim's past to be put into evidence, e.g. the US, Canada, and England, defence attorneys have ways of circumventing this limitation by resorting to irony, innuendo, and other rhetorical devices to destroy the victim's character in court (Matoesian 1993; Conley and O'Barr 1998).

2. The *British Criminal Justice and Public Order Act 1994* has recognized male and female buggery as 'rape' (Edwards 1996). Male buggery is now treated as 'anal rape' (Edwards 1996). However, while collecting the data for the present study in 1996 and 1998, I did not find any RAD

dealing with a case of male buggery prosecuted as rape. I found only one case of sexual assault by a woman on a man, but it was prosecuted as 'indecent assault on male' (see Sharon Kristine B (1994) 15 Cr App R (S)).

3. Some countries have introduced 'rape neutral laws'. This is the case in some Australian jurisdictions, e.g. Victoria, South Australia, and New South Wales where the legal definition of rape no longer requires penetration of the vagina by the penis, but any type of forced sex. However, official statistics from the 1980s indicated that 92.5 per cent of the complainants were women (Graycar and Morgan 1992).

4. This difficulty is not restricted to the law-and-order apparatus. Marital rape is a relatively new concept, and it still receives little attention in comparison with other forms of rape such as stranger rape or even date rape. Bergen (1996) argues that research on wife rape is still scarce if compared with the amount of research on other forms of violence against women and children. In her survey of American agencies that give help and support to rape victims, she found that wife rape was not widely seen as a serious social problem; in some rape crisis centres she found no available literature on wife rape, and members of staff were not trained to deal with this specific type of sexual abuse.

5. Referring to wife rape, Bergen (1996) claims that it is unclear how many victims of marital rape identify themselves as such and seek help at a rape crisis centre or battered women's shelter. She believes that surveys involving women who volunteer to describe their experiences of marital sexual abuse might be unrepresentative of the actual number of women raped by their partners.

6. I am not disputing the fact that a rape, be it of any kind, is indeed an appalling attack against a woman. The point I want to make is that appeal judges do not usually resort to negative adjectives such as 'appalling' to describe and construct cases of marital rape which are seen by the courts as less traumatic and serious than stranger rapes. Marital rapes are only described as 'appalling' when the victim succeeds in portraying herself positively in court, e.g. as a 'forgiving wife' (de Carvalho Figueiredo 2000).

References

Adler, Z. (1987) *Rape on Trial.* London: Routledge and Kegan Paul.

Bergen, R. K. (1996) *Wife Rape: Understanding the Response of Survivors and Service Providers.* Thousand Oaks, CA: Sage Publications.

Campbell, A. (1993) *Men, Women and Aggression.* New York: Basic Books.

Coates, L., Bavelas, J. B., and Gibson, J. (1994) 'Anomalous Language in Sexual Assault Trial Judgements', *Discourse and Society,* 5(2): 189–206.

Collin, P. H. (1992) *Dictionary of Law* (2nd edn). Teddington, Middlesex: Peter Collin Publishing.

Conley, J. M. and O'Barr, W. M. (1998) *Just Words: Law, Language and*

Power (Language and Legal Discourse). Chicago, IL: University of Chicago Press.

The Criminal Appeal Reports (1998) 1 Cr App R (S). Part 1. London: Sweet and Maxwell.

The Criminal Appeal Reports (1997) 2 Cr App R (S). London: Sweet and Maxwell.

The Criminal Appeal Reports (1997) 1 Cr App R (S). Part 1. London: Sweet and Maxwell.

The Criminal Appeal Reports (1996) 2 Cr App R (S). Part 1. London: Sweet and Maxwell.

The Criminal Appeal Reports (1995) 16 Cr App R (S). London: Sweet and Maxwell.

The Criminal Appeal Reports (1994) 15 Cr App R (S). London: Sweet and Maxwell.

The Criminal Appeal Reports (1988) 86 Cr App R (S). London: Sweet and Maxwell.

de Carvalho Figueiredo, D. (2000) 'Victims and Villains: Gender Representations, Surveillance, and Punishment in the Judicial Discourse on Rape', Ph.D. Dissertation. Florianópolis, Santa Catarina: Universidade Federal de Santa Catarina.

Edwards, S. (1996) *Sex and Gender in the Legal Process*. London: Blackstone Press.

Edwards, S. (1981) *Female Sexuality and the Law*. Oxford: Martin Robertson.

Fairclough, N. (1995) *Media Discourse*. London: Edward Arnold.

Fowler, R. (1996) *Linguistic Criticism* (2nd edn). Oxford: Oxford University Press.

Graycar, R. and Morgan, J. (1992) *The Hidden Gender of the Law*. Annandale, NSW: The Federation Press.

Hall, R. (1985) *Ask Any Woman: A London Inquiry into Rape and Sexual Assault*. Bristol: Falling Wall Press.

Halliday, M. A. K. (1985) *An Introduction to Functional Grammar*. London: Edward Arnold.

Jalbert, P. L. (1983) 'Some Constructs for Analysing News', in *Language, Image, Media*, ed. by H. Davis and P. Walton. Oxford: Basil Blackwell, 282–99.

Lees, S. (1997) *Ruling Passions: Sexual Violence, Reputation and the Law*. Buckingham: Open University Press.

Liebes-Plesner, T. (1984) 'Rhetoric in the Service of Justice: The Sociolinguistic Construction of Stereotypes in an Israeli Rape Trial', *Text*, (4): 173–92.

Matoesian, G. (1993) *Reproducing Rape: Domination through Talk in the Courtroom*. Chicago, IL: University of Chicago Press.

McLean, S. A. M. (1988) 'Female Victims in the Criminal Law', in *The Legal Relevance of Gender: Some Aspects of Sex-based Discrimination*, ed. by S. A. M. McLean and N. Burrows. Basingstoke: Macmillan Press, 195–215.

Meurer, J. L. (1998) *Aspects of Language in Self-help Counselling*. Florianópolis: PGI-UFSC.

Rhode, D. L. (1989) *Justice and Gender: Sex Discrimination and the Law*. Cambridge, MA: Harvard University Press.

Smart, C. (1989) *Feminism and the Power of Law*. London: Routledge.

Temkin, J. (1987) *Rape and the Legal Process*. London: Sweet and Maxwell.

Winter, E. (1994) 'Clause Relations as Information Structure: Two Basic Structures in English', in *Advances in Written Text Analysis*, ed. by R. M. Coulthard. London: Routledge, 46–8.

Wood, L. A. and Rennie, H. (1994) 'Formulating Rape: The Discursive Construction of Victims and Villains', *Discourse and Society*, 5(1): 125–48.

12 Bureaucratic Discourse: Writing in the 'Comfort Zone'

Claire Harrison and Lynne Young

Bureaucratic discourse, which is generally marked by bureaucratese, has been thought in the past to be an effective strategy for managers running hierarchical organizations. Today, this strategy is in question because leaders are no longer supposed to practise 'command and control', but openly engage and clearly communicate with staff in decision-making. A Phasal Analysis of a memo from a senior manager in a Government of Canada department – Health Canada – demonstrates that he fell back into the 'comfort zone' of bureaucratese to conceal decisions that would adversely affect employees and to place himself at arm's length from commands that staff might resent. Although the Government of Canada has declared that a goal for the next decade is to become an 'employer of choice' in order to attract highly skilled workers, this paper suggests that written bureaucratic discourse, as it is currently practised, will be a major obstacle to achieving that goal.

Introduction

Bureaucratic discourse refers to the language used in large and complex organizations such as governments and national corporations. While this type of language can be as clear and straightforward as discourse found in any social setting, it has long been associated with the pejorative term *bureaucratese*, because it is often characterized by jargon, abstractions, and convoluted syntax or as Safire (1993: 91) puts it, 'gobbledygook, bafflegab ... [and] buzzwords'. Such written bureaucratese often makes it appear as if the writers are attempting to hide behind a thick veil of verbiage and, in doing so, creating documents with writing that is so bad that it would fail even a basic composition course. Yet, as Iedema (1994/1996, Chapter II.3: 1) notes,

> Bureaucratic discourses have been and are powerful enough to organize whole armies, government diplomacies, and, eventually, whole (pacified) nation-states ... To appreciate the *constructive* power of administration and its language, we need to 'unpack' the discourse, i.e. go to the grammar and show how the features of administrative language contribute to its power over social organisation.

The purpose of this paper is to illustrate how one could go about 'unpacking' bureaucratese through the Phasal Analysis of an e-mail office memo issued within Health Canada (HC), a department of the Government of Canada. A major reorganization of HC in 2000 had resulted in a new Branch, entitled Healthy Environments and Consumer Safety (HECS). The memo was the first piece of official communication from its new head, the Assistant Deputy Minister (ADM), to his 1,200-member work-force – an amalgamation of employees from several entire Divisions as well as bits and pieces of others. As his introduction to the Branch, the ADM was well aware (personal communication, 2000) that the memo was his opportunity to make a good first impression, set a managerial tone and style that would enhance Branch relations, and begin to build a positive corporate culture among disparate groups.

In many management meetings and retreats prior to the official launch of HECS, senior managers urged the ADM to write a first memo that would set a standard for good communications, make staff feel included in the process of building the new Branch, and reduce stress and improve morale by addressing the concerns of staff. Although the ADM agreed, his memo failed on all three counts as evident from senior managers' reactions during a post-memo meeting. The research questions posed in this paper are: 'How and why did the memo fail?', 'What is it that caused good intentions to go awry?' and 'What role did bureaucratese play in contributing to this failure?'

As the analysis of the memo reveals, the ADM's bureaucratese did not reflect bad writing, but it did provide him with a 'comfort zone' where strategic wordings allowed him to camouflage managerial decisions and activities that would alarm his new employees, potentially cause dissension, and challenge the hierarchy. It allowed him to hide behind the memo and keep his ADM 'mask' firmly in place when he might have removed it and begun a process towards a more egalitarian management style. However, as this paper will argue, this rhetorical strategy, in terms of internal staff communications, is likely to adversely affect the Canadian government's ability to retain highly skilled workers in the labour market during the next decade.

The Context: Canada's Public Service

Canada's public service has undergone massive changes during the past decade. As detailed in a report by the Advisory Committee on Labour Management Relations in the Federal Public Service (2000), the public service has been downsized by 25 per cent, employees work longer and harder hours, and job security has declined. The result is a high-stress workplace. Another study (as reported by May 2002) found that federal public servants 'take more "mental health" days off work, take longer absences from the job and spend more on prescription drugs than other workers surveyed across Canada'. This report put the blame for low employee morale squarely on the shoulders of poor management and promises of institutional reforms that had never been fulfilled.

Furthermore, the increasing age of the average federal employee is causing alarm for the public service's future. As the Advisory Committee (2000: 5, 7) noted,

> The aging of the public service makes it imperative for the government to establish itself as an employer of choice so that it can compete for new employees over the coming years ... [and] To attract capable young graduates and retain existing employees in the face of competition from the private sector, the federal government will need to become a more attractive place to work.

How the government can create a more appealing work environment, given its problems, requires vast and complex systemic changes that are well beyond the discussion in this paper. However, this evolving work environment puts the spotlight on organizational communication. As Iedema (1994/1996, Chapter I.4: 16) notes, 'The weakening of either (or both) task boundaries (classifications) or (and) interactional boundaries (framings) places huge demands on intra-institutional communication and communication skills.' Government organizations have long realized the connection between good internal communications and job satisfaction. As the two following excerpts from in-house policy documents demonstrate, the 'rhetoric' suggests good intentions although the achievements have been negligible.

> The goal of effective, timely and on-going communications does not exist in isolation from other goals ... Rather, good communications are integral to the achievement of other goals. Good communications support the development of clear directions, a good working environment, a competent and committed workforce ... (*The Drug Directorate's Communication Plan*, Drugs Directorate, Health Canada 1995)

> Analysis of the recent employee survey and reports from the members of a Task Force convened to study internal communications ... confirm that there are a number of areas that need improvement. In terms of 'top-down' communication, only 30% of staff agree that managers clearly communicate their goals. (*Internal Communications Strategy*, Earth Sciences Sector, Natural Resources Canada 2000)

It is clear that, despite good intentions, traditional bureaucratese continues to flourish in federal office documents, hindering clarity in communications, contributing to morale problems, and undercutting the government's need to become an 'employer of choice' in the labour market.

Phasal Analysis: Putting the Memo under a Microscope

Phasal Analysis provides a means of discovering the ways in which speakers and writers structure and organize discourse (Young 1990: 83). A document can have two discourse 'plots': an overt, linear, 'static' structure, and a more subtle, non-linear, 'dynamic' structure. The latter can best be revealed through Phasal Analysis. As Gregory (2002: 321) points out, 'Phase characterizes stretches within discourse (which may be discontinuously realized in text) exhibiting their own significant and distinctive consistency and congruity in the selections that have been made from the language's codal resources'. What is at issue are similar selections from the ideational, interpersonal, and textual choices that form patterns of choice and show great consistency across a particular Phase. Phases are what Gregory (1985: 127) has called 'dynamic instantiations of registerial choices in a particular discourse'. In this paper, we carried out a Phasal Analysis at primary level of delicacy using Gregory's classification of process types instead of Halliday's since one of the authors has worked primarily within that framework. We examined α (independent) clauses and β and γ (dependent) clauses and did not probe further into relations of dependency. (A text of the memo, separated by clause, can be found in the Appendix.)

As Table 12.1 demonstrates, the memo had a linear, 'static' structure or 'story' that appeared to meet the ADM's goals of communicating clearly with staff about the reorganization and the role they could play in building the new Branch.

However, Phasal Analysis of the memo demonstrates a different 'story' – a 'dynamic' interweaving of other intentions that recurred and were constructed in and around the 'static' structure. In other words, the memo had a hidden agenda that was revealed in four Phases mapped incongruously at times onto the 'static' structure (see Table 12.2). These Phases, labelled to illustrate their purpose, were:

- Phase 1: 'I'm On The Level'
- Phase 2: 'Show-and-Tell'
- Phase 3: 'Concealment'
- Phase 4: 'Arm's-length Commands'

Table 12.1 The 'static' structure of the memo

Sections of the memo	Intention
Introduction (Sentences 1–3)	Welcomes staff to the new Branch.
Transition (Sentence 4)	Introduces the memo's subject matter.
Setting the Stage (Sentences 5–11)	Brings the reader up to date and provides a quick summary of the Branch's new organizational structure.
Becoming Operational (Sentences 12–20)	Elaborates on how HECS will set up its structure and processes.
Looking Ahead (Sentences 21–40)	Describes future 'moves' and the importance of staff in the reorganization.

Table 12.2 The memo's dynamic structure as revealed by Phases

Memo sections	Phase 1	Phase 2	Phase 3	Phase 4
Introduction	1, 2a			2b, 3a, 3b, 3c
Transition		4		
Setting the Stage		5a, 5b, 6c, 8	6a, 6b, 7, 9, 10a, 10b, 10c, 11a	11b, 11c, 11d
Becoming Operational		12, 16, 17, 18, 19a, 20	13, 14a, 14b, 14c, 15, 19b	
Looking Ahead	22a, 24a, 24b, 31a, 31b, 31c, 33, 34a, 34b, 35b, 39a, 40	21, 25, 26, 27a, 28, 29a, 30a, 35a, 36a, 38, 39b	23, 31d, 37	22b, 27b, 29b, 30b, 30c, 32a, 32b, 32c, 36b

Each of these Phases shows internal similarities in ideational, inter-personal, and textual metafunctions that are distinct from one another and clearly identifiable as they weave through the memo's 'static' structure. The Phasal Analysis demonstrates how the ADM, in fact, made other meanings within the 'static' structure in terms of his own personal experience of reality, his attitudes towards the reorganization and staff, and his own particular ways of expressing these experiences and attitudes through textual choices. The analysis reveals the conflicts within the ADM as he sought to reconcile management styles. As a long-time bureaucrat, he was accustomed to the traditional management style of hierarchical 'command and control'. As a manager in the new millennium, he was supposed to support a new style of management marked by sharing and delegation, not only with his senior managers, but also with those further down the line. His experience in hierarchical organizations led to the discoursal enactment of ideologies frequently below the 'surface' of the text (Fairclough and Wodak 1997: 258) with the 'pull and tug' of these two differing management styles causing discoursal contradictions that were sufficient to ensure that the memo did not achieve the results he had originally seemed to desire.

The Phases: Revealing a Discourse Plot

Analysis of the memo, overall, shows macro-consistency in all the metafunctions. Ideationally, the majority of processes realized by predicational structures as well as Grammatical Metaphors are mental processes. In fact, of the 170 processes, 102 are mental, 39 relational and 29 action. What this reflects, not surprisingly, is how much of the work involved in the reorganization is 'mental' work, particularly cognitive processes such as deciding and planning.

Interpersonally, there is consistency in Mood. Of the 69 clauses, 67 are Declaratives with only two Commands realized congruently. The tenor of this memo clearly points to the type of social relationship between the speaker as the giver of information and the audience as processors or listeners. Given this unequal power relationship, it might be expected that the memo would include more than just two Commands and, in fact, such is the case. The Phasal Analysis shows numerous, less overt Commands, strategically placed at arm's length from the ADM.

Textually, the most significant cohesive devise in each of the Phases are the collocational chains that both distinguish each Phase from the other and connect parts of each together.

Phase 1: 'I'm On The Level'

Phase 1 includes 14 clauses, i.e. 20 per cent of the text (all percentages are rounded off to the nearest whole number). Lexicogrammatically, this Phase includes only brief α and β clauses and their internal structure is generally simple. Furthermore, there are no passivizations, and the embedding of ideational processes, when it occurs, is not deep. The result is that the sentences in this Phase have the greatest readability of all of the content within the memo. For example:

2a: I look forward to working with you
24a: I believe in transparency and consultation
31c: and I ask for your patience and co-operation

Phase 1 clauses serve as the 'book-ends' of the memo with two clauses in the introduction and the majority clustered at the end. The purpose of this Phase is to portray the ADM as a caring leader who is speaking 'plainly' about his intentions, decisions, and actions and is eager for staff consultation. By establishing these credentials, the ADM seems to be attempting to make more palatable the decisions and commands which form the 'meat' of the memo, and his metafunctional sets of choices result from this intention. Serving ideational as well as textual purposes, the collocational chain highlights the image of a warm and open boss with choices such as 'transparency', 'consultation', 'patience and co-operation', 'keeping communications open', and 'appreciating suggestions'. At the same time as the ADM illustrates his willingness to engage in such processes, i.e. being transparent, consulting, having patience, and so on, he encourages staff to engage through phrases such as 'volunteer your talents and experience', 'commitment', and 'expertise and participation'. Such selections are designed to 'rally the troops' although the exclusivity of the 'we' in 31d and 35b hint at the ADM's conflicting ideologies. On one hand, the ADM wants to motivate staff through an emotive, 'first among equals' pitch; on the other, he is strongly attached to the traditional hierarchy. He reaches out to staff, but his 'reach' only goes so far. The exclusive 'we' reinforces the hierarchical structures of the Branch and establishes a subtle separation between the 'us' of management and the 'them' of staff.

Interpersonally, this Phase is the only one of the four Phases to include Mood choices other than the Declarative with two of the clauses realized as Jussive Commands. The use of such 'bald' Commands is unusual in this text and, as Iedema (1994/1996, Chapter II.2: 2–3) argues, in most administrative discourse because such 'imperatives tend to be used in situations where interpersonal solidarity [i.e. organizational cohesion] is not at issue'. However, the ADM tempers the 'must-ness' of these Commands by the use of the interpersonal Theme, 'Please' (34a), seemingly giving the addressee the option not to comply (Iedema 1994/1996, Chapter II.1: 5).

Phase 2: 'Show-and-Tell'

Phase 2 includes 22 clauses, i.e. 32 per cent of the text. As in Phase 1, the clauses in Phase 2 are generally clear and straightforward as a result of their lexicogrammatical simplicity. With the exception of 39b, they are all brief α clauses with only shallow embedding. As its label suggests, the purpose of the Phase is to provide employees with information about actions already taken and those planned for the future – actions that can be openly described because they align with the new management style of caring, honest leadership. For example:

5a: During the last few months you have undoubtedly followed closely the evolution of the realignment
20:   This meeting will begin to map out the design of Branch processes.
38:   Everyone will have an opportunity to input into the building of the new organization.

What makes this Phase distinct are two sets of choices: ideationally in the types of predications; and interpersonally in terms of mood and modality components. Although this Phase has a variety of ideational processes – mental (11), relational (8), and action (3), there is a relative consistency of action processes (8), such as 'work', 'make', 'set' and 'present', realizing mental and relational processes. This use of action processes enhances this Phase's focus on accomplishments by making them seem concrete actions. Another type of consistency is evident in the realization of 17 of the processes in the active voice which the ADM uses for talking about decisions that he is most comfortable discussing, i.e. those already made that can no longer be negotiated, and those regarding minor future actions which he can be sure will be positively interpreted by employees or which he presents in positive terms, e.g. 39b.

The five passivizations (6b, 16, 19a, 27a, 29a) are significant, however, and demonstrate the ADM's discomfort when writing about activities that involve decisions not yet made at the time the memo was written. The working groups, generally made up of senior managers, had been established to make recommendations regarding HECS structure that would only be finalized at the July post-memo retreat and then reported to employees. Further, to avoid personalizing these decisions, the ADM makes strategic use of nominalization, i.e. 'working groups' and 'meeting'.

Phase 3: 'Concealment'

Phase 3 includes 17 clauses, or 25 per cent of the text. The purpose of this Phase is to provide staff with information on what Iedema (1997: 3) calls 'Guidance':

> The area of institutional Guidance is concerned with planning and rationalising future actions and directions (whereto and why), with determining who (or rather what kind of people) should do it, with deciding what exactly needs to be done, and how it needs to be done. (Original emphasis)

Therefore, this Phase contains the 'hot' issues around the realignment – 'hot' because they include the major decisions that would affect employees' futures and because Guidance, particularly in a new organization, involves extensive negotiation as senior managers fight for 'turf'. As shown in Table 12.2, Phase 3 clauses are interwoven throughout the three sections of the memo carrying the most text, a strategically good move since putting all the clauses together would have drawn attention to their content which was attempting to downplay contentious issues. In this Phase, the ADM's high level of discomfort with these issues led to concealment of agency and intent through the use of nominalizations and a deep embedding of ideational processes, i.e. this Phase contains the only two γ clauses and many relative clauses. These transformations allowed the ADM to make an oblique command without revealing his identity or pointing a finger at who has to do what. Iedema (1994/1996, Chapter II.3: 2) refers to this as *demodalisation*: 'the backgrounding of the features of control and hierarchy in the discourse of administration', and notes that this backgrounding means that 'issues to do with control, with must-ness, and with hierarchy and rank . . . are de-emphasized by the use of "short-hand" wording [such as grammatical metaphors] which presume basic agreements about administrative issues and practices'. For example:

13:     The purpose of these meetings was to develop a shared under-standing of the issues and challenges we face in bringing together the various components of the Branch, the Branch and Pro-gramme systems and processes we need to construct, and the link-ages that will need to be strengthened or created across Canada, both with staff and with stakeholders.

14b: in providing direction for the transformation processes,

37:     Success for the endeavours of the new Branch can only come from the synergy created by all of us working together.

Ideationally, Phase 3 is very consistent in process type in part due to the preponderance of Grammatical Metaphors – 13 of the 17 clauses realize relational processes with most nominalized processes in the subject position. The relational processes of 'being' tell the story about the past, current, and possible future state of activities in HECS as opposed to those in Phase 2, which are about activities completed or those definitely about to occur. Phase 3 has a high number of impersonal participants, such as 'challenges', 'purposes', 'responsibilities', 'goals', and 'commitments', removing people, as it were, from the activities and plans. The only human actors/agents are, significantly, the inclusive 'we'. Whereas in Phase 1 the ADM used the exclusive 'we' as a counter-balance to the intimacy of 'reaching out' to staff, the reverse occurs in Phase 3, where the inclusive 'we' provides human intimacy as a counter-balance to the 'coolness' of the impersonal participants. This strategic wording is designed to conceal the fact that Guidance involves decisions made by managers, not by staff. (However, the ADM does make a telling 'misstep' in 10c where the 'we' of staff becomes 'they'.)

Textually, this Phase includes three interesting marked Themes. In 6a, the ADM was handling a sensitive subject: that of staff engagement in Branch planning and decision-making. While senior managers at meetings had agreed, in principle, that staff must be involved in these activities, the reality was that no one actually knew how to undertake and manage such an activity, and the ADM had neither the time nor perhaps the inclination to even start such a process. The Theme pays 'lip service' to staff participation, by offering staff the opportunity to make minor decisions, e.g. choosing names of the new Programmes, but no opportunity to make major ones, e.g. altering the structures being in place. In fact, the marked Theme in 10a tells the tale, so to speak, since the ADM's phrase, 'By using the concept of a Programme', lets staff know that the basic structures of the Branch are already in place.

The marked and predicated Theme in 23 is interesting because it introduces a clause whose change in tone and style from the rest of the memo is remarkable, bearing the traces of promotional, marketing language. The increasing use of advertising language within other forms of discourse is described by Fairclough (1995: 139, 138) as 'the colonization of discourse by promotion' in which discourse is 'a vehicle for "selling" goods, services, organizations, ideas or people'. The fact that this type of discourse has crept into the memo is not entirely congruent with the purpose of this Phase to conceal certain decisions. However, it is congruent with the purpose of the memo, which is to persuade staff to accept and adjust quickly to change and to be productive as soon as possible. Therefore, this sales pitch is not entirely misplaced.

Phase 4: 'Arm's-length Commands'

Phase 4 includes 16 clauses, i.e. 23 per cent of the text. As its label suggests, the ADM's purpose in this Phase is to 'distance the commander from the commandee' (Iedema 1997: 10). For example:

3a: While this process must be moved along as quickly as possible,
11c: [in order] to stabilize our management team,
30b: and I urge you to contact your manager

Although this Phase includes a variety of processes: mental (10); action (4); and relational (3), its consistency lies interpersonally in the modality of obligation. This modulation is explicit as in the use of 'must' as in 3a and 3b although here the Command is tempered because it is realized by a Declarative rather than an Imperative and has an inclusive 'we', which lends it a less hierarchical 'aura'. The 'must-ness' in this Phase is also made less explicit because of the nature of the structure in which it occurs, namely, the 'to + an infinitive in the "[in order] to" ' clauses, and because of the presence of subjective interpersonal metaphors.

According to Iedema (personal communication, 2000), the '[in order] to' clauses are the most dissimulating of the arm's-length Commands.

> the 'in order to' structures create room for an infinitive which means there is a dissimulating modal responsibility . . . the more the desired action is distanced from the tensed verb, the more the actor whose responsibility it is to do X and the person commanding are dissimulated . . . At the same time, the level of dissimulation is an indicator of the level of 'invoked' non-negotiability: the less 'congruent' the clause, the more institutionalized, the less negotiable, the Command's imperative force.

Very specific tasks form predications such as (11b) 'create structures', (11c) 'stabilize team', and (36b) 'answer questions', and, underlying each, is the most direct Command in 3b: 'we must take the time' (to do each of the activities: mental or physical).

Some arm's-length Commands are created through the subjective interpersonal metaphors that are realized by 'I urge' and 'I would like' (as mentioned above). Iedema (1994/1996, Chapter II.2: 7) notes that subjective interpersonal metaphors of modulation serve in administrative discourse to distribute responsibility among participants, e.g. the clause, 'I would like you to remain engaged in this process', places the onus both on *I* and *you* with the 'Subject of the projecting clause . . . as Source . . . the modally responsible Subject which has *ultimate* responsibility for the happening of the action'. This choice allows the ADM to mitigate his command by reducing what Iedema refers to as the 'institutionalizing of administrative need' by making the projecting clause subjective rather than objective, e.g. 'It is required that you remain engaged in this process' (Halliday 1994: 355–7).

The two remaining arm's-length Commands, 3a and 29b, are further distanced through use of the passive voice and lack of agents. The participants in this Phase are, with the exception of 'we' in 3b, all impersonal, e.g. 'consultations', 'programmes and services', 'process', 'issues', 'questions', and 'challenges', thereby allowing the ADM to maintain his arm's length relationship with 'command and control' discourse.

Conclusion

Fairclough (1992: 89) suggests 'ideology is located both in the structures (i.e. orders of discourse) which constitute the outcome of past events, and the conditions for current events, and in events themselves as they reproduce and transform their conditioning structures'. Furthermore, he adds that ideology in human discourse and actions is inevitable and constantly undergoing change: 'It is an accumulated and naturalized orientation which is built into norms and conventions . . . [and it is] an ongoing work to naturalize and denaturalize such orientations in discursive events.'

The HC reorganization provides fertile ground for the study of discourse because such social and institutional changes create an inevitable clash of beliefs and opinions as new people are thrown together and, in the case of HECS, must accomplish tasks within a short period of time. The ADM, we suggest, tried, to the best of his ability, to provide good information, raise employee enthusiasm, offer staff different ways to participate in change, and attempt a more egalitarian management style. In fact, his choice of an e-mail memo as a first vehicle of communications is itself symbolic of a less formal type of management. According to Yates and Orlikowski (1992: 315), today's e-mail memos are characterized by far greater informality in format and language than those written before the advent of e-mail communications, and, in the ADM's experience (personal communication, 2000), e-mail now allows even an employee at the lowest level of a hierarchy to feel free to communicate with the most senior manager. By sending the memo by e-mail rather than as a formal letter, the ADM was not only choosing the most efficient method of communications, we suggest he felt that he was choosing the most democratic method as well.

However, it was early in the process of reorganization; there were still many unknowns; and it is likely that some of the decisions being made would have a negative impact on some employees. However, for the ADM to say so directly in the memo would have required coming out of the administrative 'closet' and risked opening issues to further negotiation with more players. As Iedema notes (1997: 9),

> To achieve high levels of behavioural cohesion and institutional stability, bureaucrats/administrators apply a discourse which resists (renewed) negotiation of issues to do with the nature of control (must-ness); the source and target of control (hierarchical structures); and the object of control (the desired action).

The memo, therefore, reflects the conflicts inherent in the situation and the ADM's own personal issues concerning traditional versus modern management styles, and these conflicts are played out by the 'dynamic' interweaving of phases throughout the 'static' structure of the discourse.

Finally, while it is not surprising that the ADM fell into the 'comfort zone' of bureaucratese, it is also not surprising that his audience – bureaucrats themselves – understood the hidden agenda. They knew that decisions were being made that they were powerless to change; they knew that the invitation to participate was not real; and they knew that they were being moved around like pawns on a chessboard. The memo failed because of this: it did not make employees feel heard, valued or respected. Bureaucratic discourse, long considered to be useful in maintaining institutional cohesion may, in fact, contribute to the very opposite of its desired effect by creating staff resentment and resistance to the hierarchical status quo reinforced by such discourse. It does not contribute towards the kind of systemic changes required to create a work environment that will make the government 'an employer of choice' and attract the type of high-quality, skilled workers required in today's and tomorrow's workplace. In fact, quite the contrary.

Appendix: The Memo and Its Clauses

1	α	Welcome to your new Branch, Healthy Environments and Consumer Safety (HECS).
2a	α	I look forward to working with you
2b	β	[in order] to design and deliver the programmes and services that are our responsibility.
3a	β	While this process must be moved along as quickly as possible,
3b	α	we must take the time
3c	β	[in order] to do it right.
4	α	Today I would like to talk to you about some of the challenges and opportunities that we will face together in delivering on our commitments, about some of the decisions the new executive team have already made, and about the processes we have planned over the summer.
5a	α	During the last few months you have undoubtedly followed closely the evolution of the realignment
5b	α	and [you] have seen the latest organizational structure for HECS announced by the Deputy Ministers on June 19th.
6a	β	While the names of these Programmes are open for consideration
6b	γ	as we undertake our strategic planning,
6c	α	HECS will initially be composed of five Programmes – Drug Strategy and Controlled Substances, Tobacco Control, Safe Environments/Environmental Health, Product Safety, and Occupational Health and Safety.
7	α	We also have the departmental responsibility for the co-ordination of Health Canada's Sustainable Development activities.

8	α	It should be noted that we will be calling these new organizational units Programmes and not Directorates.
9	α	One of the principal challenges facing the Branch will be to integrate effectively the activities of staff in the regions with those in Ottawa.
10a	β	By using the concept of a Programme
10b	α	we can be all inclusive of all staff working at HECS Programmes,
10c	β	regardless of where they work and to whom they report.
11a	α	Much work remains to be done
11b	β	[in order] to create some of the new Programme structures,
11c	β	[in order] to stabilize our management team,
11d	β	[in order] to start dealing with the most pressing challenges facing our new organization.
12	α	In preparation for this, we have already started a dialogue, through a series of meetings with key executives and managers of the new organization.
13	α	The purpose of these meetings was to develop a shared understanding of the issues and challenges we face in bringing together the various components of the Branch, the Branch and Programme systems and processes we need to construct, and the linkages that will need to be strengthened or created across Canada, both with staff and with stakeholders.
14a	α	The advice and comments received on organizing the common Branch management processes and structures, such as those that support strategic and business planning, policy and regulatory affairs, risk management, human resources management, and communications will be useful
14b	β	in providing direction for the transformation processes,
14c	γ	as they unfold in the coming months.
15	α	Other areas that will need immediate attention include the creation of Branch Executive Committees and the integration and strengthening of newly transferred or consolidated Programmes.
16	α	The development of regional structures and the best ways for the regional delivery of the HECS Programmes will be worked out jointly with Regional Staff.
17	α	We have set a simple timetable for the summer.
18	α	The Branch came into being on July 1st.

19a	α	An extended executive planning meeting has been set for July 17–19
19b	β	to include all Directors-General and Directors or equivalents.
20	α	This meeting will begin to map out the design of Branch processes.
21	α	By September 1st, we should have all key Branch management positions occupied and all key Branch processes in place at least in a rudimentary manner.
22a	α	I would also like to be in a position
22b	β	[in order] to begin consultations with all HECS staff on our mission and guiding principles.
23	α	It is our goal to be ready for business by the Fall!
24a	α	I believe in transparency and consultation
24b	α	and [I] make a commitment to keep you informed and involved.
25	α	Reports and information from the deliberations of the management team have been and will continue to be available to you all.
26	α	We will set up the necessary structure on Lotus Notes as quickly as possible.
27a	α	Working groups have now been created
27b	β	[in order] to start identifying the issues, and the options for dealing with them.
28	α	These groups will present their proposals at the meeting planned for July 17–19.
29a	α	A report on the results of this meeting will be made available
29b	α	and follow-up work will have to be undertaken quickly.
30a	α	We will need your support and involvement
30b	α	and I urge you to contact your manager
30c	β	[in order] to volunteer your talents and experience whenever possible.
31a	α	I appreciate
31b	β	that each of you has your regular programme and service responsibilities
31c	α	and I ask for your patience and co-operation
31d	β	as we work through the transformation into the new Branch organization.
32a	α	I would like you to remain engaged in this process and

32b	α	[I would like you] to work within your management structures
32c	β	[in order] to keep the business of your organization on track through this transformation process.
33	α	I would like to keep the channels of communication open in both directions.
34a	α	Please feel free to e-mail me,
34b	α	[Please feel free to] contact any member of my staff.
35a	α	We will put into place an electronic suggestion box as soon as possible
35b	α	and [we] would appreciate suggestions on other mechanisms that you feel might enhance the flow of two-way communications.
36a	α	Your managers will also make themselves available
36b	β	[in order] to answer any questions about the next steps.
37	α	Success for the endeavours of the new Branch can only come from the synergy created by all of us working together.
38	α	Everyone will have an opportunity to input into the building of the new organization.
39a	α	Indeed, I am counting on your expertise and participation,
39b	β	which will be key in creating an effective and excellent new organization.
40	α	Thank you.

References

Advisory Committee on Labour Management Relations in the Federal Public Service (2000) *Identifying the Issues: First Report*, May 2000. Government of Canada at: http://dsp-psd. pwgsc.gc.ca/Collection/BT22–70-2000E.pdf (consulted August 2002).

Fairclough, N. (1995) *Critical Discourse Analysis: The Critical Study of Language.* London: Longman.

Fairclough, N. (1992) *Discourse and Social Change.* Cambridge: Polity Press.

Fairclough, N. and Wodak, R. (1997) 'Critical Discourse Analysis', in *Discourse as Social Action*, ed. by T. A. van Dijk. London: Sage Publications, 258–84.

Fowler, R., Hodge, B., Kress, G., and Trew, T. (eds) (1979) *Language and Control.* London: Routledge and Kegan Paul.

Gregory, M. (2002) 'Phasal Analysis within Communication Linguistics: Two Contrastive Discourses', in *Relations and Functions Within and Around*

Language, ed. by P. H. Fries, M. Cummings, D. Lockwood, and W. Spruiell. London: Continuum, 316–45.

Gregory, M. (1985) 'Towards "Communication" Linguistics: A Framework', in *Systemic Perspectives on Discourse, Vol. 1: Selected Theoretical Papers from the 9th International Systemic Workshop*, ed. by J. Benson and W. Greaves. Norwood, NJ: Ablex Publishing Corporation, 119–34.

Halliday, M. A. K. (1994) *An Introduction to Functional Grammar* (2nd edn). London: Edward Arnold.

Health Canada (1995) *The Drug Directorate's Communication Plan*. Drugs Directorate internal document.

Iedema, R. (1997) 'The Language of Administration: Introduction to Systemic Functional Linguistics and Social Semiotics', unpublished lecture, Linguistics Department, University of New South Wales, Sydney.

Iedema, R. (1994/1996) 'The Language of Administration: Write It Right Industry Research Report Vol. III [Disadvantaged Schools Program (Met. East)]', draft copy. Sydney: Erskinville.

May, K. (2002) 'Bad Bosses Break Morale of PSL Survey', *The Ottawa Citizen*, 26 August: A1.

Natural Resources Canada (2000) *Internal Communications Strategy*. Earth Sciences Sector internal document.

Safire, W. (1993) *Safire's New Political Dictionary*. New York: Random House.

Yates, J. and Orlikowski, W. J. (1992) 'Genres of Organizational Communication: A Structurational Approach to Studying Communication and Media', *Academy of Management Review*, 17(2): 299–326.

Young, L. (1990) *Language as Behavior, Language as Code*. Philadelphia, PA: John Benjamins.

13 Charismatic Business Leader Rhetoric: From Transaction to Transformation

Arlene Harvey

Two styles of leadership have been distinguished in mainstream business research. Transactional leadership encompasses managerial and pragmatic processes while transformational leadership, often associated with increased effectiveness in organizations, is inspirational and visionary. This paper examines the discourse interaction of these two leadership styles in a short dialogue between a well-known transformational business leader, Steve Jobs of Apple Computer, and his employees. A Systemic Functional Linguistics (SFL) analysis of the ideational patterning of the text shows how Jobs shifts into transformational mode through the combined strategies of abstraction, metaphor, and negative material processes. A second, interpersonally oriented analysis uses Appraisal Theory (a recent development within SFL) to demonstrate how a rhetorically skilful leader such as Jobs can evoke employees' sense of their own self-worth and efficacy to try to inspire them to perform beyond expectations, a feature of transformational leadership.

Introduction

Over the past several decades, business leadership research has focused on transformational leadership, a style of leadership that encompasses both visionary and charismatic processes. Transformational leaders such as Steve Jobs (Apple Computer), Anita Roddick (The Body Shop), and Jack Welch (General Electric) have been promoted as visionaries with a social conscience – leaders who have a profound impact not only within their own organizations, but also beyond because they often change the way companies and organizations interact with and influence society at large.

The ability of transformational leaders to motivate their employees to 'take on board' and pursue a particular vision depends to a large extent on the leader's rhetorical skills. While the rhetorical processes through which transformational leaders make such an impact have been studied, it remains unclear how transformational (and charismatic) rhetoric achieves these effects and how transformational processes interact with transactional, more managerial, and pragmatic processes. To explore these questions, this paper offers an analysis of a short dialogic text between Steve

Jobs (co-founder and current CEO of Apple Computer) and his staff at NeXt Computer (Jobs 1995), the company he formed after being ousted from Apple in 1985. The analysis demonstrates the kind of rhetorical work a leader in transformational mode needs to do when confronted with staff firmly embedded within a transactional mode. It offers further insights into the rhetorical features that make Steve Jobs' discourse so persuasive (Awamleh and Gardner 1999; Harvey 2001a, 2001b), many of which have been found to characterize the discourse of other charismatic leaders in the business and political domains. The analysis lends support to Shamir *et al.*'s (1993, 1994) suggestion that charismatic leader rhetoric achieves its effects by appealing to followers' self-concept. Finally, the analysis provides evidence that charismatic discourse relies on a delicate balance between positive and negative attributions, self and other identity, and power and empowerment (Harvey 2001a, 2001b).

Differences between transactional and transformational modes of leadership discourse are revealed through patterns of process type, agency, metaphor, negation, and personal pronouns in the text. These features are often the focus of attention in Critical Discourse Analysis (CDA), which seeks to determine how discourse constructs and reflects sociocultural practices and which often involves a critique of the disempowering effect of dominant (usually capitalist) discourses and ideology. The analysis presented here, however, approaches capitalist discourse from within, mirroring to some extent the approach of transformational leaders themselves. In other words, although I do not explicitly question the legitimacy of the capitalist system that supports transformational leaders, I do challenge aspects of the system to which they belong.

The process by which employees' self-concept is invoked is also explored using Appraisal Theory, a relatively recent development within Systemic Functional Linguistics (SFL) that provides a framework for analysing lexical choice to reveal how interpersonal and social relations are negotiated in texts.

Transformational Business Leadership and Rhetoric

In the 1970s, there was a major shift in business research away from the more mundane and managerial, or 'transactional', forms of leadership to the more extraordinary forms of leadership referred to as 'charismatic', 'visionary', and/or 'transformational'. Transactional leadership is a managerial style of leadership based on an exchange process that appeals to employees' self-interest; for instance, in return for compliance, employees receive tangible rewards, such as pay and status (Bass 1985). In contrast, transformational leadership appeals to employees' ideals, values, and emotions (e.g. Bass 1985; Burns 1978; Conger and Kanungo 1987; House 1977; Sashkin 1988). According to Fiol *et al.* (1999: 450), transformational (or 'neo-charismatic') leaders 'articulate visions that are based on normative ideological values, offer innovative solutions to major social problems, stand for non-conservative if not radical change, and generally emerge and are more effective under conditions of social stress and crisis'. Although transformational leadership has been shown to be more effective in a variety of leadership situations and contexts, it has been suggested that effective leadership requires a 'full range' of leadership behaviours (Bass and Avolio 1994), including both transactional and transformational styles.

A distinctive feature of transformational leaders is their ability to successfully communicate a coherent and appealing vision of the future, articulated in such a way as to make these proposed future events seem achievable, desirable, and, in fact, necessary. Visions tend to be ambitious and are often accompanied by high performance expectations (Awamleh and Gardner 1999). They are also usually framed in an abstract and inspirational manner as idealized goals (Conger and Kanungo 1987) and spoken of in transcendent, ideological, and moral terms (Kirkpatrick and Locke 1996). In other words, visions do not make reference to 'detailed business plans or goals and rarely mention market share percentages, revenue targets, or return on investment figures' (Conger 1989: 40–1).

The other essential ingredient in transformational leadership is charisma (Bass 1985), a term which Weber (1947) used to refer to exceptional and gifted leaders who emerge in times of crisis. While the term has been redefined and applied in numerous and sometimes conflicting ways in business leadership research (Yukl 1999), most theorists would agree that charisma does not reside purely within the leader as a set of inherent qualities but involves a relationship between leader and followers that develops within particular sociocultural contexts. At the same time, however, it is acknowledged that certain types of leader behaviours are more likely to encourage followers' attributions of charisma than others. These behaviours include an ability to motivate followers; insight into followers' needs, values, and hopes; and consideration for individuals and groups (Bass and Avolio 1994).

A second point of agreement is that the ability to encourage or convince employees to perform 'beyond expectations' (Bass 1985) requires the kind of rhetorical skills commonly associated with charismatic leaders (Awamleh and Gardner 1999; Conger and Kanungo 1987; den Hartog and Verburg 1997; Shamir et al. 1993, 1994; Willner 1984). Rhetoric can be interpreted either positively, as language that is persuasive, or negatively, as language that is potentially empty (Fairclough 2000), the interpretation depending on a complex of factors such as the perceived intent of the speaker, the effect of the rhetoric on the listener, and the extent to which the rhetoric is used as an evasion tactic. Rhetorical strategies commonly used by charismatic leaders include collective personal pronouns, negation, metaphor, and lists (typically, three-part lists). While these are recognized as features of charismatic rhetoric, the process by which these rhetorical patterns achieve their effects on listeners is less transparent.

One proposition is that the leader's rhetoric works by invoking followers' self-concept (Shamir et al. 1993, 1994). Shamir and associates have suggested that charismatic leaders make more reference in their speeches (than non-charismatic leaders) to collective history and a better future; morals and values; follower efficacy and self-worth; long-term (rather than short-term) goals; and hope and faith (see also den Hartog and Verburg 1997). However, this process of invoking self-concept can be fraught with conflicting desires, tensions, dialectics, and paradoxes, which must be successfully reconciled for the desired effect to be achieved (Harvey 2001a; Fairclough 2000). An area of potential conflict, explored here, is in finding an appropriate balance between the transactional and transformational leadership behaviours required for effective leadership.

Steve Jobs of Apple Computer

No stranger to paradox and conflicting desires is Steve Jobs, co-founder and current CEO of Apple Computer. Jobs has frequently been portrayed in academic studies (Awamleh and Gardner 1999; Conger 1989; Conger and Kanungo 1987), the media, and biographies as a charismatic leader. In the 1970s, his vision, counter-cultural ethos, and formidable powers of persuasion (among other factors) afforded him a cult-like status. In the 1990s, he was largely responsible for the resurgence of Apple and its revived reputation for innovative computer technology and design. Jobs' major contribution to computer technology (along with Stephen Wozniak) was in popularizing personal computers, making them user-friendly, and encouraging their use in education. As Jobs himself comments: 'The contributions we tried to make embodied values not only of technical excellence and innovation – which I think we did our share of – but innovation of a more humanistic kind' (Jobs 1995).

The text analysed here (see Appendix) comes from the television documentary *Beyond Excellence: The Superachievers* (Nathan 1986).[1] Part of this documentary records two retreat meetings between Steve Jobs and his senior staff at NeXt Computer, the company he formed after leaving Apple in 1985. Two of the key Apple personnel Jobs took with him to NeXt (George Crow and Susan Barnes) are co-participants in the dialogue. While the first retreat was characterized by the enthusiasm and optimism to be expected of a new company, the mood of the second retreat (from which the text is drawn) was significantly more subdued and pessimistic because the deadlines and goals that had been set during the first retreat were beginning to appear unachievable.

Conger (1989: 134–6) used this text to illustrate how the goal of shipping NeXt's first computer is framed by Jobs in such a way that its accomplishment becomes absolutely critical to the company's success or failure. The situation is therefore characterized by extreme pressure, high uncertainty, and urgency. In high technology industries and computer firms, in particular, tasks tend to be non-routine, requiring especially high levels of performance. At the same time, performance goals 'cannot be easily specified and measured ... leaders cannot link extrinsic rewards to individual performance' (Shamir *et al.* 1993: 589). High levels of creativity are, therefore, required and tight deadlines need to be met for fledgling and more established companies to gain or maintain competitive advantage or, indeed, survive. The dual demands of creativity and tight deadlines may well require a transformational leader like Steve Jobs (Shamir *et al.* 1993), that is, a leader who can inspire, motivate, goad, and occasionally threaten employees to perform well under pressure.

The *Beyond Excellence* text provides an excellent example of the kind of skilful rhetorical work a leader needs to do to defuse the tensions that can result from the conflicting demands of pressure and creativity. It also illustrates how transformational and transactional styles interact and potentially clash.

From Transaction to Transformation

In the excerpt, one of Jobs' staff members (George Crow) poses a question, which can be generalized as 'How are we going to ship this computer on time?' Although this question seems to be aiming for a transactional answer, Jobs' response effectively evades the question and reframes it as two transformational questions, namely: 'Why do we have to ship the computer on time?' and 'What will happen if we don't?' Whereas the initial transactional question is framed in instrumental, concrete, and immediate terms, the transformational answer is constructed as inspirational, abstract, and longer term. These differences are reflected in the lexicogrammatical choices made by Jobs and his staff. Of interest here is how the ideational semantics of action and symbolism collude with the interpersonal semantics of individuality/collectivism to construct organizational action, responsibility, and identity.

Significant differences between Crow (in transactional mode) and Jobs (in transformational mode) can be detected in these speakers' choice of material processes (Halliday 1994). Crow's initial question and comment (1–6) contain concrete and effective (agentive) material processes in which the Agent/Actor has the capacity to act upon the other participant in the clause (Goal/Medium), i.e. the computer and the schedule. (In the following examples, the Process is in small capitals.)

2:   if we [Actor/Agent] HAVE TO SHIP this computer [Goal/Medium] by the summer of '87

3:   how are you [Actor/Agent] GOING TO MOVE that [Goal/Medium] up?

4:   price [Actor/Agent] IS NOT GOING TO CHANGE the schedule [Goal/Medium] that much

Jobs' material processes, in contrast, are mostly grammatically low impact in the sense that they are middle (non-agentive), with the Actor as Medium not Agent:

9:   yes, we [Actor/Medium] COULD [GO to the spring of '88]

18–21:   since we've proved that we [Actor/Medium] CAN'T DO something
         great [Range] in eighteen months, why should we believe that we
         [Actor/Medium] COULD DO [something *great*] a year later?

The diminished grammatical impact of these material processes is further weakened through strategies of abstraction, metaphor, and negation.
First, Jobs' material processes are often expressed in a 'do' + Range of the
action construction (as in the above example and illustrated further
below). The Range is a quasi-participant, which, unlike the Goal, cannot be
impacted by the process (Halliday 1994); as a consequence, the process is
vague.

51–2:   so I don't think we have a company if we [Actor/Medium] DON'T
         DO this [Range]

Moreover, the process is often part of a metaphor.

16:      all the work we've done we THROW down the toilet
22:      we HAVE TO DRIVE a stake in the ground
46–7:   we 'VE BEEN GIVEN it (a window) and thank God we 'VE BEEN
         GIVEN it

Jobs' metaphors tend to speak of 'the inevitability and irresistibility of
change' (Fairclough 2000), evident in his reference to 'windows' (presumably of opportunity) that open and close, and his proclamation that 'there
are certain realities here . . . [that ARE GOING TO COME into play]' (44).

Finally, Jobs' material processes are mostly expressed in negative form,
thereby focusing attention on what cannot be done as opposed to what can
be done. Such negative assertions allow him to break current frames (Fiol *et
al.* 1999) and to 'implicitly [take] issue with the corresponding positive
assertions' (Fairclough 1989: 154).

25:      we CAN'T SELL enough units . . .
57–8:   we WILL NOT BE ABLE TO ATTRACT great people, we WILL NOT BE
         ABLE TO RETAIN the ones . . . we have

Jobs also makes use of three-part lists, an (ideational) logical device
whose sense of 'unity or completeness' (Atkinson 1984: 57; den Hartog and
Verburg 1997) reinforces the idea of inevitability expressed in his windows
metaphor. Lists are a particularly effective rhetorical strategy that can
'favour a logic of appearances . . . rather than an explanatory logic which
tries to go beneath appearances to find explanations' (Fairclough 2000:
53). For instance, in his first three-part list (25–7), Jobs attempts to lead his
staff to the conclusion that not selling enough units will necessarily lead to
an erosion of credibility, while in his final list (57–9), the (un)natural conclusion that emerges is that not meeting the deadline will lead to staffing
problems which will, in turn, lead to a loss of company identity. In both lists,
Jobs' logic is implicit and ambiguous.

At the same time that Jobs makes reference to actions that are semantically underspecified, metaphorical, negative, and/or presented in list form, he constructs action as an organizational responsibility, as reflected in his use of the inclusive personal pronoun 'we'. This pronoun allows Jobs to present himself and his staff as a collective characterized by shared values, purpose, and trust (Fiol *et al.* 1999; Gardner and Avolio 1998; Harvey 2001a, 2001b). On the other hand, Jobs reserves the exclusive pronouns, 'I' and 'you', for symbolic mental and verbal processes, which has the effect of individualizing the various participants in the organization.

38:     What DO you WANT [Mental] me to DO [Material]?

40–2:   I DON'T WANT TO HEAR [Mental] just because we BLEW [Material] it last time, we 'RE GOING TO BLOW [Material] it this time.

43:     What I WANT [Mental] is probably irrelevant.

53–5:   No matter what I SAY [Verbal] or anybody else SAYS [Verbal], that is my deepest BELIEF [Mental/nominalized].

In only two material processes does Jobs refer to himself as an exclusive identity ('I', 'me') – one of these clauses is effective (agentive), the other is middle (non-agentive).

37:     Well, George, I [Actor/Agent] CAN'T CHANGE [Material] the world [Goal/Medium], you know.

38:     What do you want me [Actor/Medium] TO DO [Material]?

In these two clauses, Jobs explicitly challenges the romanticized view of transformational leaders as change agents – extraordinary individuals who have all the answers and who can and do change the world. In his 'social contagion' approach to charismatic leadership, Meindl (1990, 1995) argues that a romanticized attributional bias can cause followers (and others) to overestimate the leader's role in the success or failure of the company while simultaneously underestimating the influence of external factors beyond the control of the leader. Jobs certainly attempts to de-emphasize his own agency here and to shift the focus onto these external realities. The rhetorical question that follows these two clauses (39: 'What's the solution?') does not expect an answer and effectively closes down this part of the dialogue. Individualizing George (by naming him) heightens the engagement but also has the effect of driving a wedge through the collective identity of the company. These three clauses also highlight the dilemmas inherent in the high-risk computer industry as well as an important paradoxical aspect of the leader/follower relationship: the balance of power and responsibility between leader, followers, and other participants.

Fiol *et al.* (1999) suggest that rhetorical strategies such as those just out-lined enable a leader to shift followers' acceptance, over a period of time, from conventional values towards values that are unconventional, and ultimately towards those that are innovative. The cluster of strategies Jobs uses in the text do seem to be aimed at shifting or realigning the values of his staff with his own, in this case from the postponement option towards meeting the deadline. It needs to be emphasized that the low grammatical impact of Jobs' responses does not detract from the 'real world' impact of his discourse. Indeed, in combination with his use of personal pronouns which draws attention to paradoxes of identity, action, and power, the effect of his material processes is to shift from the transactional and mundane to the transformational and inspirational.

Evoking Self-concept: Appraisal Analysis

As noted earlier, it has been hypothesized that charismatic leader rhetoric appeals to followers' sense of their own efficacy and self-worth, and their need for long-term goals; it also makes reference to the crucial role that hope and faith play in pursuing a path or vision (Shamir *et al.* 1993, 1994). A promising framework within which to explore issues to do with self-concept is Appraisal Theory. Situated within SFL, Appraisal Theory offers a rich and evolving framework with which to analyse the negotiation of interpersonal and social relations in text (Iedema *et al.* 1994; Martin 2000; White 2000, forthcoming). Appraisal Theory concerns itself with how speakers and writers adopt intersubjective and ideological positions in their texts through positive or negative evaluations of and attitudes towards people, objects, and events. One application of the theory is to illuminate the stylistic and rhetorical workings of texts within different genres (Iedema *et al.* 1994; Christie and Martin 1997; White 1998; Martin and Macken forthcoming). A major benefit of the theory lies in its accessibility to non-linguists, mainly due to the use of semantics (rather than grammar) as the way into the analysis (Martin 2000: 143). It is, therefore, especially well suited to an analysis aimed at potentially multiple readerships, e.g. linguists, critical discourse analysts, organizational behaviourists, and leadership rhetoric scholars.

The appraisal system of ATTITUDE, which represents the focus of the present text analysis, includes the evaluative sub-systems of AFFECT, APPRECIATION, and JUDGEMENT (Iedema *et al.* 1994). As outlined in Martin (2000), AFFECT models resources expressing emotions, while APPRECIATION and JUDGEMENT model resources to do with feelings that have been institutionalized, for instance, as 'norms about how products, performances, and naturally occurring phenomena are valued' (APPRECIATION) or 'norms about how people should or shouldn't behave' (JUDGEMENT) (Martin 2000: 155–9). The aim of JUDGEMENT, then, is to exert control over people's behaviour while the goal of APPRECIATION is to evaluate their achievements. Drawing on Halliday's (1994) description of English modality, two types of JUDGEMENT have been proposed (Iedema *et al.* 1994): the SOCIAL ESTEEM of the appraised refers to their NORMALITY (FATE) (usuality), CAPACITY (ability) or TENACITY (inclination); alternatively, the SOCIAL SANCTION of the appraised may be at stake, for example their VERACITY (probability/truth) or PROPRIETY (obligation/ethics) (Martin 1995). APPRECIATION also offers more delicate choices, for instance, between REACTION, COMPOSITION, and

VALUATION while AFFECT includes choices between SECURITY, FEAR, INTEREST, and DISQUIET, among others.

Instantiations of appraisal can be explicit (inscribed) through attitudinally laden lexis, e.g. 'problem,' 'great,' 'the worst thing' (shown in italic in the text analysis in the Appendix), or they can be evoked (as 'tokens') through ideational meanings; for instance, the clause 'all the work we've done we throw down the toilet' (16) evokes (in this context) an appraisal of failure and incapacity. Instances in which the appraiser is not the same as the speaker, that is, when the appraisal is projected onto another participant, are indicated in Column 2; the targets of the appraisals are shown in Column 6. Sub-types of ATTITUDE – that is, AFFECT, APPRECIATION, and JUDGEMENT – are shown in Columns 3, 4, and 5, respectively. Appraisals are also interpreted as carrying negative or positive connotations in the context, indicated by the symbols '+' or '–' following the sub-type of appraisal.

The appraisal analysis, like the analysis of material processes, reveals significant differences between Jobs and his staff in their approach to the deadline issue. While Crow focuses on the risks involved (APPRECIATION: REACTION) and the negative affect brought about by the pressure (AFFECT: SECURITY: DISQUIET), Jobs emphasizes JUDGEMENT: SOCIAL ESTEEM, in particular CAPACITY, TENACITY, and NORMALITY (FATE). These are mostly expressed implicitly as tokens rather than explicitly in attitudinally laden lexis. As perceptions of capacity and efficacy provide powerful motivational impetus to organizational members (Bandura 1986; Shamir *et al.* 1993, 1994), it is not surprising that Jobs relies on appraisals involving CAPACITY. What is surprising is that Jobs' appraisals are mostly concerned with incapacity, i.e. negative appraisals. The actions and events evoking these appraisals of incapacity are unrealized future events that are usually concrete (rather than metaphorical), e.g. 'If we don't do this . . .' (56), and 'We can't sell enough units in '87 to pay for our operating costs . . .' (25). Although Jobs focuses primarily on (IN)CAPACITY, he cleverly embeds appraisals of APPRECIATION within some of his judgements. In particular, he positions a positive APPRECIATION of the computer being created against his company's potential incapacity to create the computer, a juxtaposition drawing on an intertextual reference to the highly successful Apple Macintosh (once mythologized by Jobs as 'insanely great').

18–21:   [INCAPACITY: since we've proved that we can't do] [APPRECIATION: <u>something great</u>] in eighteen months, why should we believe we could do [APPRECIATION: <u>something great</u>] a year later?]

This strategy seems especially effective since Jobs, Crow, and Barnes (and some of the other staff present) share a collective history of the positive social esteem that accrued from the incredible success of the Macintosh. Had these staff members never tasted success, the spectre of failure and its accompanying fall from grace might not have had such a motivating effect.

Thus, Jobs presents two possible futures: one great (success and survival), the other dire (failure and demise).

The other main judgement expressed is TENACITY, which refers to the resolve of the appraised, i.e. the extent to which he or she is reliable or dependable (Martin 2000: 156). Jobs' instances of TENACITY are mostly expressed in positive but metaphorical terms. In his assertion that 'we have to drive a stake in the ground' (22), he urges his staff to strengthen their belief in the need to stand up and be counted (Shamir et al. 1994). However, as noted above, Crow challenges Jobs' TENACITY metaphor by querying whether everybody will believe the stake is in fact in the ground (32–3). Crow also questions the VERACITY of various participants in the company (34–5), separating the collective identity of the organization into a potentially divisive 'us' versus 'them' ('they' referring to the software department). This breakdown of trust is significant in terms of the critical role trust plays in organizational effectiveness.

Crow's lack of faith motivates Jobs to try another tactic. Having already made strong appeals to his employees' sense of self-esteem, he shifts to an appeal to faith. NORMALITY (FATE) captures meanings to do with how (un)usual or special the appraised is (Martin 2000: 156). It is expressed in the text in positive yet metaphorical terms, and is mostly concerned with luck, fortune, and opportunity, e.g. 'And I think this is a window that we've got. We've been given it, and thank God we've been given it' (45–7). Jobs' appeal to God, tantamount to an appeal to faith, not only heightens the involvement of this utterance but also emphasizes forces beyond his own control and that of his staff and company.

In his appeal to SOCIAL ESTEEM, then, Jobs emphasizes the need to be tenacious enough (TENACITY) to capitalize on transitory opportunities (FATE) so as to avoid perceptions of incapacity (CAPACITY). His patterns of JUDGEMENT (and to a lesser extent, APPRECIATION) provide support for Shamir et al.'s proposition (1993, 1994) that charismatic leaders are concerned with the collective identity of their organization, the self-worth of their followers, shared history, and faith in positive outcomes. Charismatic and transformational leadership, thus, speaks in abstract terms of non-specific (but nonetheless critical) action that must be undertaken so that the organization does not lose an identity based on competence and accomplishment. As demonstrated in Jobs' use of ATTITUDE, the evaluation is not always couched in positive terms; Jobs uses potentially negative future outcomes to inspire his staff to do the impossible. For instance, his statement 'Nobody else has done this' (48) can be interpreted in two ways – positively, in the sense that no other company has created such a great product to date because the competition is not capable of such excellence, or negatively (an interpretation perhaps preferred by his staff at this point), that no one else has done it because it is not possible.

Finally, there are important differences between Jobs and his staff in their use of AFFECT. Crow, for instance, frames his responses within the AFFECT of problem and worry (INSECURITY), in other words, as non-institutionalized emotion. Jobs, however, is more inclined towards institutionalized feelings in the form of JUDGEMENT and APPRECIATION and has no time for AFFECT ('I don't want to hear . . .' (40), 'What do you want me to do?' (37)). It is here that the organizational identity breaks down into individuals; Jobs is not prepared to tolerate faintheartedness, i.e. insecurity, and talk of failure is not an option.

Conclusion

In this paper, I have undertaken a text analysis that deals with issues of potential interest to both leadership researchers and to discourse analysts, namely, the discourse interaction between transactional and transformational leadership styles. Analysis of select ideational and interpersonal patterns in the text demonstrates how a skilful leader can reframe a discussion so as to encourage employees to achieve particular goals, the appropriateness and achievability of which, of course, are open to question. Other resources of Appraisal Theory could be drawn on to illuminate aspects of the dialogue (and charismatic discourse, more generally) not covered here. For instance, GRADATION would allow us to analyse Jobs' use of hyperbole, and ENGAGEMENT would reveal how Jobs (and other leaders) negotiate intersubjectivities with their subordinates and naturalize various ideological positions. ENGAGEMENT would be especially useful in examining the power-empowerment paradox, which presents ongoing dilemmas for organizational behaviour researchers and leadership theorists.

Appendix: Appraisal analysis of the *Beyond Excellence* text

No.	Text	AFFECT	APPRECIATION	JUDGEMENT	Target
	CROW:				
1	If we really do believe			Esteem: veracity	Jobs? & staff
2	that we have to ship this [computer] by summer of '87,				
3	then how are you going to move that up?				
4	I don't think price is going to change the schedule that much.				
5	I think the *real risk* is in the technology		Reaction: quality –		technology
6	it's [the *real risk*] not in the cost.		Reaction: quality + (not risky)		cost
	BARNES:				
7	There's another option.				
8	You can go to the spring of '88. . . .				
	JOBS:				
9	Yes, we could [go to the spring of '88].				
10	But the *problem* is		Reaction: quality –		going to the spring of '88
11	if we do that				
12	no, that's not the *worst* thing		Reaction: quality –		spring of '88 (not the worst but still bad)
13	the *worst* thing is the world isn't standing still,		Reaction: quality –		spring of '88
14	so by the spring of '89, well we want color				
15	and the technology window sort of passes us by			Esteem: capacity –	Jobs & staff
16	and all the work we've done we throw down the toilet			Esteem: capacity –	"
17	and [we] start over			Esteem: capacity –	"
18	and, you know, since we've proved			Esteem: capacity –	Jobs & staff/ [product]

		Security	Valuation	Esteem/Sanction	Topic
19	that we can't do something *great* in eighteen months,		[Valuation + 'something great']	Esteem: capacity –	Jobs & staff/[product]
20	why should we believe			Esteem: veracity	Jobs & staff
21	we could do [something *great*] a year later?		[Valuation +, 'something great']	Esteem: capacity –	Jobs & staff/[product]
22	I think we have to drive a stake in the ground somewhere,			Esteem: tenacity +	Jobs & staff
23	and I think if we miss this window			Esteem: capacity –	"
24	then a whole series of events come into play.				"
25	We can't sell enough units in '87 to pay for our operating costs,			Esteem: capacity –	"
26	word gets out that we're *not doing that well*,			Esteem: capacity –	"
27	a lot of credibility starts to erode.			Esteem: capacity –	
28	I don't know,				
29	you can make-up all these fantasies,			Sanction: veracity –	Crow/Barnes/staff?
30	we've got to have a stake in the ground.			Esteem: tenacity +	Jobs & staff
CROW:					
31	The *problem* I've got, though, is,	Security: disquiet –			meeting the deadline
32	one, will everybody believe			Sanction: veracity	Jobs' metaphor
33	the stake is in fact in the ground?				
34	and, two, when Software comes back and says what they can do by summer or spring of '87,			Sanction: veracity	software
35	will they be telling us the truth?	Security: disquiet –			"
36	That's what I'm worried about.				
JOBS:					
37	Well, George, I can't change the world, you know.			Esteem: capacity –	Jobs
38	What do you want me to do?				
39	What's the solution?				

#	Clause	Valuation	Esteem	Target
40	I don't want to hear		Esteem: capacity –	Jobs & staff
41	just because we *blew it* last time,		Esteem: capacity –	"
42	we're going to *blow it* this time.			what Jobs wants
43	What I want is probably *irrelevant.*	Valuation –		
44	I mean there are certain realities here, both psychological and market that are going to come into play, in my own personal judgment.			
45	And I think this is a window that we've got.		Esteem: normality (fate) +	Jobs & staff
46	We've been given it,		Esteem: normality (fate) +	"
47	and thank God we've been given it.		Esteem: normality (fate) +	"
48	Nobody else has done this.		Esteem: capacity –	industry
49	This is a *wonderful* window.	Valuation	Esteem: normality (fate) +	window/Jobs & staff
50	We have eighteen months!		Esteem: normality (fate) + *	Jobs & staff
51	So I don't think we have a company		Esteem: capacity –	"
52	if we don't do this.		Esteem: capacity –	"
53	No matter what I say		Esteem: veracity –	Jobs
54	or anybody else says,		Esteem: veracity –	anybody else
55	that is my deepest belief.		Esteem: veracity +	Jobs
56	If we don't do this,		Esteem: capacity –	Jobs & staff
57	we will not be able to attract *great* people,		Esteem: capacity –	"
58	we will not be able to retain the ones, some of the ones we have,		Esteem: capacity –	"
59	and, you know, it just won't be us.		Esteem: capacity –	"

* This clause seems to be operating as a positive token of the NORMALITY: FATE appraisal that has been constructed in the preceding clauses; that is: 'we're really fortunate because we have a whole eighteen months in which to achieve this' (cf. 'we have only eighteen months').

Note

1. Every effort has been made to trace the copyright holders of the original material contained in this paper. Grateful acknowledgement for this material is made to Nation/Tyler Productions, Video Arts.

References

Atkinson, J. M. (1984) *Our Master's Voices: The Language and Body Language of Politics.* London: Routledge.

Awamleh, R. and Gardner, W. (1999) 'Perceptions of Leader Charisma and Effectiveness: The Effects of Vision Content, Delivery, and Organizational Performance', *Leadership Quarterly*, 10(3): 345–74.

Bandura, A. (1986) *Social Foundations of Thought and Action: A Social Cognitive Theory.* Englewood Cliffs, NJ: Prentice Hall.

Bass, B. M. (1985) *Leadership and Performance Beyond Expectations.* New York: Free Press.

Bass, B. M. and Avolio, B. (1994) *Improving Organizational Effectiveness through Transformational Leadership.* Thousand Oaks, CA: Sage Publications.

Burns, J. M. (1978) *Leadership.* New York: Harper and Row.

Christie, F. and Martin, J. R. (eds) (1997) *Genres and Institutions: Social Processes in the Workplace and School.* London: Cassell.

Conger, J. A. (1989) *The Charismatic Leader: Behind the Mystique of Exceptional Leadership.* San Francisco, CA: Jossey-Bass.

Conger, J. A. and Kanungo, R. N. (1987) 'Toward a Behavioral Theory of Charismatic Leadership in Organizational Settings', *Academy of Management Review*, 12: 637–47.

den Hartog, D. and Verburg, R. (1997) 'Charisma and Rhetoric: Communicative Techniques of International Business Leaders', *Leadership Quarterly*, 8(4): 355–91.

Fairclough, N. (2000) *New Labour, New Language?* London: Routledge.

Fairclough, N. (1989) *Language and Power.* London: Longman.

Fiol, C. M., Harris, D., and House, R. (1999) 'Charismatic Leadership: Strategies for Effecting Social Change', *Leadership Quarterly*, 10(3): 449–83.

Gardner, W. L. and Avolio, B. J. (1998) 'The Charismatic Relationship: A Dramaturgical Perspective', *Academy of Management Review*, 23(1): 32–58.

Halliday, M. A. K. (1994) *An Introduction to Functional Grammar* (2nd edn). London: Edward Arnold.

Harvey, A. (2001a) 'A Dramaturgical Analysis of Charismatic Leader Discourse', *Journal of Organizational Change Management*, 14(3): 253–65.

Harvey, A. (2001b) 'Constructing Charisma and Identity: A Comparative Analysis of Business Leaders in the Computer Industry', paper presented to the Academy of Management, Washington DC, August.

House, R. (1977) 'A 1976 Theory of Charismatic Leadership', in *Leadership: The Cutting Edge*, ed. by J. Hunt and L. L. Larson. Carbondale, IL: Southern Illinois University Press, 189–204.

Iedema, R., Feez, S., and White P. R. (1994) 'Media Literacy (Write it Right Literacy in Industry Project: Stage Two)'. Sydney: Metropolitan East Region's Disadvantaged Schools Program.

Jobs, S. (1995) Interview with Daniel Morrow of the Smithsonian Institution at: http://www.americanhistory.si.edu/csr/comphist/sj1.html (consulted July 2001).

Kirkpatrick, S. A. and Locke, E. A. (1996) 'Direct and Indirect Effects of Three Core Charismatic Leadership Components on Performance and Attitudes', *Journal of Applied Psychology*, 81: 36–51.

Martin, J. R. (2000) 'Appraisal Systems in English', in *Evaluation in Text: Authorial Stance and the Construction of Discourse*, ed. by S. Hunston and G. Thompson. Oxford: Oxford University Press, 143–75.

Martin, J. R. (1995) 'Reading Positions/Positioning Readers: JUDGEMENT in English', *Prospect: A Journal of Australian TESOL*, 10(2): 27–37.

Martin, J. R. and Macken, M. (forthcoming) *Text* (Special Edition).

Meindl, J. R. (1995) 'The Romance of Leadership as a Follower-centric Theory: A Social Constructionist Approach', *Leadership Quarterly*, 6: 329–41.

Meindl, J. R. (1990) 'On Leadership: An Alternative to the Conventional Wisdom', in *Research in Organizational Behaviour: Volume 12*, ed. by B. Staw and L. Cummings. Greenwich, CT: JAI Press, 159–203.

Nathan, J. (1986) *Beyond Excellence: The Superachievers* (Video). London: Nation/Tyler Productions, Video Arts.

Sashkin, M. (1988) 'The Visionary Leader', in *Charismatic Leadership: The Elusive Factor in Organizational Effectiveness*, ed. by J. A. Conger and R. N. Kanungo. San Francisco, CA: Jossey-Bass, 122–60.

Shamir, B., Arthur M. B., and House, R. J. (1994) 'The Rhetoric of Charismatic Leadership: A Theoretical Extension, a Case Study, and Implications for Research', *Leadership Quarterly*, 5(1): 25–42.

Shamir, B., House, R. J., and Arthur, M. B. (1993) 'The Motivational Effects of Charismatic Leadership: A Self-concept Based Theory', *Organization Science*, 4(4): 577–94.

Weber, M. (1947) *The Theory of Social and Economic Organization*, trans. by A. M. Henderson and T. Parsons. New York: The Free Press.

White, P. R. R. (forthcoming) 'Beyond Modality and Hedging: A Dialogic View of the Language of Intersubjective Stance', *Text* (Special Edition on Appraisal).

White, P. R. R. (2000) 'Dialogue and Intersubjectivity: Reinterpreting the Semantics of Modality and Hedging', in *Working With Dialog*, ed. by M. Coulthard, J. Cotterill, and F. Rock. Tubingen: Max Niemeyer Verlag, 67–80.

White, P. R. R. (1998) 'Telling Media Tales: The News Story as Rhetoric', unpublished Ph.D. Dissertation. NSW: University of Sydney.

Willner, A. R. (1984) *The Spellbinders: Charismatic Political Leadership*. New Haven, CT: Yale University Press.

Yukl, G. (1999) 'An Evaluation of the Conceptual Weaknesses in Transformational and Charismatic Leadership Theories', *Leadership Quarterly*, 10: 285–305.

14 Ideological Resources in Biotechnology Press Releases: Patterns of Theme/Rheme and Given/New

Inger Lassen

Institutional practices 'constrain' in that they influence our behaviour, but at the same time they 'enable' complex social processes through particular discourse patterns (Iedema 1997: 73). This observation is particularly relevant to biotechnology research aimed at solving food problems in developing countries. In an ongoing public debate, biotechnology advocates have claimed that the population of the Third World need genetically engineered (GE) food to survive while environmentalists have contended that food scarcity is a result of the unequal distribution of resources. Assuming that institutions with high stakes at risk are less direct about their intentions, this article argues that, while the debating parties claim to be representing the 'truth', different *discursive resources are used to promote* different *ideologies. Using Fairclough's Critical Discourse Analysis (CDA) framework and Halliday's theory on Thematic structure and Grammatical Metaphor, I shall explore an aspect of patterns of Theme/Rheme and Given/New for expressing implicit meaning.*

Introduction

Ideological contestation in biotechnology discourse may be explored by studying various discourse types within the field, and a relevant focus area is the press release because it is often used as a channel in the public debate. Institutions issuing press releases are often under pressure to improve their public image and, therefore, want to ensure that journalists do not simply discard their texts. As a result, content as well as style both reflect a process of negotiation – a process that lends to the press release a touch of vagueness which may well be a characteristic stylistic feature in this type of discourse. This point is substantiated by discourse analyst Geert Jacobs (1999), who undertook a corpus-based study of press releases relating to the Exxon Valdez accident and describes (1999: x–xi) press releases as 'a type of indirectly targeted, projected discourse ... whose *raison d'être* is to be retold'. The title of Jacobs' book, *Preformulating the News*, is illustrative of this point and captures the main purpose of this discourse type. According to Jacobs (1999: 1), press releases are meant to be ' "continued" as accurately as possible, preferably even verbatim, in news reporting', and he illustrates (1999: 303) this point by demonstrating not only the similarity between some press releases and their corresponding news reports, but also the ways in which the contents and style of both types of discourse are being constantly negotiated. Referring to press releases as divided discourse, Myers (1996, quoted in Jacobs 1999: 311) suggests that 'In divided discourse, vagueness is often used strategically to allow a written text to take on a range of meanings for different audiences with different interests.' By inference, the press release might, therefore, be an effective vehicle for the naturalization of ideology since style that is unmarked may be presumed to have been naturalized and institutionalized through the imitation of news reporting.

In this paper, therefore, I shall focus on two biotechnology press releases, with the primary purpose of exploring one stylistic strategy that is available for naturalizing ideologies. The two press releases represent conflicting interests: one issued by biotechnology advocates from the large multi-national company, Monsanto (4 August 2000), the other written by biotechnology critics and published by the InterPress Third World News Agency (IPS) (22 June 2000) – an agency that focuses primarily on Third World issues. In my analysis, I shall combine Fairclough's three-dimensional Critical Discourse Analysis (CDA) model with the Systemic Functional Linguistics (SFL) framework of Theme/Rheme and Given/New – a framework that imports significantly on the flow of discourse as it involves the notion of Grammatical Metaphor (Halliday 1994; Martin 1992).

Fairclough's CDA Framework

Fairclough's CDA theory is based on the notion of dialectics as he perceives discursive practice as reproducing as well as transforming society in a dialectical process in which discourse and social structure enter into a dynamic relationship (1992: 65). As a result, any type of discourse will always be a reflection of social practice, and because social practices are unstable due to changing ideologies, the same instability can be observed in their discursive representations. Fairclough (1992) suggests that the analyst engage in a description stage as well as in an interpretation stage. Furthermore, results should always be seen as preliminary due to the instability of the 'orders of discourse' studied. To achieve these purposes, analysis should be done, taking into consideration the following three levels, but not necessarily in the order mentioned.

- Social practice
- Discourse practice
- Text

Social Practice

The two press releases focus on the same topic within the broader conceptual framework of biotechnology. By means of genetic engineering (GE), a Zurich-based professor, Dr Ingo Potrykus, has found a method for introducing genes from daffodils, peas, bacteria, and virus into rice seeds where they produce beta-carotene, an important source of vitamin A. One of the arguments in favour of the new method has been that a large percentage of the world population depends on rice for their staple food, and because conventional rice has a very low content of vitamin A, millions of children develop blindness caused by vitamin A deficiency, and some of these children may even die (Christensen 2000). The marketing rights of the new product, which has been referred to as 'golden rice', are owned by the Swiss agribusiness company Astra Zeneca, but in 2000 the company offered to donate the grains to poor farmers in Asia. Proponents have referred to the offer as generous while critics have suggested that the agribusiness companies were only trying to repair their tarnished image caused by their aggressive marketing of GE crops. According to critics, what GE agribusiness companies really needed was a new brand like 'golden rice' with a number of morally acceptable ingredients. But, as argued by Klein (2000), the question is whether the new brand solves 'the crisis of malnutrition or the crisis of credibility plaguing biotechnology'.

An argument also often used by critics is that since, around the world, millions of people are undernourished, there is a world food crisis. However, despite the sad fact that many people are starving, there is no crisis of world food production. If governments and international organizations would implement policy changes that would enable a redistribution of resources and guarantee food security, there would be sufficient food for everybody in spite of a growing world population. Relying on GE crops would not solve the problems of inequitable access of resources, but rather aggravate the trend that began during the Green Revolution in the late 1970s (Oxfam 1999). Now, critics fear that GE crop reliance could be a new 'green revolution' with devastating consequences for everybody apart from the agribusiness companies.

The two press releases analysed should be understood against this background because the ideological and political effects of the discourse are very much a function of past history leading up to the present situation. The beginning of what might be seen as a proposal for a hegemonic relationship between the proponents and the critics can be found as the former try to appeal to the latter for their co-operation in what they believe to be a good and noble cause. If proponents succeed, a new kind of hegemony will be created between the agribusiness companies and peasants in Asia. In such a relationship, the agribusinesse will provide the know-how needed to grow the new types of rice, and the peasants will agree to use the seeds, which have been distributed freely as part of a goodwill package. The role played by critics seems to be that of a third force whose primary objective is to try to disclose the strategies used by the proponents. The critics, thus, try to assist societal transformation rather than societal reproduction by counteracting the creation of new hegemonic relationships based on the old economic world order.

Discourse Practice

By convention, press releases are used for public image-building, and this is clearly a primary purpose of the Monsanto press release. The IPS press release, on the other hand, is not concerned with image-building, but instead makes counter-claims against the propositions made in the Monsanto press release. Consequently, the structures and strategies used in the two press releases are not the same. The primary purpose of the Monsanto press release is to reproduce and cement existing practice on the basis of the naturalized ideological platform of globalization while the primary purpose of the IPS press release is to disclose this kind of naturalization with the purpose of redirecting the course of action in order to transform society. This is seen in the way in which claims and counter-claims are continuously being substantiated in the text. Having been naturalized through conventions, such discourse becomes an obvious carrier of ideologies and, thus, facilitates the endeavour by institutions to gain popular consent for a particular paradigm.

Using Hasan's (1985) method for a linear description of the generic structure potential, the generic structure of the Monsanto press release may be illustrated as follows:

Introducing and promoting an innovative idea or product ^ ↓ *Listing and praising purposes* * ↓ *Substantiating purposes* * ↓ *Offering background information* * (*promoting the initiator*)

which should be read as: The obligatory, fixed order stage of introducing and promoting an innovative idea or product preceding the obligatory, fixed order, and recursive stage of listing and praising purposes preceding the unordered, recursive stage of substantiating purposes preceding the unordered, recursive stage of offering background information preceding the unordered, optional stage of promoting the initiator. On the basis of the generic structure suggested for the Monsanto text, it is possible to characterize the discourse type as belonging to the genre of *promotional writing*.

An analysis of the IPS press release shows the following rather different generic structure:

Raising an issue ^ ↓ *Presenting claims and/or counter-claims* ^ ↓ *Substantiating claims* * ↓ *Offering background information*

which should be read as: The obligatory stage of raising an issue preceding the obligatory, recursive, and fixed order stage of presenting claims and/or counter-claims preceding the obligatory, recursive, and fixed order stage of substantiating claims preceding the unordered, obligatory, and recursive stage of offering background information.

A quick glance at the four moves introduced suggests that the communicative purpose of the IPS press release differs from that of the Monsanto text because none of the stages tends to promote a product or ideology. Instead, all stages address claims made in past discursive events. The only similarity that can be found is the background information present in press releases and where the purpose in both is to place the issue debated in a historical perspective. I suggest that the primary communicative intention of the IPS press release is counter-argumentation and, therefore, belongs to the genre of *rebuttal.* In other words, it contests the ideas expressed in the Monsanto press release. This would suggest that press releases do not make up a single genre category but, instead, may be seen as a special kind of mode used for conveying different kinds of news of interest to the general public.

Text Analysis: Combining CDA with SFL

In SFL, social analyses focus on social systems interacting with language. Figure 14.1 illustrates how each level realizes and is realized by adjacent levels, but it also helps to explain why observations at two levels that are not immediately adjacent may seem to be independent of each other. It may, for instance, be difficult to explain how ideology influences genre conventions because there seems to be no one-to-one relationship between the two concepts. According to Martin (1992), they both influence and are influenced by register and, as such, are observable in language through the

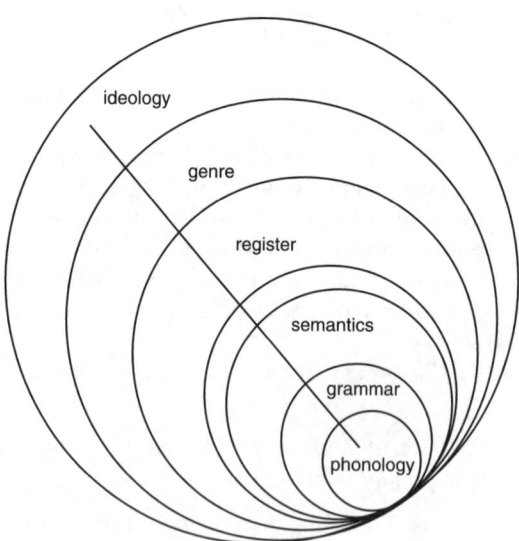

Figure 14.1 Interrelated language strata (Martin 1992: 496)

levels of lexicogrammar, morphology, graphology, and phonology. As a result, text analysis becomes crucial to the understanding of social context and social practice. A second inference is that analysis at separate levels becomes meaningless without interpreting the results in the light of other levels of the meta-redundancy model. In other words, it is not possible to draw meaningful conclusions on the basis of analyses that explore a single stratum in isolation. I would suggest that the same observation is valid also when considering Fairclough's CDA model for analysing social practice, discourse practice, and text. In order to be able to draw meaningful conclusions about one of these levels, it becomes necessary to include observations about the other levels of analysis. Therefore, the strength of both approaches lies not only in their descriptive capacity, but also in their interpretative ability.

Against this background, it becomes possible to integrate SFL and CDA at the text level, combining Fairclough's CDA model with Halliday's ideational, interpersonal, and textual metafunctions as organizing principles. By using SFL's range of tools, CDA proponents can analyse power and ideology within social contexts because of the resources SFL provides for talking about language in a way that relates grammatical functions to social activity (Martin 2000: 276).

Organizing Principles in SFL: Theme/Rheme, Given/New

In his treatment of thematic structure, Halliday (1994: 37) has referred to Theme as 'the element which serves as the point of departure of the message' and Rheme as the part of the clause which develops the Theme. In English, the Thematic structure determines the organization of constituents and interacts with the information structure of Given and New in interesting ways. The Theme is usually picked from within a chunk of Given information and the Rheme often coincides with New information. But it is important to note that the Thematic structure is not the same as the information structure. As noted by Halliday (1994: 299), the Theme is what the speaker/writer chooses as the starting point of the clause while the Given is what the speaker/writer assumes the listener/reader to know already. It is through the interplay of Theme + Rheme and Given + New that Halliday's notion of Grammatical Metaphor comes to life as a rhetorical resource.

The principle behind ideational Grammatical Metaphor is that a Process or a Classifier is mapped onto an Actor such as 'commit', which becomes 'commitment' or 'blind' which becomes 'blindness'. This change in clause structure makes it possible to develop an extended nominal group with 'commitment' or 'blindness' as Thing, which may then be pre-modified by a Deictic (determiner), Epithet (adjective), and Classifier (noun or adjective) as in Monsanto's phrase: 'deficiency-related disease' (Halliday 1994). Besides, in the new position of the nominal group as Theme and Given, it is no longer possible to challenge the truth value because the proposition presupposes that Monsanto showed a commitment that was, in fact, generous. Another advantage of the nominal group is that it removes the ability to negotiate what was present in the finite verbal group.

Thus, if the clause (1) 'biotechnology scientists opened their databases to Third World countries' is rendered as (2) 'the opening of databases to Third World countries by biotechnology scientists took place', the verb 'open' which was Rheme in clause (1) has now been included in the Theme of clause (2) where it is positioned as Given information and hence assumed to be a mutually agreed-upon fact and not open to negotiation. This is what makes Grammatical Metaphor suitable as a carrier of implicit information, inviting ideological contestation (Halliday 1994).

Analysing Theme/Rheme and Given/New

To accommodate these ideas, I explored how textual, ideational, and inter-personal meaning complexes interact as resources for naturalizing ideol-ogy and hegemony in the Monsanto text (henceforth, Text 1) and the IPS text (henceforth, Text 2). A more detailed Theme/Rheme analysis can be found in the Appendices. Following Halliday (1994), I examined the inter-play of Theme/Rheme and Given/New information at the textual level and the potential formation of Grammatical Metaphor at the ideational level. In both texts, Theme tended to coincide with Given information, while Rheme generally coincided with New, which according to Halliday (1994) characterizes the unmarked text. Moreover, both texts developed their Themes by frequently resuming an earlier Rheme as a Theme in a new sentence such as 'More than 90% of rice (Theme/New) is produced and consumed in *Asia,* where it is a staple (Rheme/New). *The region* (Rheme → Theme/Given) is also home to the world's largest rice exporters, including Thailand and Vietnam (Rheme/New).' However, as shown in Tables 14.1 and 14.2, the two texts use this organizing method for different purposes. In Text 1, 'Monsanto' and 'Monsanto's commitments' are frequently used Themes, which are described in very positive terms in the Rhemes as shown in Table 14.1.

In Text 2, on the other hand, we find great variation in the Themes. These include basically three areas, viz. 'the product', 'agriculture activists', and 'proponents' (or their synonyms). However, while the Rhemes in Text 1 are all very positive towards Monsanto, the Rhemes in Text 2 are generally negative concerning the new method, actions, and motives of those advo-cating GE crops – an impression reinforced by the host of Rhemes reflect-ing the critical voices of the opponents in Table 14.2.

As mentioned earlier, treating Rhemes – New information in a preceding sentence – as Given information in a subsequent sentence where it func-tions as Theme has the effect that its information can no longer be chal-lenged. However, while cohesion is ensured in both texts by developing new Themes on the basis of preceding Rhemes, there are clear differences in the way this organizing principle is used. As Table 14.3 demonstrates,

Table 14.1 Predominant Themes in Monsanto extract
(see Appendix A for full text)

Themes	Line no.	Rhemes
Monsanto		*About Monsanto*
Monsanto	3	announced today [. . .] that it will provide royalty-free licenses for all of its technologies that can help further development of 'golden rice' [. . .]
The company	9	also announced the recent launch of a new Internet website [. . .] opening its rice genome sequence database to researchers around the world
We	18	want to minimize the time and expenditure that might be associated with obtaining licenses [. . .]
Monsanto	44	has also developed technology to increase levels of beta-carotene in oils, and is working to share it with researchers in the developing world
Monsanto	54	has already completed the transfer of its rice genome draft sequence data and other materials to the Japanese Ministry of Agriculture [. . .]
Monsanto's commitments		*About Monsanto's commitments*
Successful development [. . .]	7	could help millions of people suffering from vitamin A deficiencies
These two actions	11	are part of the company's ongoing commitment to global agricultural research [. . .]
Monsanto's commitment [. . .]	14	is expected to aid researchers working in this area who wish to make use of existing proprietary technologies

Text 1 relies more on ideational Grammatical Metaphor for resuming preceding Rhemes as Themes than does Text 2.

A comparison of the two texts in terms of their use of Grammatical Metaphor demonstrates that the Monsanto text uses this device more frequently for resuming preceding Rhemes as Themes with a Given propositional content. As suggested above, Text 2 also has some examples of Grammatical Metaphor. However, in most cases these are not used to resume preceding Rhemes to present them as Themes with a Given prepositional content. Therefore they are not used as an argumentative strategy as in Text 1 where Grammatical Metaphor serves as an important text organizer.

Table 14.2 Predominant Themes in IPS extract
(see Appendix B for full text)

Themes	Line no.	Rhemes
The product (GE rice)		*About the product (GE rice)*
Rice seeds fortified with Vitamin A	2	are the new genetically engineered food item
[. . .] critics say (Theme in embedded clause)	3	it is a public relations move to fix the image problem of genetically altered products and should be kept away from rice-dependent Asia
[. . .] these seeds [. . .] (embedded Theme)	7	will not help reduce malnutrition and the lack of Vitamin A found in developing countries [. . .]
Agriculture activists		*About agriculture activists*
Agriculture activists	17	do not want the product used in South-east Asia
Coordinator for [. . .]	26	[said] 'the motive of these TNCs is not really to help humanity'
Proponents		*About proponents*
Proponents	33	call the rice friendly to developing countries
Zeneca	41	quoted [. . .] Professor Ingo Potrykus, as saying the giving of commercial rights to the firm 'will help us to deliver Golden Rice more speedily to those that need it most'

Conclusion

I have aimed at identifying some of the stylistic strategies used to naturalize ideology in two biotechnology press releases with opposing views. In the process, I have combined Fairclough's three-dimensional CDA framework with SFL to provide deeper insight into the ways in which readers are unknowingly being exposed to, and made part of, ideological positions. A Theme/Rheme analysis in the two press releases showed that unsurprisingly, the Rhemes that Monsanto had included about the company and its achievements were very positive towards Monsanto while the Rhemes picked in the IPS News Agency text about Monsanto and other GE proponents were all negative. My analysis of the interplay of Theme, Rheme, and Grammatical Metaphor demonstrates that the rhetorical device of Grammatical Metaphor was used much more frequently in the press release written by GE proponents (Monsanto) than in the one written by critics

Table 14.3 Grammatical Metaphors in the two extracts

Text 1 (19 sentences): Monsanto			Text 2 (19 sentences): IPS		
			Ideational metaphor with textual implications		
Grammatical Metaphor	*Line no.*	*Derived from*	*Grammatical Metaphor*	*Line No.*	*Derived from*
Development	7	Rheme 1	Public relations move	4	
Adoption	7		A sustainable solution	9	
Launch	9	Rhemes 1+2	The testing of the Golden Rice	22	
Actions	11		Free access	34	
Commitment	12		Fortification	35	Theme 1
The use	13	Rhemes 1+4	Adequate Vitamin A intake	38	Theme 1
Commitment	14	Rheme 1	Deficiency-caused blindness	39	
The development	15				
Collaboration	26				
Delivery	27				
The development	32	Rheme 3			
The launch	47	Rheme 3			
Transfer	34				
Blindness	37	Rheme 11			
Vitamin A intake	38				
Activity	40				
Announcement	48				
Research	51	Rheme 15			
The transfer	54	Rheme 16			
The use	59				
Decoding	60				

(IPS). Therefore, the argumentative direction was monitored to a greater extent and by more implicit means in the Monsanto text than in the IPS text, with the result that the Monsanto text appeared to be vaguer and more abstract. The differences in style and communicative purposes of the two press releases corroborate the observation made earlier that it might not be possible to categorize press releases as a uniform genre, but rather as a special mode or channel used for conveying news of interest to the general public.

One explanation of the varying degrees of vagueness in the two texts might be that agribusinesses that depend on shareholders' goodwill see GE as a solution to their constant need for maximizing profits. On the other hand, opponents of the new technology have nothing to lose by being outspoken. Rather than having pecuniary motives, their goal is to struggle for a more equitable distribution of global resources because they believe Third World countries should be protected against profit-oriented exploitation – a point of view that, in most people's opinion, is ethically more acceptable than the profit motive. However, in order to maintain or even improve a company's reputation, it is important to avoid issues that are less acceptable from a moral point of view and, instead, focus on issues that may help boost the company's image. In contrast, observers who are critical of GE foods have a morally acceptable cause and can, therefore, voice their opinions in much more direct terms and even take pride in doing so. In other words, implicitness seems to grow with the risk of loss; the greater the risk, the subtler the message.

Appendix A

Text 1: Monsanto Press Release of 4 August 2000

[Theme is to be read as Topical Theme unless labelled otherwise]

1 **Monsanto Adds Support For 'Golden Rice'; Opens Its Genome Sequence Data To**
2 **Worldwide Research Community**
3 **ST. LOUIS, August 4, 2000** – Monsanto *(Topical Theme 1/Given)* announced today
4 at an agricultural biotechnology symposium in Chennai, India, that it will provide
5 royalty-free licenses for all of its technologies that can help further development of
6 'golden rice' and other pro-vitamin A-enhanced rice varieties *(Rheme 1/ New)*.
7 Successful development and adoption of enhanced rice *(Rheme 1 → Theme 2/Given)*
8 could help millions of people suffering from vitamin A deficiencies *(Rheme 2/New)*.
9 The company *(Theme 1/Given)* also announced the recent launch of a new Internet web
10 site, www.rice-research.org, opening its rice genome sequence database to researchers
11 around the world *(Rheme 2/New)*. These two actions *(Themes 1+2/Given)* are part of the
12 company's ongoing commitment to global agricultural research and are aimed at
13 facilitating the use of its technologies and data for the common good *(Rheme 4/New)*.
14 Monsanto's commitment to offer royalty-free licenses for all the company's technology
15 that may be useful in the development of rice varieties with increased levels of pro-

16 vitamin A (or beta-carotene) *(Rhemes 1 + 4 → Theme 3/Given)* is expected to aid

17 researchers working in this area who wish to make use of existing proprietary

18 technologies *(Rheme 5/New)*. 'We *(Theme 4/Given)* want to minimize the time and

19 expenditure that might be associated with obtaining licenses needed to bring "golden

20 rice" to farmers and the people in dire need of this vitamin in developing countries,'

21 *(Rheme 6/New)* said Hendrik Verfaillie *(Displaced Theme)*, Chief Executive Officer of

22 Monsanto Company, a subsidiary of Pharmacia Corporation. The grain known as

23 'golden rice' *(Part of Rheme 6 → Theme 5/Given)* was developed by Professor Ingo

24 Potrykus, professor at the Swiss Federal Institute of Technology, Zurich, and Dr Peter

25 Beyer, University of Freiburg, Germany, with the support of the Rockefeller Foundation

26 *(Rheme 7/New)*. In May 2000 *(Theme/New)*, the inventors announced a collaboration

27 with Greenovation and Zeneca to enable delivery of this technology free-of-charge for

28 humanitarian purposes *(Rheme 8/Given)*. Zeneca *(Rheme 8 → Theme 7/ Given)* pledged

29 to provide regulatory, advisory and research expertise to assist in making 'golden rice'

30 available in developing countries *(Rheme 9/New)*.

31 'I *(Topical Theme 8/Given)* very much hope that others having intellectual property

32 rights used in the development of "golden rice" *(Theme 8.1/Given/Rheme 10/New)* will

33 follow the generous example of Monsanto and also provide a royalty-free license for the

34 humanitarian use of the technology and its transfer to developing countries,' *(Rheme*

35 *10.1/New)* Prof. Potrykus *(Displaced Theme)* said. The modified rice *(Theme 5/Given)*

36 is expected to provide nutritional benefits to those suffering from vitamin A deficiency-

37 related diseases, including irreversible blindness in hundreds of thousands of children

38 annually *(Rheme 11/New)*. Adequate vitamin A intake *(Rheme 11 → Theme 9/Given)*

39 can also reduce the mortality associated with infectious diseases such as diarrhea and

40 childhood measles by enhancing the activity of the human immune system *(Rheme*

41 *12/New).*

42 In March 1999 *(Experiential Theme/New)*, Monsanto joined the Global Vitamin A

43 Partnership, which includes the US Agency for International Development, UNICEF

44 and the World Health Organization *(Rheme 13/Given)*. Monsanto *(Theme 1/Given)* has

45 also developed technology to increase levels of beta-carotene in oils, and is working to

46 share it with researchers in the developing world *(Rheme 14/New)*.

47 The launch of the www.rice-research.org database also announced today *(Rheme 3 →*

48 *Theme 10/Given)* follows on Monsanto's April 4, 2000, announcement that it had

49 produced a draft sequence of the rice genome, the first crop genome to be described in

50 such technical detail *(Rheme 15/New)*. In order to facilitate and encourage basic

51 research to improve rice and other crops *(Textual Theme)*, the data *(Theme 11/Given)*

52 are being made available at no charge to registered researchers through this website

53 *(Rheme 16/New)*.

54 Monsanto *(Theme 1/Given)* has already completed the transfer of its rice genome draft

55 sequence data and other materials to the Japanese Ministry of Agriculture, Forestry and

56 Fisheries (MAFF) as the lead agency of the International Rice Genome Sequencing

57 Project (IRGSP) *(Rheme 17/New)*. The IRGSP *(Rheme 17 → Theme 12)* is a ten-

58 member consortium of rice genome sequencing projects around the world *(Rheme 18)*.

59 According to MAFF *(Textual Theme)*, 'the use of this data by the international

60 consortium *(Theme 13 → Rheme 19)* will significantly accelerate decoding' of the entire

61 rice genome.

Appendix B

Text 2: Interpress Third World News Agency Press Release of 22 June 2000

[Theme is to be read as Topical Theme unless labelled otherwise]

1 **'GOLDEN RICE' HAS NO SHINE, SAY CRITICS by Kelvin Ng**
2 **Bangkok, 22 Jun 2000 (IPS)** – Rice seeds fortified with Vitamin A *(Theme 1/Given)*
3 are the new genetically engineered food item *(Rheme 1/New)*, but *(Textual Theme 2)*
4 critics *(Theme 2/Given)* say it is a public relations move to fix the image problem of
5 genetically altered products and should be kept away from rice-dependent Asia *(Rheme*
6 *2/New)*.
7 They *(Theme 2/Given)* say these seeds, called 'Golden Rice', will not help reduce
8 malnutrition and the lack of Vitamin A found in developing countries, or be a
9 sustainable solution to food security *(Theme 1 → Rheme 3/New)*.
10 Under a May 16 agreement *(Theme 3/New)*, the UK-based agro-technology giant
11 Zeneca Agrochemical and Germany-based Greenovation acquired exclusive rights to a
12 new strain of genetically engineered Vitamin A rice *(Rheme 4/New)*. Swiss and German
13 scientists *(Theme 4/New)* had engineered the rice to produce beta-carotene, a precursor
14 of Vitamin A *(Rheme 5/New)*. This *(Rheme 5 → Rheme 5/Given)* gives the rice a golden
15 hue.
16 Zeneca *(Theme 3/Given)* will license and distribute the seed free to poor farmers
17 *(Rheme 7/New)* – but *(Textual Theme)* agriculture activists *(Theme 6/Given)* do not
18 want the product used in South-east Asia *(Rheme 8/New)*. More than 90% of rice
19 *(Theme 7/New)* is produced and consumed in Asia, where it is a staple *(Rheme 9/New)*.
20 The region *(Rheme 9 → Theme 8/Given)* is also home to the world's largest rice
21 exporters, including Thailand and Vietnam *(Rheme 10/New)*.
22 However *(Textual Theme)*, the testing of the Golden Rice *(Theme 9/Given)* is still in
23 progress *(Rheme 11/New)* and *(Textual Theme)* it *(Theme 9/Given)* is unlikely to end up

24 on dinner plates before 2003 *(Rheme 12/New)*, Zeneca *(Displaced Theme)* says.

25 'The motive of these TNCs (transnational corporations) is not really to help humanity,'

26 Withoon Lianchamroon, coordinator for BIOTHAI, a biodiversity and farmers' rights

27 group *(Displaced Theme)*, said in an interview. 'Their goal *(Theme/Given)* is profit.

28 We *(Theme)* can't hand over the future of our farmers to them like that.'

29 'Small farmers *(Theme)* can't achieve security when transnational corporations control

30 these technologies and give away GE (genetically engineered) seeds like others give out

31 food aid. It *(Theme)* doesn't work,' BIOTHAI *(Displaced Theme)* said in a statement

32 issued earlier in June.

33 Proponents *(Theme 10/Given)* call the rice friendly to developing countries because

34 poor farmers will be given free access to it, while it will be sold commercially in the

35 developed world *(Rheme 13/New)*. Likewise *(Textual Theme)*, fortification with

36 Vitamin A *(Theme 1/Given)* is designed to address concerns in poorer countries about

37 malnutrition in micronutrients, including Vitamin A, iron and iodine *(Rheme 14/New)*.

38 Adequate Vitamin A intake *(Theme 1/Given)* would help reduce infant mortality by

39 about a third in developing countries, and prevent some 500,000 cases of deficiency-

40 caused blindness from occurring each year *(Rheme 15/New)*.

41 In a May 16 statement *(Theme 11/New)*, Zeneca quoted the Swiss co-inventor of Golden

42 Rice, Professor Ingo Portrykus, as saying the giving of commercial rights to the firm

43 'will help us to deliver Golden Rice more speedily to those that need it most' *(Rheme*

44 *16/New)*.

References

Christensen, J. (2000) 'Golden Rice in a Grenade-Proof Greenhouse', *The New York Times on the Web*, November 21 at: http://www.nytimes.com/2000/11/21/science/21RICE.html (consulted April 2001).

Fairclough, N. (1992) *Discourse and Social Change*. Cambridge: Polity Press.

Halliday, M. A. K. (1994) *An Introduction to Functional Grammar* (2nd edn). London: Edward Arnold.

Hasan, R. (1985) 'The Structure of a Text', in *Language, Context and Text*, ed. by M. A. K. Halliday and R. Hasan. Geelong, Victoria: Deakin University Press (republished by Oxford University Press 1989), 52–69.

Iedema, R. (1997) 'The Language of Administration: Organizing Human Activity in Formal Institutions', in *Genre and Institutions. Social Processes in the Workplace and School*, ed. by F. Christie and J. R. Martin. London and Washington, DC: Cassell, 73–100.

Jacobs, G. (1999) *Preformulating the News: An Analysis of the Metapragmatics of Press Releases*. Amsterdam: John Benjamins.

Ng, K. (2000) ' "Golden Rice has No Shine", Say Critics' at: http://www.twnside.org.sg/title/golden.htm (consulted February 2001).

Klein, N. (2000) 'There's Nothing Like a Feel-good Bowl of Golden Rice. Or Not', *Globe and Mail*, 2 August, reprinted at: http://members.tripod.com/~ngin/feelgoodrice.htm (consulted March 2001).

Martin, J. R. (2000) 'SFL and Critical Discourse Analysis', in *Researching Language in Schools and Communities*, ed. by L. Unsworth. London: Cassell, 275–302.

Martin, J. R. (1992) *English Text. System and Structure*. Philadelphia: John Benjamins.

Monsanto (2000) 'Monsanto Adds Support For "Golden Rice"; Opens Its Genome Sequence Data To Worldwide Research Community' at: http://www.monsanto.com/monsanto/layout/media/00/08–04–00.asp (consulted February 2001).

Oxfam (1999) 'Genetically Modified Crops, World Trade and Food Security', GB position paper at: http://oxfam.org.uk/policy/papers/gmcrop.htm (consulted March 2001).

15 *We* have the Power – Or do We: Pronouns of Power in a Union Context

Maurice Ward

The language of industrial unions seems little studied but the phrase 'them and us' stereotypifies its image as a 'polarizing' and 'antisocial' force in capitalist society. This paper looks at the pronoun we *in a union meeting text as an exponent of distance and solidarity between a group of workers in a factory in New Zealand and their democratically elected union officials. It looks at how the deictic function of* we *is constrained by its prior use as a narrative referent and the spatial structure of the meeting. Using corpus and Systemic Functional Linguistics (SFL) analysis, the paper shows how union negotiators in the process of settling a labour contract are alienated from their electorate by the contradictions in the division of labour that constructs unionism and how this articulates with the semiotic construction of the meeting. It further describes initial collaborative efforts by the unionists and the researcher to re-articulate union discourse with a view to building union power.*

Introduction: The Language Context

Language is systemic internally as well as in relation to other texts and events (De Beaugrande 2000: 160). Chouliaraki and Fairclough (1999: 139–40) note within the Systemic Functional Linguistics (SFL) paradigm that 'although lexicogrammar does not directly interface with the social, it is historically shaped through processes of semogenesis – the historical production and change of the discoursal – which opens the language system to social shaping'. Similarly there is '(n)o construction of reality without negotiation of social relations and identities, but neither of these without the unfolding of text' (Chouliaraki and Fairclough 1999: 152). Much of what follows investigates how the deictic *we* helps construct polarized identities in a union meeting and also indicates broader discoursal reproduction of oppression within the union.[1]

Unionism: A Dialectical Perspective

To understand language we must first locate it in the material world

(Voloshinov 1973: 15), particularly for the labour movement which is in conflict with capital over material issues (Mumby and Clair 1997: 182). Profitable production in capitalist society is a dialectical relationship realized through the combination of segmented skills with technology, a division reproduced in other aspects of society (Marx and Engels 1966). Thus unionists engaged with transnational capital require skills such as legal and economic expertise and professional negotiation and management skills (Pocock 2000). Complementing this is the organization of workers' collective labour power as it interfaces with capital. Unionism may be characterized, then, as a division of labour reflecting a context of production and a discoursal superstructure.

1. The first aspect is direct struggle for share of surplus production through the limitation of hours of work and the extraction of wages.
2. The second is a collective consciousness that can realize the material aspect, a discoursal process consisting of meetings, discussions, pickets, newsletters, negotiations, banners, and so on.

The division of union labour socially manifests an aspect of production that workers are already familiar with – alienation: they produce goods and services but have no control over them. The negotiation of labour contracts through representatives is also a removed and potentially alienating process. As a discoursal task, it is principally but not solely linguistic.

The Research Context

The combined effects of a protracted crisis of capital and anti-union legislation unparalleled in OECD (Organization for Economic Co-operation and Development) countries saw union density halved in New Zealand between 1991 and 1996 (Kelsy 1997) and, where workers remain organized in workplaces, severe economic and political restraints are forcing unions to rethink their roles and methods of work. The union and the industry where the data were collected for this study remain anonymous to protect those involved; some workers have been fired for their union activism over the period of the study. Despite a repressive atmosphere, the majority of workers on the work site are union members, and the overworked, underresourced union organizers must find new ways to organize them (Howells 1999). New Zealand unions are moving towards a model of 'doing union' that focuses on increased membership participation and responsibility (Kelsy 1997; Duncan 1999). The data considered come from a 90-minute stopwork meeting of 43 unionists to discuss contract negotiations with their employers. The meeting falls into three sections: a presentation from the company manager of the company's position; a report from the union negotiators; and membership discussion of two resolutions presented by the union negotiators. The resolutions, according to informants, were aimed at building membership support for the union negotiators and to show solidarity to the company. The practice of starting union meetings with a company representative is relatively common in New Zealand as a part of contract negotiations and is supported by unions as a way of enabling workers to meet at the workplace for union purposes with a minimum of opprobrium from the company. Usually members are paid by employers to attend if the meeting is short and, as in the present case, the company representative leaves the meeting after his contribution. Arguably, there are two meetings, the first a presentation of the company view of the negotiations and the second from the union perspective. It is argued here that the company presentation contextualizes and intertextually defines the following union-only section of the meeting, and in practice they are one discoursal event (Bahktin 1981).

We Realizing Union Relations

Brown and Gilman (1960) say social intimacy or distance are expressed in *tu/vous* pronoun systems including the English variant. *We* intrinsically creates an opposition and exclusion, but this externalized entity may not be fixed throughout an utterance. Speakers use deixis to build co-operative involvement in meetings, and this is complex when more than one 'community' is involved (Johnson 1994: 207–13). The fuzziness of this linkage is used by politicians at times to manipulate texts and disguise agency (Wilson 1990). The union process studied here focuses on the negotiators and members as two groups with socioeconomic and political 'borders' separating them that are constituted by context, and the dynamic nature of discourse links to this. Pronouns as deictic exponents of how talk is both constructed and, in turn, constructs its contexts have been approached from a range of perspectives (Lyons 1977; Levinson 1983; Mühlhäusler and Harré 1990), and particularly from political and social identity perspectives (Wilson 1990). From an SFL approach, deictic realization of meaning is a key element textually revealing the complex of social relations, particularly in spoken genres (Halliday and Hasan 1976: 48–55). SFL further demonstrates a role for exophoric pronouns in broader deictic textual meaning-making that is also aligned with the concepts of Given and New (Halliday 1994: 298).

Reference and Deixis: Two Functions of We

Pronouns have two principal functions in text, that of indexing speaker roles and that of reference. Anaphoric reference defines objects already introduced into discourse, deixis realizes extra-linguistic processes and things which are 'spatial, temporal, social, personal aspects of a situation . . . [and is party to the] degree of power or control over another . . . [as well as for] acceptance or rejection of responsibility of the speech act itself' (Mühlhäusler and Harré 1990: 9–10). Only participants can fully grasp the indexicality of time and place; the rights of speakers and the force of their utterances are likewise locally realized. First and second person pronouns are indexical and co-indexical with *I* and *you* alternating with speaker turns; however, the third person pronoun is referential rather than indexical. These three roles – the speaker, the hearer, and the one talked about – each present a differing view of the speaker and are progressively distant both spatially and socially (Mühlhäusler and Harré 1990: 63–5). The union negotiators in the present study weave two voices together, initially as reporters of events prior to the meeting and later as organizers of action to follow the meeting. In these roles, they use the pronoun *we* initially in its referential function and subsequently in its deictic function. These uses are functionally complementary in that they aim to engage worker power in the negotiations, but they are based on two conflicting material bases – organizing and reporting, each a division of labour within the social milieu reflected and refracted in the deictic and referential uses of the pronoun that creates a contradiction.

In the SFL paradigm, 'The personal pronoun represents the world according to the speaker in the context of a speech exchange. The basic distinction is into speech roles (*I*, *you*) and other roles (*he, she, it, they*) . . . the referent is defined interpersonally' (Halliday 1994: 189). Speaker use of the deictic *we* describes a cline of listener inclusion from speaker plus listener (most inclusive) to speaker plus other-than-listener (most exclusive). Each of the ideational, interpersonal, and textual metafunctions defines a constituent in a discoursal process: the ideational having the clearest role, the interpersonal 'scattered' throughout the process, and the textual by the boundaries ordering it (Halliday 1994: 189). In its capacity as a marker of speech roles, the personal pronoun is 'typically exophoric . . . [it] can become anaphoric however in quoted speech [such as in narrative]' (Halliday and Hasan 1976: 50). So *we* in its interpersonal capacity is determined by context, both textual and extra-textual (Johnson 1994: 208–9) as data excerpts (a), (b), and (c) exemplify.

(a)   we want to renew the contract
(b)   there's a couple of things that we need to address
(c)   we were at loggerhead[2] with the company

Excerpt (a) is from the company manager's address to the union stop-work meeting and his use of *we* indexes the company. Excerpt (b) is from a union negotiator's speech to the same meeting and indexes the union representatives. Different participants take up the speaker role at different points of the meeting. Conversely, as part of the union negotiators' report on their earlier interaction with the company, *we* is referential to the negotiators' reported role as participants in another process. In excerpt (c), the *we* anaphorically links to a previous section of the text rather than realizing a speaker role. The use of an inclusive *we* in a meeting sets up rapport and involvement with listeners for the current and following speakers and, further, subtly establishes a textual and interpersonal coherence that extends beyond a single gathering (Johnson 1994: 228).

Most inclusive   ==================== Least inclusive

we<I>   we<I?>   we<R>   we<E>

Figure 15.1 Cline of inclusiveness for *we* in the data

SFL analysis enables researchers and participants to look at how discourse realizes and reproduces social formations at a systemic and instantial level. In conjunction with a concordance analysis, this paper now turns to look at how *we* as an exponent of distance and solidarity in the stopwork meeting text arises out of discoursal and non-discoursal contexts to produce a dichotomy between the union negotiators and the base members. By foregrounding lexicogrammatical structures and their functions, we are able to see both how these contribute to meaning-making and how they reflect and help reproduce social formations (Halliday 1978: 21–31).

There are 253 instances of *we* in the text. I have annotated these further on the basis of my interpretation of their inclusiveness as it is manifest in the surrounding text and context as portrayed in Figure 15.1.

- we⟨I⟩ is Halliday's 'speaker plus listener', the most inclusive and paraphrases as 'you and I together'
- we⟨I?⟩ infers inclusiveness but is vague
- we⟨R⟩ infers the exclusive we⟨E⟩ but invokes inclusiveness, paraphrased in usage as 'I' similar to the royal 'we' but is indexically less personal, less responsible
- we⟨E⟩ is Halliday's 'speaker plus other' and is exclusive and paraphrases as 'our group excluding you'

Text Analysis

Text 1 is an excerpt from an address to the meeting from company manager 'Charlie Christie' (CC), and I have provided a contextualized analysis of his use of *we*.

Text 1:

CC: I haven't rehearsed it so I may have to muddle through a bit, but we⟨I⟩'ll see how we⟨I⟩ go. And and what just to kick it off I'll just state, I'll just state our⟨E⟩ position where we⟨E⟩'re coming from and then we⟨R⟩'ll leave you to it with with your union representative. Okay as a background to today um we⟨E⟩ want to renew the contract,

Initially, the company manager is introducing his contribution, and the first instances of we⟨I⟩ include himself and the listening unionists as he refers to his ability to present his material adequately to them.

but we⟨I⟩'ll see how we⟨I⟩ go.[3]

In his next statement, the first instance of we⟨E⟩ appears, gaining its exclusiveness from the ideational and extra-linguistic fields. Christie is representing the company and stating its position, and the we⟨E⟩ follows a first person singular pronoun and another exclusive first person plural pronoun, 'our':

I'll just state our⟨E⟩ position where we⟨E⟩'re coming from

The lexicogrammatical cluster 'state (one)'s position' intertextually invokes broader formal negotiation discourses and 'where (nominal + verb "to be") coming from' – a casual embedded clause (Eggins and Slade 1997: 19–20) that expands on the nominal group *our position* – also ideationally constructs the company-union confrontation. The thematic progression of formal to casual is mitigating and attempts to construct an inclusive tenor to the clause as an entity and locally to the interpersonal marker *we* in its task of constructing deixis. The need for mitigation marks the dichotomy of the context.

The single instance of we⟨R⟩ clearly refers only to Christie as none of the other managers are in attendance and logically cannot 'leave' the meeting so is best paraphrased as 'I'll leave you to it'. Again the deixis is mediated by the juxtapositioning of the generically exclusive *we* and *you* as Subject and Complement and the material process of separation engendered in 'leave'.

In the section of the text where the company manager addresses the meeting, there are 31 instances of *we* and these are set out in Table 15.1.

Given that he is presenting argument in opposition to the claims of the unionists, it is scarcely surprising that his usage of the distancing variety of *we* is markedly higher than that of the inclusive.

In the remaining portion of the meeting where the union negotiators report on their progress and then discuss it with the members, there are 222 instances of *we* as set out in Table 15.2.

Here, surprisingly, the ratios are remarkably similar to that for the manager's presentation. Even with the we⟨I⟩ and we⟨I?⟩ taken together, the exclusive variety is more highly instanced.

As with Text 1, the ideational aspect is a determinant factor: the negotiators report extensively on their separate activities in the negotiating

Table 15.1 Instances of *we* in the company manager's address

	Instances	*Per 1,000 words (%)*
we⟨I⟩	11	09.17
we⟨I?⟩	0	0
we⟨R⟩	1	00.83
we⟨E⟩	19	15.83

Table 15.2 Instances of *we* in the union-only section of the meeting

	Instances	*Per 1,000 words (%)*
we⟨I⟩	87	10.87
we⟨I?⟩	23	02.80
we⟨R⟩	0	0
we⟨E⟩	112	13.66

process as samples exemplify. Text 2 is the initial explanation of the negotiators' activities explained by organizer 'Phil Travers' (PT):

Text 2:

PT: What happened is you had a claims meeting with Diane conducted in about August last year from there we⟨E⟩ assembled ah a whole raft of claims which essentially Billy you know six per cent and a number of other improvements and that was our⟨E⟩ starting position we⟨E⟩ were at loggerhead with the company so the negotiating team got together and we⟨E⟩ thought well we⟨E⟩'ll try and make progress, we⟨E⟩ identify the key issues and we⟨E⟩ essentially come up with just really a two-part claim

Here, all six instances of *we* are exclusive because the negotiators had discussions with the company and the ordinary members did not. This divides the meeting into those who participated and those who did not. Again, the lexicogrammar of the co-text both helps to index the pronoun and realize a spatio-temporal dichotomy generated by the need to report on an earlier event at a separate location, this at the clause level:

Adjunct of circumstance	Subject	Predicate	Complement
in about August last year from there	*we⟨E⟩*	*assembled*	*(ah) a whole raft of claims*

The thematization of time emphasizes a disjuncture with the present and is unmarked in narrative; the lexical specification of 'August last year' adds to this sense. The assembling of claims is a union task that falls within the division of labour that negotiators are principally responsible for and base members only marginally. The transitivity highlights the negotiators as active, doing material things, and their position of grammatical Subject further stresses their centrality. The listening members are textually not party to the reported discourse at all.

Corpus analysis can provide valuable insight into Critical Discourse Analysis (CDA) (Stubbs 1997: 112; De Beaugrande 2000: 180–3). Inspection of some of the concordance lines from the union-only portion of the meeting shows how the pattern of language, itself derived from the organizational frame of the meeting, emphasizes and reproduces a divided group in which the negotiators are the focus of the discourse and the members are de-focused, as Table 15.3 demonstrates.

Table 15.3 Section of the we⟨E⟩ concordance

No.	Instance	
27	we⟨E⟩ never agreed to it	we⟨E⟩ said it would be
28	not even considering that. All	we⟨E⟩ said to the company,
29	to be easily attainable so	we⟨E⟩ said right, we⟨E⟩'ll
30	We⟨E⟩ just as Billy said	we⟨E⟩ saw them as being
31	that was for a two year term –	we⟨E⟩ sort of were making
32	started in oh when did	we⟨E⟩ start Billy? November
33	got nowhere with that so	we⟨E⟩ started that (. . . hitting)
34	I'll just (. . .) what he said cos	we⟨E⟩ started in oh when
35	this today [FM laugh] PT	we ⟨E⟩ started at ten and
36	settle it BH (. . .) PT what	we ⟨E⟩ then thought this was

A total of 60 out of 112 instances of we⟨E⟩ position the negotiators as the Subjects of narrative clauses, realized in simple past tenses, as being in temporal and spatial isolation from the stopwork meeting. Importantly, these are substantially at the start of the union-only section of the meeting as a dispersion plot of we⟨E⟩ instances (see Figure 15.2) in that section of the meeting shows.

Spatial Analysis

Investigation of language alone is no longer adequate for understanding social issues; that is, analysing how boundaries between text and other modes are articulated is crucial (Kress *et al.* 1997: 272). Chouliaraki and Fairclough (1999: 144–6) suggest that text types, although generically different, articulate with each other to produce new conjunctural combinations. In Western society, texts are read from left to right and top to bottom, and the domains of Given and New, Ideal and Real respectively assigned to these zones. Given is what is assumed and New where developments are directed. Ideal may mean distant in time, ideal in form, a wish, and so on. Real is conversely present now, specific or empirical. Relations of attitude and power are reflected in these constructs with size and spatial relations realizing distance or solidarity. The relative division of the zones reflects interactants' interests (Kress *et al.* 1997: 272–6). The physical layout of the stopwork meeting, then, is in itself a text, one that comes first temporally and spatially as it is the given broader context. It expresses an ideology of proceedings and a hierarchical frame for a non-participatory membership to be realized.

N	File	Words	Hits	per 1,000	Plot
1	utqb-m~3.txt	8,202	60	7.32	

Figure 15.2 Dispersion plot for we⟨E⟩

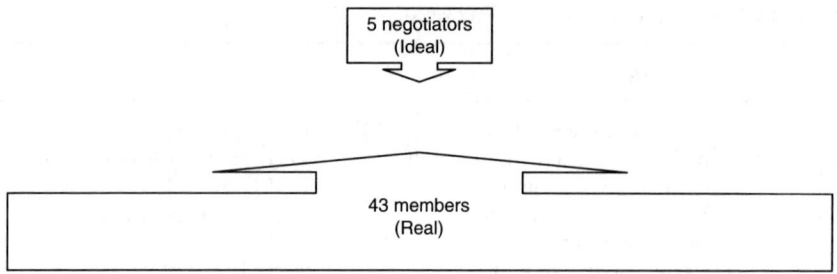

Figure 15.3 Numerical and spatial relations in the union meeting

Figure 15.3 shows the meeting layout schematically with the numerically small and socially elevated negotiators at the front and the recipient mass of members facing them. According to Kress *et al.*'s matrix, this spatial mode is also found in classroom and church interactions, and it helps construct an exclusive textual meaning for *we* in the union meeting. The third part of the meeting where the members should have engaged more dialogically with the negotiators is severely restricted by the material and discoursal context that precedes it.

The report from the negotiators is the Given, the Idealized commodity, in exchange for the discussion that follows. However, it comes to the meeting process fettered with the earlier processes and contradictions that are alluded to above. Ordinary union members are predominantly alienated in the production process, in the process of assembly contract claims, in the process of negotiation with the company, and from the company presentation at their own meeting. These are the Given to the negotiators' report to the meeting and the chain of exclusion is presented schematically in Figure 15.4.

Narrative uses of *we* in the negotiators' report have a high potential to invoke the alienation aspects of the Given and, thus, produce the potential for low membership participation in the rest of the meeting. Following the report, much of the meeting is polarized between its presenters and the ordinary members. This contradiction becomes accentuated when a member, 'Steve Williams'(SW), challenges the negotiators' proposals and they feel obliged to defend themselves. In this third portion of the meeting, the negotiators have put a resolution to the members to consider a company proposal for a productivity-related payment. They have no intention of accepting the company scheme, and the purpose of this request from them

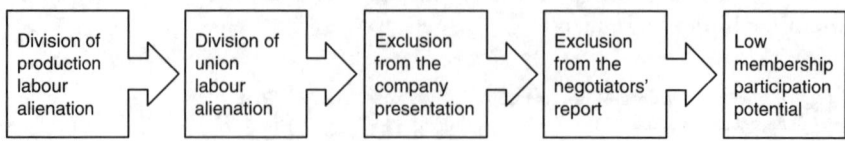

Figure 15.4 The chain of exclusion potential in the negotiators' report

is tactical – it aims to buy time and 'good faith' with the company so that other site contracts can be brought into line with the contract being discussed here. The tactic is complicated and the participants are discussing its implications. Williams' query is responded to by organizers 'Diane Dewars' (DD) and Phil Travers (PT). Turns in Text 3 are enumerated for further analysis.

Text 3:

1. SW: are you asking us⟨E⟩ to move that we⟨E⟩ agree with their seven principles pathway
2. DD: no
3. PT: no
4. DD: no what we⟨E⟩'re saying is we⟨I?⟩'re going to think about it
5.   [murmur]
6. SW: (. . .) just no I just was I just
7. DD: you just, if you want me to be brutally honest we⟨E⟩'re just trying to drag it out [murmur/laughter]

Discourse is about the negotiation of meaning, and this interaction indicates a lively part of 'doing union'. Here, it is also an instance of the reproduction of the systemic division within the group. Williams' challenge opens with an exclusive *us* shortly followed by a similarly polarizing *we*. Both deictics gain their exclusiveness from their projection in the verbal process 'asking', which has a dichotomizing *you* as sayer in thematic position in the projecting clause as Figure 15.5, a simplified analysis, shows.

In this respect, Williams is positioned among other things by the negotiators putting the proposal to the meeting and by their repeated use of the referential we⟨E⟩ prior to this point. Opposition to the proposal becomes opposition to the negotiators. The next two turns (3:2–3) are polar and followed by a turn (3:4) from Dewars explaining the negotiators' position in which the first *we* identifies them as a separate entity; the fact that this is we⟨E⟩ is recoverable from the use of the deictic *you* in 3:1, and the spatial context of participants facing each other. The second we⟨I?⟩ is vague and might be interpreted as inclusive in context. In her next utterance, she

Sayer	Verbal process	Verbiage
are you	asking us<E>	to move that we<E>

Theme	Rheme

Theme (projecting)	Rheme (projected)

Figure 15.5 Williams' use of we⟨E⟩

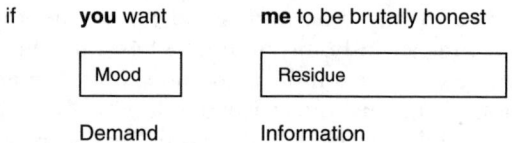

Figure 15.6 Analysis of Dewars' turn (3:7)

further identifies the negotiators as separate, and this is again manifest in a we⟨E⟩ pronoun, again partially recoverable from the modality and the exclusive *you* and *me* deictics in the hypotactic *if* clause.

The Mood element of the clause indexes speaker relationships (Halliday 1994: 68) and, as shown in Figure 15.6, Dewars thematizes her assessment of Williams' utterance as a demand for information and, in doing so, denotes her view of their present exchange relationship as distant, and herself contiguously constructing that distance between them. By making him the grammatical Subject, she is further placing the burden of the distance on him (note, for example, the alternative 'if I'm to be brutally honest'). The force of this is mitigated with the conditional conjunction *if*, but the marked thematization of the dependent clause as a whole adds to the profiling of the interpersonal, and the lexical evocation of violence in the demand suggested by 'brutally' leaves Williams in no doubt that the subsequent *we* is well framed by ideational and interpersonal distance. The echoing and support of Dewars' denial by Travers is also a feature of the negotiators' part in the meeting, as inspection of the whole text would show and, in the following section of the debate between them and Williams (Text 4), it is intense. Here, two of the negotiators, Dewars and Travers, attempt to reduce the contradiction between themselves and Williams in the first instance, but critically between themselves and the members collectively as they perceive the split in the meeting at this point. A third member of the negotiating team, 'Trevor Taite' (TT), is less adroit and more intent on isolating Williams as a perceived disruption, a process exacerbated by an unidentified member (UM) from the floor. Text 4 turns are enumerated for analysis.

Text 4:

1. SW: yeah it also says that you're considering looking at their proposed seven principle pathways
2. DD: yeah it does but
3. PT: we⟨I?⟩'re only we⟨I?⟩'re only looking at it we⟨I⟩'re only
4. TT: IT'S LIKE IT'S LIKE a gorgeous Asia Asian sheila going past in the other direction on a bike mate [laughter]
5. SW: we⟨I⟩ discussed that before
6. TT: you're looking at it that's all you're doing
7. SW: (. . .) we⟨I⟩ all virtually said (. . .) [voluble murmur]

 8.   UM: what's what's wrong with a good old kiwi girl mate
 9.   TT: no Steve's got a thing for Asians [laughter murmur]
10.   DD: Steve I don't [murmur] Steve, I don't disagree with what
             you're saying and I expect that the other sites will have
             exactly the same view but (. . .)

Disagreeing with an aspect of the resolution, Williams personalizes the matter with *you're* (4:1) rather than addressing the substance of the resolution, and three of the negotiators reply to him in a series of responses that are taken up by another member from the floor (4:8). *We* in Phil Travers' turn (4:3) may be inclusive as the resolution is being discussed by the meeting at this point, and Williams seems to take it that way in 4:5 and 4:7, the post-modifier 'all' lexically identifying which sense should be understood (Johnson 1994: 214). Turns from the negotiators in this section are intended also for listening members as 'over-hearers' and 'audience' (Goffman 1981) as well as dialogue with Williams. Trevor Taite articulates the racist and sexist humour of the Anglo-Australian/New Zealand 'mateship' genre in pejorative appraisal of Williams, aiming to distance him from group mores (Eggins and Slade 1997: 140–3), a point dialogically elaborated on by a member from the floor in 4:8 and a section of the meeting with laughter after Taite's turn (4:9). Taite's demand for recognition of his perspective by the meeting is underpinned by his marked increase in volume. Dewars attempts to repair the situation with use of the vocative 'Steve' (4:10) together with a first person deictic which distances her from what has become a negotiator-led attack on Williams and his effort to negotiate meaning for the resolution. A revision of the resolution, taking account of Williams' contribution, is subsequently approved by the meeting but, unsurprisingly, there are no other challenges to the negotiators' position.

The meeting is framed by a chain of alienation and its process dominated by the company and union negotiators' talk, and this highlights and reproduces a unionism where members are consumers not producers of unionism. Spatial and organizational discourse structures of the meeting, such as who talks and seating layout, reproduce the hierarchical capitalism that underpins the meeting. The language structure reflects and reproduces these divisions within. The discourse focuses the negotiators as the Subjects of the union talk, and instances of the pronoun we⟨E⟩ in the negotiators' talk, replicating patterns of management talk they follow temporally, isolate them from the members. The effect for members is, at least partially, of a group of union/management negotiators making decisions for them. A challenge from the floor configured by this dichotomy is aggressively responded to by the negotiators and reproduces the division acutely, and, subsequently, no membership activity comes out of the meeting and the negotiators are the only ones left with any apparent responsibility.

CDA Contribution

'Finding ways to dialogue across difference is . . . crucial to the survival of democracy' (Chouliaraki and Fairclough 1999: 92). The present research aims to help the union be more effective by increasing its membership power and by eliminating non-productive differences in the group. CDA is about identifying how language contributes to power imbalances in society and how analysis of this might contribute to change in favour of the oppressed (Fairclough 1989; Mumby and Clair 1997; Oktar 2001). Following is a reconstruction of Text 2, showing how the union negotiators' report to the members might have been refocused to identify the negotiators as linguistically and contextually separate from the company report and working to bridge the gap the division of labour in 'doing union' within capitalism produces.

Reconstruction of Text 2

> Reconstruction: We⟨I⟩ had a claims meeting with Diane in about August last year from there our⟨I⟩ negotiators assembled a whole raft of claims which essentially Billy you know six per cent and a number of other improvements we⟨I⟩ wanted and that was our⟨I⟩ starting position the company rejected these so your negotiating team got together with them and tried to make progress, the two sides identify the key issues and essentially come up with just really a two-part claim

If this text is taken in isolation, the first *we* gets its inclusiveness from the transitivity relationship of identity realized in 'had' (Halliday 1994: 132) and implicitly from cataphoric reference to the union contract claims meeting, which logically and factually included members and union negotiators (Halliday and Hasan 1976: 72). In fact, the preceding text and narrative's non-linguistic setting makes it clear that, indeed, both union parties are being referred to – a situation realized by the lexicogrammar. The following *we* and *our* continue this reference chain, and grammatical thematization of the collective instantly maintains this united focus clause-by-clause. In the next major clause, the company is lexically identified and grammatically responsible for agency in a material process that confronts the preceding union claims. There is no question of union negotiators being implicated. As topical theme of the next clause, they are, however, identified as initiating progress. '(T)he two sides' lexically refers to the company and the union negotiators in distinction, not as the unitary we⟨E⟩ which prevents the union negotiators from identifying with the members in Travers' original text. The contrived text avoids the polarizing *you* of the original; instead, it focuses on the members and the union parties as acting in concert. Where there is confrontation with the company in the negotiating process, agency is clearly identified, and the union negotiators are ref-

Re-articulation

Division of production labour alienation	Division of union labour alienation	Exclusion from the company presentation	Inclusion in the negotiators' report	Membership participation potential increases

Figure 15.7 Re-articulating the participation potential

erentially located as separate from their company counterparts. The textual change potentially offers a slightly, but critically, different contextual flow as shown in Figure 15.7.

Research Outcomes

The data presented here suggest that more attention on activities that involve members in discoursal roles, such as broadening participation in actual negotiation processes, and base-member responsibility for informing unionists on other work sites and non-unionists on their own work site, may offer practical means towards bridging division-of-labour roles, reduce systemic alienation of members, and relieve over-burdened organizers. One of the outcomes of the research has been a union proposal to refocus report-back meetings on member-driven activities along the lines suggested in the reconstructed Text 2 above. Training for delegates and organizers in focusing on member activity in oral reports will be a part of ongoing union education plans. Small group discussions and report-backs based on a written report of the contract negotiations is being considered as an alternative to the present system of limited-participation mass meetings. Finally a list of meta-discoursal monitor questions could assist participants to critically assess their own and others' contribution to meeting outcomes. For example:

- Who is talking?
- What are they talking about?
- How long have they been talking?
- When will I get to participate?
- What have I got to contribute?
- How will I contribute after the meeting?

The practice of 'doing union' currently is substantially discoursal and who does it determines what 'union' is.

Conclusion

This paper avoids a simplistic conclusion that a clique of union officials is manipulating their membership for personal or political gain, and examines the systematic discoursal framing of a group fighting oppression by highlighting a chain of intertextuality and intermodality. It shows how detailed instantial analysis of the deictic *we* in one meeting using SFL tools can contribute to understanding systemic disempowerment and offer some small steps towards empowering workers within their union, affirming that linguists in concert with other activists do have the power to contribute to change.

Acknowledgement

The concordancing software *Wordsmith* (1999) from Oxford University Press was used in the analysis provided in this paper.

Notes

1. The data were collected by audio-taping and this analysis scrutinized by the participants for accuracy and interpretation. Samples of transcribed text are presented with minimum annotation: turns are denoted with speaker initials, 'CC', inaudible text with (. . .). Capitalization denotes a marked increase in volume of sound, comment on paralinguistic features is enclosed within [ ] brackets and tags are denoted by ⟨⟩ brackets.
2. The original data use this variation of the more standard 'loggerheads'.
3. *We* is mitigating here and might also be paraphrased as *I* but by textual inclusiveness Christie requests ideational leniency from his listeners, so I have interpreted it as inclusive.

References

Bahktin, M. (1981) *The Dialogical Imagination,* trans. by C. Emerson and M. Holquist. Houston, TX: University of Texas Press.

Brown, R. and Gilman, A. (1960) 'The Pronouns of Power and Solidarity', in *Style in Language,* ed. by T. A. Sebeok. Cambridge, MA: MIT Press, 253–76.

Chouliaraki, L. and Fairclough, N. (1999) *Discourse in Late Modernity: Rethinking Critical Discourse Analysis.* Edinburgh: Edinburgh University Press.

De Beaugrande, R. (2000) 'Text Linguistics at the Millennium: Corpus Data and Missing Links', *Text,* 20(2): 153–95.

Duncan, A. (1999) 'Lions into Lambs: What Went Wrong with the N.Z. Council of Trade Unions – And Can It Be fixed?', *New Zealand Political Review,* September: 24–33.

Eggins, S. and Slade, D. (1997) *Analysing Casual Conversation.* London: Cassell.

Fairclough, N. (1989) *Language and Power.* London: Longman.

Fairclough, N. and Wodak, R. (1997) 'Critical Discourse Analysis', in *Discourse as Social Interaction: Volume 2,* ed. by T. A. van Dijk. London: Sage Publications, 258–84.

Goffman, E. (1981) *Forms of Talk*. Oxford: Blackwell.

Halliday, M. A. K. (1994) *An Introduction to Functional Grammar* (2nd edn). London: Edward Arnold.

Halliday, M. A. K. (1978) *Language as Social Semiotic*. London: Edward Arnold.

Halliday, M. A. K. and Hasan, R. (1976) *Cohesion in English*. London: Longman.

Howells, J. M. (1999) *The Background and Work of New Zealand Trade Union Officers: Evidence and Commentary*. Dunedin: University of Otago.

Johnson, D. M. (1994) 'Who is We: Constructing Communities in US-Mexico Border Discourse', *Discourse and Society*, 5(2): 207–31.

Kelsy, J. (1997) 'Employment and Union Issues In New Zealand, 12 Years On', *California Western International Law Journal*, 28(1): 253–74.

Kress, G., Leite-Garcia, R., and van Leeuwen, T. (1997) 'Discourse Semiotics', in *Discourse as Structure and Process: Volume 1*, ed. by T. A. van Dijk. London: Sage Publications, 257–91.

Levinson, S. (1983) *Pragmatics*. Cambridge: Cambridge University Press.

Lyons, J. (1977) *Semantics*. Cambridge: Cambridge University Press.

Marx, K. and Engels, F. (1966) 'Feuerbach. Opposition of the Materialistic and Idealistic Outlook', in *Selected Works of Marx and Engels*. Moscow: Political Literature Publishing House, 1: 16–79.

Mühlhäusler, P. and Harré, R. (1990) *People and Pronouns: The Linguistic Construction of Social and Personal Identity*. Oxford: Basil Blackwell.

Mumby, D. K. and Clair, R. P. (1997) 'Organisational Discourse', in *Discourse as Social Interaction*, ed. by T. A. van Dijk. London: Sage Publications, 181–205.

Oktar, L. (2001) 'The Ideological Organization of the Representational Processes in the Presentation of *Us* and *Them*', *Discourse and Society*, 12(3): 313–46.

Pocock, B. (2000) *Union Renewal: A Theoretical and Empirical Analysis of Union Power*. Adelaide: University of Adelaide.

Stubbs, M. (1997) 'Whorf's Children: Critical Comments on CDA', in *Evolving Models of Language. Papers from the 1996 BAAL Annual Meeting*, ed. by A. Ryan and A. Wray. Milton Keynes: Multilingual Matters, 100–16.

Voloshinov, V. I. (1973) *Marxism and the Philosophy of Language*. New York: Seminar Press.

Wilson, J. (1990) *Politically Speaking: The Pragmatic Analysis of Political Language*. Oxford: Blackwell.

Index